# With the Boer Foreign Legion

# With the Boer Foreign Legion

Two Accounts of Foreigners Who Fought for the
Boer Cause During the Anglo-Boer War

Ten Months in the Field With the Boers
Anonymous
(An Ex-Lieutenant of
General de Villebois-Mareuil)

A West Pointer With the Boers
J. Y. F. Blake

*With the Boer Foreign Legion*
*Two Accounts of Foreigners Who Fought for the Boer Cause During the Anglo-Boer War*
*Ten Months in the Field With the Boers*
by Anonymous
(An Ex-Lieutenant of General de Villebois-Mareuil)
and
*A West Pointer With the Boers*
by J. Y. F. Blake

First published under the titles
*Ten Months in the Field With the Boers*
and
*A West Pointer With the Boers*

# FIRST EDITION

Leonaur is an imprint
of Oakpast Ltd

Copyright in this form © 2013 Oakpast Ltd

ISBN: 978-1-78282-122-9 (hardcover)
ISBN: 978-1-78282-123-6 (softcover)

http://www.leonaur.com

Publisher's Notes

The views expressed in this book are not necessarily those of the publisher.

# Contents

Ten Months in the Field With the Boers   7
A West Pointer With the Boers   129

Ten Months in the Field With the Boers

General De Villebois-Mareuil

# Contents

| | |
|---|---|
| Sailing to War | 15 |
| The British | 28 |
| Joining the Boers | 33 |
| Outside Kimberley | 45 |
| Retreat | 54 |
| The European Legion | 63 |
| Tugela | 78 |
| Invasion | 87 |
| Worn Out | 97 |
| Johannesburg | 105 |
| P.O.W. | 114 |
| Conclusion | 125 |

*To you, General, who, from the Paradise of the Valiant, can read in my heart the sentiments of respect and affection that guide me, I dedicate these lines in token of the profound admiration of your former Lieutenant.*

Transvaal, 1899-1900.

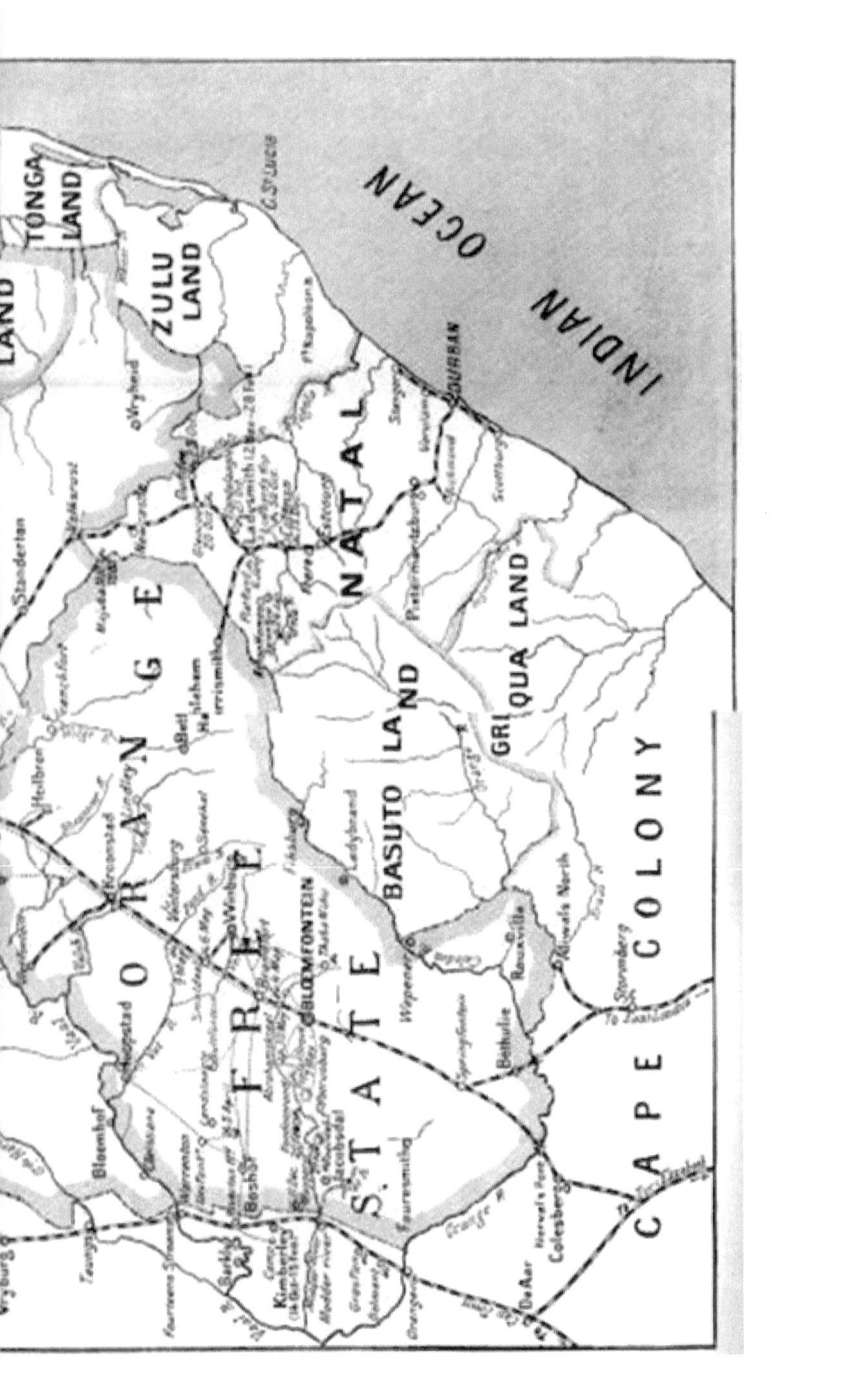

## Chapter 1

# Sailing to War

'No room, sir!'

This was the phrase that greeted my friend De C—— and myself at the door of every carriage we tried.

The fast train for Marseilles leaving Paris at 8.25 was, indeed, full to overflowing that night of December 23; by eight o'clock not a place was left.

Finally, after treading on a good many toes, and exchanging a good many elbowings, we installed ourselves more or less comfortably—a good deal less, to be accurate—one in the front of the train, the other close to the luggage-van.

A last clasp of the hand to the comrades who have come to the station with us, and we are off.

The lights of Paris begin to die out in the distance; conversation languishes; the monotonous rumble of the train lulls the travellers into drowsiness; heads nod and droop in the dim light of the lamp.

'La Roche! Wait here five minutes!'

We jump out. C—— and I meet again.

'Well, how are you getting on?'

'Not very well. And you?'

'Very badly!'

And, much depressed, we return to our respective carriages.

At last the patience under discomfort habitual to men of our unsettled lives asserts itself, and we sleep soundly till we reach Arles, when we find two seats together.

At Marseilles we were kindly received by a pleasant cousin of mine, and by a delightful lady, also of my kindred.

The 24th we spent with some comrades, officers of the neighbouring garrison, and on the 25th we and our baggage were safely on board the *Natal*, of the Messageries Maritimes.

I make special mention of our baggage, which, in preparation for the campaign we are about to undertake, consists of two little canteens. The two together weigh exactly 38 kilos, making about 19 kilos each. They hold all our belongings, including our two revolvers and two hundred cartridges. We are not overloaded with baggage.

The *Natal* is one of the 'fine steamers' of former days, fairly large.

We first take possession of our cabin, which opens into the dining-saloon. Then we go up on the bridge, where we are introduced to Colonel Gourko, who is also on his way to the Transvaal, as Russian military attaché. We had met him the evening before at the station, for he arrived by the same train as ourselves. But his fluent French, and his rosette of the Legion of Honour, which he always wears by courtesy in France, had made us take him for some important functionary on his way to Madagascar! . . .

We ask his pardon. But the minutes pass. Hand-shakings, good wishes, bursts of emotion, the time-honoured formula of departure have been gone through; the gangways are taken up, the ropes cast off; we steam out of port. The handkerchiefs that flutter on the quay and on the pier gradually diminish, the houses seem to flatten, Notre Dame de la Garde dwindles, becomes smaller and smaller, till at last it is a mere speck on the horizon. Then it disappears altogether; we are on the open sea.

I shall not thrill with ecstasy, nor pour out a tribute of emotion to the 'blue immensity,' for, though I have many parts—as you, my readers, will readily believe, especially such of you as do not know me—I am no poet. The dinner-bell finds De C—— and me prosaically wrangling over 150 points at piquet.

The dining-saloon is large, but there are few diners. We take a general survey.

The captain, who is supposed to preside over the meals, is not well, and does not appear. In fact, we scarcely see him at table during the passage.

Colonel Gourko, Captain Ram, and Lieutenant Thomson, the Dutch military attachés, Captain D—— of the Marines, with his charming young wife and their son Guy—who is soon one of our firmest friends—an engineer, a naval doctor, a young lady on her way to set up as a milliner at Tananariva, an English journalist, and Henry de Charette, a volunteer for the Transvaal, where his health will prevent him from playing a very active part, make up the sum total of diners, or very nearly so.

We further discovered on board Messieurs de Breda, a former cavalry officer, Pimpin, Michel, a distinguished artillery officer, and a few others destined to be our pleasant comrades in the future.

As at least fifteen of us are bound for Lourenço Marques, and as we have reason to fear a visit from some English cruiser not unaccustomed to such travellers, we have all adopted the most extraordinary callings. One of us is a commercial traveller in the wine or drug trade; another is a dealer in apparatus of various kinds. I also met a bird-seller, a manufacturer of blinds, and an agent for bitumens!

C—— and I are modest! We are in quest of purchasers for 'Calaya,' a febrifuge of extraordinary virtues, a specific for fever, dysentery, headache, toothache, etc.

The weather is superb; but our boat is slow, and we rarely make 300 miles in the twenty-four hours.

We reach Port Said on December 31. For New Year's Day we get up an entertainment with a lottery on board, and, thanks to Madame D——, it proves a great success.

The profits, amounting to nearly a thousand *francs*, were handed over to the Widows and Orphans' Fund of the Messageries Maritimes.

The prizes offered by the passengers were of the most curious description, and as we were bound for sunny climes, there were more than twenty umbrellas among them. Chance, with perhaps a little extraneous help, made a good many of these fall to the share of Colonel Gourko, who took the little joke in excellent part.

Breda undertakes the refreshment buffet, with the help of a charming young girl, and presides with great dignity.

After leaving Port Said the company is increased by the members of a Russian ambulance going to the Transvaal. They keep very much to themselves, and every evening they meet together on the lower deck to sing their vesper prayer. The sacred chant, in itself very imposing, takes on a solemn grandeur in the picturesque setting of the Red Sea.

At Aden we go on shore, and make an execrable lunch, washed down, however, by some excellent Chianti and Barolo; then we go to see the famous cisterns, in which there is hardly ever any water now.

We also pick up a new passenger, Captain B——, of the Royal Field Artillery, who also is for Durban on warfare bound. Our approaching hostility does not prevent us from being the best of friends throughout the passage. He wears the medal of the Soudan, too, which gives him a further title to our sympathies. He describes his very interesting campaigns in India and Egypt. He was present at Omdurman—'the great battle,' as he calls it.

Ever since we started we have been hearing terrific accounts of Guardafui. Few vessels, it appears, escape disaster at this point! But the sea is like oil, to the great mortification, no doubt, of all our ancient mariners.

Now we are bound straight for Madagascar. For eight days we shall be between sky and water. Let us turn them to account for a rapid retrospect of the causes which have led to the war in which we are about to take part.

It will not, I think, be necessary to dwell on the origin of the Boers.[1]

Colonists sent out in 1652 by the Dutch East India Company, they landed at the Cape of Good Hope, discovered two centuries before (1486), and settled there, employing themselves in agriculture and cattle-breeding.

At the time of the Revocation of the Edict of Nantes, 300 French Huguenots joined them, bringing up the number of the colonists to about 1,000. The fusion of the two races was rapid, and the French tongue disappeared among them. Many of the French names even were corrupted—Cronje was originally Crosnier—but many, on the other hand, have persisted in their Gallic form—Villiers, Marais, Joubert, Du Toit—and their bearers are very proud of their French descent. But England, anxious to acquire the colony when it began to prosper, sent out a number of emigrants, reinforcing them steadily, till they became an important factor in the community.

From 1815, when Cape Colony was recognised as a British possession by the Treaty of Vienna, English policy has been hostile to the Boers, who, for their part, received the English settlers in no friendly spirit.

About 1835 the Boers, under the pressure of the vexations to which they were subjected, began their exodus to the north—the Great Trek, as they still call it—and founded the Orange Free State, recognised in 1869 by Europe, and the Transvaal.

They were not left long in the enjoyment of the territory they had wrested from the *kaffirs*. Diamondiferous deposits were discovered in the Orange Free State in 1871; the English promptly confiscated

---
1. Boer means peasant; Burgher denotes a citizen.

the find on the pretext that it belonged to a native chief under their protection.

In 1877, the Zulus having risen against the Boers, England intervened for the alleged pacification of the country, sent her troops to Pretoria, and annexed the Transvaal.

But in 1880 the Boers revolted, and under Joubert inflicted a crushing defeat on the English at Majuba Hill, on the frontier of Natal, February 27, 1881.

The treaty of August 3, 1881, recognised the independence of the Transvaal under the suzerainty of the Queen. Another treaty, signed in London, February 27, 1884, recognised the absolute independence of the Transvaal.

On January 2, 1896, the famous Jameson Raid, still fresh in men's memories, was checked at Krugersdorp.

Wishing to satisfy the claims of the Uitlanders, the President reduced the term necessary for the acquisition of electoral rights from fourteen to nine years. Finally, in 1899, England, constituting herself the champion of the foreigners, instructed Sir Alfred Milner, Governor of the Cape, to demand a further reduction of the term to five years.

This measure meant the rapid intrusion of the alien into the administration, and the gradual swamping of the Boers. It would have been the ruin of Boer autonomy. The President refused. 'Her Majesty's subjects,' he said, 'demanded my trousers; I gave them, and my coat likewise. They now want my life; I cannot grant them that.'

All these demands were but so many pretexts intended to mask the true designs of England from the European Powers. But they are manifest to the least discerning. On the one hand, there are gold-mines in the Transvaal, and speculators demand them. On the other, Cecil Rhodes has declared that 'Africa must be English from the Cape to Cairo.' War had therefore long been foreseen, and the Transvaal quietly prepared for the struggle.

Under cover of an expedition into Swaziland, which was nothing but a march of some few hundred Burghers who had never fired a shot except at game, considerable armaments had been made from 1895 onwards.

Krupp supplied them with field-guns of 12 and 15 pound. Maxim-Nordenfeldts were bought. These quick-firing guns throw percussion-shells to a distance of about 5,000 metres; their calibre is 35 millimetres. The English have a great respect for these little pieces, which they have christened 'pom-poms,' in imitation of the noise made by their rapid fire. The same firm supplied small calibre Maxim guns for Lee-Metford cartridges. The cartridges are fixed to strips of canvas (belts), which unroll automatically, presenting a fresh cartridge to the striker the instant its predecessor has been fired.

Lastly, the Creusot factories received orders for guns of the latest pattern: four 155 centimetres long, with a range of about 10,000 metres, which the Boers call 'Long Toms,' and two batteries of 75 millimetre field-guns.

These cannon (model 95) were furnished with all the latest improvements. They fire very rapidly, and the brakes, situated on either side of the piece, absorb the recoil, the carriage being the fulcrum, and the trunnions the points of contact with the piece. They have a range of about 7,000 metres. They are loaded by means of cartridges, the whole charge enclosed in a single metal case. When efficiently served, they will fire from fifteen to twenty shots a minute.

We have advanced indeed since the year 1881, and the cannon made in the Transvaal itself, with cartwheel axle-trees riveted and braised together![2]

A large stock of Mauser, Martini-Henry and Steyr rifles (1887 pattern), with plentiful ammunition, was also bought by the Boer Government.

The weapon most in favour is the Mauser rifle of 1891, calibre 7.5 millimetres. It is sighted up to 2,000 metres. It has a magazine containing five cartridges. The movable straight-levered breech-block has a safety-bolt.

The cavalry carbine, also much appreciated, is a reduced model of the rifle. The mechanism is the same, and it also has a magazine holding five cartridges, but the movable breech-block has a bent lever. This carbine is sighted up to 1,400 metres.

These two weapons are of great precision, but I have heard it objected since my return that the wooden grip which covers part of the barrel causes an unequal heating and cooling of the metal between the covered and uncovered parts, giving rise to occasional explosions or distortions. Personally, I saw no instance of this.

The Martini-Henry rifles, carbines, and muskets are sometimes preferred by the older Boers. They are of an obsolete pattern, and have an insignificant range of only 800 metres for carbines and mus-

---

2. This is preserved in the museum at Pretoria, side by side with a *mitrailleuse* labelled 'Meudon,' given to the President by the Emperor William.

kets. They are 11 millimetres in calibre, and their leaden bullets have no casing of harder metal. To some persons they have the advantage of disabling a man more rapidly and effectually at a short range than bullets of smaller calibre.

Events now follow closely one on another. On September 26, 1899, the Volksraad issued the following proclamation from Bloemfontein:

> The Volksraad, considering paragraph 2 of the President's speech, and the official documents and correspondence submitted therewith, having regard to the fact that the strained state of affairs throughout the whole of South Africa, which has arisen owing to the differences between the Imperial Government and the Transvaal, threatens to lead to hostilities, the calamitous consequences of which to the white inhabitants would be immeasurable, being connected with the Transvaal by the closest ties of blood and confederacy, and standing in the most friendly relationship with the Imperial Government; fearing that, should war break out, a hatred between European races would be born which would arrest or retard peaceful developments in all States and colonies of South Africa, and produce distrust in the future; feeling that the solemn duty rests upon it of doing everything possible to avoid the shedding of blood; considering that the Transvaal Government during the negotiations with the Imperial Government, which extended over several months, made every endeavour to arrive at a peaceful solution of the differences raised by the aliens in the Transvaal, and taken up by the Imperial Government as its own cause, which endeavours have unfortunately had only this result, that British troops were concentrated on the border of the Transvaal, and are still being strengthened—resolves to instruct the government still to use every means to maintain and insure peace, and in a peaceful manner to contribute towards a solution of existing differences, provided it be done without violating the honour and independence of the Free State and the Transvaal; and wishes unmistakably to make known its opinion that there exists no cause for war, and that a war against the Transvaal, if now undertaken by the Imperial Government, will morally be a war against the whole white population of South Africa, and in its consequences criminal, for, come what may, the Free State will honestly and faithfully fulfil its obligations

towards the Transvaal, by virtue of the political alliance existing between the two Republics.'

On the 29th Mr. Chamberlain, more aggressive than ever, laid down certain impossible conditions:

1. The franchise to every Uitlander after five years of residence, unencumbered by any formalities that might restrict the privilege.
2. An absolute separation of the executive and judicial power in the Transvaal.
3. Abolition of the dynamite monopoly.
4. Dismantlement of the fortress of Johannesburg.
5. A special municipal government for Johannesburg.
6. Official recognition of the English language, and an equal use of it and the Dutch tongue.

During the first days of October the situation became more and more serious. Certain attempts at conciliation were still made. On October 5, President Steyn demanded that the massing of troops on the frontier should cease. But on the 6th Sir Alfred Milner replied that he could not accede to his request. Mr. Steyn accordingly wrote to the Governor of Cape Colony:

That the success of further negotiations was very doubtful, as the Transvaal would refuse any conditions whatever laid down by Her Majesty's Government if British troops continued to arrive while negotiations were in progress.

Finally, on October 10 the Boer ultimatum was handed to Mr. Conyngham-Green. The Transvaal Executive had demanded an answer within twenty-four hours, but the delegates of the Orange Free State got the term extended to forty-eight hours.

War was declared on October 11. The Boer commandos grouped themselves in two principal centres, the Orange Free State and Natal. In the Free State, Du Toit and Kolby invested Kimberley on October 14. Cronje advanced against Methuen in the south-east, Schoeman against Colesberg, and Olivier to meet Gatacre south of Aliwal North.

In Natal, Botha, Schalk Burgher, Lucas Meyer and Prinsloo, under the Commander-in-Chief Joubert, marched upon Ladysmith.

On October 20 a desperate engagement took place at Glencoe. General Symons, himself mortally wounded, lost sixty killed, 300 wounded, and 300 prisoners. The Boers had seventy men killed.

On October 21, at Elandslaagte, the German Legion and the Scandinavians, surprised by the enemy, were slaughtered by the English Lancers after a heroic resistance.

On the 23rd, at Dundee, Generals Yule and White were obliged to fall back on Ladysmith.

Finally, on October 30, under the very walls of the town, at Lombard's Kop, General White, beaten again, lost 300 dead and wounded, 1,200 prisoners and ten guns.

On November 2 Ladysmith was invested.

To judge by the behaviour of the Boers at this juncture, it would have seemed that the siege of the three towns, Mafeking, Kimberley and Ladysmith, was the end and object of the whole campaign.

They had at this stage of the war one of the most magnificent opportunities imaginable. Full of confidence, flushed with success, well equipped, and more numerous than they would ever be again, they might have reckoned on the co-operation of the Cape Boers, who, believing in the possible success of their brethren, were preparing to throw in their lot with them.

Against them they had some 40,000 English, half of them only just disembarked, unacclimatized, untried in warfare, the other half discouraged by recent events and scattered over a vast area.

Order and effort prolonged for one week only would have overwhelmed and annihilated the English army. Cape Colony and Natal would have thrown off the yoke, associating themselves with the Transvaal and the Orange Free State, and the United States of South Africa would have been a power to reckon with. But no! Nothing was attempted. Joubert seemed to be hypnotized before Ladysmith, Du Toit before Kimberley.

And, quietly and undisturbedly, England gradually disembarked the 200,000 men Lord Kitchener thought necessary for the work in hand. Nevertheless, for two months more the incapacity of the English generals all along the line thrust the flower of the Queen's battalions under the deadly fire of the Mausers, without a chance of fighting for their lives, so to speak.

On November 10, at Belmont, Lord Methuen was repulsed with heavy loss. A month later, at Stormberg, General Gatacre ventured an advance without scouts, without a map, blindly following a guide whose course he did not even verify by a compass.

The advance took place in the utmost disorder, though it had been arranged forty-eight hours, previously. The ambulance lost touch with the detachment, and went its own way. The 2nd Battalion of the Northumberland Fusiliers lost its ammunition-waggon. The column advanced in close order to within 100 yards of the Boer entrenchments without any warning, and was decimated. Gatacre lost 100 men killed and 700 prisoners.

On December 11, at Magersfontein, Lord Methuen had a second disaster to deplore. Half an hour after midnight, after twenty-four hours of artillery preparations and bombardment of the Boer entrenchments, five Highland regiments advanced in line of quarter-column. The night was dark, and rain was falling in torrents. At half-past three in the morning the English halted, not very sure of their route. In an instant a deadly fire poured out from the rocks. They were less than 200 yards from the trenches occupied by Cronje's men.

The Black Watch was decimated. General Wauchope fell, crying: 'My poor fellows! 'twas not I who brought you here!' The Marquis of Winchester was also killed.

The whole body was demoralized, and it was not possible to make the fugitives lie down till they had reached a distance of several hundreds of yards. 'It was,' says an eye-witness, 'one of the saddest sights that could wring the heart of an English soldier of our times.'

In this turmoil of confusion and indecision, Lord Methuen only gave the order to retire towards four o'clock in the afternoon. More than a thousand dead strewed the battle-field, and no help was given to the wounded till the following day.

In the last letter he wrote to England, Wauchope said: 'This is my last letter, for I have been ordered to attempt an impossible task. I have protested, but I must obey or give up my sword. . . . The men of the Modder River army will probably never follow Lord Methuen in another engagement.'

Finally, on December 15, the Battle of Colenso was fought. I borrow an account of it from Sir Redvers Buller's telegram despatched from Chieveley Camp in the evening:

> I regret to report serious reverse. I moved in full strength from camp near Chieveley this morning at 4 a.m. There are two fordable places in the Tugela, and it was my intention to force a passage through at one of them. They are about two miles apart, and my intention was to force one or the other with one brigade, supported by a central brigade.

General Hart was to attack the left drift, General Hildyard the right road, and General Lyttleton in the centre to support either.

Early in the day I saw that General Hart would not be able to force a passage, and directed him to withdraw. He had, however, attacked with great gallantry, and his leading battalion, the Connaught Rangers, I fear suffered a great deal. Colonel Brooke was severely wounded.

I then ordered General Hildyard to advance, which he did, and his leading regiment, the East Surrey, occupied Colenso Station and the houses near the bridge.

At that moment I heard that the whole of the artillery I had sent to that attack—namely, the 14th and 66th Field Batteries and six naval 12-pounder quick-firing guns, the whole under Colonel Long, R.A.—were out of action, as it appears that Colonel Long, in his desire to be within effective range, advanced close to the river. It proved to be full of the enemy, who suddenly opened a galling fire at close range, killing all their horses, and the gunners were compelled to stand to their guns.

Desperate efforts were made to bring back the guns, but only two were saved by the exertions of Captain Schofield and two or three of the drivers.

It was here that Lieutenant Roberts, of the 66th Battery of Artillery, son of Field-Marshal Lord Roberts, met a glorious death.

Some of the waggon-teams got shelter for troops in a *donga*, and desperate efforts were made to bring out the field-guns, but the fire was too severe, and only two were saved by Captain Schofield and some drivers, whose names I will furnish.

Another most gallant attempt with three teams was made by an officer whose name I will obtain. Of the 18 horses, 13 were killed, and as several of the drivers were wounded, I would not allow another attempt.

As it seemed they would be a shell mark, sacrificing loss of life to a gallant attempt to force passage unsupported by artillery, I directed the troops to withdraw, which they did in good order. 'Throughout the day a considerable force of the enemy was pressing on my right flank, but was kept back by the mounted men under Lord Dundonald and part of General Barton's brigade.

The day was intensely hot and most trying to the troops, whose conduct was excellent.
We have abandoned ten guns, and lost by shell-fire one.
The losses in General Hart's brigade are, I fear, heavy, though the proportion of severely wounded is, I hope, not large.
The 14th and 66th Field Batteries also suffered severe losses.
We have retired to our camp at Chieveley.
The Boer losses are said to be over 700 men.[3]

No, General, we did not lose 700 men that day.
General Botha's report gave 8 dead and 20 wounded, while more than 2,000 English lay on the battlefield.
Round about the batteries especially the carnage had been terrible. The Boers, ambushed on a little kopje on the further side of the Tugela, 300 metres from the cannon, kept up an unerring fire for an hour.
December 15, be it noted, has long been a day of rejoicing in the Transvaal. It is the anniversary of the Battle of Bloedriver, when Pretorius, to avenge the massacre of Pieter Retief and over 500 Boers, defied the bands of the Zulu chief Dingaun. This was on December 15, 1838, and on that eventful day Pretorius and his 400 men left 3,000 Zulus on the field, with a loss of only three wounded themselves.
After Colenso the victors had another splendid opportunity. They might have pushed forward with the armies of Natal and the Free State. The English troops had, it is true, been reinforced, but the arms of the Republics were still victorious in every direction.
In the beginning, on the whole, the elements of success were overwhelmingly with the Boers. These were superiority of numbers, of marksmanship, a profound knowledge of the country, of which no accurate maps exist, and the great distances between their opponents and such reinforcements as the latter could depend on. It might have been said that the fortune of war, taking into account the right and justice of their cause, had been pleased to place all the elements of victory in their hands. But neither the advice offered by the most authoritative voices and based on the great teachings of military history, nor the entreaties dictated by the most generous devotion to the cause of the Boers, could rouse the superiors in command from the apathy that seemed to have overtaken them.

---

3. This statement does not appear in the *Times* report of General Buller's telegram.—Translator.

Christmas passed in rejoicings on both sides. The belligerents exchanged Christmas and New Year good wishes by the medium of shells specially prepared, containing sweets, chocolates, etc. New Year's Day found them all much in the same positions. The bombardment of the three towns, Mafeking, Kimberley, and Ladysmith, continued.

However, on January 6 Joubert made up his mind to attack—if, indeed, that strange encounter, aimless and incoherent, can be called an attack. Was it an assault by the besiegers or a sortie of the besieged? Perhaps both. It took place at Platrand. Four or five hundred of Prinsloo's men were seriously engaged; the others (there were 6,000 round the town) took up positions early in the morning, quitted them towards ten o'clock to come back and breakfast in camp, returned to them later, and remained for the rest of the day 1,800 yards from the town, which was no longer defended, without firing a shot, without a thought of throwing themselves against it or of going to the help of their comrades, hotly engaged close by. In the evening they went back quietly to camp, while the commandos of Zand River, Harrismith, Heilbron, and Kroonstad had fifty-four killed and ninety-five wounded. The English lost 138 killed and over 200 wounded. A little dash, decision, and cohesion, and the town might have been taken. Such was Colonel de Villebois-Mareuil's opinion.

But even in the full flush of success we shall never find among the Boers that eagerness, that scorn of death, that enthusiasm which sweep troops forward and make great victories.

The same day, at Colesberg, an *accident* (this word is a happy invention of General French's to denote a reverse) cost the English 150 lives, among them that of Colonel Watson.

The sieges followed their—I will not say normal—course, for the ill-defended towns ought long ago to have been taken by the Boers. Such was the general situation, more or less, when we landed.

## Chapter 2

# The British

Time passed, the screw laboured round, and on January 12 we arrived at Diego Suarez.

'Passengers for Lourenço Marques change steamers!'

For the *Natal* is bound for Mauritius, along the east coast of Madagascar. We shall therefore spend the night on shore.

Wandering about the town, we meet Colonel Gourko, whom we invite to dinner, as we are in a French colony. I can't pride myself much on this meal, in the name of French culinary art.

The next day I lighted on a quartermaster of the Marine Artillery, whom I had known in the Soudan when he was only a gunner. He went off to find the other Soudanese campaigners of the settlement, and in a quarter of an hour I was surrounded by half a dozen old comrades. They were all in high spirits, for it had been a day of promotions, and several of them were toasting their new stripes.

I spend a full hour with them, recalling the old days spent in the colony that all who have once known regret.

The hour of parting draws near; several subalterns return to their duties, while my old friend and a newly-promoted officer come to see me off.

The *Gironde*, also of the Messageries Maritimes, plies from Diego Suarez to Durban and *vice versâ*. Several artillery and marine officers, having heard of my presence, have come to wish me Godspeed on board. I am much touched at this token of sympathy from unknown friends, for, setting my humble personality aside, it is a homage to the noble cause I am on my way to uphold.

But the bell rings, the anchor is weighed, and we are off. If the *Natal* was an old 'fine steamer,' the *Gironde* is a *very* old one. She was formerly one of the swift and elegant Indian liners, but now, obsolete and worn-out, is reserved for this little auxiliary service till such time as some sudden squall shall send her to the bottom.

Nevertheless, we arrived safely at Mozambique, where some few days before a terrible cyclone had destroyed part of the native village. Huts were overthrown and lying in fragments, trees torn up by the roots, telegraph-wires broken; an air of mournful desolation hung over the district.

Meanwhile, the buxom negresses of the quarter went about their daily work, apparently unmoved at the ruin of their dwellings.

We pay a visit to the fort, a very curious sight, with its medieval battlements bristling with cannon two hundred years old, and its soldiers armed with flintlock muskets. All these excellent Portuguese warriors seem to be impressed by a sense of their lofty mission. They even demurred a little before admitting us into their 'citadel.'

We take up the Archbishop of Mozambique, I believe; he is brought on board by a military launch, with all the honours due to his rank, and saluted by the guns of the fort.

We leave Mozambique the same evening.

Every day there were superb sunsets, glories of deep purple, blue, blazing red, green, yellow and pink, vivid pieces of impressionism that beggar description.

Thus, still avoiding shipwreck, we come to Beira, where we land our prelate, who is received by a numerous staff of officers; troops line the quays, and salutes are fired!

Portugal has certainly a remarkable colonial army. Among the others there is a huge captain, bursting out of his tunic. Each of his long commands, incomprehensible to me, seems to produce consternation in his troop, followed by a series of perfectly diverse manoeuvres.

We turn away that we may avoid laughing aloud, for the moment is a serious one... Two or three trombones attack the Portuguese national air. A good many of the worthy soldiers have shouldered arms, and the majority have presented them.... His lordship passes. He gets into a little 'lorry' pushed by natives, and goes off quickly, while the troops disperse. They are worthy of those I have several times seen at Lisbon.

I think if I were the Portuguese I would prefer none at all to such as these.... And, then, the suppression of the military budget would perhaps enable them to pay their dividends. In the afternoon we embark a band of Englishmen coming from Rhodesia to enlist as volunteers at Durban and Cape Town. They invade the saloon with their friends, and sing 'God save the Queen.' Some of the Frenchmen present retort with the Marseillaise; the situation becomes strained, fists are clenched, and finally a certain number of blows are exchanged. We have on board a grandson of President Kruger's, whose home is in Holland. After having been arrested once, conducted to Durban and sent back to Europe, he is making a second attempt to enter his country. Thanks to a strict *incognito*, only laid aside for two of us, he succeeds in his design.

At night we arrive off Lourenço Marques, where, without let or hindrance, we disembark on January 21.

We order a bottle of Moët in the saloon to drink the health of Captain B——, whom we are leaving, and against whom we are going to fight presently.

'Your good health,' he says, 'and I trust we shan't meet later on!'

We part with a hearty shake of the hand. At the Custom-house we easily get our artistically-concealed revolvers through, but the Customs officers fall upon the uniforms, arms and harness belonging to Colonel Gourko. They decline to pass anything, in spite of all explanations. The Colonel is obliged to go and fetch the Russian Consul and the Governor. We take up our quarters at the Hotel Continental, which, we are told, is the best. Five of us are packed into one small room on improvised beds, where we are devoured by mosquitoes ... and this costs fourteen shillings a day!

Colonel Gourko, having recovered his baggage, joins us there, and, in his turn, invites us to dinner. He does things in a princely fashion, and the bill must have been one that Paillard himself would have hesitated to present.

All sorts of obstacles are invented to prevent our departure. Firstly, of course, our passports have to be *visé*, but before this can be done we have to get stamps, which are only to be had at the opposite end of the town; we have, further, to produce a certificate of good conduct (having only arrived the night before!). Then more stamps, then a note from the French Consul, then more stamps; and the office where you get the signature or the paper is never the same as the one that sells the stamps.

At last all formalities have been carried out. Our pockets are bulging with some dozen papers covered with innumerable signatures and a shower of stamps. Cost: over 50 *francs*—10,850 *reïs*!

We go to the station at seven o'clock the following morning. There are a great many police officers on duty. By the governor's orders no one is to be allowed to start for the Transvaal with the exception of the Russian ambulance. We all exclaim shrilly, and hurry off to the consul.

Upon our formal declaration that this order will injure us in our business, he proceeds to the governor and remonstrates, with the result that we are authorized to start next morning, there being only one train a day.

We spend the day wandering about the town, which is of little interest. The great square planted with trees is pleasant, however.

We see the funeral procession of an officer of the English man-of-war stationed here. The coffin, covered with the Union Jack, is placed on a little gun-carriage drawn by sailors; others line the way. Officers in full uniform follow, and a company of red-coats bring up the rear.

This is our last encounter with the 'soldiers of the Queen' before we open fire upon them. They are already numerous in South Africa, and every day brings reinforcements.

At the beginning of hostilities there were about 25,000 men distributed over Natal and Cape Colony. From November 9 to January 1 seventy-eight transports have brought 70,000 men, completing the fifth division; 15,000 volunteers have been raised on the spot, making in all 110,000 men.

The sixth and seventh divisions, a contribution from the colonies, will bring them up to 22,000; 3,000 yeomanry and 7,000 militiamen will complete the total of 152,000 promised for the month of February. The seventh division started from January 4 to January 11, bringing nearly 10,000 men and eighteen cannon.

Engagements at the rate of 3,600 *francs* (£124) are being made on every side—1,600 (£64) on enlistment, 2,000 francs (£80) at the end of the war. Enlistments in our Foreign Legion are affected and fall off considerably.

The City of London, by means of a public subscription of £100,000, raises a corps of volunteers. This desperate system of enlistment is severely criticised, even in England.

'What a humiliation,' says Mr. Frederick Greenwood in the *Westminster Gazette* of January 2, 'to have to cry Help! help! at every crossway to pick up a man or a horse.'

Seventeen new battalions are to be raised after January 15. The choice of men rests with the colonel or the lieutenant-colonel commanding the regimental district. They are required to be aged from twenty to thirty-five, to have gone through a course of instruction in

1898 or 1899, and to hold a certificate of proficiency in shooting. But, as a fact, many of these certificates are given by favour, and a third of the volunteers are from eighteen to twenty years old. The effort made by the country has been considerable.

On January 19 the eighth division was mobilized. It comprised the sixteenth and seventeenth brigades under the command of Major-Generals B. Campbell and J. E. Boyes; Batteries 89, 90, and 91, and the 5th company of Engineers, making a strength of 10,540 men, 1,548 horses, eighteen cannon, and eight machine guns.

The eighth division is under the command of General H. M. L. Rundle, aged forty-four, who has already served in the Zulu campaign, at the siege of Potchefstroom in the Transvaal in 1881, and in the Egyptian and Soudanese campaigns from 1884 to 1898.

CHAPTER 3

# Joining the Boers

To return to our journey. On the morning of the 24th, at 10 o'clock, we took the train and departed, happy to leave Lourenço Marques. The last station on the frontier is Ressano-Garcia; again our papers are examined. If we paid highly for them, they at least do good service.

The train rolls on again, and in a few minutes we are on the soil of the Transvaal. All along the line, at every little bridge, bands of armed Boers are posted. Komatipoort Station is also occupied by troops. Everyone gets out. There is a minute inspection of all papers, even of private letters, and we are conscientiously searched. Having satisfied our challengers, we are allowed to go on. The trains travel very slowly in this very broken, varied country. We ascend almost uninterruptedly, and the line seems to run either along the sides of rocky mountains or the edges of bottomless abysses. Many of the spots we pass are extraordinarily picturesque. In the evening we arrive at Watervaalonder, and the train stops; for in this country neither trains nor men are in a hurry.

A Frenchman, named Mathis, keeps a hotel, at which we sleep. He receives us with much affability, and talks enthusiastically of the game in the neighbourhood. He is a Nimrod.

The next day we start again, and in the evening we are at Pretoria. My friend Gallopaud is at the station, and takes us to the Transvaal Hotel, where the guests of the government are quartered.

On the 26th, thanks to the good graces of M. Grunberg, we are presented to M. de Souza, Mr. Reitz's secretary, for whom we have letters of introduction.

We take the oath of fealty as Burghers, and receive our weapons, Mauser carbines, the stock of which is getting low, cartridges and belts.

Horses and saddles are already giving out. We are impatient to be off, but shops and offices are all closed on Saturday at one o'clock and throughout Sunday.

We take advantage of the holiday to inspect the town. Pretoria, as everyone knows, is the capital of the Transvaal. It is the seat of the government, which is composed of two Chambers, the First Volksraad and the Second Volksraad. Each is composed of twenty-nine members, elected by direct suffrage. The President of the Republic and the commander-in-chief are elected by the members of the First Chamber, the former for five, the latter for ten years. They are eligible for re-election for any length of time.

The President, Paul Kruger, familiarly known as 'Oom Paul,' was commander-in-chief for a long time before he became President. The present Generalissimo, Joubert, was his rival in the Presidential elections.

The Transvaal revenue is drawn for the most part from heavy royalties on the mines, and a crushing tax on explosives; in 1897 an income of 112,005,450 *francs* (£4,480,218) was received, against an expenditure of 109,851,400 *francs* (£4,394,056).

The general aspect of Pretoria is depressing; only two or three streets show any animation. The circumstances of the moment are not certainly such as to enliven the town, but I have been told that even in times of peace it is never very cheerful.

Stretching over a wide area, it is intersected by little tramways, the cars drawn by two consumptive horses. In the centre is Government House, a huge building of freestone, massive and ungraceful, though not without certain pretensions to the 'grand style,' I believe. On each side a sentry of the Presidential guard paces up and down. Under the colonnade of the main entrance, which faces a large open space, a few steps lead up to a vast hall, with a monumental staircase at the end. On each side of the hall two wide corridors run round the building, and give access to all the different offices. We find the whole place, hall, corridors and offices, crowded with busy people, some soliciting, others solicited, all hurrying hither and thither. With the exception of some few buildings of several storeys grouped round the palace and in the main street—the post-office, the clubs, the banks, the hotels and the large shops—all the houses are little one-storey cottages surrounded by gardens.

******

On Monday morning we are able to have horses, which we go

and catch ourselves in the great courtyard which serves as a *dépôt*. We have also some old English saddles, and after buying some rugs and some indispensable provisions, we are ready to start at about five in the evening.

Our departure is fixed for eleven o'clock, by the special train which is to take *Long Tom* to Kimberley, where we are to join Colonel Villebois. This *Long Tom*, a 155 millimetres Creusot gun, is a personage, a celebrity. It weighs 2,500 kilogrammes; its carriage weighs the same. Its fame is derived from its history.

One night last November, at Lombard's Kop, in front of Ladysmith, where the gun was mounted, sixty English, taking advantage of the slumbers of the Boer sentinels, stormed the hill, seized the cannon, and finding it impossible to displace it, damaged the two ends with dynamite. After this the Burghers, coming up in force, retook the gun, brought it to Pretoria, and repaired it in a remarkable manner. It was, however, shortened by about 25 centimetres.

After these adventures it has become a sort of prodigal son, a legendary weapon beloved of those great children we call the Boers. It is, therefore, no small honour to be called upon to escort *Long Tom*. We share this honour with a gunner named Erasmus, a strange being, who, after being severely wounded at the taking of 'his cannon,' had sworn only to return and fight in its company.

On this Monday night, accordingly, at eleven o'clock, in a downpour of rain, we and our horses take our places in the train, which, profiting no doubt by its being a 'special,' starts an hour after time. It consists of three or four first-class coaches with lateral corridors. These coaches, which are comfortable enough, and very high in the ceiling, have in each compartment two seats of three places each, covered with leather, and in the centre a folding-table about 50 centimetres wide. At night a second seat, which is raised in the daytime, or serves as a luggage-net, makes a sleeping-berth, so that four travellers in each compartment can rest comfortably, a convenience highly desirable in a country where journeys often last forty-eight hours, and even six or seven days, as from Cape Town to Buluwayo and Fort Salisbury.

Travellers install themselves as they please, without any sort of constraint. Luggage is not registered, and the carriages are invaded—I use the term advisedly—with weapons, saddles, bridles, bandoliers, provisions, dogs, if one has any, rugs, trunks and bundles. No officials, no staff, no warning cries, no notices forbidding travellers to get out while the train is in motion. A station-master, and hardly anything more.

A bell rung three times at short intervals announces the departure of the train. You get in, or you don't get in; you stand on the footboard, climb on to the roof of the carriage, leave the door open or shut it, get into a truck or cattle-van—it's your own look out. You are free, and no one would dream of interfering with you in the matter.

In the carriages passengers sleep, drink, eat, sing, shoot and gamble, and every morning a negro comes and cleans up.

There is a little of everything among the debris—old papers, empty preserve-tins, fruit-parings, tobacco-ash, cartridge-cases, empty, and sometimes broken, bottles. An inspector on the P. L. M. would go mad at the sight.

While the cleaning goes on, we go and ask for a little hot water from the engine, and make our morning coffee. On trucks that we go and fetch ourselves we load up heavy carts of provisions, ammunition, and cannon. Finally, we heap up pell-mell in open cattle-vans, mules and horses in some, oxen in another. And casualties are no more numerous than in Europe, where we arrange them like sardines in a box—'thirty-two men, eight horses.' The beasts of these regions, like the men, have apparently learnt to take care of themselves from their earliest infancy.

During the journey of Tuesday a springbock, a kind of antelope, startled by the engine, is so imprudent as to run along by the train at a distance of about 300 metres. From the tender to the last van a brisk fire suddenly opens. The engine-driver slows down, then, as the creature falls, stops altogether. A man gets down, fetches the quarry, and comes quietly back. The train goes on again, the springbock is cut up, and at the next station the engine-driver gets a haunch as an acknowledgment of his good-nature. This is indeed travelling made enjoyable!

But there are always folks who like to cut down the cakes and ale! In April, 1900, a penalty of £5 sterling was decreed for persons who fire a gun or a revolver in a railway-station or a village.

In every station—and they are legion—the whole feminine population has gathered, and sings the Boer hymn as soon as the train appears. And at every station the following ceremony takes place: A deputation comes to Erasmus, and begs him to show *Long Tom*. Erasmus mounts on the truck where the cannon is installed, and opens the breech. Each woman passes in front of it, putting either her head or her arm in, with cries of admiration. Then Erasmus closes the breech, gets down, and the Transvaal hymn, sung in chorus, alternates with that of the Orange Free State until the departure of the train.

On Tuesday evening at six o'clock we arrive at Brandfort. It is too late to unload the gun, and we spend the night in the village, where we are very well received.

Early on Wednesday we begin our task, with the help of the whole village, and to the accompaniment of the national hymn. The young girls all have sharp, forced voices, but from a distance the effect of these voices in chorus is not unpleasant. As to the male choirs, which are heard on every possible occasion, they are really charming and very impressive. Their music is very slow, and almost exclusively devotional in its rhythm.

Towards three o'clock on Thursday the convoy is ready. Thirty bullocks have been harnessed to *Long Tom*. The rest of the convoy consists of some twenty waggons of provisions and ammunition. As we set off, two or three photographers make their appearance.

The column, escorted by some sixty Boers, moves off towards Kimberley, in the midst of enthusiastic demonstrations. The waggons are heavy four-wheeled carts, with powerful brakes; the back part is covered with a sort of rounded tent stretched over hoops. This tent is the home of the travelling Boer. In it he keeps his mattress, his blankets, his utensils, his arms, while the front part is reserved for the heavy stores—millet, flour, biscuits, etc.

The driver walks beside his team, armed with a long whip, which he wields in both hands. The thick cane handle is often about 10 feet, and the lash, of strips of undressed hide, from 15 to 20 feet long. The management of this whip is no easy matter, and it is curious to see a good driver, at the moment when an effort is required, giving each of his twenty or thirty bullocks the necessary stroke in an instant.

The Burgher himself is mounted, shabby and ragged, dressed in a faded coat, a shapeless hat, and long trousers without straps.

For some time on the march we had a neighbour whose ulster, formerly, no doubt, of some normal hue, had turned, under the rains of years (I had almost said of centuries), a pinkish colour, with green reflections, like a sunset at sea. And the happy owner of this prism seemed quite unconscious that, amidst much that was extraordinary, he was perhaps the most extraordinary sight of all.

One warrior was mounted on a wretched old English saddle, to which were slung pell-mell a mackintosh, a many-coloured rug, a coffee-pot, a water-bottle, and a bag containing a medley of coffee, sugar, tobacco, biscuit and *biltong* (dried meat). Two *bandoliers*, and sometimes his rifle, were slung across his body, the latter horizontally on his stomach, when he was not carrying it upright in his hand, like a taper. His braces hung down his back. He had a single spur, for the Burgher rarely uses two, thinking a second an unnecessary luxury. Indeed, he relies much more on his *shambock* (a thong of hippopotamus hide) than on his single spur for the control of his horse.

Thus equipped, he shambles along on his jade, which trots, canters and gallops at intervals, silent, his legs well forward, his feet stuck out, catching at his over-long stirrups. His military organisation is on a par with his equipment.

The *'commando'* is the only military division known among the Boers. A *commando* is a levy of the men of a district, under the leadership of a field-cornet or a *commandant*. These grades, which are ratified by the government, are independent of any hierarchy, and merely imply a difference in the number of electors.

I say electors advisedly, for the field-cornets are chosen by their men, and, in their turn, take part in the nomination of the generals. This arrangement works well enough when electors and elected are of one mind. But when the leader wants to carry out some plan which his electors disapprove, he runs the risk of being cashiered and replaced by one of the majority.

I do not know what are the results of this system in politics; but, applied to an army, it is disastrous, for very often the leader, brave enough himself, dares not engage his men, lest he become unpopular; and this, I think, has been the main cause of the total absence of offensive action on the part of the Boers. Perhaps, indeed, it will prove one of the main causes of their final overthrow.

The *commandant*, or field-cornet, chooses among his men a 'corporal,' who acts as his auxiliary. These *'commandos,'* the effective numbers of which are essentially variable, are called after the chief town of the district from which they are drawn: Heidelberg Commando, Carolina Commando. And not only do they vary considerably, according to the population of a district, but the field-cornet himself never knows how many men he has at his disposal, for the Burghers have no notion of remaining continuously at the front; when one of the number wants to go back to his farm nothing can stop him. He goes, though he will come back later for another spell of service. Desertions of this kind often took place *en masse* the day after a reverse.

The Johannesburg Politie and the Artillery are the only troops in the Transvaal which can be described as more or less disciplined. The

Politie are the police-force of Johannesburg and Pretoria.

In times of peace the men wear a uniform consisting of a black tunic, cut after the English pattern, and black trousers. On their heads they wear a little hard black cap, with a button at the end, and for full dress a white peaked cap with a badge bearing the arms of the Transvaal. On the collars of their tunics are three brass letters: Z. A. R. (Zuid Africa Republic). But during the campaign their uniform has disappeared, and they are not to be distinguished from the ordinary Burghers. A certain discipline obtains among them, and they receive regular pay, which is reduced in time of war, as their families are then in receipt of indemnities in kind.

These men are the only ones who can be relied on to hold a position they have been told to keep. The other Burghers will only fight if they choose, and if they can do so without much risk.

The fighting strength of the Johannesburg Politie is about 800 men, with four lieutenants, under Commandant van Dam, an energetic and intelligent man.

The guns, of which I have already given a brief description—four *Long Toms*, a dozen 75 millimetres Creusot guns, some thirty Krupp field-pieces and old Armstrongs—are served by a body of artillery whose barracks are at Pretoria. I do not say nineteen or twenty batteries, for there are no groups or detachments. Each gun is used separately, according to the needs of the generals or the fancy of the artillerymen.

The corps consists of thirty officers and about 400 men. They wear a black tunic and breeches, and a sort of shako much like that of the Swiss army. In the field this shako is replaced by a large felt hat looped up on one side, and the rest of the costume undergoes any modification that suggests itself to the wearer.

They were at first under the command of Commandant Erasmus, who was superseded after the affair of Lombard's Kop, below Ladysmith.[1]

The artillery of the Free State, composed of old Armstrong guns and a few Krupp guns lent by the Transvaal, is served by a corps who look like the artillerymen of a comic opera. They wear a drab tunic and breeches with a great deal of orange braid, and are inferior even

---

1. Commandant Erasmus must not be confused with the Adjutant Erasmus who was with our party. The same names are very frequent throughout the Republics, the natives of which are mainly sprung from the few families who originally settled there. Thus there are some twenty Bothas, thirty Jouberts, etc.

to their colleagues of the Transvaal.

All told, then, the army consists of some 40,000 to 50,000 Burghers, without cohesion and without discipline, field-cornets who do not obey their generals, and who cannot command the obedience of their men. Over them are titular generals and *vecht*-generals (generals appointed for the term of the campaign only), for the most part ignorant of the very elements of the art of war, and at variance one with another.

How often during this campaign are we led to ponder over the phrase we have been mechanically ———

We have a six days' march before us. The bullocks are accustomed to travel by short stages of two hours, followed by an hour's rest. At night, however, we advance by stages of four or five hours.

The soil over which we pass is bare and sandy, of a uniform grayish-yellow tint, and produces nothing but short, coarse grass, which serves as fodder for the oxen and horses.

At every halt the cattle are let loose, and when the rest is over the *kaffir* 'boys' go off in pursuit of them, often to a considerable distance. Water is scarce, and generally bad.

Very often on the way we are received with delightful hospitality at the farms we pass. These houses are clean, and often even those which stand quite alone in the bush have a parlour adorned with photographs, religious prints, and Scripture texts in large characters. The furniture is simple, but there is very often a harmonium, for the singing of hymns is a frequent exercise in a Boer household.

Nevertheless, a respect for musical instruments is not carried to extremes. At Dundee, for instance, a Burgher had made a shelter for himself with a piano taken from an English villa.

The head of the family, often an old man with a white beard, is an absolute and much respected master in his home. He presides at meals, waited on by the women, who do not eat till the men have finished. The menu invariably consists of eggs and mutton cooked together in a frying-pan, bread or biscuit, and fruit. The drink is coffee with milk.

The Boer women are not well favoured. As a rule, they are thick-set and weather-beaten. They wear large pink or white sun-bonnets, very becoming to the young girls.

The traveller is a guest, received as if he were an old acquaintance; and whatever the hour of his appearance, he is at once offered coffee with milk, and, when they are in season, peaches.

At the time of our journey a good many men were at the front; but there are often some dozen children with the women, making large households. They all live pell-mell in two or three rooms.

In time of peace the Burgher is a keen sportsman; this is, indeed, the reason of his wonderful skill as a marksman, for he always shoots with ball-cartridge; shot is never used. In time of war he is a hunter still. He fights as he hunts, the game alone is changed; but as the quarry has means of defence more efficacious and violent than those of the ostrich or the springbock, he is often less persevering in pursuit of it.

When the Burgher halts to hunt or to fight, he dismounts, shelters his horse behind some rock, and leaves it loose, taking care to pass the bridle over its neck. All the horses are trained to stand perfectly still when they see the reins hanging in front of them thus, and, no matter how heavy the fire, they will not stir.

The Boers have a way of their own of reckoning distances. When, for instance, they tell you that it is seven hours from a certain place to another, don't imagine that you will be in time for dinner if you set off at noon; the seven hours in question are a conventional term. They are hours at the gallop, and it is supposed that a swift horse, going at his utmost speed, could cover the distance in seven hours.

The immense concessions given by the government are not cultivated, for the Boer has a rooted dislike to work; his black servants grow the necessary mealies, and keep his numerous flocks. As his wants are very primitive, this suffices him. To procure sugar, coffee, and other necessaries, he goes to town and sells two or three oxen.

The rifle and cartridges furnished by the State in time of war become the Burgher's property.

✶✶✶✶✶✶

On the march in war-time this system of halting the oxen because they are hot, and the men because they want to drink coffee at every farm, is neither very rapid nor very practical. We do not arrive at Boshof till the fifth day. This is the spot fated to be the grave of our venerated leader.

Boshof, in contrast to its surroundings, is a gay little oasis, traversed by a cool stream. It boasts green trees and pretty villas. Two ambulances are installed here, but they shelter only two or three wounded as yet.

At the end of the village is a pool, which delights us vastly. We spend the afternoon in it, after lunching with the field-cornet.

The town is *en fête*, as at Brandfort, to receive us, or rather—away with illusion!—to receive *Long Tom*.

We start again in the night, and reach Riverton Road. We are now on English territory, in Cape Colony.

Towards noon, M. Léon comes to meet the cannon, the arrival of which has been anxiously expected for the last two days.

We are only an hour from the camp, which we reach at a gallop. There, at Waterworks—the reservoir that supplies Kimberley—we find Colonel de Villebois-Mareuil.

Need I describe that frank and energetic face, with its searching blue eyes, and its benevolent smile, sometimes a little ironical, always subtle; the clear voice; the concise manner of speech, brief without being brusque? Even at that stage a look of sadness had stamped itself upon his face; he saw that the men for whom he was to lay down his life would not follow the counsels dictated by his profound knowledge and unquenchable devotion.

✶✶✶✶✶✶

We had been expected for two days, and twice the colonel had had good luncheons prepared. Then, giving us up, he had ordered nothing, and we took his kitchen by surprise.

We find with him Baron de Sternberg, that charming Viennese, whose inexhaustible good spirits are famous throughout London and Paris. In the evening he works in his tent at a history of the war, and composes the most delicious verses in German. The colonel also works hard.

*Long Tom* arrives some time after us.

Our laager at Waterworks is a large square, measuring some 200 metres on every side, planted with trees, and containing the machinery for distributing the water. It looks like an oasis in the midst of the vast yellow plain. In the distance are a few *kopjes*. We are about 700 metres from Kimberley. The camp is commanded by General du Toit.

Kampferdam, where the cannon has been taken, is 3 kilometres to the south, and 5,500 metres from Kimberley. It is a kind of whitish peak, about 50 metres high, formed of the refuse from the diamond mine below.

The night of Tuesday to Wednesday is spent in the construction of the wooden platform on which *Long Tom* and his carriage are to be mounted.

The English searchlights fix their great round eyes upon us from time to time, but there is nothing to show that the enemy has noticed anything abnormal in our proceedings.

All night long the work goes on with feverish activity, for Léon, who is superintending the operations, wants to fire his first shell at daybreak. But it is no easy task to hoist up that mass of 5,000 kilos, especially with inexperienced, undisciplined, and obstinate men, and the cannon is not ready till ten o'clock.

One of our party, Michel, an old artilleryman, the holder of some twenty gunnery prizes, gives the workers the benefit of his experience, and as he cannot find any sights, Erasmus artlessly proposes to make one of wood!

At last the first shot is fired! I am certain that at this moment not a single Boer is left in the trenches. Everyone has rushed out to see the effect produced. It is of two kinds. Firstly, our shell, badly calculated, bursts far off in the plain; then, no sooner has it been fired, than an English shell from the Autoskopje battery, 3,500 metres to our right, falls and explodes among the machinery of the Kampferdam mine. This exchange of compliments goes on till near twelve o'clock. This is the sacred hour of lunch. The fire ceases.

As coffee is a liquid which has to be imbibed slowly, firing does not begin again till nearly four o'clock. It is very hot, for it is the height of summer.

During this interval, the colonel has been several times to General du Toit, to ask for fifty volunteers.

The colonel's plan is to batter the town with a storm of shells (we have 450) for two hours, from four to six, and thus demoralize it; then, with fifty men, whom the French contingent would lead, to seize the Autoskopje battery, which is but poorly defended, at nightfall, and thence to gradually creep up to the town through a little wood, which would mask the advance. The plan was very simple, requiring but few men, and had every chance of success, because of the surprise it would have been to the English, who had never been attacked hitherto.

'Wait a bit,' said Du Toit; 'I will lay your plan before the council of war tomorrow.'

In vain the Colonel tells him that the success of the plan depends on its immediate execution. He can get no answer. The evening is wasted.

General du Toit is a big, bronzed man, with a black pointed beard and a straight and penetrating gaze. Though very brave personally, he has never dared to engage his men.

The latter are very well pleased with their role of besiegers. They will appreciate it less when the *Long Cecil* comes upon the scene. Hitherto, the long *far niente*, comparatively free from peril—the town, under the command of Colonel Kekewich, was defended by such a small garrison that *sorties* were impossible—has only been broken by the singing of hymns, the brewing of coffee and cocoa, and the occasional pursuit of a springbock.

Every evening a guard, composed, I fancy, of anyone who chose to go, went off, provided with a comfortable stock of bedding, to do duty round the camp.

Others, the valiant spirits, remained at the three batteries where were installed *Long Tom*, the three Armstrongs, and the Maxim.

*Long Tom's* battery was by far the most popular, for several reasons. In the first place, its processes were much more interesting than those of the small guns; then, its defenders were much more sheltered, owing to the proximity of the mining works; and finally, a good many former miners were always on the look-out for a stray diamond or two.

Among the besiegers of Kimberley, indeed, we met with a good many adventurers who took no other part in the campaign.

Men of all nationalities, many of them familiar with the town, having worked in the mines here, they came in the hope of finding some diamond overlooked in the sudden cessation of mining operations.... Then, too, they knew that Cecil Rhodes was in the town, having had no time to fly or to carry off his treasure.

Then, again, there are bankers and jewellers in Kimberley, and if the Boers had taken the town . . .

It appears that Cecil Rhodes was quite aware of this danger, and I have heard that he attempted to manufacture a balloon which was to have carried 'Cecil and his fortunes' to a safer city.

In any case, his gratitude to his defenders was very lively. And, in addition to other liberalities, he presented a commemorative medal to them all.

CHAPTER 4

# Outside Kimberley

Failing an assault, we resume the bombardment. The firing is slow and inaccurate. The English reply in much the same fashion, when suddenly their new cannon appears on the scene, not altogether to our surprise, for some intercepted letters had warned us of its manufacture. It was the famous *Long Cecil*.

The *Long Cecil* was a gun of about 12 centimetres, made in Kimberley itself during the siege with a piece of steel taken from the machinery of the De Beers mine.

The piece was drilled and rifled with the means at the disposal of the besieged.

The closing of the breech, a somewhat fantastic arrangement, was based on the Canet system. In default of a trial field, the range was arrived at from observations of actual firing against us.

*Long Cecil* accordingly began to speak, and to speak very much to the point. Several times we were covered with earth, and I am certain that out of twenty shells, the extreme error was not more than 200 metres. One fortunately fell diagonally on *Long Tom's* very platform, rebounded, and burst a little way off. Seven men were killed.

The next day, Thursday, passed in almost precisely the same fashion. Towards five o'clock the interchange of amenities between *Long Tom* and *Long Cecil* began, and lasted till 8.30; at 8.30, breakfast. After breakfast, the guns went to work again till 11. At 11, lunch, rest. From 4 to 6, another cannonade. At 6, dinner.

This respect for meal-times is charming, and greatly facilitates life in the field.

It is a pity the attention of the Powers is not called to this subject by an international convention! Many affections of the stomach would be hereby avoided.

Encouraged by the example of their big brothers, the little 12 and 15-pounder Krupps and Armstrongs join in the concert.

The English have five, and we have four. It is delightful, and one can't complain of a single second of boredom.

On Friday, the colonel's request is still unanswered.

'Wait a little while!'

Sternberg has had enough of it. Recognising the impossibility of persuading Du Toit to take decisive action, he starts off to Jacobsdal, where the English make him a prisoner. He was a great loss, for he had an extraordinary repertory of adventures, which he told in a very amusing manner, and, besides, he was a capital cook.

The 'boys' in these regions, greatly inferior to those of the Soudan in this respect, claim to be cooks as soon as they know how to light a fire. Accordingly, we prepare our meals ourselves. Tinned meat, a bit of roast mutton, or a stew, are the usual dishes.

The Colonel eats very little, and only takes grilled meat; he drinks tea or milk, and never touches wine or spirits. He does not smoke. He is a striking contrast to the rest of us, who eat like ogres, drink like sponges, and smoke like engines!

Our contingent, consisting of Breda, Léon, Michel, Coste, my friend De C—— and I, remain with Villebois.

Michel has calculated the ranges, and we fire all Friday night. The points aimed at are: the searchlights, Cecil Rhodes' house, the Grand Hotel, the last high chimney on the left, and that on the right.

Erasmus was unable to suppress a gentle amusement at the sight of our preparations for night-firing. But when he grasped the idea that we were in earnest, and that his *Long Tom* was being loaded, the benevolent smile with which one would watch a spoilt child engaged in some innocent folly changed to a look of real anxiety. He thought poor Michel had gone mad. He finally got used to the novel proceeding.

Firing ceased on both sides about 12.30 a.m. Early on Saturday morning it began again. One of our shells fell on the De Beers magazine, transformed into an ammunition factory, and caused an explosion and a fire.

The English, despairing of silencing our *Long Tom* with their *Long Cecil*, replied to every shot at the town by a shell into our laager. The accuracy of their fire with this gun at a range of about 7,000 metres was remarkable. We were indeed a capital target: a green rectangle of 200 metres in the midst of a yellow, arid plain.

The shell arrived in thirty-four seconds, but did no great damage, for a watchman gave the alarm, '*Skit!*' each time when he saw the smoke, and we retreated into shelter.

The telegraphists of the staff, who were working in a little house, were placed in communication with the watchman by means of a bell, and, warned half a minute before the arrival, they had time to take refuge in a neighbouring trench.

We learnt later that a similar system had been adopted in Kimberley as a protection against *Long Tom*, and hence the small number of killed during the siege. One of the first victims of *Long Tom*, however, was the engineer of the *Long Cecil*, who had just finished his work. A shell burst on his house and killed him in his bedroom. Another cause of the slight mortality on both sides was the bad quality of the fuses for the projectiles, which often burst imperfectly, or not at all. Thus, one of the English shells fell in the machinery of the waterworks, only a few inches from our reserve of a hundred shells, and happily failed to explode. Another went through a cast-iron pipe, over a centimetre thick, and buried itself in the earth without exploding; its fuse was completely flattened on the projectile by contact with the pipe.

Nevertheless, a good many, too many indeed, *did* burst with satisfactory results—to those who fired them.

A good many of the Boers accordingly took the precaution of digging a sort of tomb several feet deep, in which they piled mattresses and blankets. They spent all night and part of the day lying in this shelter.

On Saturday morning, on arriving at the battery, we were surprised by a whistling sound. The English, harassed by the fire of *Long Tom*, had dug trenches during the night to a distance of about 1,200 yards, and had manned them with riflemen. Their fire was not yet very galling, because of the distance between us.

Colonel de Villebois, seeing clearly what would happen, renewed his request for a party of men. He now only asked for twenty-five to make an assault that very night, for he pointed out that the *shanjes* (trenches) would be pushed forward during the night, and that our battery would become untenable. But he was repulsed by the eternal 'Wait a little while!'

Long convoys of *kaffirs* that the English could no longer feed came out of the town every day, preceded by huge white flags. Some were allowed to pass after a parley, others were sent back again.

The colonel feared that an attempt would be made against *Long*

*Tom* by night, as a sequel to the offensive movement on the part of the garrison indicated by the making of the trenches.

Everyone goes to spend the night at the battery, and we take the opportunity of firing at the town. It proves to be merely a pastime. The English reply, but do not attack us.

On Sunday, February 11, we rest all along the line. The Burghers sing hymns in chorus, and do not cease till late in the evening. A sort of patriarchal simplicity obtains among them. Yesterday the colonel was shaving. A Boer entered without saying a word, sat down on his little camp-bed, and remained there motionless. The colonel, used to their ways, took no notice, but waited for the visitor to explain his visit. As this was prolonged considerably, the colonel continued his toilet by a tub taken *puris naturalibus*. The Boer remained, staring silently at him. At last, his toilet ended, the colonel explained to the visitor that he must go, as he wanted to close his tent. The Boer departed without a word. About ten minutes afterwards he came back with a friend, who explained that he wanted the colonel's razor. He would bring it back-*afterwards*. It was very hard to make him understand that the colonel wished to reserve the implement for his private use.

On this Sunday, the day of rest, we accordingly went off to bathe at a spring four kilometres from our laager. We enjoy this peaceful pastime in the company of a young clergyman who was at one time in the camp. When *Long Cecil* began to bombard us, he judged its warlike thunders to be incompatible with his sacred function, and set up his tent beyond its range.

On Monday morning the firing began again early. Léon and the colonel went off to the battery. Our horses had been turned out to graze by mistake, so we did not start till an hour after them. On arriving, we found the balls whistling more smartly than on Saturday. We could plainly distinguish the buzz of the dum-dum bullets amidst the whir of the ordinary charge.

During the two nights, the English had pushed forward their trenches to a distance of from 700 to 800 yards from us. We went up on the platform, where the Colonel, his glass in his eye, was talking imperturbably to General du Toit. At the same moment we saw Léon, who was standing behind them, spin round and fall across the gun-carriage. The poor fellow had been shot right through the forehead just above the eyes.

The colonel at once raised him in his arms, others started off in haste for an ambulance; but the bullets were now falling round us like hail. Two horses were wounded in an instant, and a Burgher fell, a bullet clean through his body.

Poor Léon was still conscious. He bid us all good-bye calmly, taking a particularly affectionate leave of the colonel, to whom he was greatly attached. The colonel took a little water to wash the blood from his face, and placed the empty *pannikin* on the parapet of sacks filled with earth behind which we were sheltered. So heavy was the English fire that the *pannikin* instantly fell to the ground pierced by a bullet.

At last a cart appeared with an attendant and a stretcher. The wounded, who numbered about a dozen by this time, received first aid; then Léon was carried off on a stretcher.

What a journey was that march of three kilometres, the first part of which was performed under a rain of bullets! The head of the wounded man was swathed in cloths, which we kept wetting continually, holding an umbrella over his head, for the heat was intense—it was eleven o'clock in the morning. Blood poured from his mouth and nose. Poor fellow! we made up our minds that it was all over with him.

We reached Waterworks in two hours. But the little house that had been turned into a hospital was no longer safe since the bombardment of our camp had begun. A telegram had therefore been sent to Riverton Road, where there was an ambulance-station with a good doctor. Towards one o'clock an ambulance-carriage arrived and carried off our comrade.

On Tuesday, the 13th, we missed the salute *Long Tom* had been in the habit of giving the enemy at daybreak. What had happened? We sent off for news. General du Toit replied that Erasmus declared the gun was broken, and could not be fired. He himself had not been to inquire into the damage, and seemed to be no more concerned than if he had been told it was raining at Chicago. We set off to Kampferdam in great distress, expecting to find the gun a wreck.

As we approached, however, we saw that it was still in place, apparently wondering at its own silence. We examined it carefully all over, but could find nothing to account for the catastrophe, and, in despair, we sent for Erasmus.

Standing back a couple of paces, he showed us that one of the beams of the platform, which had received the full force of the recoil, had sunk some few centimetres. It was a matter of no importance, and did not interfere with the firing in any way. But Erasmus, I suppose, did not feel inclined to work the gun that day. He had told Du Toit that it was broken, and the general had at once accepted the statement. After a severe reprimand to the recalcitrant gunner, the firing recommenced as usual.

Our provisions began to run out in camp, in spite of a stock of potatoes we had discovered at the waterworks. It was accordingly arranged that we should start off with two others of the party to get fresh stores, and a cart and mules, at Pretoria.

The colonel, believing that the lack of offensive action among the Boers would prolong the siege indefinitely, determined to set out himself on the 15th for Colesberg, where we were to rejoin him in a few days. We started on the 14th, bound for Brandfort and Pretoria.

On setting out, my mare, an excellent mount, but very fiery, brought me suddenly to the ground, to the great amusement of the colonel. The same accident having happened to Breda a day or two before, it began to be looked upon as a special privilege of the ex-cavalry officers!

At nightfall we arrived at Riverton Road, where Léon was lying. During the evening the colonel himself came over to inquire for him. He had had a good day, and the operation that was judged necessary had been fixed for eleven o'clock that night, to avoid the heat of daylight. We waited about the door of the baggage-shed, which had been converted into an ambulance.

The operation, which proved perfectly successful, lasted an hour and a half. The doctor, a Scotchman called Dunlop, assured us that our poor friend was out of danger.

At daybreak on the 15th we started, the colonel for the camp, we for Brandfort. It was terribly hot, and we were in a hurry, for a rumour of Lord Roberts' arrival had got about. It seemed likely that there would be some more lively work on hand very soon, and we were anxious to get through the drudgery of revictualling as quickly as possible.

In the evening we reached Boshof, where a good many wounded had been brought since our last visit. We rode all day on the 16th, slept in the bush, and started again at daybreak on the 17th. Towards noon we took a rest of an hour and a half, and consumed a tin of corned beef.

It was nearly two when we mounted again under a sky of fire, not to draw rein till we reached Brandfort at ten o'clock on Sunday morning, save for a compulsory halt of two hours from three to five in the morning, when the darkness made it impossible for us to continue our journey in the trackless sand and tangled bush.

We had been in the saddle twenty-six hours out of thirty to accomplish our journey of 120 miles, and had taken three and a half days, riding over sixty kilometres a day, in average heat of from 38° to 40° (centigrade), without fodder and almost without water, in a wild, unknown country.

Our horses were dead-beat, and we entered the village on foot, dragging the poor brutes by their bridles. What was our stupefaction to hear that the siege of Kimberley had been raised without any engagement the very day after our departure!

The surprise, it seems, had been complete. There was a cry of 'The English!' and then a panic, which barely left time to carry off the guns and waggons. Part of the ammunition was left behind, some provisions, *Long Tom's* break and its platform. The colonel had escaped with Breda. But in the confusion one of our comrades, Coste, was lost, and eventually joined Cronje.

A story which amused us all at the time may be told here. A volunteer, no longer in his first youth—well over fifty, in fact—had come to join the colonel just at the time of the English attack. A very eccentric character, and slightly bemused by drink, he found himself in the thick of the stampede, without any clear idea of what it was all about.

Suddenly the Burghers, who had never seen him in the camp before, struck by his odd behaviour, demanded his passports. Not understanding a word of Dutch, he had some difficulty in making out what they wanted.

At last he produced the necessary paper. The pandours of the moment scrutinized them carefully, then, shaking their heads in the fashion which among all races implies negation, they said:

'No good! *Obsal!*' (mount).

Two men ranged themselves on either side of the unlucky wight, a complete novice in horsemanship, and galloped off with him to a farm several miles off.

'Dismount! Your passports!'

About fifteen persons, men, women and children, were grouped round a table. The passport, handed round once more, is discussed by the assembly, each person present giving an opinion. The general verdict is unfavourable, for heads are again shaken.

'No good! *Obsal!*'

The poor volunteer, aching from his furious gallop, begins to think things rather beyond a joke; but, anxious to conciliate, he remounts, and gallops off again under escort. On arriving at another farm another inspection, also unfavourable, takes place.

'No good! *Obsal!*'

This time the worm turns. Pale, exhausted and racked with pain, he opposes the force of inertia to the rigour of his tormentors, who, convinced that he is a spy, set him against a wall and load their rifles. This argument is so convincing that he remounts, and finally makes them understand that he will be able to find someone to answer for him at Brandfort.

Two days later he arrived there, fasting, exhausted, and still guarded by his escort. Fortunately he was recognised and released. He never returned to the front.

✶✶✶✶✶✶

We leave for Pretoria by the first train, and arrive on the evening of the 20th. We at once set to work on our re-victualling mission.

Two days later, I got a telegram from Colonel de Villebois-Mareuil. Having heard of the arrival of a good many French volunteers at Pretoria, he agrees to take the command of them, and orders me to get them together. A letter to M. Reitz, sent off at the same time, explains the project.

Among the new arrivals are ex-petty officers, ex-sailors, ex-legionaries . . . a motley crew. Their equipment will take several days, and it is arranged that they are to join us at Colesberg, for which we start by that evening's train.

During this short sojourn at Pretoria I was presented by Colonel Gourko to Captain D——, the French military *attaché*, one of the most charming men I have ever met.

We noticed numerous placards on the town walls, giving notice of thanksgiving services for February 26 and 27. It is the anniversary of Majuba Hill, which is celebrated every year with great pomp. This year, in spite of the national pre-occupation in current events, the traditional custom is to be kept up. The usual review of the troops by the President and the Commander-in-Chief cannot, of course, take place; but the shops and offices will be closed for forty-eight hours, and the whole population will flock to the churches.

Shortly after our departure, at a station the name of which I forget—perhaps intentionally, for I feel a qualm of remorse at the recollection of it—a little fox-terrier playing about the train jumped into our carriage. We were just starting.... It would have been cruel to throw the poor little beast on to the platform at the risk of maiming it or causing it to be run over.... In short, we kept her, and christened her Nelly. She was very pretty, pure white, with a black patch on her head and another on her back. I felt remorseful—until the next station; then I overcame my scruples. I am so fond of dogs.

At Brandfort, a counter-order awaits us, directing us to go to Bloemfontein, where the colonel awaits us, in consequence of Lord Roberts' latest operations. We land our cart, our mules, and our provisions. But our worn-out horses have to be replaced. The colonel, impatient to be gone, will not wait for us, and starts for Petrusburg, where we are to join him as quickly as possible.

On the 28th, the news of Cronje's capitulation reaches us. We know nothing of the details, but the moral effect is terrible.

We had got together hastily at Pretoria a cart, harness, mules, and three black boys. Individually, each of these acquisitions is highly satisfactory. The cart is a superb omnibus, freshly painted gray; the harness is almost new, the mules very handsome—a little black one in particular. The boys were chosen to suit all tastes: one tall, one short, and one of medium height. But it proves very difficult to establish any sort of cohesion between these various elements.

At the first attempt the harness breaks, the mules bite and kick. It needs the cunning of an Apache even to approach the little black one. The boys are stupid, and speak neither Dutch nor English, nothing but *Kaffir*. The omnibus alone remains stationary, but it creaks and groans in a pitiable fashion when touched.

A second experiment is no more successful than the first. The third gives a better result: the vehicle moves, and even goes very near to losing a wheel.

This remarkable result is achieved, firstly, because all the rotten leathers of the harness are in pieces, after a double series of joltings and strainings; only the solid ones are left. Secondly, the pretty little black mule has run away, after breaking some dozen halters, so that we are saved the trouble of harnessing her. Lastly, we have stationed the three boys at a safe distance, begging them on no account to help us, and Michel, who as an old artilleryman is an adept in harness, does wonders. Finally we get off, escorting our omnibus, which groans aloud at every step.

We look like 'The Attack on the Stage Coach' in Buffalo Bill!

CHAPTER 5

# Retreat

On the morning of the 7th, the road to Petrusburg was blocked, and the guns were roaring in front of us. Marais, Botha's adjutant, joined us. At the first sound of the guns we left the waggons, and galloped off in the direction he pointed out. The Battle of Poplar Grove was about to be fought under our eyes, though we were unable to take a very active part in it.

The engagement went on mainly on our right; we were on the left of the Boer lines. In front of us was a *kopje* occupied by a hundred rifles.

About 11 o'clock the English cavalry charged at the guns, about two miles away. The firing slackened. Then about 2 o'clock the English began to shell us furiously with shrapnel, also the kopje forming the Boer centre. An outflanking movement completed the demoralisation of the Boers, and at 3.30 the retreat became general.

President Kruger came by this morning to announce that he had made the following peace proposals:

> Bloemfontein,
> March 5, 1900.

The blood and tears of the thousands who have suffered by this war, and the prospect of all the moral and economic ruin with which South Africa is now threatened, make it necessary for both belligerents to ask themselves dispassionately, and as in the sight of the Triune God, for what they are fighting, and whether the aim of each justifies all this appalling misery and devastation.

With this object, and in view of the assertions of various British statesmen to the effect that this war was begun, and is being carried on, with the set purpose of undermining Her Majesty's authority in South Africa, and of setting up an administration over all South Africa, independent of Her Majesty's Government, we consider it our duty solemnly to declare that this war was undertaken solely as a defensive measure to safeguard the threatened independence of the South African Republic, and is only continued in order to secure and safeguard the incontestable independence of both Republics as sovereign international States, and to obtain the assurance that those of Her Majesty's subjects who have taken part with us in this war shall suffer no harm whatsoever in person or property.

On these two conditions, but on these alone, are we now, as in the past, desirous of seeing peace re-established in South Africa, and of putting an end to the evils now reigning over South Africa; while, if Her Majesty's Government is determined to destroy the independence of the Republics, there is nothing left to us and to our people but to persevere to the end in the course already begun, in spite of the overwhelming pre-eminence of the British Empire, confident that that God who lighted the inextinguishable fire of the love of freedom in the hearts of ourselves and of our fathers will not forsake us, but will accomplish His work in us and in our descendants.

We hesitated to make this declaration earlier to your Excellency, as we feared that, as long as the advantage was always on our side, and as long as our forces held defensive positions far in Her Majesty's colonies, such a declaration might hurt the feelings of honour of the British people; but now that the prestige of the British Empire may be considered to be assured by the capture of one of our forces by Her Majesty's troops, and that we are thereby forced to evacuate other positions which our forces had occupied, that difficulty is over, and we can no longer hesitate clearly to inform your Government and people in the sight of the whole civilized world why we are fighting, and on what conditions we are ready to restore peace.

Lord Salisbury replied as follows:

Foreign Office,<br>March 11, 1900.

I have the honour to acknowledge your Honours' telegram, dated the 5th of March, from Bloemfontein, of which the purport is principally to demand that Her Majesty's Government shall recognise the "incontestable independence" of the South African Republic and Orange Free State "as sovereign international States," and to offer on those terms to bring the war to a conclusion.

In the beginning of October peace existed between Her Majesty and the two Republics under the Conventions which were then in existence. A discussion had been proceeding for some months between Her Majesty's Government and the South African Republic, of which the object was to obtain redress for certain very serious grievances under which British residents in the South African Republic were suffering. In the course of these negotiations the South African Republic had, to the knowledge of Her Majesty's Government, made considerable armaments, and the latter had, consequently, taken steps to provide corresponding reinforcements to the British garrisons of Cape Town and Natal. No infringement of the rights guaranteed by the Conventions had, up to that point, taken place on the British side.

Suddenly, at two days' notice, the South African Republic, after issuing an insulting ultimatum, declared war upon Her Majesty; and the Orange Free State, with whom there had not even been any discussion, took a similar step. Her Majesty's dominions were immediately invaded by the two Republics, siege was laid to three towns within the British frontier, a large portion of the two colonies was overrun, with great destruction to property and life, and the Republics claimed to treat the inhabitants of extensive portions of Her Majesty's dominions as if those dominions had been annexed to one or other of them. In anticipation of these operations, the South African Republic had been accumulating for many years past military stores on an enormous scale, which, by their character, could only have been intended for use against Great Britain.

Your Honours make some observations of a negative character upon the object with which these preparations were made. I do not think it necessary to discuss the questions you have raised. But the result of these preparations, carried on with great secrecy, has been that the British Empire has been compelled to confront an invasion which has entailed upon the Empire a costly war and the loss of thousands of precious lives. This great calamity has been the penalty which Great Britain has suffered for having in recent years acquiesced in the existence of the two Republics.

In view of the use to which the two Republics have put the position which was given to them, and the calamities which their unprovoked attack has inflicted upon Her Majesty's dominions, Her Majesty's Government can only answer your Honours' telegram by saying that they are not prepared to assent to the independence either of the South African Republic or of the Orange Free State.

It was to be war, then, to the bitter end.

✶✶✶✶✶✶

At the beginning of the retreat, a field-cornet came to ask my advice, as often happened. He disregarded it, as always happened. I wanted them to destroy the reservoirs, burn the forage, and poison the wells all along the line of retreat.[1] He would never consent.

Later on, when I was a prisoner, an English officer of rank, who had taken part in the march across the Orange Free State, told me he had suffered terribly from thirst, and he assured me that if the measures I had advised had been taken, Roberts' 40,000 men, for the most part mounted, would never have achieved their task.

But at the moment time failed me to prove to the brave field-cornet, by the teaching of history in general, and of the wars in Spain in particular, what excellent results might be obtained by such a method of defence. Minutes were becoming precious, and we made off as fast as we could, while in the distance we saw half our convoy blazing, fired by bursting shells.

Towards half-past nine we lay down on the veldt, without pitching any tents, and keeping a sharp look-out. By eleven the last of the Boer stragglers had passed. Colonel Gourko and Lieutenant Thomson had been made prisoners.

On the 8th we were astir at daybreak. Our three boys went off to find our beasts, which had strayed far in search of pasture, on account of the scanty herbage, in spite of their hobbles. They were all recovered, however, with the exception of one mule, which remained deaf to every summons, a most inconsiderate proceeding on his part, seeing that the English were at our heels.

---

1. The writer apparently made this monstrous suggestion quite seriously.—Translator.

Time being precious, we started off as well as we could with our reduced convoy. Suddenly one of our boys, big John, stood tiptoe on his long feet, gave a sweeping glance around, and went quietly on his way. Half an hour later, he began again to increase in height and to study the horizon. . . . We could see absolutely nothing. As my acquaintance with John was slight, I imagined that he probably suffered from some nervous affection. But this time he sniffed the air loudly, and, without a word, darted off obliquely from our track.

An hour passed, and he did not return. Grave doubts of his fidelity began to afflict us. At last, two hours later, we noticed a speck on the horizon, then two. It was John with the missing mule. John is an angel—a black angel!

All the farms we passed on the road had hoisted the white flag. At noon we reached the point where the road to Bloemfontein bifurcates. A few Burghers were gathered there. We pitched our tents.

During the evening the French Military *Attaché*, Captain D———, passed, and told us that Colonel de Villebois was only about an hour distant from us.

On March 9 we set out to join him. We found him with about fifty men, coming from Pretoria. These men were divided into two companies, the first under Breda, the second under me. Directly we arrived it was agreed to start at ten o'clock. We stopped long enough to add our cart to the colonel's convoy, which we were to pick up near the farm of Abraham's Kraal. The 'French Corps' was formed!

About four o'clock we arrived on the height of Abraham's Kraal. The farm so-called lies along the Modder River, which flows from east to west. Its steep, bush-entangled banks are bathed with yellow, turbid water, whence its name—Modder (Mud) River. A line of *kopjes*, starting from the edge of the river, stretches several miles south of it. In front of them, to the west, lies a barren yellow plain. Far off on the horizon lie the *kopjes* of Poplar Grove, where we were forty-eight hours before.

The colonel, who has gone off on a scouting expedition with his troop, is not to be found. We wait for him vainly all the evening with General Delarey's staff, in company with Baron von Wrangel, an ex-lieutenant of the German Guards. In this expedition a young volunteer named Franck, a quartermaster of the Chasseurs d'Afrique, whose term had just expired, distinguished himself by his coolness and his boldness under fire. He was a brave fellow, as he was to prove later on.

Night came on fast, our chief was still absent, and we went off to sleep at a little deserted farm, with the officers of the Johannesburg Politie. We lay down beside them and slept like men who have been in the saddle for twelve hours.

On March 10, at 5 a.m., we started for General Delarey's bivouac. It might have been 6.30, when Vecht-General Sellier passed us at a gallop, crying: '*Obsal!* The English!'

Our positions, chosen the night before, were as follows: Our right, with the Modder River beyond, consisted of about 400 men of the Johannesburg Politie, with a Krupp gun, an Armstrong, and two Maxims. Then a space in the plain, where a commando of 200 men, with three cannon and a Maxim gun, constituting our centre, had taken up a position early in the morning. Finally, to the south, on our left, 300 men on a round *kopje*, fairly high.

At Poplar Grove two days before we had numbered several thousands; but the Boers, discouraged by the check they had undergone, had returned to their farms, refusing to fight. This was a proceeding very characteristic of these men, slow physically and morally, profoundly obstinate, astute rather than intelligent, distrustful, sometimes magnanimous. Easily depressed and as easily elated, without any apparent cause, they are a curious jumble of virtues and failings, often of the most contradictory kinds. The sort of panics frequent among them are due, I think, rather to their total lack of organisation than to their temperament; for, not to speak of individual instances of valour, by no means rare among them, the Johannesburg Politie, with their very primitive discipline, have shown what might have been done by the Boers with some slight instruction and some slight discipline.[2]

They alone had remained, with a handful of foreigners and some

---

2. Ten years ago the Duc de Broglie, in his *Marie-Thérèse Impératrice*, wrote as follows of the campaign of 1744 against Frederick the Great:
'Prince Charles had not even all his force at his disposal.... All that had been left him were the Hungarian levies, who had indeed been the main strength of the Austrian army; but these irregular troops, passing from ardour to discouragement with that mobility proper to men with whom enthusiasm does duty for experience and discipline, now thought of nothing but of a speedy return to their homesteads, and entered reluctantly upon every enterprise that retarded this return. Whole companies deserted the flag and took the road for Hungary.'
These words, written of the Hungarians of the seventeenth century, are literally applicable to the Boers of today, and it is curious to note—though I do not for a moment compare Lord Roberts to Frederick the Great—that the Hungarians often inflicted a check on the King of Prussia, just as the Boers have occasionally stopped the English marshal.

stray men from various *commandos*.

The Heilbron Commando, consisting of over 200 men, was represented by the corporal and three men. All the rest, the commandant at their head, had gone home; hence their reduced fighting strength. At last all the remnant of the force was in its place, behind little rocky entrenchments hastily thrown up.

In the distance a long column of 'khakis' defiles, marching from north to south, presenting its left flank to us from a distance of seven or eight miles, and preceded by a body of mounted scouts.

We go to inspect the mounting of our guns, which are arriving on our left and in the centre of our line. Then we return to the *kopje* where we were before with the Johannesburg Politie. Captain D——, the French Military *Attaché*, is there following all the movements.

About eight o'clock an English detachment essays a movement against us, and we open fire with our Krupp gun. English regiments defile against the horizon till eleven o'clock. Some Maxims and a battery of field-guns have been mounted against us.

Between the English and Boer lines a herd of springbock are running about in terror under the shells. The poor beasts finally make off to more tranquil regions and disappear.

The Maxims fire short, but after a few seconds the field-guns find the range, and fire with a certain precision. Two shrapnel-shells fired one after the other burst over our heads. My right-hand neighbour gets a bullet just below his right eye, and falls against me; I am covered with his blood. He died soon after.

As I bathe his face, I see Captain D——hobbling back. I go to him. He has been struck on the hip by a ball, which, having fortunately spent most of its force, has not penetrated the flesh. The wound was not dangerous, but it swelled a good deal at once, and caused a numbness in the leg. I hastily applied the necessary dressing, which the captain had with him, and then went to fetch his horse.

After his departure, we return to the *kopje*. The Mounted Rifles advance in force. We wait till they are about 500 metres off, and then open a heavy fire upon them, supported by the two Maxims. They retreat rapidly, leaving some dozen of their number on the field. We make four prisoners. They are sailors who have been mounted, lads of barely twenty. There is a lull after this attempt.

About four o'clock the artillery fire begins again with redoubled fury, heralding a violent charge by the infantry, who have been concentrated under the shelter of the field-guns. A simultaneous charge is made on our left wing. All along the line and on both flanks we sustain a heavy fusillade from the enemy. Although protected to some extent by our rocks, our losses are pretty heavy.

The English come up to be killed with admirable courage. Three times they return to the charge in the open, losing a great many men. At nightfall they are close upon us.

I go in search of Colonel Villebois, who means to rest his men in a little wood behind a *kopje* on the banks of the Modder. We have eaten nothing since the night before.

At eight o'clock comes an order for a general retreat. We learn that an outflanking movement is to be attempted against us. In the evening General Delarey telegraphed as follows:

> The English are advancing upon our positions in two different directions. They have begun to bombard General Sellier, and are keeping up a sharp rifle-fire. We have been heavily engaged from nine o'clock this morning till sunset. The federated troops fought like heroes. Three times they repulsed a strong force of the English, who brought up fresh troops against us every time. Each attack was repulsed, and at sunset the English troops were only about forty metres from us. Their losses were very heavy. Our own have not yet been ascertained. A report on this point will follow.

We found afterwards that Roberts' entire army was present, some 40,000 men, and that he had engaged over 12,000. Our losses were 380 men out of about 950.

At 8.30 we set out hastily for Bloemfontein, carrying off our prisoners and wounded on trolleys drawn by mules. About eleven o'clock we pass some English outposts, which are pointed out to us on our right at a distance of only a few hundred metres.

At three in the morning we arrive at the store where we had bivouacked two nights before. We leave our horses to graze in a field of maize, and take a short rest. About five we are greeted by distant volleys.

'*Obsal!*'

But my horse is dead lame in the right hind-leg. I try to bind it up with the remains of an old waistcoat. Impossible. He cannot drag himself along. I am forced to 'find' another which is grazing nearby.

I seem to be forming predatory habits. Here I am now with a dog I 'found,' which follows me faithfully, on a horse I also 'found'! But it is in the cause of liberty.

Besides, these habits are so much in vogue among the Boers. I could tell a tale of one of my comrades, to whose detriment some half-dozen horses had been 'found' by the Burghers (the process is called by them *obtail*). And, to conclude, my find was no great acquisition.

We finally arrive at Bloemfontein about three o'clock in the afternoon. Here we meet numbers of English men and women, smartly dressed in summer costumes, smiling and cheerful, starting out in carriages to meet the victors. They are not aggressive, however; our sullen bearing perhaps warns them that a misplaced exuberance might have unpleasant consequences.

We find our convoy at the entrance of the town, and we pass through to our camp on the east.

Poor capital! What terror, what disorder shows itself on every side! The shops have been hurriedly shut; men, carriages, riders pass each other in every direction, and the two main streets are encumbered with an interminable string of bullock-waggons. In the market-place and in the market itself an improvised ambulance has been set up, and the wounded are being tended. On every threshold stand women and children, whose anxious eyes seem to ask: 'Where are they?'

CHAPTER 6

# The European Legion

We start again on the 12th, at three in the morning. Not a Burgher remains with us. They have all gone off in the directions of Wynburg and Kroonstad.

On the 13th we are on the bridge of the Modder River. We establish ourselves in a deserted farm, and execute some stray ducks, which would no doubt have died of hunger but for our timely appearance—a most painful end, I believe.

Scouts are sent out. In about an hour the English are suddenly sighted. We rush to the road, and in ten minutes a barricade is thrown across it. I am in the centre with the others. But the English hang back, and finally go off.

Towards noon we start in the direction of Brandfort, where our convoy, which was to travel day and night, is expected to be by this time. It is about 4.30 when we come in sight of the village.

There is a cloud of dust on our left, then two despatch-riders on bicycles fly past us. The lancers!

We set off at a gallop to get to the houses before them. It is a steeplechase between us. After an hour's ride we arrive at the same time as the head of the enemy's advanced guard, which falls back at a gallop. We try to pursue them, but our broken-down horses can carry us no further.

We rush into the village, while our men hastily harness our carts. The colonel sends us to take up a position to cover their retreat, for there are two squadrons of lancers in the little wood 500 metres from the village. The *landdrost*, fearing reprisals, comes to beg me not to fire. I give him these alternatives—to hold his tongue or to be shot. He prefers the former, and I see him no more.

Meanwhile, C—— and Michel get down a cannon from a truck

at the railway-station. The terrified artillerymen refuse to work it. But the English, not knowing what our numbers are (we are barely twenty-five), dare not attack us, and we get away in the night.

Our rallying-point is Kroonstad, the new capital of the Free State.

On the 15th we are at Wynburg. We leave it again on the morning of the 16th by the last train, setting fire to the railway-station and destroying the reservoirs. Comfortably installed in a train we made up ourselves, at Smaldeel we are invaded by a whole *commando*. . . . Six men to every carriage, with their six saddles, six bridles, six rifles, six cloaks, a dozen blankets, and some twenty packages. . . . Ouf!

These good Burghers, who smoke as long as they can, are without the most elementary ideas of ordinary civility of behaviour. Their familiarity of manner is extraordinary; happily, they show no resentment if one retorts in like fashion. One of them, to steady himself during his slumbers, thrusts his foot—and such a foot!—into the pocket of C——'s coat. C——, put quite at his ease by this proceeding, does not hesitate to increase the comfort of his own position by a reciprocal thrusting of his foot into the waistcoat of his sympathetic *vis-à-vis*. They form a touchingly fraternal group, and in this position they sleep for ten hours. At every sudden stoppage, the rounded paunch of the good Burgher acts as a buffer, deadening the violence of the jolt for my friend.

My *vis-à-vis*—I had almost said my opponent—much more formal, is content to plant a bag on my knees, and a box on my feet. . . . How beautiful is the simplicity of rustic manners!

At last, on March 17, we reach Kroonstad and establish our camp there. We take advantage of this sojourn to pursue the education of our 'boys.'

In consequence of our having 'chummed' with other comrades, our suite has taken on alarming proportions; we look like a company of slave-dealers.

The biggest and oldest of our boys is called John. He seems to have an inordinate affection for straws, with which he delights to adorn the calves of his legs.

The second is also called John; he is one of the best. We have christened him 'Cook,' in allusion to his functions. An old stove, found in a house that had been burnt, gives him quite an important air when he prepares our meals.

The third is called Charlie. He is very intelligent, an excellent mule-driver, but a thorough rascal.

The fourth, who is chocolate-coloured, is good at guarding the mules at the pasture. He is called 'Beguini,' which means little.

The fifth is not of much use for anything, but he is very fond of his master, a sympathetic survivor of 'Fort Chabrol.'

The sixth belongs to no one. But noting that his compatriots seem happy enough with us, he has established himself in our kitchen, and serves us more or less like the others.

The Walsh River, a very remarkable stream, for there is water in it,[1] flows past Kroonstad, and we occupy our leisure moments with the bucolic occupation of fishing.

All the members of the government have assembled at Kroonstad; the two Presidents, the generals, the military attachés, and Colonel de Villebois-Mareuil are present at their deliberations.

There seems to be a tendency to energetic measures. A martial law decreeing the death-penalty against deserters is passed and proclaimed. Unfortunately, it was never enforced. The confidence of the Burghers has been somewhat shaken. The Executive begins to understand that he who foretold the consequences of their blunders so unerringly may perhaps be able to remedy them.

On the 20th, accordingly, Colonel de Villebois-Mareuil is appointed Vecht-General, and all the Europeans are placed under his command. But scarcely had this just and intelligent resolution been passed, when jealousy, pride, and fear of seeing a stranger succeed where they themselves had failed took possession of the Burghers, and the orders to concentrate were never carried out.

It is much to be regretted that sentiments so injurious to the national cause should have deprived the government of the inestimable services that might have been rendered by a corps of 1,500 or 2,000 resolute Europeans, all formerly soldiers, under the command of a man of the science, the valour, and the worth of General de Villebois-Mareuil.

Nevertheless, about 200 men of all nationalities, drawn by the confidence such a leader alone could inspire, came of their own free will to place themselves under his orders. With these he organised the 'European Legion.' It included the two divisions of the French corps, a Dutch corps, and a German corps.

Everything General de Villebois asked for was promised, but nothing was carried out. His plan consisted primarily of raids like those which marked the War of Secession.

---
1. Most of the rivers are dried up in summer-time.

On the 20th he addressed this stirring proclamation to us and to those who were scattered further afield:

To the Legionaries who have known me as their comrade:
Officers, non-commissioned officers, and soldiers! I know you have not forgotten me, and that we understand each other, hence this appeal to you.

We see around us a worthy people, who are threatened with the loss of their rights, their property, and their liberty, for the satisfaction of a handful of capitalists.

The blood which flows in the veins of this people is partly French blood. France, therefore, owes them some manifestation of sympathy.

You are men whose martial temperaments, to say nothing of the great obligations of nationality, have brought together under the banner of this people. May success and victory attend their flag! I know you as the ideal type of a corps made for attack, and ignorant of retreat.

Influenced mainly by the unfriendly attitude of certain generals to whom his promotion had given umbrage, Villebois determined to strike a great blow in all haste.

Without waiting to complete the organisation of the Legion, he formed us into a corps of 100 men, which he made up by the addition of twenty-five Afrikanders, under Field-Cornet Coleman; and as soon as the cartload of dynamite he had been awaiting arrived, he set out on the 24th, at eight o'clock in the evening.

His parting orders to me were to hold myself in readiness, with the rest of the men (about 100) and the new arrivals, for Saturday next, March 31, and to collect horses and provisions. On the 31st, he would come back and explain the second part of the operation he was then beginning.

Absolute secrecy was preserved as to the object of his expedition. To Breda's question as to the direction he proposed to take, he replied: 'To the right.'

Our poor general was very nervous. On March 23, the eve of his departure, he telegraphed to a wounded friend who was returning to France:

You, at least, know your fate, whereas I am uncertain what lies before me!

A dark presentiment, perhaps. In any case, what melancholy underlies that short phrase! I do not say *discouragement*, for there are some stout hearts who know not the feeling, and Villebois was of these.

Two days after, one of my men returned in the evening; his horse had broken down on the road. They had made a very rapid march, taking only four hours' rest at night and four in the day, in two fractions. Nevertheless, after thirty-six hours of marching at this rate, this man, unmounted, and separated from the rest of the column, had found a horse in a *kraal*, and had been able to return to Kroonstad in two hours.

Where then had the guide led them? If I could have communicated with the General, I would have warned him, but this was out of the question. On the 31st, there was no news; on the 1st, 2nd and 3rd of April, still none. On the 4th, after a notice from Colonel Maximoff, our detachment moved to Brandfort.

We are at a loss to account for the delay in the return of our comrades. But in a campaign delays are so common, the unexpected happens so constantly, that our anxiety is not very great.

The special train that takes us to Smaldeel consists of fifty-three coaches, the number found necessary for the men, waggons, and horses of our contingent. We found that the railway had been cut beyond Smaldeel, and we were obliged to go on to Brandfort by the road.

Brandfort had been occupied by the lancers for several days, but they had fallen back. The village is now the centre of Generals Delarey, Kolby and Smith.

We arrive on April 7 at 8.30. In the afternoon a telegram is posted up announcing that General Christian de Wet, who is operating to the east of Bloemfontein, has arrived near Sanna's Post, cutting off the water-supply of the Bloemfontein garrison, and carrying off 375 men, 7 cannon, 1,000 mules and 400 waggons. Three days later, on April 4, at Dewetsdorp, he took 459 more prisoners and 12 waggons.

This was the beginning of that series of *razzie* and surprises he has been carrying on incessantly ever since, astonishing the most audacious by his audacity, and by the rapidity and suddenness of his movements defeating the most scientific and elaborate devices for his capture. Broadwood, Rundle, Hunter, even Kitchener have been forced to give up the chase, and to wait till Fortune, unfaithful for a day, shall deliver the valiant Burgher into their hands.

We met the *landdrost* of Brandfort again, now more patriotic than ever; but he seemed slightly embarrassed when he saw us.

On April 7, the day of our arrival, we made a reconnaissance towards the south with four men. As we left the Boer lines we met a man, who, hearing us talking French, came to bid us *'Bon jour!'* We entered into conversation, and he seemed to take a great interest in European news. At last he told us he was a Belgian, and suddenly asked:

'You had a war with the Germans one time, didn't you?'

The war of 1870 was news to him. He had been on the *veldt* since 1867.

'Do you know if our Leopold is still on the throne?'

After assuring him of the health and even vigour of his Sovereign, we continued our reconnaissance, not without moralizing a little over a man who had so completely broken with Europe and the old civilization.

The English positions were visible from Brandfort, on Tabel Kop and Tabel Berg, the other side of the plain that stretches south-east of the little town. Towards five o'clock we received a few volleys, hastily fired, which did no damage. But our object was attained: we had discovered that the enemy's positions extended a good way to the south.

The 8th was a Sunday. In the evening I received this telegram from President Steyn:

> The *landdrost* of Hoopstad sends me the following:
> Field-Cornet Daniels reports that the troops under Methuen's command at Boshof have marched upon Hoopstad, and I have received from Methuen himself the letter I communicate below. The native who brought the letter tells us that an engagement took place with General de Villebois in the neighbourhood of Boshof, that ten men were killed on our side, and fifteen on that of the enemy, among them a superior officer, but that all our force was finally made prisoner. Field-Cornet Daniels supposes that the enemy will march upon Christiana and Hoopstad, and thence upon Kroonstad.
>
> Headquarters, Swartz Kopjefontein,<br>April 8, 1900.
>
> To the Commandant of the Free State Laager.
> Sir,
> I have the honour of sending you a copy of Lord Roberts' proclamation to the Free State, laying down the

conditions under which you are invited to surrender.
Two days ago the Foreign Legion was taken prisoner by me, and their General, Villebois, was killed.
The English army is advancing on every side, and I beg you to consider the very liberal conditions now offered you, which would not be renewed at a later date.

I have the honour to be, sir,
Your obedient servant,
Methuen,
Lieutenant-General commanding the 10th Division.

This telegram was a thunderbolt for us. The anxiety we had felt at the general's delay had not been such as to have caused us to dream of such a catastrophe. Yet we could not doubt the news.

Two days ago the Foreign Legion was taken prisoner by me, and their General, Villebois, was killed.

That evening two reconnoitring parties were sent out; the first, from the Tabel Kop direction, came in next morning with a wounded man. The second, under Wrangel, started for the neighbourhood of Hoopstad, and could not return for several days.

On the 9th we made an inventory of the property belonging to the General, to Breda, and to the rest of our poor comrades, all of which was packed for transmission to Pretoria. The same day I received the following telegram from Colonel Gourko:

> Thomson unites with me in the expression of our profound grief at the cruel loss you have sustained in the person of Colonel de Villebois-Mareuil, a valiant soldier and distinguished leader.

This homage from the Russian and Dutch attachés to the memory of our great compatriot touched us deeply.

On the 10th one of Ganetzki's men was killed in a reconnaissance. Comte Ganetzki had his day of Parisian celebrity in connection with La belle O———.

On the 11th I had a telegram from Wrangel:

> I reached here (Hoopstad) at 5.30 this evening, with five men. The English are at Knappiesfontein, an hour and a half's march from Boshof. There are no Burghers at Hoopstad. I shall start for Boshof tomorrow, and send you a report later on. I await

your orders.

I at once communicate this news to General P. Botha. He believes that the environs of Hoopstad are occupied by the Burghers, and that the English will march upon Smaldeel to cut off communication (April 12). Events proved him to have been entirely mistaken; but I might have talked to him for hours without altering his convictions an iota.

Cannon had been thundering all the evening in the distance, but we had not been able to determine in what direction they were. On April 13, Commandant Delarey, brother of the general, was appointed honorary commander of the European Legion—'honorary' because he could not act save in concert with the heads of the different corps—Rittmeister Illich for the Austro-Hungarians, Captain Lorentz for the Germans, myself for the French.

An official telegram announces that General de Villebois was buried at Boshof with military honours. Lord Methuen was present, and the prisoners of the Legion were represented. There was even a funeral oration, to which Breda replied.

In the engagement of April 5 there had been 11 killed, the general being one, and 51 wounded, out of 68. The rest had been made prisoners.

*Easter Day*, 1900.—A second telegram from Wrangel, dated from Hoopstad, reports as follows:

1. Braschel (a former officer of the German artillery) informs us that 10,000 men and 700 cavalry are marching from Boshof on Bultfontein. He counted thirty-six gun-carriages, cannon, and waggons.
2. There are about 700 Burghers at Landslaagte.

On the 16th, we take horse at noon with every man available to join Kolby. This excellent general, one of the best men that ever lived, is not remarkable for the originality of his combinations. He witnessed our arrival with delight, smiling—he is always smiling—received us very cordially, and asked us what we had come for! He had had no instructions about us; however, it was all the same to him whether we slept there or elsewhere, so we remained. We came in for a perfect deluge of rain all night, and at four the next morning we started to take up a position with Delarey's, Botha's, and Kolby's commandos.

We number from 1,000 to 1,200 Burghers, with two Creusot guns, a Krupp and a Nordenfeldt.

At 4.30 in the evening, orders are given to retire to the different camps. We arrive at 10 o'clock.

On the 18th, it rains again in torrents. In the evening, about 9 o'clock, Wrangel's reconnoitring party comes in. I will transcribe the account given me by one of his men, Meslier, that it may lose nothing of its interest by a paraphrase.

Starting on Monday, the 9th, in the evening, we marched secretly and rapidly towards Hoopstad, following first the Vedula and then the Wet River across the *veldt*. We crossed rivers without any fords, passing through a country without roads or paths, and through the dense bush that grows on the banks of the water-courses. Out of ten picked horses two died, and three men fell out on the road exhausted. One of them went into hospital at Smaldeel.

On Wednesday, the 11th, we reached Hoopstad at five o'clock in the evening, and slept at the President Hotel, which is kept by a German.

At six o'clock next morning (April 12) I started with Braschel and Brostolicky in the direction of Boshof. The English, after having advanced upon Bultfontein, as reported in our telegram of the 15th, returned for the most part towards Boshof. We slept that night at Landslaagte, where the Johannesburg Politie are encamped. They number about 200, and expect a reinforcement of 300 men.

We left again on the morning of the 13th, separating at a given point, Braschel and his companion going towards the camp of Commandant Cronje (brother of the General taken prisoner at Paardeberg), and I towards Boshof.

Towards noon I passed Driefontein, which was supposed to be occupied by the English. The inhabitants of the farm told me that when Colonel de Villebois arrived an English corps had been in the neighbourhood for several days, apparently waiting. The people at the farm heard the noise of the battle, which lasted about four hours, and helped to collect the dead and wounded afterwards. Among our men they noticed one who had a handkerchief bound round his head and a very large nose. Another had a very long beard.

Towards one o'clock I arrived at Muyfontein, where there was a little outpost of thirty lancers under an officer. I sheered off to the east, and arrived near Boshof about half-past four.

Boshof was full of troops. From the neighbouring *kopjes* one could distinctly see the "khakis" moving about in the village. Skirting Boshof, I arrived at Kopjefontein on the south-west. There I was a good deal disturbed by strange hissing noises coming from about 800 metres away, and the pursuit of a party of twenty Lancers, who followed me for about half an hour.

I returned to Rothsplaats Farm, where I spent the night. I had fastened my horse to a cart, and had laid down myself under a tree. About ten o'clock eight marauders approached from the path. Not seeing me, some of the party installed themselves in the farm, while the rest chased a young pig, which, flying in terror before them, came quite close to the corner where I was lying in ambush. Fortunately he changed his mind, and made off in another direction. Finally, to my great satisfaction, they caught him, and the whole party returned to the farm. They stayed about two hours, and then departed.

At four in the morning I continued my journey, and at eight o'clock I arrived at Landslaagte, where I joined the Johannesburg Politie.

Between Landslaagte and Driefontein I met Cronje with about 2,000 men, a Krupp and a Nordenfeldt gun. His intention was to attack Kopjefontein. I reported what I had seen, and went on towards Hoopstad; but my worn-out horse fell when we were still some four hours distant from the town. I was obliged to sleep at a farm, and was unable to reach Hoopstad till the afternoon of Sunday, the 15th. All our seven horses had broken down. We asked for others, which the Landdrost refused. Wrangel accordingly telegraphed to President Steyn, who replied by an order to give us everything we required.

We took some excellent horses and a few necessary garments, for a three days' journey through the thorns and bush that border the Wet River had reduced us to absolute rags.

These negotiations and a brief rest occupied Monday and Tuesday. We started on Wednesday at one o'clock, and knowing the road to be safe, we passed through Bultfontein, accomplishing our return journey in a day and a half.

At Hoopstad we were told that when the Villebois contingent had passed through, all had remarked the gaiety of the General, who had kept the piano going all the evening, and the depression of Breda.

These last words gave a fresh poignancy to our regrets. Just as the general had been the ideal of the brilliant and revered leader, so had Breda been the ideal of the devoted friend, the good comrade, the man of sound judgment and charming amenities.

★★★★★★

From this report we gathered certain facts hard to explain. We group them here together with others which reached us from a different source.

1. Wrangel and his men, who left Brandfort on the evening of the 9th, arrived at Driefontein at noon on the 13th—in four nights and three and a half days. The general, under the conduct of his Afrikander guide, took twelve nights and eleven days (from the evening of March 24 to the morning of April 5) to cover an equivalent distance. Now, the length and irregularity of this march were utterly irreconcilable with the object the general had in view, with the dates he had himself fixed, and with the length and severity of the distances he was in the habit of exacting from his men.

2. Numerous desertions took place among the Dutch and the Afrikanders, men who spoke the same language.

3. Finally, and this is a very serious coincidence, a whole English brigade, which retired as soon as it had made the *coup* determined on, was lying in wait for the contingent, the itinerary of which had been kept so strictly secret that only the guide could have known it exactly.

This fact was confirmed by the following statement made to me by an English officer present at the engagement. The general, finding himself surrounded at daybreak, after having marched all night, took up a position on a kopje near the farm of Driefontein. Artillery fire began almost immediately, opened by Battery No. 4 of the Royal Field Artillery.

Throughout the four hours of the engagement the general was seen walking up and down, encouraging first one and then another, and pointing out the spots at which his followers were to fire. His death was followed by the surrender of the decimated band.

The general wore the costume he always put on for expeditions and for the field—a brown hat, fastened up on one side with a badge bearing the arms of the Transvaal; an old black tunic, the large metal buttons of which had been replaced by large black ones; brown corduroy trousers, and shooting-boots, laced in front and buckled at the sides; his revolver in a cross-belt, and at his waist a yellow leather case, containing a chronometer, a barometer and a compass. He always wore brown kid gloves, and carried a bamboo cane. I will not yet express the melancholy thought which, with me, has become a firm conviction; but when I learned the fate of my revered chief, 'the La Fayette of South Africa,' as one of the most distinguished generals of the French army called him, how could I but remember the disappointments he had suffered during the last six months, the petty jealousies by which he had been pursued, and the ill-will which had hampered all his bold and intelligent initiative?

Pondering these things, I recalled the day when, before Kimberley, the general had received from France a little gold medal, which he showed me with proud emotion. It bore this inscription: 'To a great Frenchman, from the companions of his daughter.'

Yes, a great Frenchman! For in him flourished all high thoughts of duty and abnegation, all the noble virtues that make up a great leader and a great patriot. He was a man and a soldier.

In this connection it will be of interest to record what my friend and comrade Breda told me, on his return from Saint Helena, of the engagement of April 5. He cannot believe that there was treachery, yet he cannot explain certain strange coincidences.

> We started, as you know on the evening of March 24. Our guide began by losing his way the first night and the first day. (This confirmed the story told by my man, who came back in two hours, after marching out for thirty-six.)
> At last we arrived at Hoopstad, where an important group of the Dutch contingent refused to advance.
> The general, determined to advance with the French alone, ordered the names of the Dutch who remained faithful to be taken down. A sudden revulsion of feeling made the majority of them give in their names, and the detachment set off in the direction of Boshof.
> At the farm of Driefontein a messenger came in search of the general. A most important communication from a distinguished personage awaited him at Hoopstad. A serious scheme was on foot for the formation of a large legion.

This project appealed strongly to the general, who left me at Driefontein with the detachment, returning himself to Hoopstad to confer with the envoy. He returned in three days, and the march towards the south was resumed.

The general supposed that there might be about 200 or 300 men at Boshof, and, on being assured of this, a Boer *commando* of about 200 men joined us. But on the 4th, information was received that Boshof was much more strongly occupied, and that it might hold from 800 to 1,000 men. The general, believing this story to be an invention of the Burghers to excuse their defection—of which they immediately gave notice—disregarded it, and continued his march.

We arrived near a farm where, it appears, the English officers at Boshof were in the habit of coming to picnic on Sundays. The general made for a point a little way from this, and halted beside a small *kopje*. We unsaddled the horses and sent them to graze, and the tired men lay down to sleep.

I remained talking with General de Villebois, when we suddenly caught sight of a few horsemen.

"The English!"

I went off to wake the men quietly, for we hoped to surprise this little reconnoitring party. There were so few of them that we did not fetch in our horses.

They came nearer. All of a sudden, behind them in the distance a long column of "khakis" came in sight. It was no longer a question of surprising a patrol. We had to defend ourselves.

The general at once recognised the gravity of the situation. He arranged his men on two little *kopjes*, the Dutch on one, the French on the other, remaining himself with the latter. Each man had his place assigned him, his rock to defend.

And the battle began—a furious, hopeless encounter. For three hours we replied as well as we could to the tremendous fusillade that soon made gaps among us.

Almost at the outset the Dutch hoisted the white flag and surrendered. Two or three of them who chanced to be with the French contingent came and asked General de Villebois to surrender. He pointed to the *kopje* where their compatriots had already laid down their arms.

"Here we do not surrender," he said.

By degrees, however, the first shelters were abandoned, and the men fell back on some rocks beyond. The general noticed this. "Return to the first positions!" he ordered.

Bullets were falling like hail. There was a moment's hesitation. "Shall I go myself?" cried the chief, advancing.

But a brave fellow springs forward. It is Franck, who had already distinguished himself at Abraham's Kraal. Waving his rifle with a grand gesture, he cried: "*Vive la France!*"

He fell instantly, struck by two bullets. But the impulse had been given; the positions were resumed.

On all sides, however, the "khakis" were closing in upon us. They fixed their bayonets and charged. Suddenly the general fell back without a word. He was dead.

★★★★★★

Whatever the strength and vitality of a man may be, the inert body will fall when the soul takes flight. Villebois was the soul of the legion. Accordingly, when he was killed, the survivors surrendered, after four hours of heroic resistance.

Out of twenty-seven Frenchmen, the General, Le Gilles and Robiquet were killed, Bardin, Bernard, Franck and the others were wounded.

The English officers told us that they had been informed several days before of the arrival of 100 Frenchmen at Hoopstad, thus confirming the story of the Driefontein farmers.

The Comte de Villebois, one of the youngest colonels in the French army, had been severely wounded as a sub-lieutenant in the army of the Loire in 1870. His conduct had been such as to merit the Cross of the Legion of Honour at the age of twenty.

I will transcribe here, as a touching homage to his memory, the order of the day which Colonel de Nadaillac addressed to his regiment, informing them of the glorious death of their former chief:

> Colonel de Villebois-Mareuil, who had the honour of commanding the 130th Regiment, has died a soldier's death in the Transvaal, shot through the breast by the fragment of a shell.
> Retiring at an early age, at his own request, he took his sword and the resources of his fine intelligence to the aid of the little Boer nation.
> His chivalrous soul could not resist the appeal of those generous sentiments which have so long been a tradition in our fair France. He wished to defend the weak against the strong.

Let us respectfully salute this victim of the noblest French virtues, this valiant soldier who has fallen on the field of honour.

The former Colonel of the 130th will be held in loving remembrance by us, and we offer the just tribute of our patriotic regrets to his memory.

May God have mercy on the brave man who left child, friends, and fortune, to defend the oppressed.

The death of Colonel de Villebois-Mareuil will be recorded in the regimental annals of the 130th.

CHAPTER 7

# Tugela

On the 18th we heard that De Wet, after his successes at Taba N'chu and Sanna's Post, was at Wepener, where he had surrounded 2,000 men of Brabant's Horse.

******

Without orders, and without precise tidings of any kind, we remain five days longer at Brandfort.

General Delarey seems uncertain what to do. While he is casting about for a plan of action, we may take a glance at our enemies, and study them a little.

In this campaign the English army has collected together elements the most diverse. About one half of it consists of regular troops, the other half of volunteers, colonial troops, and contingents from every country. Their behaviour under fire varies greatly, according to their origin.

Tommy Atkins the regular, cold, calm, advances under a hail of projectiles, marching steadily in time, as if on the parade-ground. Scornful of danger, his head held high, he seems to say: 'Make way! I am an Englishman!'

The colonial, on the other hand, the cowboy, the volunteer from the Cape, from Rhodesia, and from Australia, a hunter by profession, fights in the same fashion as the Boers. He has their qualities and their defects: great precision as a marksman, but a lack of cohesion and of discipline. Crouching behind a rock, taking advantage of every scrap of cover, like his adversary, he hunts rather than fights.

But a good many militiamen, volunteers from various towns, and yeomen are even less brilliant, and exchange perils, privations, and fatigue for a sojourn in a Boer prison with great readiness. Some of the regular regiments, too, brought up to their fighting strength by hasty recruiting at the last moment, are not exempt from the shame of unnecessary capitulations.

But such proceedings are not characteristic of Tommy. The Englishman knows very little of the art of war, but he is brave, very brave.

The officers, with some few exceptions, are ignorant of everything an officer should know. The operations (?) of Sir Charles Warren, Lord Methuen, and Sir Redvers Buller seem to be a sort of competition of lunatics.

General Buller appears to have some inkling of it himself; on December 28 he writes as follows from the camp of Frere:

> I suppose our officers will in time learn the value of scouting; but in spite of all one can say, up to this our men seem to blunder into the midst of the enemy, and suffer accordingly.

These words from the pen of the general who, on January 24, was to 'authorize' the Spion Kop fiasco are delicious!

The profession of arms in England is an occupation not at all absorbing, but very fashionable, very 'sporting.'

War itself is a sport, which has its special costume, its accidents proper to the soldier, but which is not supposed to engross the man. The fact that a great many officers brought with them, in addition to their khaki uniforms and braided tunics, tennis, football, and polo costumes, dress-coats and smoking-jackets, is significant of this state of mind.

The programme they had mentally drawn up was something of this sort: From 7 to 8 a.m., football, breakfast; from 9 to 10, lawn tennis; from 10 to 11, a battle; then a rest, a tub, massage, lunch!

The English officer is a gentleman, always perfectly well bred, often very well educated, and extremely affable; but he is a gentleman, and not an officer.

War entered upon by men of this type demands neither serious preliminary study nor effective progress in an army; and as regards military art and science, the English are still at the stage of the pitched battle.

It is but just to add that they have also preserved the cool, tenacious courage and the indomitable energy of their race, qualities which none can deny them. I saw some superb charges by English troops in Africa, but they always reminded me of Marechal Pelissier's remark after the heroic charge at Balaclava: '*C'est magnifique, mais ce n'est pas la guerre!*'

I am no Anglophile, as my campaign of over eight months on the Boer side sufficiently proves, but it is the duty of a loyal soldier to recognise the qualities and the courage of his adversaries.

After this short digression, let us resume our survey of the English Army.

During the first months, up to March, their artillery ammunition seems to have been very defective, often exploding imperfectly, or not at all. The fire took a long time to regulate, and was nearly always independent, rarely in salvoes. Nevertheless, I several times saw guns served in a remarkably efficient manner.

The horses are superb, and were constantly renewed; throughout the campaign they had from five to six *quarterns* of oats a day.

Their artillery equipment consists of a variety of very ordinary patterns. They have not yet any field-guns with breaks. The mounted artillery (Royal Horse Artillery) is a picked body of men. Its officers must have served four years in the Field Artillery, and must also be possessed of a certain private income.

Their guns, Armstrongs of 76.2 millimetres, are called 12-pounders (from the weight of the projectile). The Field Artillery uses 89 millimetre guns with 22-pound shells. The breech-blocks are screwed in. The mountain-guns (1882 pattern) are loaded at the muzzle.

The batteries consist of six pieces, with the exception of the volunteer batteries, which have only four.

Their shell-guns, of which even during their operations on the open plain they had a certain number of batteries (notably No. 61 Battery at Spion Kop, and No. 65 Battery at Paardeburg), are howitzers of the latest pattern; they are loaded at the breech, and are specially constructed for fire at a high angle of elevation.

Their naval guns and siege guns, dragged about by teams of from twenty to thirty oxen, were able to follow the troops in a satisfactory manner.

The lyddite shells did not prove very effective. They explode with a loud and violent report. The green smoke has a stupefying effect; objects such as stones or fragments of shell that come in contact with the explosive take on a sulphur-green tint.

The English used over 300 guns; and if we add to these thirty-five large naval guns, mounted upon siege-gun carriages, and those of the volunteer batteries, we get a total of about 400.

The cavalry has played but a secondary part; but the charges of General French's division at Poplar Grove were vigorously executed, and cost the lives of two officers and some fifty men. The relief of Kimberley by this same division was rather a raid of great rapidity than a cavalry action properly so-called.

The Boer method of warfare explains the powerlessness of the cavalry to take any prominent part in the operations; reconnaissances were carried out by *kaffir* spies and Afrikander irregulars. Cavalry pursuit would, I think, have been perfectly useless, for the Boers would have immediately taken up defensive positions in kopjes inaccessible to horses, and the precision of their fire would soon have proved extremely harassing to the horsemen.

The infantry, to give it greater mobility, was relieved of every kind of impedimenta. The uniform is extremely practical as a whole.

The foot-soldier wears a khaki tunic with pockets, made in the summer of canvas, in the winter of cloth; trousers to match, the lower part bound up in strips of khaki flannel, on the same pattern as those of our Chasseurs Alpins. His helmet is absolutely unsuitable; heavy and ugly, it does not even protect him from the sun.

A big dark-gray cloak, a blanket, and a waterproof tent canvas, which theoretically are supposed to be carried on the back in two little rolls, are as a fact transported on trolleys drawn by mules marching on the left of each company.

The man carries only his canteen and his bandolier. The latter seemed to me too large and heavy to be practical, but the canteen, the lid of which makes a saucepan, seems convenient. It is the same for officers and privates. Each battalion is followed by a little Maxim gun, firing Lee-Metford cartridges.

The Mounted Infantry is, theoretically, an arm of the first importance. In practice it has its partisans and its detractors. I leave the task of authoritative pronouncement to critics more expert than myself, and shall only say that Colonel Martyr's and General Hutton's Mounted Rifles rendered very considerable service to Lord Roberts. The Mounted Rifle has an ordinary cavalry saddle, with a black cloak rolled up on the holsters before him. His uniform is the same as that of the infantry: a tunic, trousers, and flannel bandages. He wears the felt hat of the country. He carries two bandoliers and is armed with the Lee-Metford rifle and with a short bayonet like that of our artillerymen. The butt-end of his gun rests in a bucket hanging on the right of his saddle, and the stock is supported by a leather thong round the right arm like a lance.

The Mounted Rifle fights on foot, sheltering his horse behind a piece of rising ground. His horse to him is merely a rapid means of transport.

Belts and straps, swords, sheaths and hilts, guns and waggons, are all painted khaki colour.

After enumerating all the weapons used by the belligerents, it would be an unpardonable omission to say nothing of the famous dum-dum bullets.

Have they been much used? Yes, certainly, and on both sides.

The story that the Boers only used those they had captured from the English is quite inadmissible, for the Mauser rifles, which were used exclusively in the Transvaal, were largely provided with them.

I will try to describe the patterns chiefly used:

1. Section in the nickel casing, leaving the extremity of the leaden bullet exposed; the lead, getting very hot, emerges partly from the casing, flattens at the slightest resistance, and expands.

2. Four longitudinal sections in the nickel casing allow the bullet to flatten at the moment of contact, and to exude lead through the apertures.

These two first patterns, the ones most in use, are made for Lee-Metford and Mauser rifles.

The English also use hollow-nosed bullets, the extremity of which is cut or rubbed off.

The Boers, for their part, have manufactured solid projectiles, which show the lead through a straight section, and have the four longitudinal slits.

A few expansive Lee-Metford cartridges, hollow, and filled with fulminate, certainly existed, but I do not believe that they were ever in general use.

I need not insist upon the terrible injuries inflicted by all these projectiles. I have seen the whole of the back of a man's hand carried away by a bullet entering the palm, where it had only made a hole of the normal dimension.

During this war, in an arid country without any towns, Tommy has suffered terribly. Accustomed to the comfort of English barracks and to abundant meals, he was ill-prepared to spend his nights on the hard ground in cold and rain, with stones that bruised his ribs for his only bed, and half a biscuit for his dinner.

Now that we have inspected the English Army, let us see what it has accomplished since our arrival.

First of all in Natal. In January, Ladysmith was still invested. The garrison of nearly 10,000 men and the inhabitants were decimated more by disease than by the occasional shells the Boers threw into the town every day as a matter of duty. Provisions had become scarce. An officer's ration was two biscuits and 240 *grammes* of horseflesh a day.

A dozen eggs cost £2 8s.; a dozen tomatoes, 18s.; a tin of preserved meat, £3; a tin of condensed milk, 10s.; a pot of jam, £1 11s.; a quarter of a pound of English tobacco, £3; a case containing a dozen bottles of whisky, £140, nearly £12 a bottle.

Nevertheless, a newspaper published by the besieged, the *Lyre*, is still facetious. It publishes the following notes:

> Telegram from London.—A shell thrown by *Long Tom* fell in the War Office. General Brackenbury received it with resignation.... A good many reputations have been damaged. The 2nd Army Corps has been discovered in the War Office portfolios.

Meanwhile, Buller was still trying to cross the Tugela and relieve Ladysmith. Without any definite plan, perplexed and irresolute, he runs up and down the bank of the river like a cat afraid of the water.

At last he 'permits' Warren to attack Spion Kop. It is strange indeed to find Warren's 15,000 men (the 5th Division) and Buller's 25,000 setting out without a map, without information, and without a guide.

On January 16 Lieutenant Flood luckily discovered a ford, by which two battalions crossed the river; but then the Engineers were obliged to await the arrival of Lieutenant Mazzari's sailors to make a ferry.

At Trichardt's Drift two pontoon bridges were built, and the whole of Warren's division crossed.

On the 19th this general essays an out-flanking movement in the direction of Acton Homes; but this manoeuvre at the base of escarpments occupied by the enemy is found to be too dangerous; the division falls back upon Trichardt's Drift with its convoys and the 420 bullock-waggons intended for the Ladysmith garrison.

A frontal attack, facing east, is decided upon for January 20. The infantry is engaged 800 yards from the Boer trenches. It is three o'clock; an assault is about to be made on the position. But a counter-order arrives, the reason for which has never yet been explained.

On the 21st, 22nd and 23rd the English try to gain a few hundred yards. Clery and Warren confess themselves powerless, and turn the attack towards the south-east.

On the night of the 23rd General Woodgate receives orders to seize Spion Kop. General Woodgate, commanding the 9th Brigade, took part in the Abyssinian campaigns of 1868, the Ashanti campaign of 1873, and the Zulu campaign of 1879. Later he was in command of the English forces in West Africa, during the rising of 1898.

He took with him eight companies of the 2nd Battalion Lancashire Fusiliers, six companies of the 2nd Battalion Royal Lancashire Regiment, two companies of the 1st Battalion South Lancashire Regiment, 194 men of Thorneycroft's Mounted Infantry, and a half-company Royal Engineers. To these were added two battalions from General Lyttelton's Brigade.

At 3.30 in the morning, after mounting the hill in silence, Lieutenant Audrey, in command of the advance-guard, took two of the Boer trenches with the bayonet. They were held by Boers of the Vryheid commando, who were few in number, and had been completely surprised.

But the Heidelberg and Carolina *commandos*, under Schalk Burger, came to the rescue. Urged forward by a German *commando* and by Ricciardi's Italians, they crossed an open space under a hail of bullets and lyddite shells, and established themselves on one of the three spurs formed by the kopje at this point.

The struggle was very fierce. Between nine and eleven the English charged three times with the bayonet and were repulsed. Under the deadly fire of the Mausers and the Maxim-Nordenfeldts they were obliged to fall back gradually, before any serviceable reinforcements had reached them.

Woodgate, mortally wounded, was replaced by Colonel Thorneycroft; the latter received neither orders nor instructions, though it would have been easy to have established optical telegraph communication, as the heliograph was working between Mount Alice and Bester Farm (Redvers Buller and White).[1]

His position had become most critical; a council of war was hastily called, on the decision of which the height was evacuated under cover of night.

On January 25 Sir Redvers Buller, who had hastened to Warren's camp, was informed of this catastrophe, which upset all his combinations. A general retreat was determined on, and the troops recrossed the Tugela.

After this bloody check, General Buller's report of the movement

---

1. A heliograph *was* working on the height, but 'the signallers and their apparatus were destroyed by the heavy fire' (*vide* Sir Charles Warren's report).—Translator.

is delicious:

> The fact that we were able to withdraw our ox-waggons and mule transports over a river 85 yards broad and with a rapid current, without any interference from the enemy, is, I think, a proof that they have learnt to respect the fighting powers of our soldiers.

The 'lesson' he had given the Boers had cost him 307 killed, thirty-one of whom were officers; 175 wounded, of whom forty-nine were officers; and 347 prisoners and missing, among them seven officers.

The Boers had 168 men killed. And, as Ricciardi has pointed out, but for the incomprehensible opposition of General Joubert, this retreat across the Tugela would have been, not a proof that the enemy had learnt to respect the fighting powers of the English, but a terrific rout. For General Louis Botha, surrounded by a dozen guns, was watching the English passing over their pontoons from the heights he had defended the night before. They were well within range, and the gunners were at their posts. It wanted but an order, the pontoons would have been destroyed, and Warren's division, hemmed in by the river, would have been massacred to a man. Why was this order not given?

In March, even before the death of the *generalissimo*, a terrible word had been whispered—treason! At any rate, his inaction was highly culpable, for if the struggle seems hopeless now, there was a time when he might have turned it into victory, and made it another Majuba Hill campaign.

We know that Joubert's ignorance was almost incredible, that he could not even use a map, and that he stubbornly refused to learn. His attitude at the time of Warren's retreat and in certain other circumstances no doubt gave colour to the rumours of poisoning which followed the general's sudden death in March. It is conceivable that some Burgher, carried away by patriotic zeal, did not hesitate to commit a crime that the supreme command might pass into more faithful or bolder hands. . . .

Later on, when I was a prisoner in the English camp, I said one day in jest to a young sub-lieutenant:

'You lost one of your best generals in March.'

'Who do you mean?'

'Joubert.'

Seeing his air of surprise and annoyance, a superior officer who was present said, with a smile:

'You are right!'

On February 1 the positions of the belligerents had undergone no very notable modification since the beginning of the war. We will recapitulate them for the last time, for English reinforcements were arriving from every side. Lord Roberts had assumed the supreme command, the besieged towns were shortly to be delivered, and the war was to enter upon an active phase.

In the north, in Rhodesia, General Carrington was at Marondellas, and Colonel Plumer at Safili Camp, near Buluwayo.

At Mafeking, Colonel Baden-Powell is made a lieutenant-general. 'The Wolf who never sleeps,' as his men call him, is still besieged by Snyman.

Colonel Kekewich at Kimberley is surrounded by the troops of Du Toit, Kolby, Delarey, and Ferreira.

General Cronje, to the south of Kimberley, is well informed as to Lord Roberts' preparations, but he pays no heed to them, and meets all Villebois' far-seeing counsels with the stock phrase: 'I was a general when you were still a child.'

Schoeman is near Colesberg, facing General French.

Olivier, to the north of Burghersdorp, confronts Gatacre.

Botha and Schalk Burgher, on the north bank of the Tugela, hold in check Buller and Warren on the south bank, near Colenso.

Finally, Joubert, Prinsloo, and Lucas Meyer are round Ladysmith, where General White is still imprisoned.

On February 5 Buller, after deploying his troops as if for a frontal attack in the direction of Potgieter, at last crossed the Tugela at the foot of Dorn Kop. If perseverance deserves a reward, he has certainly earned one.

But the period of sieges draws to a close. The war is entering on another phase. Lord Roberts has completed his concentration, his orders are given, the invasion begins.

CHAPTER 8

# Invasion

On February 10 the field marshal concentrated three divisions on the Modder River: Kelly-Kenny (6th), Tucker (7th), and Colvile (9th). Then he secretly assembled the cavalry, grouped into three brigades (those of Broadwood, Porter, and Gordon), under General French. The latter, supported by seven mounted batteries and six field batteries, started in the night of the 11th-12th, reached Rooidam, continued by way of Potgieter's Farm, brushed aside General Ferreira, and entered Kimberley on Thursday, February 15, at half-past five in the evening.

The surprise was complete, as we know!

Meanwhile, Lord Roberts had not been idle. On the 15th, Maxwell's Brigade occupied Jacobsdal, and Lord Kitchener was pressing Cronje, who was retiring upon Paardeburg.

French, his raid accomplished, joined Kitchener by way of Koodoesrand, and on the 17th the whole of Roberts' force surrounded the Boer General.

After a ten days' defence, more heroic than reasonable—for he might have broken through with De Wet's help—Cronje, crushed by the terrible fire of 90 cannon,[1] bore out Colonel de Villebois' prediction, being forced to surrender unconditionally on February 27, at 7.30 a.m.

Lord Roberts telegraphed as follows to the War Office:

Paardeburg, 7.45 a.m.

General Cronje is now a prisoner in my camp. The strength of his force will be communicated later. I hope Her Majesty's

---

1. Lord Roberts had 6 field batteries, 1 howitzer battery, 7 horse batteries, and 5 naval guns—90 pieces in all, to be exact.

Government will consider this event satisfactory, occurring as it does on the anniversary of Majuba.

It was afterwards announced by the War Office that the general had surrendered two Krupp guns, one belonging to the Orange Free State, and two Maxims, one of these also belonging to the Orange Free State, 4,000 men, of whom 1,150 were Free Staters, and 47 officers, 18 of them Free Staters. Among the officers was the artillery commandant Albrecht, formerly an Austrian officer.

In Natal, on the 28th, Lord Dundonald entered Ladysmith, the siege of which had been raised at six in the evening, preceding a convoy of provisions which arrived on the morning of March 2.

Lord Roberts did not linger long on the banks of the Modder River. After giving his troops a short rest while he went with Kitchener to visit Kimberley, where he was the guest of Cecil Rhodes, he continued his march upon Bloemfontein. On the 7th he was at Poplar Grove, on the 10th at Abraham's Kraal—he called the battle fought here Driefontein—and on the 13th he entered the capital of the Orange Free State.

> Bloemfontein,
> March 13, 8 p.m.
>
> By God's help, and thanks to the bravery of Her Majesty's soldiers, the troops under my command have taken possession of Bloemfontein. The British flag is now flying over the President's house, which was last night abandoned by Mr. Steyn, the late President of the Orange Free State.
>
> Mr. Fraser, a member of the former executive, the mayor, the secretary of the late government, the *landdrost* and other functionaries, came to meet me two miles out of the town, and handed me the keys of the government offices.
>
> The enemy has retired from the neighbourhood, and all seems calm. The inhabitants of Bloemfontein gave our troops a hearty reception.
>
> Roberts.

Lord Roberts's first operation was accomplished; he established a solid base at Bloemfontein, accumulating a great quantity of provisions there, a very wise measure to take before throwing his troops into a hostile country, impoverished by five months of warfare, the resources of which had already been heavily laid under contribution by the Boers. At the same time his troops radiated round the former capital to drive off the little commandos that were still hovering about in the neighbourhood.

The 9th Division, under General Colvile, was broken up to keep communications open, and its chief returned to England.

Such was the situation when, on Monday, April 23, we received orders to saddle at seven in the morning. We started at 8.30, with two days' rations.

The direction is the same as before, towards the south. But after the counter-order of last Monday, we feel no great confidence as to the object of this new manoeuvre. We have christened these starts 'the Monday morning exercises.'

This time, it seems, that while De Wet is busy at Wepener with Brabant's Horse, which he is still surrounding, a strong column is to attempt to cut him off from the north, by establishing a line between Bloemfontein and the frontier of Basutoland. We are to oppose this movement and enable De Wet to pass.

We arrive in the plain watered by the Onspruit about five in the evening. We bivouac there with Lorentz's Germans, with whom we are still grouped. The nights begin to be cold. During the evening 1,000 men and two 75 millimetre Creusot guns arrive.

In Botha's camp, close by, there are still from 300 to 400 men, a Krupp gun, an Armstrong, and a Nordenfeldt.

On the morning of the 24th a reinforcement of from 200 to 300 men arrives. Our total strength is from 1,500 to 1,800 men.

We remain in bivouac, but on the 25th our provisions are exhausted, and they re-victual us by driving a flock of sheep across the plain. Each group of five or six men takes one. Part of the flesh is grilled over a fire of cow-dung—the only fuel available in the Veldt—and the rest, cut into quarters, is slung on the saddles for next day.

For the last two days the luminous balloon of the English has been visible all the evening till midnight.

In the afternoon we get orders to start for the Waterworks, to the east of Bloemfontein, which the English have recaptured from General Lemmer. We are to take provisions for several days; but the English, it seems, are close behind us. They have come down into the plain, and the road from here to Brandfort is very insecure.

At three o'clock in the afternoon Wrangel, two former officers in the German Army, Couves, De Loth, and I, set out to fetch a trolley loaded with necessaries for the two corps.

We arrive at Brandfort towards midnight. Captain D——, whom

we meet here, gives us the news from France. The Théâtre Français was burnt down on March 9, and Mdlle. Henriot was one of the victims of the catastrophe. We also hear of the explosion at Johannesburg. A telegram says that the fort blew up on the 24th. But we learn later that it was Begbie's factory and not the fort that exploded. Another telegram, relating to the fight at Boshof, says that Prince Bagration is not dead, but wounded only. A lieutenant of marines named Gilles was killed. This is all we have in the way of details, for the official list of the losses of April 5 has not yet appeared.

As regards the explosion, the following information may be of interest.

The citadel of Johannesburg was not constructed with a view to defending the town, but, on the contrary, with the idea of bombarding it. This curious arrangement calls for some explanation.

On January 1, 1896, Dr. Jameson, coming from the east, was checked at Krugersdorp with his contingent, which prevented the execution of his *coup de main*. But at the news of his arrival a number of Uitlanders, for the most part English, had armed. Forming themselves into commandos, and reinforced by a battery of Maxims smuggled in among machines for use in the mines, they bivouacked on the heights of Yeoville, commanding Johannesburg, to await and join the men of the Chartered Company.

After this escapade the Transvaal Government, in order to work upon the loyal sentiments of its good city of Johannesburg, presented it with a fort, which, situated in a prominent position in the town, would have been capable in a very few minutes of correcting any ill-timed manifestations of sympathy to which its inhabitants might be inclined to give way in the future.

The Begbie factory was used for the manufacture of projectiles. With comparatively primitive methods and absolutely inexperienced workmen, the making and charging of shells of all the patterns in use in our own artillery had been carried on here. Every evening from 700 to 800 were despatched in every direction.

For a long time past, directly after war was declared, the English who had been expelled had publicly predicted an explosion at this factory. On February 2 a telegram from Durban announced that this explosion had taken place. The manager, Mr. Grünberg, had even vainly called the attention of the police to a house close to the powder magazine.

To be brief, a terrible explosion took place on the 24th, killing some hundred persons, and destroying a quarter of the town.

This was in the main what the inquiry that took place afterwards brought to light:

A little mine containing black powder had been dug in the suspected house, close to the dynamite reserve of the powder magazine. The authors of the explosion had afterwards connected the mine with the electric light of their rooms; then they had departed quietly to a place of safety, having still half a day to spare. In the evening, at five o'clock, when the electric light works turned on the current to distribute light in the town, the explosion was produced automatically. The guilty persons were never discovered.

★★★★★★

We spent our evening discussing all this news, and then went to bed in our encampment. On the morning of the 26th we loaded a trolley, to which we had harnessed eight strong mules, with cartridges, biscuit, and a few other necessary provisions. We started at two o'clock in the afternoon, and arrived late in the evening at a farm where an ambulance was installed.

We bivouacked several hundreds of metres off, as we were urgently recommended to do by the doctor, who was accompanied by his wife. He took advantage of the Geneva Convention to protect his domestic peace, no doubt with an eye to Wrangel, who is a very pretty fellow!

I do not know if the legislator foresaw such a case as this!

Our dinner was furnished by the roosters of the farmyard, which three of our number had initiated in the laws of hospitality. Certain protestations are raised by the victims, during which I call and scold my poor Nelly, who is lying perfectly innocent at my feet. But the ambulance men will think it was she who was pursuing the poultry.... One should always try to save appearances.

We take a very light sleep, and towards three o'clock a *kaffir* comes to tell us that he has just met a numerous band of English. We harness up rapidly, and make off still more rapidly at a hand-gallop, while in the dawning light we make out the scouts of the enemy on the neighbouring *kopjes*.

All day we marched across the plain without a guide, and at six in the evening we reached Botha's camp. Our comrades, who had gone off on a little reconnaissance, which proved to be fruitless, came in at about 8.30.

A rumour that we had been taken prisoners together with the trolley had preceded us; it had been brought in by the Irish Americans, and confirmed by a heliographic message from the commissary at Brandfort.

On the 28th all the Europeans were told to hold themselves in readiness to start as an advanced guard. I meet with a very cordial reception from the officers of the staff, for I find among them the Adjutant,[2] Marais, who was with us at Poplar Grove. The order to start was given at two in the afternoon.

We have just heard that Von Loosberg, an ex-lieutenant of the German Army, whom we knew at Abraham's Kraal, and who had since taken service in the artillery, had received seven Maxim bullets at Dewetsdorp, two in the head and five in the body. He recovered!

At five o'clock we reach a little stream. Here we are to encamp for three days. From 1,200 to 1,500 are gathered here with Botha, Delarey and Kolby. The tents are set up a little apart. We are very comfortable.

At about 8.30 we had finished dinner, and were about to seek a well-earned repose; several of the party were already rolled up in their blankets. Suddenly there was a noise of the tramp of horses and strange murmurs. We went in search of information. All the camp was astir, and the Boers were making off quietly.

'The English! Be off!'

We struck our tents hastily, saddled our horses, and harnessed the mules, without getting any more precise information, and then we joined in the general retreat. The questions we ask call forth answers precisely like those given by young recruits at their first manoeuvres.

'The enemy!'

'Where?'

'Over there!'

A sweeping gesture embraces the whole horizon; the indication is all the more vague in that it is ten o'clock, and that the night is very dark.

'Are there many of them?'

'I don't know.'

'Which way are they going?'

'I don't know.'

I almost think that if one asked rather sharply, 'Did you see them?' the man would answer, 'No.'

Nevertheless, the convoy takes an easterly direction, and the men are so disposed as to cover the retreat. We are on a rocky *kopje* swept

---

2. The title of adjutant to a Boer general often corresponds to that of head of the staff, and not to the subordinate rank implied by the grade in France.

by an icy wind. Thinking we were to bivouac again further on, we had packed up our cloaks and rugs on the trolley. Our benumbed fingers can no longer grasp our rifles; we shiver, swear, and sneeze in chorus. It was a horrible experience!

After a night that seemed interminable, dawn and sunlight put an end to our torture. During the morning certain information is brought in. The camp has been broken up, 1,500 men have been mobilized, and have spent the night on the *qui vive*. A patrol of thirteen Lancers passed close by.

The 29th is a Sunday. The Boers sing hymns. We pitch our tents again about two hours' distance from our camp of the night before.

On the 30th, at eight o'clock, orders are given to transport our laager to the foot of the high kopjes we see four or five miles off in the direction of Taba N'chu.

Towards 9.30 the Maxim suddenly opens fire, without our having seen or heard anything to account for it. We gallop off to the kopjes straight in front of us, making for one of the highest, which is called Taba N'berg. But a field-cornet comes after us at a gallop, and sends us more to the left to join General Kolby. It is all the same to us, as we know nothing of what is on hand. We take up a position on a little rocky peak.

The *kopjes* form a large semicircle, slightly oval, the curve of which lies to the north-east and the opening to the south-east. A group of trees in the midst of the arid yellow basin is Taba N'chu. To the west of our position twenty miles off is Bloemfontein. All the bottom of the vast hollow is full of men in khaki.

It is ten o'clock. We have one cannon on our left, and on our right, between us and the big *kopje*, another cannon and a Maxim gun. Later in the day two or three Grobler guns appeared on the scene. One English battery took up a position about 4,000 metres from us, then another, distributing common shell and shrapnel all along our line. A brisk fusillade was also brought to bear upon us at a long range (about 2,500 yards).

Judging the distance to be too great for effective rifle-fire, we did not respond to this, but did our best with our guns. At eleven o'clock, however, our Maxim was silenced.

The Duke of Edinburgh's Volunteers and the Royal Irish charged our right wing four times, and finally succeeded in establishing themselves on the flank of the incline, which was relatively slight on their side.

Von Braschel was killed, and Brostolowsky, both former officers in the German army; also Baudin, a former sergeant of marines, who had served his fifteen years, and had come to the Transvaal while waiting for the liquidation of his retiring pension.

About 4.30 we were ourselves vigorously charged by the infantry, but a brisk fire, unerringly delivered, dispersed those who did not fall.

The fighting ceased with the day. In the evening, owing to the unexpected nature of the engagement, we had neither provisions nor coverings. A box of sardines between ten of us was our dinner, and the intense cold debarred us from the sleep that would have consoled us for our missing meal.

We remained in position, and at daybreak on May 1 the battle began again.

With the Germans, we were sent to occupy the big kopje against which the English attack had been most violent the night before. Its dominant position made it of great strategic value; but the Boers who had held it were guilty of the disastrous negligence, only too habitual with them, of retiring from it in order to sleep comfortably, instead of strengthening their position upon it.

The English, on the other hand, had spent the night digging trenches, and were firmly established on the ground they had gained in the two days. From the very beginning, therefore, our position was less favourable.

The ascent of Taba N'berg by a rocky, steep, and almost precipitous incline took about thirty-five minutes. So rugged was the hillside that it was impossible to use litters to bring down the wounded. We were forced to drag them down by the feet, or to make them slide down sitting. Our shelters were therefore often stained with long trails of blood.

Our horses were left at the bottom of the hill, without anyone on guard as usual. On reaching the top, we were greeted by steady infantry fire and by a few shrapnel shells, which we received without responding till ten o'clock. Then, leaning a little upon our right, we began to fire. We numbered about a hundred—fifty foreigners, and as many Boers; for the majority of those who had been with us the night before—perhaps 500 Europeans, and a rather smaller number of Burghers—had returned to the laager, and had not come back.

It is true that the day had been a hard one for them, and that they had had to bear the brunt of the battle under a heavy artillery fire.

Up to this moment nothing serious had been attempted. But about eleven o'clock the whole of the Royal Canadian contingent arrived in open formation. They were greeted on their passage by our two 75 millimetre guns, which had taken up a position on our left at the foot of the kopje.

I heard afterwards that the guns, though they had been remarkably well laid, had not been very effective, the shells with fuses having fallen without exploding. In consequence of this, only two or three men, who had been struck full by the shells as if they had been bullets, had been killed. Several others were knocked over by the shock, but picked themselves up unharmed. I got this information later from a superior officer of an English regiment who had been present in the engagement.

About one o'clock, without any order and without any reason, the Boers, who were occupying another little *kopje* on our left, forsook their position. The English artillerymen at once rushed forward, and now began to fire upon us at a distance of 3,500 metres. Then, all at once, there was a cry of, 'To the horses!' At our feet, behind us in the plain, a regiment of lancers, who had come round the big *kopje* where we were stranded as on an island, sweep forward in loose order, to seize our horses which are sheltered below.

There is a rush to protect them. A few Boers, coming from I know not whence, took ambush in a little *spruit*, and drove off the lancers by a withering fire; but while this feint was being carried out, the English made another rush forward, more serious than the first. A fierce fusillade was kept up on both sides.

We are now only hanging on to the kopje by the left corner.

Suddenly, not having been able to seize our horses, the enemy open a terrible artillery fire upon them obliquely. The Boers retreat before it, and the position becomes untenable; we have only just time to reach our horses. As we come down the *kopje*, one of my comrades, who is a great declaimer of verse, recites *Rolla*; but his memory fails him at a certain verse, and he asks me to help him out. I reply that I don't know *Rolla*, but my answer is cut short by a shell which, passing between us, bursts and carries off the head of a Burgher clean from the nape of the neck.

And through the crash of shells and the whistle of bullets I hear a few metres off the voice of my friend De C—— speaking to someone I cannot see:

'It was at Tabarin, you know.'

At last we reach the horses; Buhors arrives, bringing the water-bottles he has filled at a little spring a hundred metres off under a hail of projectiles. An ambulance is on the spot, riddled with bullets, and the doctor, admirably calm, tends the wounded, while the natives hastily harness the mules. We see two or three more men fall; a horse drops disembowelled by a shell; then we are in the saddle.

Four or five men, who were firing at us from a distance of about 200 metres on top of the kopje we had just abandoned, and the battery which was working away unceasingly 3,000 yards off, had got us in an angle of fire. The ground was ploughed up by a hail of projectiles, and the shower of bullets raised thousands of little clouds.

A hard gallop of 2,000 metres under these convergent fires carried us pretty well out of danger.

A German, with a long fair beard, whom I knew well, galloped past me. He had no coat, no hat, no arms; his horse had neither saddle nor bridle; he was guiding it by a halter. Pale, with staring eyes, his face contracted, he dashed past me. There was a large bloodstain on his shirt. He had been shot right through the body!

It was half-past two o'clock.

These two days cost us twenty killed, among them six Europeans, and about fifty wounded, of whom twenty were Europeans.

Scarcely had we got beyond range, when we met Botha, who posted us on a little slope. There were about sixty of us. Then Botha went off. When he had disappeared, a Burgher went slowly up to his horse, mounted it, and left the field. Another followed him, just as slowly, then a third. Soon there were only about fifteen Europeans left.

We could see nothing on the horizon, neither convoy nor retreating troops. We in our turn departed, saluted by a few shells.

Here and there a few wounded, and one or two men who had lost their horses, were going away. No one knew what had become of the army.

## Chapter 9

# Worn Out

At last we meet General Olivier's troops, marching to the north-west. They appear to know nothing of the battle. Scarcely have we gone 100 metres with them before we are stopped by a battery, which opens fire upon us. The English form a semicircle round us. The situation is serious. We make off across the *veldt*, towards the east, till far on in the night. We sleep on the ground, keeping a sharp look-out.

On the next day, Tuesday, at dawn, we set out again, describing a wide circle, first to the east, then to the north, and finally to the west. It proved lucky for us that we had done so, for we were behind the English columns marching on Brandfort and Winburg.

Finally, always making our way across the *veldt*, we arrived at Brandfort on the 4th about eight o'clock in the morning.

Oh, how thankful we were to be in our camp and in our tents again! What a tub we had! what a breakfast! and what a sleep we look forward to when night comes!

While waiting for the preparation of a serious meal, we set to work to grill a few chops. They have scarcely been on the embers more than two minutes, when we hear *Pom! pom! pom!*

There is no time for breakfast. To horse! We swallow our raw cutlets, and gallop off.

Four men stay behind to strike the camp, and we take up a position to the south-east of Brandfort, on the *kopjes* that command the plain.

In the distance, about eight kilometres off, we see the English convoys already making for Brandfort. They are pretty confident.

To the right, a battery, of which we can distinguish the escort, silences the cannon nearest us by killing the gunners. Then a second battery advances at a trot on the left in the plain, and crosses the fire of the first.

The Boers watch this manoeuvre with great interest, discussing it and giving their opinions on it. Then, as the battery halts and takes up a position, slowly but surely, they all make for their horses.

Scarcely are the first shells fired before they are in their saddles, decamping at full speed.

Our two 75-millimetre guns come up, and throw a few shells from a distance, with no result.

It is always the same. They watch the enemy's operations without interfering, and when they want to act, it is too late.

It is two o'clock. Our waggons went off long ago, but the road is encumbered with a long string of vehicles.

The roads to Smaldeel and Winburg are cut off. There is an indescribable throng on the *veldt*; each person is going in his own direction. The confusion is complete.

C—— and I go off to try and find our baggage, for since the 1st we have had no news of the trolley, which is with Michel and a few comrades. The rest of the carts may very well have been captured, like so many others, either near Winburg or near Smaldeel.

My friend, always full of foresight, had taken the precaution of putting a pot of peach jam in his pocket when we started in the morning. On this we dined without a scrap of biscuit.

Late in the evening we arrived at a farm, from whence we were shown the English outposts on a *kopje* opposite. During the night the owners of the farm went off in a cart. *Kaffirs* kept watch to warn us should any attempt be made on our refuge. We slipped away at daybreak, and arrived at Smaldeel towards noon on the 5th.

The retreat continued. Each day was marked by a skirmish, though no serious engagement took place except at Zand River on the 9th. There the fighting was pretty hot. The Boers of our right wing were driven back, while the Germans, who were in front, held the bed of the river, which makes an angle at this point. The English column advanced, greatly outnumbering the Germans, who were very nearly taken. They ordered the Boers to stand firm to allow them to disengage themselves, but the panic-stricken Burghers would not stop. Then, without receiving any orders, the Germans, moved by a feeling of deep and legitimate anger, once more summoned the fugitives to fight, and on their refusal, poured a volley into them at a distance of about 200 metres. Several fell; the rest, cowed by this prompt action, returned to their positions, held the English column in check for a few moments, and gave the Germans time to disengage themselves.

On the 12th French had arrived first at Kroonstad by one of his usual outflanking movements. The surprise had been complete. Fortunately our carts had left the day before.

Since the 8th Heilbron had become the seat of government of the Free State.

The Irish Brigade,[1] nearly all of whom were drunk after the sacking of the stores, had been made prisoners for the most part.

The railway-station, which served as a commissariat store, had been burnt to the ground with all the provisions, which there had been no time to save.

Everyone was worn out. Lorentz had been shot in two places at Zand River; Wrangel too was wounded. Everywhere where resistance had been necessary the Boers had not stood against a dozen shells.

The retreat continued to Vereeniging; we arrived there on the 14th. The most contradictory rumours were freely circulated. On the 12th, Mafeking was said to have been taken by the Boers; on the 13th the news was confirmed; on the 14th it was denied.

The town, it appeared, had very nearly been taken by a hundred foreigners; but getting no support from the Boers, they had failed in their attempt, and seventy-two of them had been killed.

On the morning of the 17th we were said to have captured eighteen guns at Mafeking. The following telegram, signed by General Snyman, had even been published:

> This morning I had the good fortune to take prisoner Baden-Powell and his 900 men.

In the evening it was reported that we had suffered a check, and had lost ten guns.

The last report was, unhappily, the only true one.

Baden-Powell, whom Lord Roberts had asked in April to hold on till May 18, had been relieved on the 17th, after a siege of 118 days.

The last few days, it seems, had been very hard ones, for on April 22 the ration had been reduced to 120 *grammes* of meat and 240 *grammes* of bread a day.

The little garrison had been greatly tried, losing more than half of its numbers during this siege, the longest in modern times after those of Khartoum (341 days) and Sebastopol (327 days), though a trifling affair as compared with the ten years of Troy, or the twenty-nine years

---

1. A certain number of Irish, commanded by Colonel Blake, had taken service with the Boers under the name of the Irish Brigade.

of Azoth recorded by Herodotus.

We found our waggons awaiting us at Vereeniging on the 15th; we were thoroughly disgusted, as may be supposed. We had been retreating and retreating continuously, without a struggle, without an effort, offering no resistance.

However, we found that a *Long Tom* had been brought up, mounted on a truck. It was protected by a steel shield and a rampart of sandbags. A second truck, also casemated with logs and sandbags, served as a magazine for powder and shell. But the kind of armoured train thus formed remained idle in the railway-station.

I inquired whether we were to attempt an attack and push forward. The answer was that we could not venture to cross the Vaal with the gun, because it was feared that the Free State Boers, who were displeased at the war, might blow up the railway bridge while the 'armoured train' was in the Orange territory, and thus deliver it into the hands of the English. Such was the spirit of confidence that reigned!

In spite of all this, we wished to try once more to organise an effective foreign legion. De Malzan, a former officer in the German Army, was appointed Adjutant of the Uitlanders' Corps under Blignault, by the Government of Pretoria; his commission was signed by Reitz and Souza. He went, his jaw still bandaged for a wound received at Platrand, to confer with General Botha. He was very badly received.

'I do not recognise anyone's right to make appointments. Blignault is not a general, and you are nothing at all. The Europeans can all go back to their own countries. I don't want them. My Burghers are quite enough for me'—a remark he might have spared the European legion, which, out of about 280, had in the last two months lost fifteen killed, nineteen prisoners and eighty-seven wounded on the battlefields of Boshof, Taba N'chu, Brandfort and Zand River.

Anxious to clear up the question definitively, I left my camp on the other side of the Vaal, and made for Pretoria on the evening of the 18th in a coal-truck.

On the 19th I found Lorentz there. He had been made a Colonel. We held a council of war—Lorentz, still lame from his two wounds; Wrangel, with his arm in a sling; Rittmeister Illich, the Austro-Hungarian, and myself. It was decided that we should lay before the President a scheme of organisation, from which I will quote a passage, as it shows the state of mind in which we all were:

We earnestly hope that on the lines we have laid down, and

with the active support of the government—which no one has yet obtained—a good result may be achieved.

This plan, taking into account the rapidity with which events are following one upon another, depends for its success on the swiftness with which it is carried out. But we much fear that a fresh rebuff from the government, after so many others, would irrevocably discourage its well-wishers.

******

We obtained an interview with De Korte, who had influence. He approved the plan, but feared to see it fail, like so many others. Our representations became more and more pressing.

On the 24th I went to Johannesburg to see Dr. Krause, who is also influential. He was very amiable, but irresolute, and did not know what to say.

******

The English continued to advance. A despatch-rider came to tell me that my convoy had arrived. It joined me, indeed, at Johannesburg on the 26th, without any 'boys,' all of them having deserted; the waggons battered and broken by fording the rivers, the beasts dead or exhausted by a journey without rest or food, the men worn out by continual vigilance, and by their double duties as 'boys' and combatants, disgusted at the retreat and the disorder.

Many of them laid down their arms, and found work at the cartridge-factory and in the mines at from twenty-five to thirty shillings a day. One, more desperate than the rest, left his arms with us, and went off to the English lines to surrender. Only a very few remained, waiting for the President's decision as a last resource.

The *landdrost* allots a piece of waste ground to the twenty mules, twenty-one oxen, thirty-two horses and two 'boys,' which constitute the debris of our convoy. The men find lodging where they can.

On Sunday, the 27th, one of my men arrived from Pretoria with a letter from Lorentz, dated Saturday morning. The scheme had been signed and approved. Afterwards he handed me a proclamation by Lorentz, dated the evening of the same day. At two o'clock everything was retracted and refused. Furious and despairing, Colonel Lorentz adjured all the foreigners to lay down their arms:

> As the honourable Government of the Z.A.R. cannot accede to our modest but just demands, we, the foreigners of various nationalities, being without means of livelihood, are no longer

in a position to sacrifice our lives for the maintenance of the Federated Republics.

I, the under-signed, hitherto commandant of the international corps, hereby invite all persons who voluntarily joined me to lay down their arms on Tuesday, May 29, 1900, at ten o'clock in the morning, at the Old Union Club at Pretoria, or at any other place where they may happen to be.

(Signed)           C. Lorentz.<br>
*Hauptmann v. L.*

I hesitated to show the proclamation to my companions, they were already so depressed.

On the morning of Monday, the 28th, a policeman, furnished with an order from the Landdrost, requisitioned our beasts at the grazing-ground without even giving us notice. I believe he sold them. I had almost certain proof of this later on. We never found them again.

In the night three of our waggons out of the five were pillaged in spite of the man on guard. Such behaviour to Europeans who were being cut up into mincemeat for them! . . . It was too much! The cup was full. I handed Lorentz's proclamation to the men. It did not raise a regret; they were all sick of the business.

Those in authority had refused them a few shillings, scarcely the pay of a *kaffir*, of which they were sorely in need, for they were utterly destitute, and had not the means to escape from the English and return to their countries.

And now the authorities were taking advantage of our exhaustion to steal our horses—under a pretext of legality—to give, or, rather, to sell them to Boers who were going back quietly to their farms. For if a few thousand still stood their ground, the majority had lost heart, and had returned to their homes, only leaving them when their wives, more patriotic than themselves, drove them back to the front.

It was generally the old men, those who had taken part in the 'Great Treks,' who set the example of resistance. These men have inherited the virtues of their ignorant and rustic ancestors. If they can read at all, the Bible is their only book; and even if they cannot read it, they know its grand pages, and try to live up to its precepts.

Many Burghers of the younger generation, on the other hand, have inhabited towns; they have become greedy of gain, very English in their habits and customs, and have lost the principal virtues of their race, substituting for them the faults, often much aggravated, of those who have given them the shady civilization of South African cities.

In the army of Natal, round about Amajuba, there were seven guns and about 200 men. Of these just *six were* Burghers, the rest were Afrikanders and foreigners. And while former officers and non-commissioned officers of the European artillery were begging for cannon, two of these seven guns were idle for want of men to serve them.

They prefer to leave them thus rather than to give them over to foreigners. I was told this by a Burgher, an artilleryman of twenty, who was going to his post. I travelled with him from Pretoria to Elandsfontein on the morning of May 24. He himself did not conceal his indignation at this method of proceeding.

At Pretoria the government had given up all pretence of action. A general panic seemed to reign. Rumour reported that influential persons were mainly occupied in dividing the public money among themselves.

It is a fact that none of the tradespeople, whether they were hotel-keepers who had lodged and fed troops on presentation of requisition warrants, or dealers in clothes and provisions, had been paid. They all now declined to lodge persons or provide goods for the State.

A woman, Mrs. S. D., who had had a contract for saddles, was obliged, after many fruitless appeals, to enter the government offices horsewhip in hand, like Louis XIV. when he intimidated his Parliament.

Thanks to this vigorous proceeding, she received a credit-note, on which a certain number of bars of gold were given her, for the national bank-notes had fallen to about two-thirds of their nominal value. But this was an exceptional case, and most of the trades-people were less fortunate.

What became of the gold that for eight months was taken out of seven mines working for the State? No one knows!

It is true that, from the highest functionary to the humblest Burgher, all were intent on the most shameless pillage. I saw army contractors, on whom no sort of check existed, charged with the provision of every kind of necessary, food, clothing, horses, oxen, etc., and making fine fortunes in no time; while the honest and worthy Boer received from the State horses and harness which he afterwards sold to it again with the utmost coolness.

I know, too, that very large sums were devoted to a press propaganda in favour of the South African Republics. And how many skilful middlemen, by means of round sums judiciously distributed, secured orders for the most expensive and useless commodities!

In all countries and in all ages it is notorious that out of ten army contractors nine are thieves and one is a rogue, especially in war-time. Their depredations date back to the institution of armies, and the Boer contractors had only to follow on a path already clearly marked out for them by their European *confrères*. But few of these have displayed such a degree of proficiency in their calling.

I might quote the case of a famous Parisian firm of balloonists, to which nearly 10,000 *francs* were paid in ready money for waterproof silk, cord, and various utensils for the construction of a balloon. An aeronaut was also engaged at a salary of 2,000 *francs* a month, all expenses paid, and when he arrived at Machadodorp, where the President was at the time, he was greeted with:

'A balloon? What for?'

After awaiting a solution for three weeks, the aeronaut returned to France, noting on his return journey a number of stray packages on the quay at Lourenço Marques. They contained the silk and the rest of the apparatus.

It was by a scientific application of these Boer principles that Mrs. S. D. came by the very pretty sum we have seen her collecting with her horsewhip!

She had engaged to deliver 500 saddles a week at £10 each; but a good many of the Burghers to whom the saddles were distributed sold them back to the worthy lady's agents for £4 or £5, and she then sold them again to the State, after changing the more conspicuous of them a little. So that these wretched saddles were always reappearing on the scene, as in a review at the Châtelet; but each of their migrations brought in a solid sum to Mrs. D——.

It is not difficult to see why there was no money for the combatants.

CHAPTER 10

# Johannesburg

After forty-eight hours of fighting from Elandsfontein to Florida, on May 29 and 30, we were cut off from the road to Pretoria by General French and his cavalry.

Without horses it was impossible for us to follow the retreat, and we found ourselves shut up in Johannesburg. We succeeded in enrolling ourselves among the police of the mines, which gave us a temporary shelter, and perhaps saved us a sojourn at St. Helena; for we were determined not to take the oath of neutrality, but to begin fighting again as soon as possible.

On May 31 the English entered Johannesburg. The English flag was hoisted with great pomp at noon in the great square, in the presence of Lord Roberts. Dr. Krause had been empowered to surrender the town.

Johannesburg is a very English town. Its behaviour at the time of Jameson's raid sufficiently proved this, and many of the more irreconcilable Burghers who had been brought into hospital there wounded ran away before they were cured rather than remain in the hostile town.

The Union Jack was accordingly greeted with loud shouts of 'Hip! hip! hip! hurrah!'

Nevertheless, we often met Burghers in the crowd who, like ourselves, were only biding their time to return to the front. I saw one old man weeping silently. I am not sentimental, but I have rarely felt a more poignant emotion than this mute and dignified despair excited in me. I hurried away. I think I should have wept myself.

The entry of the troops began at about 10.30, and lasted four hours. About 12,000 men marched through the town, and in the environs, as far off as Elandsfontein, some 50,000 passed, it was said.

But what a procession it was! There was no order; the men barely marched in ranks. No uniforms, officers and soldiers huddled together, dirty, and many of them in rags. They had eaten nothing since the day before, when the ration had been two biscuits.

On they came, or rather dragged themselves, with drooping heads, one with his rifle on his shoulder, another with his slung across his back, one with the butt-end uppermost, some without bayonets, others with bayonets fixed. Some officers had our Mauser rifles, others Lee-Enfields, others sporting rifles. Nearly all, both officers and soldiers, walked with the help of sticks.

From Bloemfontein to Johannesburg they had covered 250 miles, fighting every day, and sometimes marching 45 kilometres without a halt across country.

A few days earlier, at Kroonstad, their convoys had not come up. Lord Roberts, anxious to continue his forward movement by forced marches, asked the commissariat-officer:

'Can you serve the ration?'

'No, sir.'

'Half ration, then?'

'No, sir.'

'Quarter ration?'

'Yes, perhaps.'

On receiving this problematic reply, the Marshal explained the situation to his men. They immediately replied with acclamations: 'For Lord Roberts we would march without any ration at all!'

The Black Watch, out of a thousand men, their strength on landing, mustered about sixty behind their pipers. The others lie in the trenches of Magersfontein and at the foot of Dorn Kop.

Save for a few battalions that have arrived recently, the regiments are skeleton corps.

As we watched these haggard, exhausted troops dragging themselves along, involuntarily we called to mind him who once marched our fathers through all the capitals of Europe. In spite of fatigue, privation, and hard fighting, it was in a very different guise that the Grand Army entered Vienna and Berlin behind the Emperor and his glittering staff.

The artillery was in better form. Some fifteen batteries were drawn by magnificent horses, and I saw men on cobs that looked well worth from two to three hundred *louis*.

There were also some siege-guns, and some 15 centimetre naval guns—one from the *Monarch*—drawn by thirty-two oxen. It was behind this powerful artillery, devastating the whole region with it on principle, whether occupied or not, that the English army had advanced from Bloemfontein.

If we had had a body of cavalry, I believe that rapid and energetic action would have resulted in a considerable loss of *matériel* to the English army; for, relying on the absolute lack of offensive measures on our side, they often left their batteries defenceless.

Next came a strong train—telegraph apparatus, balloonists, engineering implements for digging wells, pumps, etc.

The troops merely passed through the town, leaving in it a garrison under the command of Colonel Mackenzie (Seaforth Highlanders), who was appointed Governor of Johannesburg.

The next day a proclamation by Frederick Sleigh, Baron Roberts of Kandahar and Waterford, K.P., G.C.B., G.C.S.I., G.C.I.E., V.C., Field-Marshal, commanding Her Majesty's Forces in South Africa:

> Assures the non-combatant population of his protection.
> All Burghers who have committed no act of violence contrary to the laws of civilization against any of Her Majesty's subjects are authorized to return to their homes, after giving up their arms and pledging themselves to take no further part in hostilities. Passports will be given them.
> Her Majesty's Government will respect the private property of the inhabitants of the South African Republic, as far as is compatible with the exigencies of war.
> All individual attempts upon property will be severely punished.
> God Save the Queen!
> Given under my hand and seal at Johannesburg, May 31, 1900.

At the same time, regulations fixing the prices of provisions for the troops were issued: 30s. for a sack of 168 lb. of oats; champagne-tisane, 160s. a case; tobacco, from 3s. to 7s. a pound, etc.

Let us take advantage of our ephemeral functions as policemen to explore the town a little. Johannesburg was not the first mining centre in the Transvaal. The first workers established themselves at Barberton in 1886. A few years later the Brothers Strubens, whilom prospectors, discovered an auriferous vein in the Witwatersrand near the farm of Landlaagte. Johannesburg then consisted of a few scattered huts. It now numbers over 100,000 inhabitants (I mean, of course, before the war).

It is a town given over to business. The centre is occupied by the post-office, a huge building, in front of which is a vast marketplace. Here in normal times trains of carts bring in all the necessaries of life—fruit, vegetables, mealies, etc. The principal streets, Commissioner Street, Market Street, Pritchard Street and President Street, are wide, clean, and bordered by handsome shops. The whole town is lighted by electricity.

The blocks of houses, three and four stories high, are called 'buildings'; often several of them belong to the same owner or to the same society, and bear their names: Ægis Building, Commissioner Street; S.A. Mutual Building; Standard Building; Heritier Building.

The houses are not numbered, but this does not inconvenience the postmen, for they do not exist. Each inhabitant pays a small sum for his own box at the post-office, and goes to fetch his correspondence when he likes.

Johannesburg has a very well organised fire-brigade, with engines, ladders and fire-escapes of the latest pattern. The captain, who is, I believe, an Englishman, served for a time in Paris, London, and New York, and wears the honorary medal of our Paris brigade. The men wear the same uniform as English firemen.

The hosiers, tailors, French milliners, dressmakers, saddlers, and music-sellers of the town are on a par with the best European specialists. Life is very expensive, and all luxuries command tremendous prices. Cabs, dirty and ill-harnessed, drawn by two miserable horses and very badly driven, cost 7s. an hour. Little light cabriolets drawn by negroes are therefore generally used for locomotion. These are much cheaper and fairly rapid, for the negroes—*Kaffirs* or Zulus—are in excellent training, and can go extraordinary distances at the double.

The currency was for a long time English, but in 1892 the Transvaal struck her first coins (pounds and shillings) with the effigy of President Kruger.

The Free State has no coinage of her own, and uses English or Transvaalian money.

Bronze money, of which the President only allowed a few specimens to be struck, is not current; the monetary unit is the 'ticket,' a small silver coin worth 3d.[1]

---

1. Some English officers, it seems, saw for the first time at Elandsfontein a Kruger's penny, and bought it for £2. The current price of a Kruger's penny is from two to three shillings.

The Johannesburg journals, the *Standard and Diggers' News* and the *Wolkstrem*, the official organ, therefore cost 3d.

At Johannesburg much more than at Pretoria, because the town is more English, the houses in the centre of the town are mainly offices, for all the inhabitants who are comfortably off live in the suburbs, either on the height beyond the fort, or at the end of Main Street, in the great park of Belgravia.

Most of these suburban dwellings are very expensive, and are comfortably and luxuriously arranged. A garden more or less large is considered an absolute necessity.

The majority of the population speculate and gamble, and it is not rare in times of peace to recognise in some barman or miner a gentleman who had dazzled the town by the magnificence of his carriages and horses a few months back. No surprise is felt by anyone, for the next 'boom' will perhaps make him a wealthy man of fashion once more.

I could quote the case of a young man I knew well who was twice a millionaire, and who, after having been ruined for the second time, was gradually building up a third fortune. He is very little more than thirty.

Johannesburg, however, is merely a city of passage. Men stay here just long enough to make money, and directly this is done, they return to their own countries. The end and aim of everything here is to make money, and to make it quickly.

Based on this principle, and composed of a number of adventurers, the cosmopolitan society one finds here hardly offers a guarantee of irreproachable morality.

Antecedents are of little account, indeed. A merchant who has been convicted of fraud in France, here enjoys the consideration due to the £500,000 he has gained with the money he stole in his fraudulent bankruptcy.

I have even heard that some years ago the extradition of a rogue was the signal for disorderly scenes and an expostulatory address, because he had not been convicted of theft since his arrival at Johannesburg. He had made a considerable sum of money there, and was accompanied to the station by a number of friends.

★★★★★★

No sketch of Johannesburg would be complete without a few words about the gold-mines.

I am no authority on the subject, but I will describe what was told me and what I saw; and as the engineer who was good enough to give me some information knew me to be ignorant, my *precis* will be a little

*Manual on Mining* for the use of novices.

In the first place, there is an essential difference between the manner in which gold is found in Witwatersrand and in other districts, such as Klondyke, Senegal, or the Soudan. In the latter, the gold is in grains, either embedded between the frozen stones, or rolling in the beds of rivers. The auriferous mud is taken up and washed, and the gold is retained. Nothing could be simpler.

In the Rand, however, the working of the mines is purely scientific. The mineral is found in blocks of quartz and silicious clay containing pyrites of auriferous copper and gold.

After calculating the direction of the reef, one must dig down to a greater or less depth to find it. Dynamite is then used to detach the gold-bearing quartz, which is brought to the surface. It has the appearance of very hard white stone, slightly veined with blue. It is carried off to the batteries in Decauville trucks, and there a crushing-mill, which looks like a gigantic coffee-mill, and sledge-hammers combined into groups of five, reduce it to a very fine powder. A current of air spreads this powder over copper-plates covered with mercury.

A large proportion of the gold, about 60 *per cent.*, amalgamates with the mercury, and once a fortnight the amalgam is scraped off. After fusion the mercury in the amalgam volatilizes, leaving a deposit of almost pure gold.

The residuum of the first process is afterwards poured into huge vats of from 10 to 12 metres in diameter, in which cyanide of potassium has been placed. A solution of cyanide of gold is thus obtained, and this is put into cases lined with strips of zinc, on which the gold is precipitated. The 40 *per cent.* lost in the first process is thus recovered.

The gold thus collected is melted down into ingots, the transport and verification of which are the objects of interminable regulations.

So much for the scientific part. The rest is simpler.

The heavy labour is mainly done by *kaffirs* or Zulus under the supervision of white miners who earn about twenty-five pounds a month, and live in the boarding-house connected with the mine.

The natives live in a compound where no alcohol is allowed. Their rations are given them, and they live on very little. Their ambition is to earn enough money to return to their native place, buy two wives, and do no more work; the wives work for them thenceforth. It takes them about two years to realize this dream. When the time is up, it is impossible to keep them in the mines.

The first year of working (1888) yielded about £1,000,000. In

1895 about £8,000,000 was extracted. Finally, from January 1 to August 31, 1899, the harvest was nearly £13,000,000. The net profits of exploitation are considerably diminished by the enormous expenses resulting from the dearness of European labour, and the heavy taxes imposed by the Transvaal Government on mining rights and on the importation of explosives.

At the time of my sojourn all the works were closed. In the town, as every hospital and ambulance was full to overflowing, the hotels were requisitioned for the sick. In front of the Victoria Hotel there were often strings of ten and twelve waggons bringing in the wounded.

Often at dusk a dray would pass, into which long, heavy cases of deal were furtively slipped... The *avowed* losses were terrible enough. What were they in reality?

About the middle of December the War Office confessed to 7,350 men. At the beginning of February this number was doubled, and Buller's three attempts on the Tugela cost 1,046 killed, 3,785 wounded, and over 1,500 missing.

In March the numbers had swelled to 14,000. It was the unhealthy season, and sickness—enteric fever especially—made wider gaps in the English ranks than bullets. On May 10 over 18,000 men were missing, 5,000 of whom were dead.

On the Boer side the statistics are much more difficult to check, especially when one is confronted with such discrepancies as these: Rumours and reports stated the Boer losses at the Battle of Colenso, on December 15, to have been 8 killed and 14 wounded. But I find a report drawn up by the Red Cross Society in which the numbers are given as 77 killed and 210 wounded.

What is one to believe? In all ages belligerents have tried to conceal their losses, and this kind of juggling is, of course, much easier among incoherent groups like the commandos than in regular battalions.

★★★★★★

One day—it was June 10, I think—all the police of the mines were requisitioned to transport the wounded from the station to the hospitals. There were a great many, and they had been forbidden to say whence they came; the police were also forbidden to speak to them on any pretext whatever. Had something very serious happened? We never knew exactly what it was.

Pretoria had been occupied on June 5. The news that reached us came at long intervals, after manipulation by the censor, and was often of the most fantastic order.

The police regulations were most stringent. Everyone was ordered to be indoors, at first by seven o'clock, later by 8.30. The streets and squares were guarded by troops. Jewellers' and wine-merchants' shops and bars were closed by order. No one was allowed to draw money without a permit from the military authorities, and a limit—of £20 a week, I think—was enforced as to the amount, unless a special permission had been granted.

Finally, residents in the town were required to get a pass and to take an oath of allegiance. Those who, like ourselves, had resolved not to do this, were obliged to hide like outlaws, to avoid being marched off to the fort, and thence to Ceylon. We give a reproduction below of the chapter of this police regulation which was posted on the walls of the town.

A few days back a German had gone into Government Place at noon and hauled down the English flag. The sentry looked on aghast at first, and then began to question him.

'It has no business here,' replied the German, going on with his work. He was arrested at last, and condemned to nine months' hard labour.

The life of inaction had become unbearable to me. At the end of June, still on the lookout for a means of returning to the front, I at last 'found' the papers of an English police-officer. And now for liberty!

\*\*\*\*\*\*

V. R.

### Police Notice

1. All civilians are required to remain in their houses between the hours of 7 p.m. and 6.30 a.m. unless provided with a pass signed by the Military Commissioner of Police.

2. No natives are allowed in the town except such as are permanently employed within its limits.

3. All liquor stores, bars, and *kaffir* eating houses are closed until further orders. No liquor will be sold except on the written order of an officer of Her Majesty's Forces.

4. All jewellers' shops are closed.

5. No civilian is allowed to ride or drive, or ride a bicycle within the town unless provided with a pass signed by the Military Commissioner of Police.

6. Any person disobeying these regulations is liable to arrest, and will be dealt with under martial law.

By Order,
Francis Davies, Major Grenadier Guards,
Military Commissioner of Police.
Johannesburg, 1st June, 1900.

### POLITIE KENNISGEVING.

1. *Alle inwoners worden hierbij bevolen om in hun huizen te blyven van 7 uur's avonds tot 6.30 uur's morgens indien niet voorzien van een paspoort, geteekend door de Militaire Commissaris van Politie.*

2. *Geen kleurlingen mogen in de stad zyn indien zy geen vast werk hebben daarin.*

3. *Alle bottel stores, bars en kleurling kosthuizen moeten gesloten worden tot nadere kennisgeving. Geen drank mag verkocht worden indien niet voorzien van een permit van den officier van Harer Majesteit's Troepen.*

4. *Alle jewelier winkels moeten gesloten worden.*

5. *Geen inwoner mag ryden te paard, rytuig of bicycle in de stad, zonder voorzien te zyn van een permit, geteekend door de Militaire Commissaris van Politie.*

6. *Eenig persoon die deze regulaties niet opvolgt, zal gestraft worden onder de krygswet.*

By Order,
Francis Davies, Major Grenadier Guards.
*Militaire Commissaris van Politie.*
*Johannesburg, 1 Juni,* 1900.

\*\*\*\*\*\*

## Chapter 11
# P. O. W.

With a brief but resolute gesture, I took off my hat in farewell to the City of Gold. With a few necessaries rolled up in a cloak, I succeeded in passing through the English lines at Boksburg, after journeying for three days, sometimes in friendly carts, sometimes on foot, to escape attention.

Near the level crossing of the railway at Boksburg a party of Lancers was encamped. Putting on the tranquil and indifferent air of a man whose conscience is at ease, I passed through them without molestation. Further along the road there were two small outposts, which I was able to avoid by passing over a dried-up pond.

When night came on, I slept at Benoni. Commandant Derksen, of the Boksburg commando, was in the neighbourhood. I hoped to fall in with him in the north-east. The nights began to be terribly cold.

At 4 a.m. on July 4 I was once more on my way. I walked till nine in the evening. My feet were sore and bleeding.

I arrived at last at a farm, where I was coldly received at first; for they took me for a spy. But when I showed the papers that constituted me a Burgher, I was petted as if I had been a son of the house. They gave me eggs, milk and biscuit, and offered me shelter for the night. As I had no rug, and the cold was terrible, I accepted the offer with joy.

My hostess had three sons with Derksen, and a fourth with De Wet. The fourth was Baby, as she called him, showing me the photograph of this little Benjamin, who may have been about forty, and had a beard down to his waist.

They were worthy folks, Boers of the old school, hospitable and patriotic. They made me up a bed in a kind of old travelling carriage in the coach-house, and after half an hour of fierce conflict with a swarm of mice, I fell asleep.

Twice I was roused by further attacks from the rodents, and a third time by a man with a long beard, who said:

'*Obsal!*'

I was a little surprised at first, but finally I grasped the situation. A patrol commanded by one of the Bothas (a cousin of the Generalissimo), had come to the farm at three in the morning. My hostess explained my case, and they had sent to ask me if I would join them.

I agreed eagerly, and rapid preparations were at once made for my equipment. They found me a lean hack, gave me a rug by way of saddle, and two pieces of cord for stirrups, and armed me with a Lee-Metford rifle, taken from the English a little while before! Don Quixote!

We consumed the usual coffee and biscuit, and started, taking a zigzag route northwards towards Irene. Derksen was rather more to the east.

Towards nine in the evening we lay down to rest on the Veldt. I think I never suffered as I did from the cold that night. It was freezing hard, and I had nothing to cover me but the rug, which, soaked through with the horse's sweat, was as stiff as a board in ten minutes. It was impossible to sleep for a moment, and the pain became so intolerable that I was obliged to walk about to warm myself a little; and then the wounds on my feet, which were quite raw, made me suffer cruelly.

A few days later an officer of the first brigade of Mounted Infantry was found frozen to death on bivouac, in spite of his blankets.

We started at daybreak on the 6th, making for a *kaffir kraal*. At about 7.30 we heard three cannon-shots fired, but could not tell exactly from what direction. Then there was silence again.

Towards eight o'clock a group of about fifteen horsemen in felt hats and long dark overcoats came towards us, then, suddenly wheeling, went off at a gallop. We were fourteen, all told.

When it reached the top of the *kopje*, the party disappeared, and when, in our turn, we rose above the crest, we were received with a fusillade. There were about forty men, some 400 metres from us. We turned back hastily, to put our horses in shelter on the other side, and then replied.

A Burgher was wounded in the head. We had the cover of the rocks to protect us, and, in spite of our inferior numbers, the two sides were about equal. Then another Burgher and my neighbour were wounded almost simultaneously, the latter in the thigh, probably by a ricochet. His wound was serious. I took his Mauser and his cartridges from him.

I am not very sure how long this little game had been going on, perhaps ten minutes. Suddenly we heard shots behind us. One of our horses fell; Botha got a bullet right through him. We were surrounded by about 300 men of the Imperial Light Horse. There was nothing to be done. A Burgher named Marais held up a white handkerchief. There were only ten of us left. I was handed over to some English officers, who received me with the greatest possible courtesy. As the action had now extended all along the line, I was taken to the rear.

In the evening I was confided to the Connaught Rangers, who had been kept in reserve. Hearing of my nationality and my former rank in the French Army, they said: 'We are allies now! We are making common cause in China!' I made many inquiries about the events in the Far East, of which we knew nothing, having held no communication with Europe since April.

Hoping to be able to take part in the Chinese Expedition by joining the Foreign Legion, I made up my mind to give my parole to General H——, who was in command of the column.

Meanwhile I heard the most interesting details from the English officers of the campaign in which we had lately been fighting against each other. There were among them survivors of Colenso and Spion Kop, and men of the Ladysmith garrison.

The Connaught Rangers were commanded by Colonel Brooke, who was seriously wounded at Colenso, near the railway bridge. He was acting as General in command of the Irish Brigade. He invited me to dine with him, and at night, though most of the officers were sleeping in the open air, he offered me half of the little shanty which formed his bedroom, and himself fetched a bundle of straw for my bed. Then I had innumerable offers of rugs, cloaks, and capes, till at last I believe I was better wrapped up than anyone in the camp.

During the evening a telegram came telling Colonel Brooke that he had been promoted and was a general. I willingly joined in the toasts that were drunk in his honour, for it is a fine and noble feature of a military career that one feels no bitterness to an adversary. When the battle is over, foes can shake hands heartily, though they are ready to slash each other to pieces again a few hours later.

On July 7 we rose at six. A captain brought me some hot water in an india-rubber basin, sponges, and soap. Then breakfast was served. We had porridge, red herrings, butter, jam, biscuits, coffee and tea.

But the Irish Brigade had received orders to saddle up, and I was handed over to the staff of the first brigade of Mounted Infantry. I was very politely received by General Hutton's staff-officer, a lieutenant. The superior officer who took me to him, Major M. D——, of the 2nd Royal Irish Fusiliers, asked him if he spoke French. I was delighted to hear him answer in the affirmative. I went to lunch with him in his tent. Conversation languished. For a long time he did not open his lips, if I may so express it, for he was eating the grilled mutton his orderly had given us with evident appetite. Suddenly he addressed me:

'*Navet du pon.*'

I bowed amiably, thinking we were to have a dish of turnips of some kind. '*Du pon*' puzzled me a little; but perhaps there were '*Navets Dupont*' just as there are '*Bouchées Lucullus*' and '*Purée Soubise.*' I was astonished at my host's culinary knowledge. At last, later on, when I had heard the phrase a great many times without ever seeing any turnips, I found out that he wished to say, '*N'avez-vous du pain.*' This was the highest flight of which he was capable in French.

Nevertheless, my sojourn with Colonel Hutton's staff was extremely interesting. I heard that we had killed the day before Captain Currie and Lieutenant Kirk of the Imperial Light Horse, and I was present at an engagement that lasted three days. On the third day, indeed, shells burst so near me that I ran a fair chance of being killed by my friends.

I will give a brief journal of events hour by hour, so to speak.

On the 7th fighting began early towards the east. We could hear it, though we could see nothing. From noon to three o'clock the cannonade was very lively towards Olifantsfontein. This was the engagement at Witklip, I believe. The English lost some fifty men, among them ten killed.

On the morning of July 8 twenty mounted men went out with picks and spades to bury the dead. They were preceded by a large white flag. At 10.30 cannon-shots were heard east-south-east, then suddenly, at 11.5, three detachments of the Mounted Rifles went off.

Officers and despatch-riders were galloping up and down everywhere. I think the English had been completely surprised by a return of the Boers.

There was rapid harnessing and saddling. All round the bivouac horsemen were bringing in oxen, mules, and horses from grazing.

The Mounted Rifles galloped off to take up a position on the crest a mile away about which there had been fighting the day before.

At 11.15 another large detachment of Mounted Rifles passed, returning the salute of the sentry on duty at headquarters.

In all they may have been from three to four squadrons. It was difficult to form any idea of actual numbers, for they were not marching in strict order, and taking into account the reduction in the strength of certain corps, a column of two or three hundred men may well have represented a whole regiment.

A captain of the Irish Brigade told me that his company consisted of seventy-eight men, completed by yeomanry, and he called his adjutant to verify the figures he had given me.

At 11.20 a battery of the Royal Field Artillery went off in the same direction at a trot. A fraction of about fifty returned at a walk.

About 100 metres from my point of observation—an old waggon—the Irish Brigade and the Borderers stood at ease. At 11.30 a battalion was moved forward. Five minutes later a second battery, a great naval 10-centimetre gun, drawn by twenty oxen, joined the fighting line with the rest of the Irish.

Everything had been done very rapidly. One could see that the men had been trained to sudden alarms by six months of warfare. Thirty-five minutes before the men were busy in camp, and the beasts were grazing. Now more than half the men were engaged, and all were ready awaiting orders to advance.

The skirmishers came back at a gallop, and a man arrived to hasten the advance of the naval gun, the oxen of which were almost trotting already.

At 11.55 two other naval guns, also drawn by twenty oxen each, went forward to join the others. A large ambulance-waggon followed.

In the camp a dog was howling dismally. The cannonade slackened a little.

At noon an ammunition-waggon, drawn by ten mules, went off to supply the line of combatants.

It is lamentable that the Burghers, clinging obstinately to their defensive tactics, know nothing of rear or flank movements.

There are no sentries either right or left. All the troops have gone off in the direction of the cannon—that is to say, towards the east—and in that immense camp, containing some hundreds of waggons, there are only a platoon of Mounted Rifles and a half-battalion of infantry. A handful of men could carry the camp and sack it.

In addition to the material result, what a moral effect would be produced on the troops engaged a mile and a half off, if they knew that an enemy, however feeble, was in possession of the road of retreat, and engaged in plundering the stores and ammunition!

It is true that the Boers did not know the state of the camp, but if they had they would have done nothing. This circumstance, confirming many other instances, would have convinced me more firmly than ever, if that were possible, that the great secret of warfare is to *dare*! This, I think, was the sole science of Murat, Lassalle and many another famous *sabreur*. And the Emperor himself, was not he, too, a type of audacity in the conception of his most brilliant campaigns, in the conduct of his most glorious victories?

About 12.30 the firing ceased. It recommenced again about 3 and 4.30. At three o'clock another great ammunition waggon was despatched. No losses were announced that evening.

The staff was at work till one o'clock in the morning, and a long telegram in cipher was sent off to Pretoria. In the evening rather late I heard the movements of troops, which recommenced the next morning at dawn.

*July 9.*—From 7 a.m. to 7.30 a battery and several detachments of the Mounted Rifles, ten or fifteen, moved off to the east-south-east, strongly flanked on the right (south) by other Mounted Rifles and by a battery.

In the early morning there were two centimetres of ice on the artillery buckets, and towards noon we were glad to be in our shirt-sleeves. This great variation, more than 37 degrees in twenty hours, is very trying. We were now in mid-winter, and the sun set at five o'clock. At eight the firing, which was very brisk, seemed nearer than the day before. The Boer shells, carrying too far, burst between the camp and the line of the English artillery, which we could see perfectly. The infantry was posted towards the east-south-east.

The staff-officer told me that the English were engaged with General Botha's 5,000 men. I offered no opinion, but I was sure he was wrong, and information I received later justified this belief. I was rather inclined to think that it was the worthy Derksen, who had collected some 500 or 600 men, and who, by rapid and unexpected movements, was trying to make the enemy believe in the presence of a very considerable force. My staff-officer further told me that General Hutton was in command of 6,000 men, three batteries, and four naval guns. This, to judge by what I saw, may very probably have been correct. At any rate, a formidable convoy was on the spot. The guns were still booming.

An old sergeant with four stripes was introduced to me. He was the senior member of Battery 66, which had been kept in reserve. He had been serving under Lieutenant Roberts, who was killed at Colenso.

During the day four ambulance-waggons were sent out to the lines. It was at first intended that I should be taken to Pretoria, but as the route of the convoy had been changed, I was conveyed to Springs. I was one of fifteen prisoners, not counting the wounded.

At 4.30 the firing was much closer, but we had to start; the convoy was ready. It consisted of fifty bullock-waggons, eight or ten of them filled with wounded men. We, the prisoners, were at the head of the convoy, strongly guarded by infantry and mounted men. A few mounted irregulars preceded us as scouts. These men, recruited chiefly among the Afrikanders, sometimes even among the Boers, know the country very well.

Our guide was a native of Boksburg, and knew all the men with Derksen, the leader of the Boksburg commando. I made no attempt to conceal the disgust I felt for this renegade. But nothing distracted him from his duties, for he had a holy horror of falling into the hands of the Boers.

During the night fires in the bush reddened the horizon on every side. They came to ask us several times if these were signals. I really had no idea, but I was inclined to think not.

On account of the meagre fuel afforded by the short dry grass of the *veldt*, the fires we saw in these regions had none of the grandeur of the bush-fires in the Soudan, where the high grass is from 6 to 10 feet high. In those whirlwinds of fire the flames seem to lick the sky, and the tallest trees are twisted and calcined like straws. Numerous as the fires were, they did not warm the atmosphere, and the cold was terrible.

At last we arrived, supperless, at Springs, at 1.30 in the morning, so frozen that we were obliged to look and see if our feet and hands were still in place. We slept huddled in the guard-room at the railway-station.

Early on the morning of the 10th, Major Pelletier, of the Royal Canadian Regiment, came to fetch me to breakfast at mess. But Captain Ogilvie, the commandant of the station, would not let me leave his jurisdiction till I had been to his quarters to make my toilet.

After this process I went off with the major. He was a charming fellow, a French Canadian, as his name indicates, and a native of a little village in Normandy. I spent the day with him. He told me the most interesting things about Canadian life, spoke enthusiastically of the fine sport there, and invited me to come and pay him a visit later on. At the same time he confided to me that both he and his men were suffering terribly from the heat. I then, being almost frozen, make up my mind never to accept his kind invitation.

I met a young doctor, too, whose name I forget, also a French Canadian. All the French Canadians, who form the majority of the contingent, speak excellent French, interlarded with old-fashioned expressions and marked by a strong Norman accent. Many of them do not know a word of English.

At six o'clock I start for Johannesburg, in the carriage reserved for officers. My pockets are full of French Canadian papers, which, though some two months old, are full of news fresh to me.

On my arrival, I presented myself to Major Davies, the commandant of the military police. He speaks French very correctly, was very agreeable, and gave me leave to go about the town on parole. I had only to leave my address with him, and to report myself at his office every morning at eleven o'clock.

On the 13th a plot was discovered to seize the town. About 500 arrests took place during the evening. As I had taken the oath of neutrality, I was not among the conspirators, and while hostilities last I can say no more on this subject.

On the 14th I received a permit to return to France, and I started by the two o'clock train that very day.

All along the line the railway-stations had been converted into entrenched camps. We continually passed trains loaded with horses, guns, and men—some twenty in all, perhaps. We arrived at Kroonstad at eleven in the morning on the 15th. Nothing remained of the sheds and the goods-station which we had burnt on May 12, with all the stores.

Involuntarily I took out my pocket-book, and read the names of the men who then composed the French corps. We were not forty altogether. Three had been killed, five had disappeared, the others were dispersed.

I tried to go out of the station to revisit all those places in the town where we spent a fortnight, gay, full of hope, almost complete in numbers. But the station was surrounded by sentries, and no one was allowed to pass.

From a distance the prospect was dismal enough. The streets were deserted, and, as if to emphasize the fact that everywhere there is suffering, the Red Cross flag floated sadly over the town. In the foreground, close to us, on the line, and in the sidings, were deserted railway-carriages, half burnt, overturned, and broken.

All round the town were field hospitals and vast camps. There were about 11,000 men in all, I was told. A feverish activity reigned at the station, a continuous bustle and movement. Convoys of provisions and arms followed each other in rapid succession. We counted sixteen during the day on the 16th.

Horses and mules were entrained in some, others brought back the worn-out horses. Many of these poor beasts had died on the road; most of them could hardly stand. They were dragged along a few steps, and a non-commissioned officer put a bullet through their heads inside the station. Thirty or forty thus executed lay heaped one on another in a pool of blood, which ran in a little stream towards the line.

On the platform stood cases of ammunition and arms. Several placed together contained Lee-Enfield cavalry carbines, and were marked 'Very Urgent.'

On the 16th we were still at Kroonstad, and a trainful of prisoners passed going to East London. It became one of the daily exercises of the garrison to walk to the station and see the travellers.

Two questions were to be heard perpetually:

'Do you think it is nearly over?' 'Have you any Kruger pennies?'

And Tommy is quite happy when they tell him that, as to being nearly over, it's not quite that; but that as to going on much longer, it won't go on much longer—at least, it depends on what you mean by much longer; or when someone gives him one or two Kruger pennies.

At last we left Kroonstad at ten o'clock in the evening, passing through Brandfort, that village to which, feted and acclaimed, we had come with *Long Tom* in January. All along the route the railway had been destroyed, and we travelled on rails laid on unballasted sleepers by the Royal Engineers.

Trenches had been dug to enable the train to pass over the shallow, dried-up streams without any very artistic labour, and sometimes the little half-destroyed bridges had been repaired with logs and made to do duty again.

It seemed wonderful that it could all hold. But it appeared—I heard this at the camp at Springs—that one of the chief engineers of the railway service was a civilian, a French Canadian, who had already distinguished himself in America by the construction of very daring railways.

He must have been extraordinary indeed to have astonished the Americans!

It is certain that the English successfully re-established railway communication with very restricted means in a very rapid manner—not that this prevents it from being constantly re-cut, however.

On July 17, at 8.30 in the morning, we were at Bloemfontein. Poor old capital of the Orange Free State! It is now the chief town of the Orange River Colony. Here again there was an immense camp, a large proportion of the Kelly-Kenny division.

We only stayed half an hour, and, after changing trains at Springfontein, we passed Norval's Pont at 6.35 in the evening. We were in Cape Colony! Here we were no longer on an improvised railway, and we got on faster. On the 18th, about 7.30 a.m., we were in the environs of Cape Town.

In accordance with English custom, many of the merchants have offices in the town, and live in little houses which give a gay and smiling aspect to the suburbs. We therefore took up a number of passengers who looked like men of business. In a few minutes we were in the town. We left the train at 8.30.

My permission to return to France was confirmed by the general commanding the garrison. I was almost a free man!

\*\*\*\*\*\*

Vague rumours reached us from the front, always carefully doctored by the censor. Prinsloo was taken prisoner with several thousand men; but on the line to Lourenço Marques Botha was still defending himself vigorously. After the taking of Pretoria the government, incarnating itself, so to speak, in the person of President Kruger, installed itself in a special train. There Oom Paul slept, received, ate, and lived. There the official printing-press was also set up, and the money that was circulated was minted there. As in the hurried departure from Pretoria it had not been possible to carry off a complete set of weights, the sovereigns issued were simple gold discs, quite plain, without image or inscription.

It was on this line, too, that the last great battles were fought, at Middelburg, Belfast, and Machadodorp, after which, renouncing all attempts at defence, the Boers began that guerilla campaign which De Wet had already successfully essayed.

In a few days our steamer sailed. It was not without a pang that we quitted the land we had hoped to see free, for which we had fought for seven months, and which had proved the grave of a venerated leader and of beloved friends.

# Conclusion

An inexperienced writer, more expert with arms than with the pen, I do not know if I have described all these events in a manner sufficiently clear and coherent to convey a distinct impression. I shall therefore try to sum up on a few broad lines the ideas I have been able to form after the experiences I have recorded.

First of all, two great questions seem to present themselves: Why, in spite of all their qualities, have the Boers been beaten? Why are the English, with over 250,000 men, held in check by a handful of peasants?

These two questions are closely connected, for, though this seems a paradox, the chief cause of the defeat of the Boers is also the cause of their long resistance. I will explain.

I think we must attribute the defeat of the federated troops mainly to their absolute lack of military organisation, for in spite of the legend of the volunteers of 1792, no undisciplined force, however brave, will ever prove a match for a regular army.

Resistance may be more or less prolonged, phases more or less heroic, but the issue is foredoomed.

This lack of organisation, of discipline—that is the great thing—explains the absence of cohesion, of combined action, of rational leadership.

I have already sufficiently pointed out the evils of suffrage as applied to the election of commanders. In addition to this, what enthusiasm or confidence can these feel, when they know that half the men of their commando will leave them on the road if they feel so inclined? And even if they do not actually do so, the leader's confidence is put to a rude test!

Yet these same Boers who have fought like lions on occasion, and on occasion have fled without firing a shot, are capable of education in the art of war.

The Johannesburg Politie is a striking proof of this. With the elementary discipline that obtains among them, this corps held their own for a whole day against Lord Roberts's 40,000 men on two occasions, at Abraham's Kraal on March 10, and near Machadodorp on August 27, almost unsupported. And each time at the price of a third of their number!

✶✶✶✶✶✶

To this chief and primordial cause we must add another, not altogether inexcusable, but very harmful under the circumstances. I mean the dread and hatred of the foreigner.

Not inexcusable, I say, for, for nearly a century, the foreigner has been to the Boer the invader, the robber, and the enemy!

The Boers therefore, as a whole, could never believe that for love of a noble cause, or a passion for adventure, men of every nation should have come to espouse their cause against the United Kingdom quite disinterestedly.

In the unfortunate state of mind that prevailed among them, the eulogies of a well-intentioned but maladroit press had the most disastrous effect.

What sort of respect, indeed, could these primitive people feel for Europeans when Lombroso and Kuyser had written in all good faith:

> As 63 *per cent.* of Boer blood is Dutch, 12 *per cent.* French, 12 *per cent.* Scotch, and 3 *per cent.* German, this mixture of the best nations of Europe ought to constitute a centre of liberty and civilization, a race superior to any in Europe!

Why, when one belongs to 'a race superior to any in Europe,' should one follow the advice of officers of the European armies, and, consequently, of the inferior races?

And, indeed, when we consider the remarkable campaign now being carried on by De Wet and Botha, we may well ask whether Europeans could obtain better results. Under present conditions, I think, it would be hard to do better.

But if General de Villebois' advice had been taken from the first, it is very probable that the guerilla war would never have been inaugurated. The campaign would have been over long ago; for whereas the Boers were content to hold the English in check, the Europeans wanted to beat them.

Not satisfied with successful engagements that gave no solid advantage, they wanted to push forward, with the enthusiasm that surprises a demoralized enemy, creates a panic, and results in total rout.

Haunted by the names that gleam in the folds of our banners—Jemmapes, Valmy, Marengo and Austerlitz—we dreamed of great victories. And if the Boers had wished it, this dream might have been realized!

We now come to the reason why the English, with over 250,000 men, are held in check by a handful of peasants.

I have said that this question is closely bound up with the cause of the Boer defeat—the absence of discipline. For how is it possible to surround, to conquer, and to crush adversaries who will never be drawn into a battle, and who make off directly a blow is struck at them?

Are they closely pressed by the enemy? Each man goes off as he chooses in a different direction, and the *commando* of 500 men which attacked a little convoy yesterday has melted away before the column of 2,000 sent in pursuit of it.

Far away in the bush, to the east, a horseman disappears on the horizon, another on the west—and that is all.

If one of these men should have been too closely engaged in the English lines, the first farm he comes to offers him an asylum. His rifle is thrust under a plank in the flooring, his horse turned out to graze, the white flag floats over the house, and Her Majesty has no more inoffensive subject than my Burgher—for the next twenty-four hours.

If need be, when the English authority is too near, an old gun—I once saw a flintlock—will be handed to him in sign of submission, and the oath of neutrality taken.

This explains the enormous number of arms that have been given up, while the Burghers have retained their good Mausers and Martini-Henrys, and still use them.

But as soon as the English, pleased at a fresh submission, have gone off, the rifle—the good one this time—is brought out, the horse stealthily mounted, and the Burgher is abroad once more.

The dispersions are merely momentary, and very often a rallying-point among the hills has been fixed on in advance. Eight days later the commando, concentrating again, appears on the scene with some unexpected stroke. This kind of thing may go on for a long time.

'*Egaillez-vous, les gas!*' was the cry of the Vendéen chiefs; and it is this manoeuvre, and the rally which follows it, that regular troops cannot execute.

This kind of warfare is obviously very painful and fatiguing for the invader. But it is a purely defensive method, and cannot have any decisive success, unless the invading army should give up the struggle.

For which side does Fortune reserve her final favours? It is certain that the English are weary, very weary, and that they have been so for some time.

Ten months ago, at the beginning of January, a soldier of the 2nd West Yorkshire Regiment wrote with mournful resignation:

'We shall all be thankful when this war is over, and this horrible butchery at an end!'

Another, less disciplined and more easily discouraged, a yeoman, wrote after Colenso:

> If I come through alive, the army will have seen the last of me! I have had enough of it, and I bitterly regret having rejoined my regiment.

I do not say that these sentiments are general, but they indicate the weariness of the combatants. And this lassitude seemed to me to be creeping over all, from the general to the private, among those I met between Springs and Cape Town.

The army itself will not be consulted, of course, but I wish to note this state of mind, which seems to me serious.

On the other hand, British prestige is too deeply engaged for the English to retreat without losing caste.

What will happen? It would be foolhardy to prophesy. 'If in doubt, refrain,' says the sage. I will take his advice, offering for the consideration of those who have followed me so far this melancholy sentence from the *Westminster Gazette* of last March:

> Each Boer will have cost us £2,000 to subdue, and no one can yet say what each will cost us to govern.

A West Pointer With the Boers

J. Y. F. BLAKE
Colonel Boer-Irish Brigade at time of general surrender
in June, 1902

# Contents

| | |
|---|---|
| Introduction | 135 |
| Preface | 137 |
| Lobengula and the Chartered Company | 141 |
| A Carnival of Murder | 148 |
| I Take Command of the Irish Brigade | 165 |
| Butchery of Prisoners By English Lancers | 171 |
| Besieging Ladysmith | 197 |
| British Treachery at Colenso | 201 |
| Spion Kop | 208 |
| White's Incapacity | 217 |
| The Fighting in the Free State | 225 |
| Magersfontein and Paardeberg | 230 |
| De Wet Looms Up | 238 |
| Paying an Instalment on the Irish Debt | 245 |
| General Buller Arrives in Transvaal | 258 |
| English Savagery | 263 |
| War Declared at an End By Roberts | 272 |
| Boers Become Aggressive | 278 |
| De Wet Alarms the English | 286 |

| | |
|---|---|
| An Exciting Trip | 293 |
| De Wet Cornered Again | 314 |
| An Irish Boy's Strategy | 321 |
| English Surprise the Boers and Are Routed | 326 |
| The Only Naval Battle of the War | 332 |
| General De Wet's Daring Work | 338 |
| General De Wet Completely Cornered | 345 |
| Peace Terms | 356 |
| Poisoning of Boer Prisoners at St. Helena | 371 |
| A Perfect Spy System | 378 |
| The English Arm Kaffirs | 386 |
| Conclusion | 402 |

To the Memory of the
Twenty-Two Thousand
Boer Women and Children
Murdered
In the English Prison Camps
of South Africa
During the Anglo-Boer War.
1899-1902

# Introduction

Friends have advised me to say a little something about myself, by way of a beginning, and to please them, I will commence with the statement that I was born in the State of Missouri, in 1856, and waked up on a horse and cattle ranch on the plains of Denton County, Texas. At least, here it was that I first saw light, as far as I can remember. As I grew up I learned to ride the Texas pony, and became fairly well acquainted with the character and habits of horses and cattle, by having, year after year, to look after them, and see that none strayed away. Happy were those days of loneliness and ignorance spent on those far-stretching plains, where roamed hundreds of thousands of horses, cattle and buffalo!

In 1871, my father started me to school at the Arkansas State University, at Fayetteville. In 1876, while still at the University, I received the cadet appointment to the U. S. Military Academy at West Point, through the kindness of Hon. Thomas M. Gunter, M. C., an old friend of my father. I entered the Academy in September, of the same year, and graduated in June, 1880. I was assigned as 2nd Lieutenant of the 6th U. S, Cavalry stationed in Arizona. I passed through the Apache wars, serving first under General Wilcox, then under General Crook, and lastly under Gen. Nelson A. Miles.

General Crook[1] put me in command of the Apache Indian scouts, and with them I roamed about the mountains till 1885, when my troop was ordered to Fort Leavenworth, Kansas. I passed through the Infantry and Cavalry school, and, on being promoted to the rank of 1st. Lieutenant in 1887, was ordered to Fort Wingate, New Mexico Now General Miles put me in command of the Navajo Indian scouts.

The Indians remained quiet and peaceful on their reservations. Post life became monotonous, and I resigned in 1889.

---
1. *Campaigning With Crook* by Charles King also published by Leonaur.

I went to Grand Rapids, Michigan, to try my hand in business, but soon found that the "tricks of the trade" were too deep for me, so I made up my mind to go to South Africa, where the gold mining prospects were attracting adventurous men from every part of the world.

# Preface

I wish the following pages to be considered as a simple narrative of some of the important events of the Anglo-Boer War and a very terse and unpolished narrative at that. I have endeavoured to tell the truth in as brief a way as possible and, to speak the truth again, I believe I have been too brief in many instances.

Ordinary readers sicken of long military details of battles and I have purposely refrained from giving them. During the first nine months of the war, many American correspondents were present and I think they can give a pretty correct account of what happened during their time, and I don't believe my account will in any way conflict with any they may give. Among many whom I know, are Rev. Peter MacQueen, Richard Harding Davis,[1] Mr. Unger, Mr. Hillegas, Allen Sangree and E. E. Easton, and such men as these will not lie because the English are happy to call themselves our *"Cousins across the Sea."*

Some criticism has been made of Captain Patrick O'Connor, Lieutenants John Quinn and Mike Enright, who were in charge of the Chicago Ambulance Corps, sent by Colonel John F. Finerty and Patrick J. Judge to South Africa to assist the Boers, for laying aside the Red Crosses and taking up the mauser. These were all good and true men and had the Boers asked them to do Red Cross duty, they would have willingly consented. But they were not needed in this line, so they were equipped for fighting.

At Spion Kop, General Buller had many of the ambulance men remove their Red Crosses and take the rifle during the battle. We captured several of these and they told the whole story. After the battle was over, all those not captured were required to pin on the Red Cross again and look after the numerous dead and wounded. If the English

---

1. *Richard Harding Davis' Great War* by Richard Harding Davis also published by Leonaur.

ambulance men could remove their Red Crosses and take up rifles at the pleasure of the British commander, I can't understand why the Boer ambulance men could not do the same.

I have not said as much about the English commanders of the war as I might have said j and now a word about them may not be taken amiss.

The Boers generally acknowledge General Buller as by far the ablest commander the English had in the field. True it is, he made mistakes on the Tugela, but it should be remembered that he had but 35,000 or 40,000 men to dislodge some 6,000 Boers entrenched for a distance of thirty miles along the river. Had Buller been in supreme command, I firmly believe the war would have been brought to an end within six months after the relief of Ladysmith.

Lords Roberts and Kitchener had treble the number of men, an open country and only about 4,000 Boers in front of them; yet Buller relieved Ladysmith by the time they could relieve Kimberley.

In fighting negroes armed with sticks both Roberts and Kitchener were enabled to add a list of letters to their names almost equal to the number in the alphabet; but when confronted with an armed Boer, both found themselves practically helpless.

Roberts for his proclamations received from the British Government $500,000, and an earldom. Kitchener received $150,000 for wiping out of existence 22,000 women and children. It must be added, however, that he was simply carrying out Lord Roberts' instructions, to his great pleasure. Though degenerate and incompetent, yet the English soldier knows a little something. The 29th of September, 1902, was the King's Procession Day. I was present and witnessed the circus. Between Trafalgar Square and St. Paul's Cathedral, Lord Roberts was violently hissed and the people called for General Buller, who had done all the fighting and reaped disgrace as his reward. Roberts bit his lip but that is all the satisfaction he got.

There is no doubt about it, the English lords and generals in command of the British Army are degenerate and incompetent and that, too, far more so than the English soldier. In hundreds of instances, I am quite sure had an English sergeant been in command, we would have been badly beaten where we gained successes. The English commanders had large numbers, but small brains-

The quiet, modest little de la Rey, with his dancing, hazel eyes, was unquestionably the ablest of the Boer generals and the greatest man of the war.

The stalwart, restless, commanding General De Wet was the great strategist and Stonewall Jackson of the war. The handsome, refined and polished General Louis Botha proved a most brilliant commander and fighter, and another war will mark him as one of the brightest military stars of modern times. He is young and cool-headed and has in him all the necessary material to make a great military leader. May the time soon come for him to make use of his material.

Although the Boers had three such able leaders, yet the two little Republics lost their liberty and independence because the 25,000 patriots under their command thought it better to surrender and save their women and children and therefore their race from extinction. Horses, mules and men from the United States of America destroyed the two little republics.

We can always point with pride to our great liberty lovers, Washington, Jefferson, Madison, Adams, Jackson, Munroe, and Lincoln, but since the days of these great patriots and Americans our leadership has degenerated; trade and greed have taken the place of lofty ideals which made the country the hope and model of every people aspiring to freedom; vulgar ambition for territorial extension has put us on the low level of all the conquering nations of old; the late war with Spain developed all the latent greed of an ambitious upstart among nations; neither the plausible protestations of one president nor the open boldness of another justified our un-American policy in the far East.

When it came to the question of acting towards the republics of South Africa as our forefathers had acted towards the republic of Texas, neither the oily McKinley nor the vociferous Roosevelt showed the honour and courage of a pure-blooded American. I do not mean they were bought by England. Our State Department is not the kind of a courtesan whose favours have to be paid for in anything but smiles and flattery. England smiled and flattered and America smiled back as she strangled the liberties of a brave people. The Philistines captured Samson, thanks to the American Delilah.

CHAPTER 1

# Lobengula and the Chartered Company

On the fifth day of December, 1894, I sailed on the *City of Berlin* from New York.

We started in a storm, continued in a storm, and landed in a mud bank off the Isle of Wight, just below the Needles. This caused quite a commotion among the passengers, and all seemed inclined to make the last stand at those points of the deck nearest to the lifeboats. By reversing the screws, the old death-trap, after a few hours' hard work, succeeded in releasing itself, and we were again on the high sea.

On the 14th, we landed, and I saw a foreign land for the first time. I spent a week in London trying to see something, but the fog was so thick that I could scarcely see myself, so I decided to move on toward South Africa.

I left Southampton December 22nd, 1894, on board the *Lismore Castle* for Cape Town where I arrived January 12th, 1895. On the voyage I could hear nothing talked but C. J. Rhodes and Dr. Jameson. We had them for breakfast, dinner and supper, and at all intervening hours.

Connected with these names was a country known as Rhodesia, lying north of the Transvaal, and it was always Golden Rhodesia, a land overladen with diamonds and gold. I made up my mind on that voyage to look up this C. J. Rhodes and his "pal," Dr. Jameson. One thing was certain in my mind, and that was that either these two men were really great men or monstrous rascals, and that Golden Rhodesia was either a marvellous land or a smartly advertised fraud. I said to myself: "I will investigate both the men and the new country before I am in South Africa many months." On arriving at Cape Town, a city that expired many years ago, I immediately went to Johannesburg, the Golden City of the Transvaal.

January 16th I beheld this lively, wonderful city that rested then and rests now on the greatest gold bed known in the world. Money was so plentiful that there were no poor men in the city and I was simply appalled by the very prosperity of the place. I had never seen anything like it before and shall probably never see anything like it again. Yet in this phenomenally prosperous city, I heard from the lips of everyone with whom I conversed, of that far more wonderful country lying far to the north, the land of Golden Rhodesia. Strange to say, however, I could not find anyone who had visited this country so heavily laden with gold.

First I will tell how Rhodesia received the name and became the property of the notorious Chartered Company.

In 1889, C. D. Rudd, R. Maguire and F. R. Thompson, aided by a missionary who knew a few Kaffir words, induced Chief Lobengula, of Matabeleland and Mashonaland, to sign a paper which was first interpreted to Lobengula and his *indunas*, (sub chiefs) by the missionary. This fellow told them that the three white men had said in the paper that they would give the chief $500 per month, 1,000 rifles and 100,000 cartridges, for the right to put up a mill on a certain piece of gold bearing ground. Lobengula told them to bring the money, rifles, etc., and then he would show them the ground and they could mine it. The white men also agreed to give Lobengula a steamboat, to run up the Zambesi River. This missionary convinced Lobengula that there was nothing more in the paper, and he signed. By the document, he had given Rudd, Maguire and Thompson, all the mining rights of his whole domain; but, of course, he did not know it, as it had not occurred to him that possibly the missionary had lied. In a short time, Lobengula learned the truth and at once assembled his *indunas* and called the white men to attend. He could get no satisfaction, so in April, 1889, he wrote the following letter to Queen Victoria:

> To Her Majesty, Queen Victoria:
> Some time ago, a party of men came into my country, the principal one appearing to be a man named Rudd. They asked me for a place to dig for gold and said they would give me certain things for the right to do so. I told them to bring what they would give me and I would show them what I would give. A document was written and presented to me for signature. I

asked what it contained and was told, that in it were my words and the words of those men. I put my hand on it. About three months afterwards,! heard from other sources that I had given by that document, the rights to all the minerals in my country. I called a meeting of my *indunas* and also of the white men, and demanded a copy of the document. It was proved to me that I had signed away the mineral rights of my whole country to Rudd and his friends. I have since had a meeting of my *indunas* and they will not recognize the paper, as it contains neither my words nor the words of those who got it.

After the meeting, I demanded that the original document be returned to me. It has not come yet, although it is two months since and they promised to bring it back soon. The men of the party who were in my country at the time were told to remain till the document was brought back. One of them, Maguire, has now left, without my knowledge and against my orders. I write to you, that you may know the truth about this thing and may not be deceived.

With renewed and cordial greetings, I am your friend,

Lobengula.

Rudd, Maguire, Thompson and C. J. Rhodes were all in the same Company, and working to the same end. They were determined to rob Lobengula of his country. The queen took no notice of Lobengula's letter, but Rudd and his men knew that they could not swindle Lobengula without a fight. He was honest, and in earnest, and did not know that he was dealing with unscrupulous people. In the past, Lobengula and his father, Umsiligaas, had befriended Dr. Livingston and other white men who had ventured into their far away land, and had always in return been treated honourably; so they were not prepared for sharpers. The English boast of fair play and justice, but they give neither, unless forced to it.

Now I will tell how just the queen was to Lobengula and how humane her subjects were to his people. Whether Lobengula told the truth or lied, in his letter to the queen, made no difference, for the British Government on October 15th, 1889, granted a charter to C. J. Rhodes, Alfred Beit, George Cawston, A. H. G. Grey, Duke of Abercorn and Duke of Fife, as petitioners, under the corporate name of the British South Africa Co., commonly known as the Chartered Company.

The Charter having been granted under the impression that Lobengula had voluntarily given his country away, the Chartered Company must continue lo keep the English people in the dark. C. J. Rhodes now employed and armed about seven hundred men, with the permission and approval of the high commissioner. That everything might appear well on paper, he sent Jameson to Lobengula to get permission for this armed, Christianising force to enter Mashonaland. Of course Jameson soon returned and reported that Lobengula was delighted with this idea of such an armed force entering his country.

Now everything being made satisfactory to the outside world, by deliberate lying, the march began and was continued for four or five months, when the band of humanity lovers reached Mount Hampden, without the loss of a single life; and, having established Fort Salisbury in honour of their Lord, declared the Chartered Company Monarch of Mashonaland. The Company then hoisted its flag, bearing its motto of "*Justice, Commerce and Freedom,*" and all set to work to spread civilization and Christianity. Sir John Willoughby, in the ecstasy of joy, now wrote for the benefit of the general public that the "Government in granting the Royal Charter, had secured 'Fairest Africa' to England and spread blessings of hope, peace and security, among all the nations of the land."

It required about two and a half years to completely relieve the Mashonas of all they possessed, spread terror among their women, and rob the innocent public of about half a million pounds sterling, by floating as gold mines a large number of sand hills. Now that their real object in Mashonaland had been gained, and that it was evident the Company would soon be forced again into hard straits, unless a new field was opened up, all set to work to prepare the public mind for the invasion of Matabeleland.

They sent out reports to the effect that Lobengula was making raids on his own people, the Mashonas, killing many of them, and taking their cattle, and that every effort was being made to convince him that such conduct was highly condemned by his loving friends in England. Such reports were sent out daily, for some time, that the public might be thoroughly aroused as to the awful state of affairs, and finally, it was made known that Dr. Jameson, Rhodes' most willing tool, had determined to invade Matabeleland, in order to instil into Lobengula and his people the principles of love and humanity, and, by example, make known to them the good effects of civilization and Christianity.

ALFRED LORD MILNER
High Commissioner of South Africa, who fell into
Rhodes' hands because of his money.

So in July, 1893, he mustered together his band of 600 full fledged angels, and Major Wilson and Colonel Forbes, of the English Army, and proceeded to old Buluwayo, the Royal Kraal; where he arrived without scarcely seeing a *kaffir*, till the end of his journey. Here he found a fellow Scotchman and another white man, and expressed himself as much astonished to see them safe and sound among a people so bent on war. Strange to say, they knew nothing about a war till Jameson arrived. He learned from them, that Lobengula was not in old Buluwayo, so having nothing to fear, he proceeded to slaughter about 800 old men, women and children.

Now they hoisted the British flag on top of a a tree, to wave in peace and love over the many hundred women and children whom they had murdered, in the name of humanity. Then the band set out to kill Lobengula, and having found him and his soldiers, on the banks of the Shangani, they turned loose upon him and his men, as so many engines of wholesale slaughter, but they soon found out that they had something else to contend with besides women and children; for in a short time, Major Wilson and his whole command, excepting two men, were completely destroyed, and then Colonel Forbes' command made a rapid retreat to old Buluwayo.

The two men who escaped were Americans, one being known as "Burnham the Scout," and the other as "Ingram the honest man." As this man Burnham often ran to America to boast and deceive, I will say half a dozen words about him. He first claimed that he was a scout in America, but all soon learned that there was no truth in his claim. At the time of the Matabele War in 1896, he showed himself in his true light. He was of no earthly use at Buluwayo, for all knew him, so he went to Hangwe, a few miles to the south. Here he shot an innocent, unarmed *kaffir*, if he shot one at all, and reported that he had shot and killed M'Limo, the Kaffir war-god. He was told that he was really a wonderful man and undoubtedly the greatest shot in the world. So ignorant is he, that Burnham did not know that M'Limo was a myth, a great Spirit, to whom the Matabele would pray and look to as their guide.

But Burnham, the scout, managed to shoot and kill the great Spirit, and, on receiving a report of this wonderful achievement, the London *Graphic* brought out his picture and his long story of how he killed M'Limo, the war-god, and the terror of the Rhodesians. The Americans in Rhodesia made it so warm for him, that Burnham left for the United States to give a course of lectures. He now wears khaki and is in the British service, (as at time of first publication), and his native land feels thankful.

Lobengula now sent in word that there was no cause for war with his white brothers, and that he could not understand why they had suddenly appeared in such a state of frenzy. Captain Blank, the famous scout, and another man,—or beast,—were now employed, and sent out to negotiate with Lobengula, and after a few days absence, returned to report that he had died suddenly on the Zambesi River, which, you know, is about three hundred miles distant. They were sure he was dead, *Because Poison Seldom Lies.*

The Matabeles had no desire to fight, and did not know that the whites contemplated attacking them, till it was too late, otherwise it might have been a very different thing. Lobengula, who had ever been a warm friend of his white brother, who had fed him, protected him and granted him his every wish, within reason, had now, in return for his many kindnesses, been foully murdered, because he was chief, and controlled thousands of cattle which the Chartered Company must have, in order to postpone, for a few years, its inevitable downfall. The truth is, that Jameson sent word to Lobengula, that some of his people had come in and killed some of the Mashonas, and that he must arrest and punish them.

Lobengula immediately sent a party to arrest the murderers, and Jameson at once, on their approach, made it an excuse to invade Matabeleland. The men who composed the police force tell the truth when they say it was a put up job, and the Chartered Company and its officials maliciously lie, when they say the war was provoked and prosecuted for the cause of humanity. Matabeleland and Mashonaland together were now christened Rhodesia. There was nothing more to fear, now that Lobengula was dead, and the great Rhodesian swindle prospered for several years, or until the Jameson raid.

CHAPTER 2

# A Carnival of Murder

Having remained in Johannesburg for just thirty days, I secured four pack donkeys, and in company with three friends, started for this fabulously rich country, Golden Rhodesia. It was the rainy season, and it was rain, rain, rain, day and night, but we were determined not to be balked by anything; we would see Buluwayo, the gold centre, 600 miles away, or go down in the attempt. We had before us eight swollen rivers, wicked rivers at this season, but almost dry beds at any other time of the year. We had to swim all of them, and what a struggle it was for us! I can't understand now just how we succeeded, and do not know how we escaped the crocodiles, yet we landed safely in Victoria, Mashonaland, on Easter Sunday, in the early part of April.

Here I found about 600 people sleeping in the graveyard, and about 300 lying on cots and on the counters in the stores and various other places, all down with the fever. I did not like the situation at all. To buy anything one had to help himself and then hand the money to the sick man on the counter. I found that Salisbury, Gwelo and Buluwayo were all practically in the same condition. It was fever, fever, nothing but fever everywhere, and all this talk of gold, gold, gold, was entirely misleading. It did not take us but about one minute to discover that Golden Rhodesia was a golden fraud, and so it was then, and so it is now, and will forever be.

However, I was not satisfied, so I traversed the whole land, penetrated into the jungles of the Zambesi, roamed about in company with the elephant, rhinoceros, the hippopotamus, the savage buffalo, giraffe, zebra, the lion, leopard, hyena, wild dog, jackal and all the many and various kinds of antelope that swarm in that far-a-way, God-forsaken, fever-stricken country, where Livingstone breathed his last, and where the natives, in thousands, naked as nature made them, swarm

CECIL J. RHODES
Notorious for his greed and inhumanity.

about you, and look at you and treat you royally in their simple way. Here was wild nature, in all its glory, and here I was supremely happy. Thousands of baboons and monkeys made music during the day, and at nightfall the lions, hyenas and jackals took up the strain and kept a curious, nature-loving white man, with his rifle on his knee, delightfully entertained. After several months of exploring, I returned to Buluwayo, on March 21st, 1896; and on March 23rd, the Matabeles broke out in rebellion against the great C. J. Rhodes, and his great fraud, the Chartered Company.

The Matabeles surrounded this miserable, drunken, fever-stricken town, and, of course, I was one of the victims. These *kaffirs*, 15,000. or 20,000 strong, would dance on the ridges about us, make sport of us, and have a good time generally during the day, and when night came, all women and children were shut up in the market building, while the men were in the *laager* surrounding it. During the night every house in town was abandoned. False alarm after false alarm was the order of the night; and how often have I seen loving mothers, with their arms around the necks of their two, three or four children, moaning, shrieking, praying, appealing to God and kissing their little ones the last farewell! Those awful scenes still haunt me, and will till the day of my death. During the day the men would go out and fight for a while, and then fly back with the Matabeles after them, and proceed to get on a big drunk, and then have a riot meeting.

During the siege, many small parties of *kaffirs* would come into Buluwayo for safety, as they would not take any part in the war. Chartered officials made use of these small parties, as a means to amuse the people with interesting street scenes. On reaching the town, the party of two, or three, or four, or possibly ten *kaffirs*, would be arrested and ordered shot. The poor devils would be marched up the street, lined up, and in the presence of a large crowd, shot down. After several hours, when all had feasted their eyes and satisfied their curiosity, the innocent whites, among the Company's convicts, were made to carry these mangled bodies in their arms to the veldt, and bury them. These convicts were not allowed to make use of wagons or carts. In order to have a change of scene, the guards would sometimes make these refugees climb the big tree on Fife Street, and having attached ropes to their necks and a limb of the tree, would make them jump for their lives.

Then again the guards would sometimes take others to the same tree, and, having tied the ropes to their necks and passing it over the

Innocent Matabele Kaffirs hung on the tree on Fife Street in Buluwayo, in 1896, by order of C. J. Rhodes and his Chartered Co., in order to amuse his fellow British subjects.

limb of the tree, would draw them up till their toes would just touch the ground, that the people might see them struggle and slowly strangle to death. Again, they would be marched into the street, and many guards being placed behind and near them, they would be commanded to run for their lives. Of course, all would be shot down, and the wounded sometimes shot five or six times before they died. These were horrible murder scenes, but Rhodesians seemed to enjoy them. Having seen all this, I do not hesitate to tell the public, that all may know just what a civilized people the English are.

In June we were relieved, by troops coming from the south, and I said farewell to the miserable hole, Buluwayo, and returned to Johannesburg in August, 1896.

I will tell in a few words the causes of that war, because I know them. The Matabeles had not forgotten that white men had poisoned their chief, Lobengula. The Chartered Company sent its police and forcibly took all the cattle from the *kaffirs*. This caused the death of thousands of their little ones, who lived almost exclusively on the milk of the cows. The Company allowed its police and its people generally to go to the *kaffir kraals*, and, with their rifles, force young girls to go to their huts, where they could use them at their pleasure. This struck the *kaffirs* to the very heart, because they are an extremely moral people, and immorality with them is punished by death. The Company allowed its police commissioners to force the *kaffirs* to work in the mines. The commissioners received from the Mining Company $2.50 for each *kaffir*, and, in return, guaranteed the *kaffir* to work for three months.

Just before the expiration of the three months, the mine captain would take his cowhide whip and so slash them that they would run away. He would then call upon the commissioners to make good their contract and bring back the *kaffirs*. The commissioner would then send his police to arrest the runaways, and, having got them in his possession, would himself give them twenty lashes and return them to work. Finally the *kaffir*, after running away, would hide in the hills. Then it was that the commissioner would arrest the fugitive's wife and children and hold them as hostages, till he came and gave himself up to receive the twenty lashes. If the *kaffir* left before his three months expired, the mine captain did not have to pay him any wages.

To get his $2.50, the commissioner had to make the *kaffir* work three months, or put another one in his place, so that the poor *kaffir* must be cut and slashed to pieces whether he worked or not. So universal was this cutting and slashing, that life to the *kaffir* became worse than hell itself, and thereupon they rebelled, and killed every white man they could lay hands on. I said, "Well done." They would have taken the country, but Rhodes paid them $2,500,000, in kind, and bought peace; and today there is no whipping, no cutting *kaffirs* to pieces, and they are as independent as kings, in Rhodesia, because they are the masters.

While I was enjoying myself in the jungles of the Zambesi, Rhodes completed all his arrangements for a raid into the Transvaal, but I must tell why it became necessary for Rhodes to make a raid into the Transvaal. He had painted Rhodesia yellow, and through flaming advertisements had led the world to believe that it was the richest gold bearing country on earth.

He knew there was no gold of any account in the country, and he knew, too, that the English public had been swindled out of more than $120,000,000. He knew also that the Chartered Company could not exist, would fall flat, and prove worse than the South Sea bubble, if something were not done, and that quickly, too. Now if he could only manage to seize the world-known, rich gold-fields of the Rand, at Johannesburg, and annex them to Rhodesia, why then he and the Chartered Company would be safe, and could easily fill their chest with many more millions.

If the Rand gold-fields were once annexed, then he could advertise the marvellous gold output of Rhodesia, and would find no trouble in floating all the sand banks of that desert land, as veritable gold mines, and thus save and enrich himself and the Chartered Company.

I will say a few words about the raid.

In December, 1895, Rhodes put about 600 of the Rhodesian police, with Dr. Jameson in command, on the western border of the Transvaal, near Mafeking. Of course, Rhodes had everything arranged in Downing Street, London, so that at the proper time the English Government could step in, with its troops, to protect its citizens and thus take the rich Rand gold-fields from the Boers. Rhodes had a telegram sent to the *London Times* that the Boers were about to murder the English women and children in Johannesburg. Many of Jameson's men refused to cross the border, but when they were called into line and told they must go and help protect the English women and children from the savage Boers, they consented. The raiding column made a rapid march, reached Doornkop, about twenty miles from Johannesburg and were there captured by 180 Boers, who had come to meet them on hearing of the raid.

There were some prominent Americans in the Johannesburg Reform Committee of seventy, who with Rhodes were implicated in this most outrageous piece of piracy, and when President Krüger refused to put Dr. Jameson and his staff, together with his seventy members of the Reform Committee, in a line and shoot them down, (and what a blessing it would have been for humanity,) he made the fatal mistake of his life and in the end lost his country, at least, temporarily. It was by wilful lying that Rhodes, Jameson and the Reform Committee induced those 600 police to make that raid, and on the tombstones of the twenty-five or thirty men killed at Doornkop, there should be engraved the words, "Murdered by C. J. Rhodes and his followers." All the miscreants who were connected with that infamous raid were soon set free, and they began at once in another way to create trouble for the Boers, and, as a result of their labour, one of the greatest wars in the history of man was fought by a handful of patriotic Boers, against the so-called mightiest empire of the world.

As a result of the raid, the names of something like a hundred low, greed-loving conspirators were made know to the world, and the Transvaal still held possession of its precious gold fields.

Rhodes had now failed, and in order to avert the catastrophe, he put up money himself, and pulled in his faithful allies, Alfred Beit, Lionel Phillips and several others, and succeeded in preventing a great financial calamity.

Immediately after Jameson and his 600 men were captured, Rhodes swore he knew nothing about the raid, and that it was a surprise to him. Of course Joe Chamberlain knew nothing about it because he *said* so. With Jameson, was captured a lot of cipher telegrams, as well as the keys. These gave Rhodes away, and proved conclusively that he was the organiser of the raid, and that Chamberlain was implicated with him. I will give one or two letters, just to show how much faith can be placed on an English official's word.

30 Mincing Lane, E. C.,<br>London, February 20th, 1897.

My Dear Grey:

Thanks for your letter of the 9th *ult.*, which I read with great interest. You will, of course, have heard that the committee was reappointed and has got to work. I send you official prints of the evidence already taken. Rhodes has done well, and I think will come out on top. He was nervous on the first day, though his evidence was good even then. Yesterday he was simply splendid. I do not think that we are by any means out of the woods, but there does not seem an off-chance of the plea of public interest being recognized, and the cables of the last of the year 1895, or rather the negotiations of that period, not being disclosed, though I am bound to say that personally I think the balance of probability is that they will have to come out. If they do, Mr. Chamberlain will have no one but himself to thank. I am very sorry I have been such a bad correspondent, but really the work and anxiety of the last fifteen months, or nearly two years, that is, since Harris came to England on the subject of the Protectorate, in July, 1895, have been most trying, and I sometimes fear that even my constitution will not stand it much longer, though, happily, I am still very well. I will try and write you more fully next week. Believe me,

Very truly yours,

Bouchier, F. Hawkesley.

P. S.—Rhodes has received your letter and cable about Lawley.
The Right Hon. Earl Grey.

The following came out in the Select Committee of the House of Commons that was appointed to investigate the Jameson Raid. The suppressed cables mentioned were never produced, because Mr. Chamberlain must be protected. The above letter, however, is pretty strong evidence and it made Mr. Chamberlain shake in his boots. Mr. Hawkesley is Rhodes' solicitor, and with him Chamberlain and the London *Times* were deeply implicated in the raid.

[Private]

39 Cadogan Square, London, S.W.

(No Date)

Dear Mr. Hawkesley:

So many thanks for yours. I knew you would feel as I do, that we owe Allingham a great deal, and must give the brother any (or every) help we could. I will tell him to make an appointment to come and see you one morning. He sails in the beginning of next month. I quite agree with you that very little good, if any, can be done with J. C. He knows what he has to expect, and will have had plenty of time to think it over, by the time C. J. R. arrives. As long as you make it impossible for C. J. R. to give away Jameson, he will be loyal to him; but I am sure from what I've said (heard), that at one time Rhodes contemplated sacrificing the Dr. The Dr. must never know this, and if anyone can keep Rhodes up to mark, you can. I want to talk to you one day about the Dr.'s future—to see what you think of my plan, which he has already taken kindly to.

You do not know how grateful I am to you for all you have done for him, but I think you can perhaps partly understand how much it means to me to feel he has got a friend like you. Can I come and see you one morning about 11.30?

   Yours sincerely,

               R. L. Chamberlain.

The above shows that C. J. Rhodes was ready to prove traitor to his most faithful tool, who had done all his dirty work. The initials J. C. stand for Joe Chamberlain and all want to know what he had to expect. The initials C. J. R. stand for C. J. Rhodes.

On the arrival of Mr. Tatton Egerton in London after the circulation of a report that Mr. Chamberlain was cognizant of the plans connected with the Jameson Raid, this gentleman was confronted by the Colonial Secretary, and asked who had told him that Mr. Chamberlain was in the raid. The reply was, "Mr. Rhodes himself." The Colonial Secretary's answer to this blunt statement of the case was, "The Traitor!"

As neither Mr. Egerton nor Mr. Chamberlain has ever denied the above report, one can draw his own conclusion. If Rhodes "peached" on Chamberlain to Mr. Egerton, then I think that he was guilty of treason to one of his most trustworthy fellow-conspirators.

Rhodes and his crew did not remain idle for a moment, they started more newspapers in Johannesburg, got possession of all the newspapers in South Africa, except three or four, and then began a paper war against the government, President Krüger, all Boer officials, Hollanders, and in fact all who were in any way in sympathy with the Boers. There was nothing too low, too mean, too maliciously false for them to say about the Netherlands Railroad Company, the Dynamite Factory, the price of coal or the treatment of some Cape niggers caught in a drunken brawl.

There were many other grievances, among them was the five *per cent* tax levied on the gold output, by the government. Then again, the capitalists wished to establish the "compound" system, and thus make

RT HON. JOSEPH CHAMBERLAIN
Colonial Secretary, who with Rhodes and Milner
is directly responsible for the death of thousands
of innocent people.

slaves of all *kaffirs* employed at the mines. This the government refused to grant.

In addition to this came the cry for the franchise. It was claimed that the *Uitlanders* furnished the money that carried on the government, that they were in a majority, and that therefore they were entitled to vote and hold office. They claimed the franchise by the fact of residence in the Transvaal. Under no circumstances, were they to forswear allegiance to their queen and thus forfeit their British citizenship. They claimed the right to vote and hold office, as long as they saw fit to reside in the Transvaal, and at the same time to remain British subjects.

The government changed the law from fourteen to seven years' residence necessary for the franchise, with an oath requiring the applicant to renounce all allegiance to the State of which he was last a citizen. The press cried this down as an act of impertinence and injustice on the part of the government, because no British subject could for one moment think of giving up his citizenship and queen for the sake of becoming a citizen in a country run by an ignorant Boer.

Remember, reader, that all this was purely the work of the press of South Africa, whose object was to give Joe Chamberlain a chance to put his mouth into the business. The *Uitlanders* of the Transvaal, including Englishmen, Americans, Germans, Frenchmen, in fact, representatives of all nationalities, took little or no interest in the reports which the press was spreading, because all knew that they were manufactured and utterly false; and besides all were freer, happier and making more money than ever before in any other country. All were making from $5 to $25 per day of eight hours' work, depending on each one's individual skill and smartness. I was there, knew them, heard them talk, and I say, there was not one in a hundred who wanted the franchise, who would have made use of it if given to him, or who ever discussed the subject. Each was trying to make his little fortune, that he might leave that far away land and return to his old home.

The horrible condition of affairs in the Transvaal existed only in the press and was the work of Rhodes, his crew and his ally in Downing Street, London. The press continued its dirty work day after day and month after month, without variation, except in a few instances where the imagination, under heavy strain, was able to squeeze out a little more venom. The English pursue the same tactics in their fighting, they bombard day after day, increasing the number of guns from time to time, and at last when they have concluded that the Boers are all killed or so demoralized that they could offer no resistance, they advance the line for the general attack. Just so the press continued to spit out its venom and spread it over the civilized world, month after month, until it was deemed that the time was ripe for making the final crushing blow that must rob the Boers of their gold-fields and their country. This brings me to that notorious petition of 21,000 names that was deliberately manufactured in Johannesburg. Excluding women and children, I think it is safe to say that there were not 2,000 genuine signatures on that petition.

A hired bar-room specimen would go from house to house and have the mother put her name down and the names of all her children, first telling her it was the wish of Rhodes and the so-called big men of Johannesburg. Cape niggers would give their names, and the bar-room specimen would write them down, for the niggers could not write their names. There were men in Johannesburg who made it a profession to get up petitions, charging so much for every hundred names. The Rhodes crew employed these fellows at $25 per hundred names. These fellows would then go to their rooms, write down a few hundred names, as they came to their minds, and would then turn in the list, receive their money, and proceed to their rooms to repeat the process. That is the way that petition was gotten up, and it recited enough grievances to stagger the world. I used to talk with the people, and many of them, too, every day, and it was a rare exception when I found one who ever saw the petition.

When completed, it was forwarded to Sir Alfred Milner, Cape Town. He looked at it, pronounced it correct, and forwarded it to Downing Street. When Sir Alfred Milner reported that he had investigated the names on that petition, and found them correct, he knows, I know, and the people of Johannesburg know, that he was guilty of a deliberate falsehood. Milner was sent to South Africa for a purpose. His predecessor would have thrown that petition into the waste basket. He could not be handled by Rhodes; so it became necessary to get rid of him, and out he went. Milner was just the man for the place, for he was an educated man, suave and gentlemanly, and, best of all, he was easily led by such a moneyed man as Rhodes.

Now you have what I call a trinity, three in one, but apparently three distinct individuals, Chamberlain, Milner, Rhodes, three names that will in time appear on the first page of the history of the decline and fall of the British Empire, as the cause of the beginning of the end. With Chamberlain in Downing Street, Rhodes and all his money in

PRESIDENT KRÜGER

South Africa, and weak Mr. Milner in the middle and ready at hand, it was inevitable that the great struggle must come, in which thousands of innocent people must fall, and the plains of South Africa be reddened with their blood.

As a result of this petition, the conference in Bloemfontein between Presidents Krüger and Stein and Sir Alfred Milner was held. This conference was simply a farce, as the world knows, for Milner had his orders and all the concessions made by Presidents Krüger and Stein were simply declined. Had President Krüger told Milner that he was willing to cut off the Rand Gold-Fields, and allow them to be annexed to Rhodesia, why, that would have prevented the war, and war could not have been avoided in any other way, for Milner positively refused to let any of their differences go to arbitration. He came there to bring on war; he succeeded, and what a pity it is that he, Chamberlain and Rhodes thought it prudent to remain so far removed from the immediate scenes of action! But that is the way in this wicked world those who are responsible for suffering and loss of life in a cruel and uncalled-for war, are the very ones who escape unharmed, and receive the congratulations of the civilized world for the masterly way they have carried out their designs.

From now on telegrams fly thick and fast, the pot is boiling, and ready to flow over at any moment. President Krüger is praying for arbitration and peace, while Chamberlain, as chief of the Trinity, is clamouring for gold and war. He had lyddite, too much lyddite, and it must be exploded; and on the mountains of Natal, and the plains of the Transvaal and the Free State, the explosion must take place. Every shell exploded means so many dollars to Chamberlain and Co., and thousands upon thousands were exploded before the bloody struggle came to an end. I am glad to add, however, that but few Boers owe their death to lyddite.

If you read the London *Times* from June to October, 1899, you will find that the British Government had no intention of going to war with the Boers. But during this time about 15,000 English Troops were assembled at Dundee and Ladysmith, on the Transvaal border, and about the same number on the border of the Free State in Cape Colony.

A goodly number were also sent to Mafeking on the western border. About $2,000,000 worth of ammunition and war supplies were put into Dundee, and about $10,000,000 worth into Ladysmith. In Kimberly and Mafeking, the same provisions were made as regards ammunition and war supplies. At the same time there were something like 20,000 troops on the water, bound for South Africa. There can be no question about it, the British Government had no idea of making war on the Transvaal, for Chamberlain said so in Parliament, Milner said so in Cape Town, and Rhodes backed up both of them with his money.

These great bases of war supplies were established, and thousands of troops landed in South Africa, simply to keep the Commissary and Quartermaster's Department in good training, and allow the troops to enjoy some holiday exercises in a far-away land. Long before the war, many English officers, disguised in civilian clothes, had laboured hard in making military maps of the Transvaal and Free State, showing every road, path, farm, *sluit*, hill, etc., and yet the British Government had no idea of forcing war upon the Transvaal; and this must be true, too, for the London *Times* said so, Chamberlain said so, Milner said so, and all were backed by Rhodes and his millions. We captured so many of these military maps that I can make the above statement without fear of contradiction.

Years ago, the Orange Free State had been robbed of the Kimberly Diamond Fields by the English, and thereafter the English Government never complained of any grievances in that Republic. The South African Republic and the Orange Free State formed an offensive and defensive alliance because it was a certainty that if the English took one of them, it would be but a question of time when an excuse would be manufactured to take the other; so they wisely concluded to stand shoulder to shoulder and live as Republics, or fall together and exist as dependencies.

> They did stand together, they fought together and although they were brought to their knees, they are not down yet, and the price the English have so far paid, if the English graves in South Africa are to be taken as an index, is certainly enough to stagger humanity. How many graves are yet to be dug on the very same battlefields, of those two little countries, in order to keep the Boer on his knees, or to put him, quite down, is the question for the future to answer.

Now I come to the point where the two little Republics are brought face to face with the military forces of war—prepared England; when war is inevitable, when the immortal gods could not prevent a clash of arms; when the first shot is fired in a struggle destined

M. T. STEYN, PRESIDENT ORANGE FREE STATE

to stir the world, humiliate the English officer and lord, and destroy the name and prestige of the great degenerate British Empire.

CHAPTER 3

# I Take Command of the Irish Brigade

Before we begin to fight I must say something about the fighters, and will commence with the Boer and his readiness for war. The Boer is a simple, unpretentious farmer, with a long beard, rather long hair, a powerful physical frame, a man inured to all kinds of hardships, who daily looks after his horses, cattle and sheep. He has a lot of *kaffir* families on his farm, to whom he gives all the land they wish for cultivation, on the condition that they put in his little patch of mealies (corn), and oats. To the *kaffir* boys who stay at the farm house, and make themselves useful at all kinds of odd jobs, he gives each a cow at the end of the year. This means a great deal to the *kaffir* boy, for when he has as many as eight head of cattle, he has the price he must pay for a wife; and to have a wife is every *kaffir* boy's ambition.

Every night and every morning the Boer has religious services in his house, and all the family attend. A visitor may attend or not as he pleases.

The Boer cares not what your religion is, nor of what your church may be, and it does not concern him whether you have any religion or not. He looks after his own soul, and grants you the privilege of looking after yours. He will never impose his beliefs upon you, nor will he ask you your religion. He simply takes it for granted that you are a Christian, a God-fearing individual. He is a domestic man whose greatest happiness is in his home, with his wife and children—and he generally has plenty of children. When he visits his neighbours on Sunday, the whole family visits with him. They all go to church on Sunday, and after the services are over, they all remind me of a happy reunion of a family that has long been separated. In his way, he is as simple as a child, hospitable and generous to a fault, ready to extend the helping hand to friend or stranger, modest and retiring; but when once you try to deprive him of his liberty, you will find that he will fight to the bitter end, regardless of the odds against him.

For months previous to the war, the English Press was busy trying to let the world know what a savage the Boer really was, and especially how intolerant he was, as regards the Catholics. There was an object in spreading broadcast all these outrageous lies; because England wished the world to believe, that in waging war against the Boer, she was really doing a service toward God and humanity. The Irish people were Catholics; so the press told how bitter the Boer is against the Catholic, how he tramples him down, and tries to drive him out of the country. All this infamous lying was for the sole purpose of inducing the Irish to enlist in the British Army, and I regret to say that the Irish fell into the trap. Thousands of them joined the British army, and today thousands of them are buried in South Africa. Few English are buried in South Africa, but the graves of the Irish and Scotch can be counted by the thousand.

Leaving aside the religious aspect of the man, the Boer reminds me very forcibly of our Southwesterners, in appearance; and especially in his riding and shooting ability. I have given a lengthy, but an honest and faithful portrait of the Boer, because the subsidized press of England spent itself in trying to disgrace him in the eyes of the world, for no other reason than to cover up the English Government's infamy in forcing a most unholy and damnable war on the God fearing Boer race of South Africa.

During the time of intense excitement in the towns of South Africa, and in London, the unmindful Boer was quietly and religiously pursuing his daily routine work on his remote farm. It never occurred to him that his quiet was liable to be disturbed at any moment by an exploding bomb that might force him to leave his wife and little ones for two years and eight months, and possibly forever. Occasionally he heard the distant rumble of impending war, but he gave it no heed, for his ear had become accustomed to such sounds during the last twenty years. He could see no reason for war and therefore dismissed the subject from his mind. The Transvaal Government and the Free State Government had, all told, a standing army of about 900 artillerymen who manned their forty cannon and sixty maxims. The artillerists were farmer boys, smooth-faced, and from sixteen to eighteen years old. They were trained by Boer officers principally. I think there were as officers, also, two young Hollanders, and two Germans, who had long resided in the Transvaal.

These young Boer officers and smooth-faced farmer boys proved themselves the most remarkable artillerists in the world. The Free State and Transvaal were exactly on the same footing as to readiness for war, and neither was, therefore, in any sense of the word, prepared for a struggle with the mightiest Empire of the world.

The total population of the Free State and Transvaal combined did not exceed 250,000 men, women and children; while that of Great Britain and her colonies runs up to something like 350,000,000. The Transvaal and the Free State are two inland countries several hundred miles from the coast; so England had no reason to fear trouble in landing her troops at any of her many coast towns. The Transvaal and the Free State are divided into districts, and each district is divided into *veldtcornetcies*. In each *veldtcornetcy* there is a *veldtcornet*, elected by his constituents, who is a civil officer in time of peace and the military leader of the men in his *veldtcornetcy*, in time of war.

A *commandant* is appointed, and given command of one, two, or more *veldtcornetcies*, depending upon circumstances. Each *veldtcornet* divides up his men into corporalships of twenty-five men, and over each corporalship he appoints a corporal. The commandant general (commander-in-chief), who is elected by the whole people, appoints a *vecht*-general (fighting general), who commands one, two or more *commandancies*, also depending upon circumstances. Assistant commandant-generals are appointed by the chief, to assist him in various districts; these, of course, hold command over the *vecht*-generals. In time of peace there is but one general, and that is the commandant-general, who is also a member of the President's staff, called the Executive Council. In time of war all the other generals are appointed as they are required.

At the beginning of the war, there existed what you might call a Commissary and Quartermaster Department. These departments load the trains with rations and clothing, and ship them to the front for the supply of the *burghers*. Each *veldtcornet*, on their arrival, sends his wagons, and gets all they can haul without requisition. The corporal in charge simply signs a receipt for what he gets. On the wagons arriving at the camp, the *burghers* go and help themselves to what they want. This never causes any trouble, for the *burghers* are always ready to divide up with each other whatever food or clothing they may have. I mention these two departments, because it is the first time in Boer history that they ever existed. They continued to exist for about ten months and then disappeared, and it is my opinion that all were better off; for then we had to come down to straight mealie pap (corn meal mush), and fresh beef. Commissary Departments kill more soldiers than are killed by bullets. When living on nothing but "mealie pap" and fresh meat, all are healthy, strong, energetic and full of fight. The Boer war has proved this; for during the last two years of the war we had nothing else to eat, and we lost but one man from sickness; and did the hardest work and best fighting, and in the end, when the general surrender came, the world had never seen 24,000 stronger, healthier and more dashing patriots than those who laid down their faithful rifles to save their women and children from extinction. I now arrive at the point when the rapidity with which telegrams were passing back and forth on the telegraph lines was such, that the iron poles were fairly melting to the ground, and when President Krüger was finally convinced that war could not by any possibility be averted, and that the so-called great Christian nation, his foe, was bent on spilling the blood of thousands of innocent people, in order to satiate its thirst for gold.

The feeble old man, the time-battered old soldier, the fervent old patriot, the bulwark of the Boer nation, now prayed God to direct him and his people and give them strength to preserve and enjoy their liberty and independence. Commandant-General Piet Joubert, being authorized to proceed to the defence of the land, sent messengers to all the *veldtcornets*, with directions to call the *burghers* to arms, and proceed to Laing's Nek, on the Natal border, to meet the invasion of the British Army. The same orders were given in the Free State, for the *burghers* to go to the Cape Colony border, and resist the British Army assembled there. A small body of *burghers* was sent toward Mafeking[1] to protect the western border. These orders were issued during the last days of September, 1899.

On October 1st, there were more than 10,000 *burghers* on the Natal border, and at the same time the Free State *burghers* had assembled on the border of the Colony.

It was at this time that the Irish and the Irish-Americans of Johannesburg and Pretoria, about 300 strong, had assembled, and asked me to take command of them to help the Boers in their battle for freedom. I accepted the command on the condition that not one of them would *expect* or *accept* one cent of money for his services, and that all

---

1. *Mafeking: a Diary of a Siege* by F. D. Baillie also published by Leonaur.

COMMANDANT GENERAL PIET JOUBERT

would fight purely for their love of liberty, and for down-trodden Ireland. This condition having been unanimously accepted, horses, arms, ammunition, etc., were at once procured, and off we went for the Natal border, where we joined the Boers on October 6th. It was quick work, but it is so easy to do things quickly, with a command of true and patriotic Irishmen, overjoyed and brimming full of enthusiasm at the prospect of giving a blow to Ireland's life-long enemy and oppressor.

Laing's Nek and Majuba Hill are on the border, between Natal and the Transvaal. We were on one side of the Nek, and the English on the other, both parties awaiting further developments. Finally, on October 9th, General Joubert sent a demand to the British Government for the recall of the English troops from the Transvaal border. The British declined, all communications were broken off, and war was declared on the following day, October 11th.

CHAPTER 4

# Butchery of Prisoners By English Lancers

The Government of the South African Republic feels itself compelled to refer the Government of Her Majesty, the Queen of Great Britain and Ireland, once more to the Convention of London, 1884, concluded between this Republic and the United Kingdom, and which in its XlVth Article secures certain rights to the whole population of the Republic; namely, that:
All persons, other than natives, conforming themselves to the laws of the South African Republic, (a) will have full liberty, with their families, to enter, travel, or reside in any part of the South African Republic; (b) they will be entitled to hire or possess houses, manufactories, warehouses, shops and premises; (c) they may carry on their commerce either in person or by any agents whom they may think fit to employ; (d) they will not be subject, in respect of their persons or property, or in respect of their commerce or industry, to any taxes, whether general or local, other than those which are or may be imposed upon citizens of the said Republic.'
This government wishes further to observe, that the above are only rights which Her Majesty's Government have reserved in the above convention with regard to the *Uitlander* population of this Republic, and that the violation only of those rights could give that government a right to diplomatic representations or intervention while, moreover, the regulation of all such questions affecting the position or the rights of the *Uitlander* population under the above-mentioned convention, is handed over to the government and the representatives of the people of the South

Mrs. Joubert Widow of
Commandant General Piet Joubert

African Republic.

Amongst the questions, the regulation of which falls exclusively within the competence of the government and the Volksraad, are included those of the franchise and representation of the people of this Republic, and, although thus the exclusive right of this government, and of the Volksraad, for the regulation of that franchise and representation is indisputable, yet this government has found occasion to discuss, in a friendly fashion, the franchise and the representation of the people, with Her Majesty's Government, without, however, recognizing any right thereto on the part of Her Majesty's Government. This government has also, by the formulation of the now existing Franchise Law, and the Resolution with regard to representation, constantly held these friendly discussions before its eyes.

On the part of Her Majesty's Government, however, the friendly nature of these discussions has assumed a more threatening tone, and the minds of the people in this Republic and in the whole of South Africa have been excited, and a condition of extreme tension has been created, while Her Majesty's Government could no longer agree to the legislation respecting franchise and the Resolution respecting representation in this Republic, and finally, by your note of the twenty-fifth of September, 1899, broke off all friendly correspondence on the subject, and intimated that they must now proceed to formulate their own proposals for a final settlement, and this government can only see in the above intimation from Her Majesty's Government, a new violation of the Convention of London, 1884, which does not reserve to Her Majesty's Government the right to a unilateral settlement of a question which is exclusively a domestic one for this government, and has already been regulated by it.

On account of the strained situation and the consequent serious loss in, and interruption of, trade in general, which the correspondence respecting the franchise and representation in this Republic carried in its train, Her Majesty's Government have recently pressed for an early settlement, and finally pressed, by your intervention, for an answer within forty-eight hours (subsequently somewhat modified), to your note of the twelfth of September, replied to by the note of this government of the fifteenth of September, and your note of the twenty-fifth of September, 1899, and thereafter further friendly negotiations broke off, and this government received the intimation that the proposal for a final settlement would shortly be made, but although this promise was once more repeated, no proposal has up to now reached this government. Even while friendly correspondence was still going on, an increase of troops on a large scale was introduced by Her Majesty's Government and stationed in the neighbourhood of the borders of this Republic.

Having regard to occurrences in the history of this Republic, which it is unnecessary here to recall to mind, this government felt obliged to regard this military force in the neighbourhood of its borders as a threat against the independence of the South African Republic, since it was aware of no circumstances which could justify the presence of such a military force in South Africa, and in the neighbourhood of its borders. In answer to an enquiry with respect thereto, addressed to His Excellency the High Commissioner, this government received, to its great astonishment, in reply, a veiled insinuation that from the side of the Republic (van Republikeinsche zyde) an attack was being made on Her Majesty's Colonies, and at the same time a mysterious reference to possibilities; whereby it was strengthened in its suspicion that the independence of this Republic was being threatened.

As a defensive measure, it was therefore obliged to send a portion of the *burghers* of this Republic, in order to offer the requisite resistance to similar possibilities. Her Majesty's unlawful intervention in the internal affairs of this Republic, in conflict with the Convention of London, 1884, caused by the extraordinary strengthening of troops in the neighbourhood of the borders of this Republic, has thus caused an intolerable condition of things to arise, whereto this government feels itself obliged, in the interest not only of this Republic but also of South Africa, to make an end as soon as possible, and feels itself called upon, and obliged to press earnestly and with emphasis for an immediate termination of this state of things, and to request Her Majesty's Government to give it the assurance.

(a) That all points of mutual difference shall be regulated by the friendly course of arbitration, or by whatever amicable way may be agreed upon by this government with Her Majesty's Government.

(b) That the troops on the borders of this Republic shall be instantly withdrawn,

(c) That all reinforcements of troops which have arrived in South Africa since the first of June, 1899, shall be removed from South Africa, within a reasonable time, to be agreed upon with this government, and with a mutual assurance and guarantee on the part of this government, that no attack upon or hostilities against any portion of the possessions of the British Government shall be made by the Republic, during further negotiations within a period of tune to be subsequently agreed upon between the governments, and this government will, on compliance therewith, be prepared to withdraw the armed *burghers* of this Republic from the borders,

(d) That Her Majesty's troops which are now on the high seas shall not be landed in any part of South Africa.

This government must press for an immediate and affirmative answer to these four questions, and earnestly requests Her Majesty's Government to return such an answer before or upon Wednesday the eleventh of October, 1899, not later than 5 p. m., and it desires further to add, that in the event of unexpectedly no satisfactory answer being received by it within that interval (it) will with great regret be compelled to regard the action of Her Majesty's Government as a formal declaration of war, and will not hold itself responsible for the consequences thereof, and that in the event of any further movement of troops taking place within the above mentioned time in the nearer direction of our borders, this government will be compelled to regard that also as a formal declaration of war.

The reply was as follows:

H. M.'s Agency, Pretoria,<br>October 11th, 1899.

Sir, I am instructed by the High Commissioner to state to you that Her Majesty's Government have received with great regret the peremptory demands of the Government of the South African Republic, conveyed to me in your note on the 9th inst., and I am to inform you in reply that the conditions demanded by the Government of the South African Republic are such as Her Majesty's Government deem it impossible to discuss.

I have the honour to be, Sir,<br>Your obedient servant,
W. Conyngham Green, C. B.

Those assembled on the Natal border, October 11th, will never forget that day, not only because it was the first day of the war which was to be recorded as one of the greatest in the annals of history, but because it was so bitterly cold and stormy. A strong wind was blowing, heavy and murderous looking clouds were rolling and tumbling about our heads. Snow was falling on the mountains, and while the heavens and the earth were thus warring with each other, the Boers filed across Laing's Nek, to defend their homes and country against aggressive and greedy England. Among the Boers there are no discipline, no drilling, no inspections, no roll calls, every man feeling himself a general with full authority to do as he pleases.

So they began the war, so they prosecuted the war, and so they finished the war. The severe cold and apparent confusion and disorder among the Boers, as they cantered off like so many Apache Indians toward Laing's Nek, did not seem to make the slightest impression on the boys of the Irish Brigade. They had something else to think about, and they were doing a lot of thinking. Of all the horses for them, there were not over twenty broken to the saddle, and among the boys themselves, there were not over a half a dozen who had ever tried to ride a horse. Now, one can easily see why the Irish boys were doing so much thinking. They did not wish to be left behind, yet each one felt that there was a great uncertainty as to how friendly the relations between himself and the horse might be.

The time came when the order was given to saddle up. Everyone, with the enthusiasm of a true soldier hastened to make good the order. After a good two hours' struggle, every horse was ready for his rider. The men were told to mount, each in his own way, and to make every effort to hold the saddle after once he found it. As they were told to lay aside their rifles until they had become on friendly terms with their horses, they were not hampered with any impediment except their inexperience. Having mounted, I scarcely know what happened during the next five minutes, but I saw men in camp, on the *veldt*, in fact, all about me, picking themselves up, shaking the sand off them, and chasing here and there and everywhere a lot of horses from which they had just separated. Having caught their horses they were told to try again and keep trying again, until they and their horses became thoroughly acquainted with each other.

For hours I sat and witnessed and enjoyed the best show I had ever seen or ever expect to see. But the men were Irish, and were not to be defeated as long as there was life in them. I kept no account of how many times each mounted his horse, and immediately thereafter turned a somersault, but, when, at the conclusion of the performance, each rode up and said he was ready for his rifle, I felt proud of them, for they showed the real Irish pluck and grit that are destined some day to free Ireland. Within one week from that day I could call each one of those Irish boys a truly good cavalryman. They learned to ride much sooner than they learned to know their horses.

A few of them, to be sure, would tie a piece of ribbon in the mane or tail, and would always hunt for their ribbons instead of their horses. This gave rise, months after, to some trouble in which Father Van Hecke, the brigade chaplain, was implicated. Father Van Hecke always tied a green rag into his horse's mane so that he could find him quickly. He rode a bay pony, and a good pony he was, that Father Van Hecke thoroughly appreciated.

One day one of the mischievous boys thought he would play a trick on the good Father. He went out, caught the Father's pony, removed the green rag and tied it into the mane of a sorrel pony, not half so good as the Father's. When the order was given to saddle-up, out went the Father, and the boys and Boers, each for his own horse. Father Van Hecke found the green rag, caught the sorrel pony and started to camp with him. At this moment up came the Boer who owned the pony, claimed him and accused the Father of trying to steal his horse. Father Van Hecke informed the Boer that he thought he had ridden that horse long enough to know him, and that the green rag was his mark. The Boer used rather strong language, but the Father would not surrender his pony to anyone. Finally I was sent for to settle the matter.

About twenty feet from the two equally certain owners of that sorrel pony, stood the Father's pony. I pointed him out to the Father and told him I thought that some of the boys had played a trick on him by removing the green rag from his pony and transferring it to the Boer's. The Father smiled and gave the Boer his horse, but I think today that that Boer is convinced that Father Van Hecke was trying to steal his horse. Father Van Hecke is a noble, good man with a warm, sympathetic heart, and as such he will always be remembered by the boys of the Irish Brigade.

Already the last of the Boers had disappeared over Laing's Nek, when the boys reported that they were ready for their rifles, so each secured his piece, and off we started without further delay. All were worrying for fear the Boers would have a fight with the English before we arrived. After travelling about twenty minutes we began to feel the biting cold and I was asked to give them a gallop.

I told them the idea was a good one, but I had grave fears about the consequences. "Oh, that's all right. We are all right, colonel, we have shown these horses what we can do." I started off on a slow gallop, and within two minutes at least one-third of the boys were deposited on the veldt, and it took the other two-thirds about half an hour to round up the loose horses and put matters into marching order again. After that I had no further delay, but I never repeated the gallop until near Dundee, where every man sat his horse in true cavalryman style. Late that night we overtook the Boers at Newcastle, the boys being very tired and stiff, but none complained, for they had, so far, not missed the first fight.

What an enthusiastic and patriotic body of men those Irish boys were! They seemed to feel that if they could give England one good blow, their happiness would be an assured fact. The very fact that the Irish, where ever you find them, so utterly despise the English, and so earnestly long to blow the whole English race into eternity, is in itself sufficient proof that the English rule in Ireland is cruel and brutal.

All had now passed over Laing's Nek and down the mountains into the valley. Here it was warm, but as disagreeable as ever, in fact more so, for it was rain, rain, rain, day and night, and the thick clouds of mist were actually rolling along the ground. At times we could not see twenty paces ahead of us, so it was necessary to move cautiously, because we knew that the English were falling back toward Dundee just ahead of us. Thoroughly soaked to the very skin, all ploughed through the mud, felt their way through the mist and clouds, passed Danhausser, and camped about seven miles from Dundee. On the following day, the clouds were motionless, but resting heavily on the adjacent mountains and foot-hills, while the valleys were quite clear. It was apparent to all now, that a battle must take place, and that, too, in a very short time.

Just as all horses were saddled and the artillery inspanned, and ready to move out, about two miles to our left and front we discovered a column of English emerging from a cloud on the foothills across the valley. Every Boer that happened to see them put spurs to his horse, and after them he went. Of course a lot of the Irish boys followed suit in great haste. The English whirled about and took refuge in a great stone cattle *kraal*. In five minutes the rifles began to speak on both sides—in another five minutes a French cannon was sent out, and fired a couple of shells, and five minutes later the white flag was waving above the heads of the English, and all was quiet again. Colonel Moller with his 196 well trained Eighteenth Hussars, had surrendered to forty untrained farmers. We now learned that Lucas Meyer, who had taken a road much to the east of us, had attacked Dundee, and been forced back because General Daniel Erasmus, who was to cooperate with him, had failed to show up. Colonel Moller had been sent out to follow up the Boers, and according to his own statement had lost himself, and hadn't the slightest idea where he was, although Dundee was only six miles away.

Of the 196 Irishmen captured, eighty-five begged to join the Irish Brigade and fight with the Boers. I wanted to take them on the spot, but the Boer officers did not consider it right, because, they said, if any of them were afterwards captured, the English would surely shoot them. When first captured, all were half scared to death and the first thing they wished to know was whether the Boers would shoot them or not. When told that they would be sent to Pretoria, where they would probably spend most of their time in playing cricket and football, they were, one and all, positively delighted that they had surrendered. They said that their officers had told them in Natal, that the Boers were savages, worse than the Zulus, and that so sure as any of them were captured, just so sure they would be killed.

While the men scarcely believed all their officers had told them, yet they were uncertain, because they had never seen a Boer and didn't know just what kind of a ruffian he was. The men of the Eighteenth Hussars had now learned what a liar and a hypocrite the English officer is.

These are harsh words, but it requires just such words to bring out the naked truth about the English officer. There were very few officers who were not branded as liars by their men, after it was learned how the savage Boer treated the Eighteenth Hussars.

Within the next few months we had captured several thousand prisoners, and they all told the same story and it was just as related above. That is enough about the English officer at this stage of the war, but I assure him that I will give him plenty of attention before this narrative is finished. To continue, we now heard that the English were moving out of Dundee to take possession of the hills lying between us and the town. The Irish Brigade were ordered to move at a gallop and reach the hills first, and we succeeded. The English were to be seen at different places in the little circular valley in which Dundee is situated.

This valley is about six miles in diameter and surrounded by hills and mountains. Several deep ravines run through it, and in them a whole army could easily be concealed. Dundee was near the hills on the east side, and Glencoe near the hills on the west side of the valley. Had the English troops taken possession of the hills and mountains around Dundee, I do not believe we could have taken the place.

General Penn-Symons had about 6,000 men there and eighteen cannon, and for defence his position was most excellent. Fortunately for the Boers, he did not take advantage of his position, and the result was that 1,000 Boers were chasing the lancers armed with cold British steel, about that little valley nearly a whole day. The English seemed afraid to move eastward of Dundee, yet there were no Boers there, as Lucas Meyer had fallen back some fifteen miles. The Boers in bands of 100 or 200 placed themselves about the north and west sides of the valley, and here it was that the lancers, in bands of 400 strong, would try to find an outlet. At every point the Boers would meet them with a few shots, and off went the cold British steel in search of another outlet. The mountains were rugged and steep on the southeast side, and there was but one pass through to the valley, and that leads to Ladysmith. At times it would rain, and then again the heavy clouds would roll over the valley and totally obscure the whole scene of action.

The whole day, however, was to the Boer something like a day of sports, for they had enjoyed themselves chasing the lancers about the valley as so many springboks. When night came, it was terribly dark, and now it was that Colonel Yule and his 6,000 men, armed with cold British steel, took advantage of the only outlet to the south and made then: escape to Ladysmith, some thirty miles away. During the battle with Lucas Meyer, General Penn-Symons was killed, and Colonel Yule succeeded him. For this masterly escape of Colonel Yule and 6,000 men from about 1,000 Boers at Dundee, the English proclaimed to the world their great victory, and promoted Yule to the rank of Major-General. In any other army he would have been put aside in disgrace. I am not sure whether he received a Victoria Cross or not, but if he didn't he certainly deserved one.

On the following day Dundee surrendered, with about 250 officers and wounded men, and almost an equal number of prisoners. Enough food and ammunition fell into our hands to provide our command for many months. The English, as usual, after one of their great victories, had forgotten to bury the dead who had fallen at Talana Hill two days before, in the fight with Lucas Meyer; they had dug a shallow pit and thrown in some of them.

But when we arrived, their hands and feet and stomachs were protruding above its surface and presented a most revolting scene. Thirty-nine dead bodies were left unburied, and the savage Boer gave them decent interment. It was near this very spot that, two days beforehand, the English, on getting possession of Dr. Van Der Merwe and his ambulance, tied ropes about his neck, and the necks of his Red Cross assistants, and then, having fastened the ropes to their wagons, dragged them off as prisoners of war.

Mr. Englishman can't deny this, but he may lie about it. Something else fell into our hands here, something that has caused Mr. Chamberlain to tell many a falsehood to the world. We captured thousands of dum-dum bullets and split bullets, and gave plenty of them to the different foreign consuls. I had the pleasure of supplying the whole Irish Brigade with these dum-dum bullets and split bullets, and the English Lee-Metford rifles captured at Dundee. The Boers thought it a pity to waste them also, so they too supplied themselves. We gave the English back their own medicine in big doses at Ladysmith, and many and numerous graves in and about that town mark the results.

The prisoners captured at Kraaipan were all carrying dum-dum bullets, and all the cartridges fired at Rietfontein near Elandslaagte were dumdum bullets; and, Mr. Englishman, we would never have known what dum-dum bullets were, had you not brought them to South Africa and given them to us. Bring some more, next time. If asked why we didn't capture Colonel Yule and his 6,000 men, as well as all they possessed, I answer that we had no generals—we had only Lucas Meyer and Daniel Erasmus, and the fighting brains of the two together, would not suffice to make an efficient corporal; much as we deplored their determination not to fight, yet we found a little satisfaction in the fact that we saw that awfully, awful death-dealing "cold British steel" in an awfully, awful, terrible tremble. How is that, Mr. Englishman?

We now passed on towards Ladysmith where we hoped to have a shake not only with Colonel Yule, but also with General Sir George White, Generals French, Hunter and other terrors of the English army. Lucas Meyer fought General Penn-Symons on October 20th, and on October 21st was fought the Battle of Elandslaagte. That good, unfortunate old soldier, General J. H. M. Koch, was in command of a mixed commando of Boers, Germans and Hollanders, numbering something like 600 or 700 men, all told. He should have closed up the only pass through which Colonel Yule could escape, but he didn't. He was persuaded by his under officers to go towards Ladysmith, and at Elandslaagte, fifteen miles from Ladysmith, his men unfortunately captured a supply train on its way to Dundee. On that train was plenty of whiskey and wines, and all the men thought it best to dispose of such beverages by drinking them; the result was that many were not in very good fighting trim.

General French was sent out with his thousands of trained soldiers, bristling with cold, British steel, to meet General Koch and his little band of 600. They met, and a bloody battle was fought, in which the Boers were defeated, General Koch mortally wounded, and many other distinguished men lost their lives, among them being that brave and patriotic Hollander and States Prosecutor, Dr. Hermanus Coster. General Koch had no position at all, for it was open to cavalry movements on all sides, and offered no protection in any sense of the word. He should have retreated at once, but he didn't, so it simply remains for me to tell what happened.

We lost forty-five men killed, about one 100 wounded, and something like 190 taken prisoners. Not over 300 escaped, so it proved a bad day's work for us, and allowed the British to boast of the prowess of cold British steel throughout the civilized world. The British officer, and the soldier, too, are both justified in their boasting, for they used their cold British steel as it had, I hope, never been used before. They went about the battlefield driving their lances through the bodies of both the dead and wounded, that each might carry his bloody lance back into Ladysmith, display it, and boast to the men, women and children of the town, of the bravery of him who carried it.

I will here insert a letter or two, to convict the boasters in their own words. These letters have often been published before, but they cannot be published too often, for the people of the world should know all about cold British steel, and how it is invariably used. Many an unarmed negro has fallen victim to cold British steel, so it is well for all to read the following letters, and, having read them, apply to the British army for lessons in chivalry, and on the best methods of carrying on civilized warfare in the twentieth century.

> After the enemy were driven out, one of our squadrons pursued, and got right in among them in the twilight, and most excellent pig-sticking ensued, for about ten minutes, the bag

being about sixty. One of our men stuck his lance through two, killing them both at once. Had it not been getting dark we should have killed more.

The above is a published extract from a British officer's letter and speaks for itself.

The lancers wrote many letters, boasting of their savagery and many acts of murder, as the following published extracts will show.

We charged them, and they went on their knees begging of us to shoot them, rather than stab them with our lances, but in vain. The time had come for us to do our work and we did it.

Another lancer, (he had taken an enemy prisoner), boasts as follows:—

I got hold of one Boer he did not know what I intended doing, so I made motions to him to run for his life. So he went, and I galloped after him with the sergeant's sword, and cut his head right off his body.

Another lancer writes:—

We just gave them a good dig as they lay. Next day most of the lances were bloody.

Now read this extract from a happy lancer, and I will pass the rest:—

Many of our soldiers are quite rich with the loot that has fallen to them. The infantry regiments profited to the largest extent. One Tommy secured a pocket-book containing 270 pounds in Transvaal money. Our boys are parading about now with gold watches, chains, and other trinkets.

He might have added with truth, that he and his comrades cut off many fingers in order to remove the rings, and that they are today wearing those rings on their fingers as souvenirs of their savage and bloody deeds.

May the day be not far distant when a humane and God-fearing people can erect a monument on that bloody battlefield to perpetuate, from generation to generation, the memory of those loathsome deeds of pelf and murder committed by self-convicted British officers and soldiers on the plains of Elandslaagte!

We now mentally resolved to deal with every British soldier caught with a lance in his hand as the interest of humanity might demand, and marched on towards Ladysmith, the last resting place of many of Elandslaagte's cowardly murderers, and the grave of cold British steel. We came in sight of Ladysmith on October 27th.

We halted to discuss and make plans. It was very necessary, too, for there was a much larger force in Ladysmith than we had, and the chances were that we would get a good thrashing. I was asked if I would go to the Tugela River and blow up the railway bridge, which was fifteen miles south of Ladysmith, that no guns and re-enforcements might come from Maritzburg. I said I would if they would provide me with a guide. The guide having been presented, I called upon my men for volunteers, and explained to them that it was a dangerous piece of work, but that I thought we were equal to it. Fifteen promptly responded, and that was all I wanted. The entire Boer force then moved on, and the fifteen men and myself remained where we were.

As we had no dynamite, I sent little Mike Halley and two other men back to a coal mine, about six miles distant, for about 100 pounds of it. A coolie was in charge of the mine, and he swore that there was no dynamite there. Mike made him get a candle and show him into the mine, that he might see for himself. On reaching a dark shaft, the candle was lighted, and at once there was an explosion. McCormick was badly burned about the face, Dick McDonough's hands suffered, and Mike looked as if his head had been submerged in a pot of boiling water. However, they did not give up their search, and at last found some dynamite, fuse and detonators. Just as they returned, General Joubert came upon us from another direction, and asked me what I was doing, and why I had not gone on with the main force. I told him what I had been requested to do, and that the boys had just arrived with the dynamite. He said he could not think of allowing us to do it, that it was too dangerous, that all of us would be killed, etc.

I told him that in war people had to take chances, and that I thought we could do the work and come out all right. But he would not allow us to go, and directed that we should go with him to the main force near Ladysmith. He afterwards acknowledged that he had made a mistake, for had the bridge been blown up, neither marines nor naval guns could have reached Ladysmith. It was this force and these guns that enabled the English to stand the siege and save Ladysmith from being captured.

This town is situated in a little valley on the banks of Klip River, and is almost completely surrounded by mountains, high and precipitous. Modderspruit runs from the east through a narrow valley between Lombard's Kop and Pepworth Hill, and empties into Klip River near the town. The distance from the tops of the mountains and from the crest of Pepworth Hill was, on an average, about 6,000 yards. General Sir George White, with his 13,000 trained soldiers and fifty cannon, held and occupied all the mountains, but ignored Pepworth Hill, lying to the north-east at a distance of about 6,000 yards from the town. Nickolson's Nek on the north did not command the town, so that, too, was not occupied by the British. Some low hills to the north-west were also unoccupied, so it was plain what we had to do in the first instance.

The Free Staters came in through Van Reenen's Pass and occupied the low hills to the north-west and a part of Nickolson's Nek. The Transvaalers were on the hills on the north, Pepworth Hill, and along the ridge near Modderspruit, and in an easterly direction from the town.

Ladysmith with its surrounding mountains is certainly a most excellent position both for offensive and defensive operations; and had a good commander been in Sir George White's place, he could have easily defeated and routed the Boers on their first appearing.

It was White's stupidity and inability that locked him up in Ladysmith, and kept him there, just as it was someone's great love of humanity that prevented us from taking the town on October 30th. The Irish Brigade and Ermelo Commando were placed in the centre, on Pepworth Hill, as a guard to Long Tom, two French field guns and two pom-pom maxims. Christian De Wet with some Free Staters, and Erasmus with some Transvaalers, together with the Johannesburg police, were in and about Nickolson's Nek on the right, Lucas Meyer and Schalk Burger, and Captain Pretorius with his cannons on our left, occupied a long ridge and some small hills near the eastern part of Lombard's Kop. The total Boer forces did not exceed 8,000 men with ten cannon.

Saturday, the 28th, passed without a shot being fired. Sunday came, and some of the Irish boys grew restless and complained that they were hungry. I am sure they were, too, for I know I was. We had precious little to eat for about two weeks, for it had been raining steadily for that time and we had been constantly on the move. Three of the boys urged so earnestly their request to go to a farmhouse near the town for a pig, that I finally gave them permission. When within about

A PART OF THE IRISH BRIGADE AT LADYSMITH

500 yards of the house they discovered and shot a fat, half-grown pig. Much to their surprise, within the wall around the house were some English soldiers, who at once opened fire upon them. Hot times then ensued, but in the end the boys came out all right and brought the pig to camp. These were the first shots exchanged between the English and our men at Ladysmith.

The Irish camp was about 300 yards in the rear of the guns, and our guards were posted in front of them and on the crest of the hill. About two o'clock on Monday morning one came down, woke me and told me that a balloon was moving along the valley not far from the hill, and he evidently felt excited about it, for he asked me if I didn't think "they were after dropping dynamite on us." When I told him that the object of the men in the balloon was to find out our strength and position, he felt perfectly satisfied and returned to his post.

During the night, Tom Haney was on guard and Mick Ryan was to relieve him. When the hour arrived, Mick picked up his rifle and went to take his post.

On approaching, Tom said "Halt! Who comes there?"

"It is Mick," was the reply, and he approached.

Tom said, "See here, Mick, you must not answer 'Mick' when you are challenged, but 'friend'."

Mick's reply was, "Now, Tom, how can I answer, 'friend,' when I haven't a friend in the world?"

From the balloon incident I knew there would be trouble in the early morning. At the first sign of dawn I got up and went to the hill crest. I had not sat there long before it became light enough for me to use my glasses. Within about two minutes, I discovered twenty-four cannon about 2,500 yards distant, and pointed right toward Pepworth Hill. Near them was a long line of lancers and some cavalry. Beyond them and nearer to Lombard's Kop, I saw a lot more cavalry. To our right and front, I saw ten companies of infantry marching towards us. They were halted and concealed behind some rocks, at about 1,500 yards from us. I had seen enough to be convinced that there was going to be a fight, and that no time was to be lost. I sent one of the guards to tell the boys to come quickly, for there was going to be a hot fight. He found them making coffee and preparing pig for breakfast. They forgot their coffee and pig and everything else, except their rifles and ammunition, and came running up that hill like a band of wild Apaches. As fast as they arrived they would call out, "Where are the English?"

After all had taken a good look at the cannon and cavalry in front of them, I simply told them to remember that they were Irishmen, and then put them in a position on the right of the guns. Commandant Trichardt had discovered the English batteries at the same time that I did, and after the Ermelo Commando had taken its position at the left of the guns, he prepared for immediate action. It was just 5.45 a. m. Sunday when a long column of curling blue smoke rising from Long Tom told us that a six-inch shell was on its way, to extend to the English an early welcome.

Within ten seconds the British batteries responded with twenty-four fifteen pound shells, and the Battle of Modderspruit was begun. The shells continued to come so thick and fast that by seven o'clock, Pepworth Hill was so enveloped with smoke that it was with difficulty at times to see the enemy.

Shells were bursting over our heads, on the ground, among us, and great chunks of iron were whizzing about from stone to stone. At times the uproar was so great that we could scarcely hear each other speak, yet the Irish boys, who had not the least protection, never once showed any inclination to waver. They were there to protect their guns, and to fight the English, and though they could be killed, they were not to be driven away. It was about this time, seven o'clock, that the Ermelo Commando could not stand it any longer, and nearly all of them fell back about one mile, and there awaited further developments.

Afterwards this same commando proved to be one of the best, bravest, and most reckless in the field.

It was about this time, too, that six of those artillery boys were killed and several wounded. This so weakened the artillery force at Long Tom that he could not be supplied with shells, and so had to stop fighting. Shells continued to rain upon us, and the English undoubtedly thought that Long Tom was disabled, as he had ceased to respond.

As no Boers could be found who would carry ammunition to Long Tom during such a shell storm, Commandant Grobler came to me about seven o'clock and asked for four volunteers from the Irish Brigade, to serve Long Tom, and I called upon the boys. In an instant Everyone clamoured to go, and I sent seven instead of four, as being necessary. In another three minutes Long Tom roared again and it was plainly to be seen by the commotion it raised in the valley, that the English were utterly amazed. Of the seven men who volunteered

MAJOR J. L. PRETORIUS
The acknowledged greatest artillerist of the world by those who know him and his deeds.

and served Long Tom, two were shot. Now Long Tom and the two French field guns made it so very uncomfortable for the English that the number of shells that had been raining upon us for the past hour and a half was reduced at least fifty *per cent*.

Between seven and eight o'clock the commandos under Lucas Meyer and Schalk Burger came into contact with French's cavalry on the extreme English right. We could plainly see warm rifle firing, and soon it grew to be terribly hot, and then we knew that the English would be so hard pushed that they would have to abandon any hope of breaking through our centre and capturing Long Tom and the French field guns. After a time that brave, keen-eyed artillerist and dashing officer, Captain J. L. Petrorius appeared on the scene with his pom-pom maxims, and so deadly was his fire that French's cavalry had to fall back.

Major Wolmorans brought his French guns into play on the English right also, and this forced some of the English guns to drop Pepworth Hill, and try their luck with Wolmorans. Wolmorans was too much for them, and we could see that the whole English line was beginning to tremble, yet the battle continued to rage and the bullets and shells were flying to and fro so thick and fast that it would seem impossible for anyone to come out alive.

It was about this time, eight o'clock, that a shell caught me, smashed both the bones of my arm near the elbow, cut the tendon, nerve and artery and completely paralysed my whole arm. I went to my horse, about 300 yards away, and was fortunate to find him alive, because most of them near him had been killed. A young Boer boy helped me to mount and I managed to reach a hospital tent about a mile away, but it was a close call, for I had grown very weak from loss of so much blood. As I passed my camp, I could not help smiling, for it was completely destroyed, and I knew that when the Irish boys saw it again, there would be plenty of Irish wit in the air.

Finally about two p. m. the Boer fire became so warm and deadly that the Lancers with their cold British steel, and the whole British army, bolted, and a pell-mell retreat followed, in which everyone seemed bent on getting into Ladysmith as quickly as possible, regardless of consequences. Such was their anxiety to escape, that they crowded together like a flock of sheep, and it may be taken as a fact that Captain Pretorius did not fail to try his pompom guns on such a magnificent target.

The lancers threw away their cold British steel, helmets, guns, ammunition, and everything of weight that might impede fast running; and so ended the Battle of Modderspruit.

On our right at Nickolson's Nek, something happened that we on Pepworth Hill knew nothing about, till the battle was over, although the Nek was in plain view. During the previous night, General White sent two regiments under Colonel Carleton to take possession of Nickolson's Nek and the adjoining big hill. Before they reached the Nek, some Boer guards saw them and fired upon them. Colonel Carleton, who was in command, had with him a lot of pack mules carrying several mountain guns. It seems these mules did not like fighting, so they deserted with their cannon and joined the Boers. However, Colonel Carleton got the Nek and the big hill much to his regret. The wily Christian De Wet (afterwards General De Wet) happened to be near at hand.

In the early morning some Pretoria town boys, Johannesburg police, and a few Free Staters discovered the unwise colonel and his men on the Nek and hill. Having placed themselves in a *sluit* about 1,000 yards away, they gave the colonel a warm rifle salute. Carleton and his men of course responded. Cunning De Wet took about 200 Free Staters, slipped around the hill, crept up it and fired into Colonel Carleton's rear. No man likes to be shot in the rear, so Colonel Carleton hoisted his white flag, and with about 900 of his men went to Pretoria to see Oom Paul. Of course General White thinks that if the mules with the cannon had not stampeded, Colonel Carleton would have been all right and would have given the Boers particular—well, I will put it mildly and say fits.

Now a word about those mountain guns. The Boers would take a good look at them, give a sarcastic smile and walk away. Those guns are about as much use in war as so many popguns would be, and it is a question with me whether I would rather fire one of them or stand 100 feet in front of it, and let someone fire at me. They might prove useful in scaring unarmed niggers, who had never heard a loud noise. The Boers are not niggers, notwithstanding the fact that the whole British press laboured hard during the year preceding the war to make the world believe they were niggers, and savage ones, too. The Boer has heard too many lions roar to be frightened to death by a popgun; but an incompetent British general must have some kind of an excuse to explain away his blunders, so General White attributes his defeat to the unfaithfulness of a mule, and receives the congratulations of his queen.

At the conclusion of the battle Commandant General Piet Joubert called up the Irish boys, thanked them, congratulated them, and told them that the brave stand they had made and their serving of Long Tom had prevented a grave disaster and enabled the Boers to gain a great victory over the enemy.

Young Tommie Gates, who carried the green flag, and young Cox, another brave boy, were both shot dead, and buried on Pepworth Hill, facing the enemies' position. Hugh Carbury was shot through the head, the bullet striking the very centre of his forehead. How he lived for even an instant no one could understand. Dr. Max Mehliss and Dr. Lilpop took him, operated upon him and within three days he was walking about the temporary hospital. Finally orders were received for all the wounded, eighty-five in number, to be sent to Pretoria. I would not go, because I knew that I must stay near the Irish Brigade. Hugh Carbury went to Pretoria and so far recovered that he was walking around the town. In about three months he had a stroke of paralysis and died, and the Irish Brigade lost one of its best and bravest boys. Andy Higgins, Olsen, Kepner, Tinen, Barnes and Gaynor were also wounded, but all recovered. Many others had holes shot through their clothing but escaped uninjured.

For months after this battle, the Irish boys and the Boers amused themselves playing a game known as "mumble peg" with the cold British steel that the lancers on their hurried retreat thought unnecessary to carry with them into Ladysmith. The lancers were now armed with rifles and converted into mounted infantry, and I don't think that a lance was ever after seen on any battlefield during the rest of the war. When we captured the Eighteenth Hussars, we asked them for their flag and we were informed that they didn't carry any. Now Christian De Wet had captured two regiments, the Dublin Fusiliers and the Gloucesters, and when asked for their flags they answered that all regiments had received orders to leave all colours and flags behind, locked up in the vaults at Durban, Pietermaritzburg and Cape Town. Of course every regiment was provided with the necessary white flag, and everyone found that flag a most useful and life-saving piece of cloth. Not a battalion and not a regiment carried either its own colours or its country's flag into the battlefield, throughout the whole war. This alone should be sufficient proof of the cowardice and degeneracy of the British Army, and at the same time explain the pig-sticking at Elandslaagte and the use of the dum-dum and split bullets by the soldiers.

There, can be neither pride nor honour among either officers or soldiers of any army when they hide away their country's flag for safe keeping, on the eve of battle. I have an idea that every regiment considered the carrying of its colours and flag into battle from a business point of view, for if their flag were not carried into battle it would not be necessary to make requisition for a new supply after the battle. However, I will guarantee that anyone visiting the various regimental headquarters throughout England, will find in Everyone of them a tattered and torn flag bearing the names of many great battles in South Africa in which it floated; and in which its brave defenders performed wonderful deeds and added another glorious victory to the British army in the face of overwhelming odds.

Everyone asks "why didn't the Boers follow up this pell-mell retreat of the English into Ladysmith?" The fact is that the Boer is too pious, too religious and, therefore, too humane to battle with such an unscrupulous people as the English. Commandant General Piet Joubert was a grand man, grown old and mellow in the service of his country, a most religious and humane man, who looked upon the English as a Christian people, and he felt that it would be unchristianlike to follow up and shoot down his retreating enemy.

When the English were well out of range, and the commandos returned to their *laagers*, they held their services, and then began to make their coffee and prepare their food, as if nothing had happened. Every pot, kettle, blanket and tent, etc., in the Irish camp was simply riddled by shells, so that they had to be supplied with a completely new outfit. This resulted because our camp was about 300 yards in the rear of the guns, and the English guns were so located that every shell that passed over our heads must fall in or near it. Judging by appearances one could easily be made believe that about all the shells fired by the British landed in the camp, for it was certainly a total wreck.

Now that the battle was over, the dead and wounded must be cared for, and our ambulances were very busy the whole afternoon, because they had to pick up a dead or wounded man here and there along a line six miles in extent.

General White sent out his white flags requesting truce after truce, for one or two days or more, that he might be permitted to care properly for his dead or wounded. His ambulance men certainly were busy; at the same time his men were very busy in another way. All were occupied day and night in building forts, digging holes and throwing up earth works of various kinds. General Joubert, being very humane, granted White all the time he wished, to take care of his dead, but, of course, never once suspected that advantage would be taken of the truce to prepare defences. The humanity of the Boer in time of war is his greatest weakness, while the unscrupulousness of the Englishman is his greatest strength in time of peace or war.

As a result of the English retreat, the Boers took possession of all the hills and mountains around Ladysmith, with the exception of one, and that one was of the greatest importance of them all. It was the Platrand, lying just south of Ladysmith. As the Boers did not occupy Platrand, the English after a time took possession of it. Had the Boers seized this Platrand, as well as the other positions, General White could not have held Ladysmith three days. About one-half the Boer forces were used to invest Ladysmith, the other half went to the Tugela River, and took position along the hills in front of Colenso, a little town about fifteen miles south of Ladysmith.

Within a week from the investment of Ladysmith, we had our maximum force in Natal, numbering nearly 12,500 men. They were distributed about Ladysmith, along Tugela River and at Helpmakaar, about fifty miles eastward of Ladysmith. The Irish Brigade took its position in the Modderspruit valley, about one mile to the east of Pepworth, and about 1000 yards from the hospital, where I could see it plainly. The Platrand and Ladysmith were in plain view, and about once a week the Irish brigade and camp was shelled. No damage was ever done, however. Although not yet recovered, I returned to duty on December 12, for I was needed. The Long Tom and howitzer on Pepworth Hill, were our especial care, and fifty of the boys slept with the guns every night during that long siege of four months. The hill is low and of very easy ascent on all sides, yet not once did the English ever try to interfere with the guns by any night attack.

Commandant General Joubert's headquarters were to our left and rear about one mile, as we faced Ladysmith, and every white flag bearer from General White had to pass us to reach General Joubert. We would stop the bearer, forward the report, and have a chat with the gentleman from the city. They were always anxious to know just where the Irish camp was, and were always told just where it was, and had it pointed out to them besides; yet the English never once attacked that camp except with cannon, either day or night during the siege. The English seemed to want us badly, but never could make up their minds to come and get us, although we offered them every inducement.

In my opinion, it was a good thing for us that they didn't come,

Col. Blake, his two sons, Aldrich and Ledyard, in America, and Lieut. Wynand Malan who was so undeservedly held partially responsible for the destruction of Long Tom on Lombard's Kop.

for we had no defences and were very few in number; still they would have had to pay a heavy price for anything they might get in that camp, for the Irish boys were fighters, and not to be frightened at the appearance of a large force of English. One Long Tom was placed on Lombard's Kop, another at Bulwana Kop, and still another on the low hills west of the town. Early in December, a strong force came out, ascended Lombard's Kop, blew up the Long Tom and a howitzer, and returned to town very jubilant, and they had reason to be, too, for it was a plucky piece of work.

There were twelve artillery boys with these guns, and no more. They managed to kill one, and wound four or five Tommies before they left their guns. Long Tom was sent to Pretoria, and in about two weeks, began to tell the English that he was well and hearty once more. Major Erasmus and Lieutenant Wynand Malan were highly censured by the Boer Government for neglect of duty, etc., in allowing these guns to be blown up, but they were truly innocent. They had tried by letter and every other way to get General Daniel Erasmus and Schalk Burger to give them a guard for the night, but no guard was ever given. If anyone or two should be censured or shot, that one or two was General Erasmus and Schalk Burger. Lieutenant Malan proved himself to be a patriotic, efficient and brave soldier to the very end of the war.

About ten days later the English made another night excursion to a high hill near Nicholson's Nek, and succeeded in blowing up a howitzer. They were about 700 strong, and to defend the howitzer, there were about 150 Pretoria town boys, and no better boys or soldiers ever shouldered the rifle. They were fighters, and met the English in a hand-to-hand combat. After the howitzer was blown up, a contest took place between the mauser and cold British steel. The mauser won easily, cold British steel was buried, and we have never heard from it from that day to this. The Boer's loss in the contest was three killed and four wounded. The British officially reported fifty-four killed and wounded, but I don't know how much truth there is in this report, because no faith can be put in any British report. The British officer always gives his report as so many killed and wounded and so many missing. The missing seldom show up, but this gives them the opportunity of fooling the British public, and creates an impression among the people that they have gained a victory and not suffered a defeat. Of course people are always convinced that the missing will turn up either during the day or the night.

CHAPTER 5

# Besieging Ladysmith

Not a day passed without a set-to taking place between one or more of the commandos and the English. If the latter did not come out, the Boers would go in, and, in many instances, some very hot skirmishes resulted. Such sports lasted usually about half an hour, when the English, almost invariably turned tail and ran back into their places of safety.

All *burghers* not directly engaged in these skirmishes, would secure good seats among the rocks and light their pipes and enjoy themselves watching these shooting matches, as much as they would Barnum's circus. One day about fifty of the Irish boys were induced to go on a visit to a big fort, right at the town, and they went; but just how they got out of the circle of fire within which they found themselves is a mystery to them and to me to this day, but all came back safe and sound, bringing with them a few good horses and mules, and reported one captain and three Tommies killed. They went without my knowledge, and certainly I would never have given my consent, for it was an idiotic act on their part. The boys themselves, however, were not to blame. They were induced to believe that the Boers were going too, and that they would be strongly re-enforced by them. The Boers had no idea of going, for they had too much sense, and had the boys known this, they would never have gone; so they told me on their return.

I was still in the hospital, and that is the reason I knew nothing about it. They complained to me that "they" were making fools of them and wanted me to return to camp and stop that kind of business. Nothing could possibly be gained by the venture, and the chances were a hundred to one that much loss of life would result. When the Boers saw them actually at the town they thought the Irish had gone crazy or had deserted to the English. For several days afterwards, some of the boys would slip around the ravines, get near the town, jump some horses and mules, and, at full speed, under cannon and maxim fire, return to camp. The English always kept some *coolies* on guard over their horses and mules, but just one shot was enough to put each *coolie* to flight. The English finally put up a trap to catch the boys and some of them came nearly falling into it. They concealed a hand maxim and two men in a pit near the horses, and with a small, but strong rope, tied each horse to a stake. The *coolie* had orders, of course, to run as soon as the Irish boys came in sight.

It was supposed that the boys would make a rush to start the horses off on a run, and, on finding the horses tied, would stop to loosen them. But the boys discovered the ropes, surmised that a trap was laid, and made a hasty retreat, though not before this concealed maxim and two men popped up above the ground and began to pepper them. Sergeant Major O'Reilly was particularly smart at this business, and he took no less than thirty horses and mules. He is Africander born, but an Irishman to the backbone, and has all the pluck and daring of his race. They were not permitted to go again after horses, because it was thought too risky.

The English were constantly trying to break through the Free Stater's line on the west side, for, having broken through them, they could cross the Tugela River near Spion Kop, go around the Boers at Colenso, and proceed to Maritzburg, so here it was that most of the heavy fighting took place during the siege. Yet with all their cannon and men, they could never break through that weak little line. The Free State men were bold, and would often rush through the English lines and bring out thousands of cattle, horses and mules. Almost every night there was an alarm, and, with two or three exceptions, it proved to be always a false one, but all had to turn out just the same, because it would not do to take any chances. The result was that everybody, at night, would roll up in his blanket with boots and clothes on, that he might be ready in an instant to use his rifle.

These alarms would generally occur between one and two o'clock in the morning, and when we heard the rifles popping away in many directions, out we would run, take our fighting positions and there sit and watch till daylight. I never rolled out of blanket but twice without feeling that the alarm was false, and on the first occasion I told the boys that we were in for a red hot fight. It was on this occasion that about 200 of the Lydenburg Commando were posted on guard to our left and front, that is, just in front of General Joubert's headquarters. It was about two o'clock in the morning when we were aroused by a rifle fire so terrific that one could easily have believed that all the forces about Ladysmith were engaged in a hot fight. Those Lydenburgers were so close that we felt we were actually in the fighting line, yet were not engaged. You may be sure that we did not lose a second in getting into our positions.

As the fighting continued, we could easily see the sparks of fire from the rifles, yet we could not see any English, nor could we discover any return fire. In this state of doubt and anxiety we sat and watched for half an hour, when the firing ceased. It ceased because the Lydenburgers, feeling that they could not hold their position any longer, retreated and took up another post at General Joubert's headquarters. For a circuit of three miles all the commandos were in a terrible state of excitement because they believed that the English had made a strong attack on Joubert's headquarters. All the men felt that the English would have to clean up the Irish boys before the general's camp would be taken, but they didn't know but that the Irish boys had been finished.

General Joubert was not in the least excited, but was very angry at the Lydenburgers for leaving their position, for he knew there were no English on the ground, otherwise they would have followed up. He sent a couple of good men to investigate. They found that a poor old mule had escaped from Ladysmith and had come out our way in search of something to eat and that poor old mule was quietly eating his grass as if nothing had happened, although at least 10,000 shots had been fired close to his ears. The Lydenburgers were then ordered back to their post and all was serene once more.

Now I shall tell about another alarm when I was sure we had a fight on hand. It was about two or three o'clock in the morning when hot firing was heard right by our camp, not to the left and front as before, but to our left and rear this time. I felt terribly frightened and hustled the men out as they were never hustled before. I felt sure that the English were actually firing into General Joubert's headquarters. The firing did not last more than three minutes; then all was quiet again. One of the Irish boys went out to investigate. He moved carefully, and after awaiting about twenty minutes, returned and reported, "Oh it is those damned Lydenburgers again." Some Lydenburgers were guarding an English *kaffir* spy that some of the Boer boys had captured, and, the night being dark, the *kaffir* made a break for liberty.

Not only the guard, but all the Lydenburgers, 1,000 strong, jumped out and began to fire, on the supposition that there must be some English somewhere in front.

That Lydenburg Commando could stir up more false alarms than all the other commandos around Ladysmith put together, yet during the whole war, I don't believe they were ever in a fight. David Schoeman was *commandant* and Piet Swartz was the chief *veldtcornet*, and wherever you found them, you might be sure you would find no English, and that you could lie down to sleep without any fear of being disturbed, except by a false alarm.

Every morning when it was sufficiently light to see moving objects in and about Ladysmith, all the Long Toms and howitzers would open up and drive Everyone into the hole provided for safety. After that, silence would reign until about ten a. m., when an artillery duel of ten or fifteen minutes' duration would be fought, just to vary the monotony. Then all would be quiet again until about four p. m. when some English cavalry would come out to see if there were any gates open in the Free Stater's line. A lively skirmish would ensue, the English would fly back to their holes, and the day's work was done. As the English were kept in their holes all day, of course they had to get out and do their necessary work at night.

The Boers thought they would hamper them somewhat in their work, so at sundown, they would load and aim all their cannon and at the hour of midnight would all fire at once. This caused the English so much annoyance that they in turn tried the same game on us, but never did us any harm. I have now given the usual program both for the day and night during the siege of Ladysmith, and while I could write page after page describing incident after incident that occurred during the long siege, yet I do not care to do it, because it would mean more work for me and prove tiresome to the reader.

In a nut-shell, the Boers had a delightful time, lived in luxury, had their sports, smoked their pipes, drank their coffee, entertained visiting friends and when there was a fight they were always ready for it.

## Chapter 6

# British Treachery at Colenso

Now I pass on to Colenso, where, in a short time some lively work was to be done, and, in passing, I must try to put the reader in a position to see the situation as it really was. Do not be frightened, however, for I am not going to give you long descriptions of positions or battles in the future, but will confine myself to relating just what I think will prove most interesting and nothing more. If my life depended upon it, I could not write even an approximately correct history of the war; and I am sure that no one else could do it, because the military operations were spread over such a large extent of country. Of course the London *Times* has published a correct history of the war, and so has Conan Doyle[1] written and published a correct history of the war; the only time that a great newspaper and a popular novelist ever competed in the art of fiction. Both won.

During the Battle of Modderspruit, General Lucas Meyer fell sick and went home. No one wished him to die, but no one was sorry that he had to go home. He was as hopelessly incompetent to command as either General Erasmus or General Schalk Burger, and that is saying a great deal. The gods were with us now, sure enough, for Louis Botha, a private, was made a general in Meyer's place. Botha was young,—about thirty-five,—energetic, brave, a quick and able soldier, and he at once put himself to work. He made the Boers dig trenches in the hills and along the river bank in front of Colenso, and built stone walls for protection, for he knew that Buller would come with a strong force and many cannon. Certain it was that a big battle was to be fought at Colenso, because Ladysmith must be relieved.

The Tugela wound along at the base of the hills, and beyond it was

---
1. *The Great Boer War* by Arthur Conan Doyle also published by Leonaur.

an open plain over which Buller must come. Botha was now ready for any army that might show itself. The railway bridge and the wagon road-crossing were just in front of his line of trenches, and there the heavy fighting must take place.

Buller with about 35,000 men and ninety-six cannon finally came into view, camped at the little towns of Chieveley and Frere, about six or seven miles away, and from there sent out his reconnoitring parties.

The Boers "laid low and said nothing," not a rifle or cannon was fired, and all was as silent as the grave.

On December 15th, General Buller made up his mind to relieve Ladysmith, as, apparently, there was no obstacle in his way. He moved out his forces in beautiful battle-array, brought his cannon into position and opened fire upon all the hills. If there were really any Boers in those hills his heavy lyddite shells would soon make them shift and abandon those parts. Soon the earth seemed to be in a tremble, gravel and stones were whizzing through the air, and the roaring of the bursting shells on the hills and mountains in the rear was simply terrific and deafening, yet the Boers "laid low and said nothing." Soon the English became convinced that there was no enemy in the hills or along the river banks, so all the cannon ceased firing and a deadly silence reigned as the English-Irish regiments with steady step advanced toward the river.

When within easy range, the silent Boers along the river banks raised their mausers, made them sing in unerring tones, and, at the same time, Captain Pretorius roared from the hills his pompom and cannon to make complete the scene of death and destruction. Soon the plain of Colenso was strewn with dead and wounded Irish Tommies, and at the very time when the battle was raging at its highest pitch, ambulances in great numbers rushed into the field, apparently to assist the unfortunate, but, in fact, to stop the Boers in their deadly work. Screened by these ambulances, twelve Armstrong cannon came into the field, but the quick eye of Captain Pretorius detected them, and at once he sent some shells that landed among them. These then scattered and fled for safety and exposed the twelve cannon to the Boer and his mauser. Artillery men and artillery horses were quickly shot down and the guns rendered useless. Rescuing parties made bold attempts to save the guns, but the Boer and his mauser mowed them down. Here it was that Lieutenant Roberts, a son of Lord Roberts, an English politician and financier, bravely met his death.

Commandant General Louis Botha.

Now the British began to fall back, and about 200 Boers and Irish boys rushed across the river, seized ten of the guns (two had been rescued), Colonel Bullock and a good bunch of prisoners, and recrossed the river, landing in safety within their own lines. Strange to say, all this was accomplished right under the eyes of the whole British force, without any resistance being offered. They all evidently felt sick, had had enough and wanted to go home, and they did, without delay or ceremony return to their homes in Chieveley and Frere.

General Louis Botha had now fought his first battle, won an easy victory and destroyed British prestige, and that, too, with a loss of but six men killed and a small number wounded. I don't know what the English loss was, and I don't believe the English know either, for it was only last September or October that Mr. Chamberlain, in answer to a question on the subject made by a Scotch member, stated that the list of the dead in South Africa was not yet completed. It is barely possible that Mr. Chamberlain is still waiting for his missing thousands to show up. Sure it is, St. Peter has completed the list, and when Chamberlain and Milner follow up Rhodes, no doubt each will be supplied with certified rolls of the names of their thousands of victims in South Africa. I can see a very warm future ahead for the South African Trinity. After all was over, the British sent a wail to the remotest part of the civilized world, to the effect that the Boers had deliberately fired upon the red cross ambulance, in utter disregard of the rules of the Geneva Convention.

Those ambulances were rushed into the immediate line of fire in order to stop the Boers from shooting down the English soldiers, and, at the same time, to serve as a screen for the two batteries in reaching their coveted position. The infamous game was detected, a shell scattered and put to flight the ambulances, the Tommies continued to fall, and ten guns of the two batteries being now completely exposed and within easy mauser range, were quickly captured. Yes, Mr. Englishman, as you cannot fight honourably and win, you must resort to infamous methods and manufacture excuses for failure out of deliberate falsehoods. Had your little game succeeded, the batteries reached their coveted position and proved disastrous to the Boer forces, it would never have occurred to you to mention this ambulance incident.

General Botha having granted General Buller all the time he wished for to care for his thousands of dead and wounded, the Boers returned to their pipes and coffee, their usual daily services and their peaceful way of camp life, without its once occurring to them that their deeds, on that day, had made them known, respected and honoured throughout the civilized world.

Of course this does not include the British Government in London, Silly Billy of Germany or the English Government in Washington, D. C. The fifty Irish boys who went down for the day and were in the very hottest of the fight, and who particularly distinguished themselves by being among the very first to seize the English cannon, now returned to camp at Modderspruit; but they were so restless and jubilant that it was plain that something must be done to pacify them, so it was suggested that we arrange for some sports, as Christmas was very near at hand. This suggestion hit just the right place with all of them, and it was decided to have horse races, athletic sports and some kind of a banquet too. Christmas day was to be the day, and the boys went to the different commandos, invited all who had fast horses to come and try their luck, and all who felt that they could run, jump, throw heavy weights, etc. Nor did they fail to tell everyone that all would have an opportunity to take a smack at Irish cooking. Every thing went beautifully, a half-mile track was prepared, plenty of food was cooked, and all was in readiness when Christmas day came.

Boers with fast horses from all the commandos were there. Athletes representing all commandos; generals, *commandants* and *veldtcornets* were there; young ladies and old ones, too, from Pretoria, Johannesburg, Dundee and other towns, were entertained by the Irish boys. All gazed in admiration at the colours that waved to and fro with the breeze, for they saw the *vierkleur*, the green flag with the harp, the star and stripes, the tricolour of France, and the German and Holland flags that floated over the Irish camp.

It was a day of jubilee without a queen, a day for brave and patriotic hearts to assemble, a day for a liberty-loving and God-fearing people to rejoice and be merry. It was not a day for a titled figurehead, not a day for dissolute lords, not a day for an unscrupulous colonial secretary, a weak, high commissioner of South Africa, or the moneyed rascals of Kimberley. For them the day must smell of rottenness, and therefore be celebrated in London. With one horse the Irish boys easily won in all the races, while the Boers captured nearly all the prizes in athletics. The Irish, however, played an English trick in the races on the unsuspecting Boers. By the art of commandeering, they had possessed themselves of a good race horse in Pretoria, and it was this horse that so easily took all the prizes. The sports having come to an end, all went to camp and enjoyed the Irish boys' meats, cakes, pies, etc., but it was a painfully dry banquet. Several cases of liquid refreshments had been ordered and they had arrived at Modderspruit, but some thirsty party had appropriated and removed all of them before the Irish boys arrived at the station, so we had to use coffee as a substitute.

Now, coffee is all right, and it is wet, but that little something is missing in it that puts such a delightful tingle into the blood. I felt sorely disappointed because it was Christmas day, the boys had distinguished themselves only a few days before, and I fondly hoped to give them a drink or two, their guests a drink or two, and besides I wanted a drink or two myself. Having feasted, all joined and sang first, God save Ireland, then the Volkslied of the Transvaal and that of the Orange Free State, and then, after giving three cheers for the Irish boys and Ireland, all, happy and satisfied, dispersed and returned to their respective camps to attend evening services. During that whole afternoon, I confess that I felt nervous, for there was a large crowd of men, women and children assembled in the camp, and I was afraid every moment that I should hear a big lyddite shell come whizzing over from Ladysmith. I was happily disappointed, however, and felt much relieved after the people had dispersed.

THE FIRST BRITISH TRENCH ON SPION KOP, SHOWING THE ENGLISH DEAD LYING THREE DEEP.

Chapter 7

# Spion Kop

From the middle of November to the end of December, someone would come around every week to ask for volunteers to rush Ladysmith. The Irish boys responded to a man every time, but for some reason the rush was never made. Personally I considered the scheme idiotic, because every foot of ground in and around Ladysmith was strongly fortified, and our investing force was very small as compared to General White's army of 12,000 men.

At the conclusion of the Battle of Modder Spruit, I strongly urged the Boers to storm the town, and I continued to urge them every day for the ten following days, but Generals Erasmus and Schalk Burger thought that all such talk was nonsense. The English as yet had practically no defences that we could not overcome. As soon as White got everything in apple-pie order and had finished all his defences and well surrounded them with barbed wire, then it was that Generals Erasmus and Schalk Burger and their kind were most anxious to rush and take Ladysmith. They really thought that the *burghers* would then refuse, but they didn't. So it happened that on January 5th a fellow came to the Irish camp, as they had often done before, for volunteers, and received the same answer, "We'll be with you." General Erasmus sent around the necessary orders and may have sent one to White, too, as far as I know,—and all the men were to be in positions agreed upon by 3 a. m. the following morning, January 6th.

During the night General Erasmus sent a countermanding order to some of the Transvaal Commandos, but forgot to let the Free Staters know that he had done so. Much to my surprise, we were ordered to go with four field guns and take position on a small hill near the Pretoria Town laager, and just in front of the English guns and forts on the Rooirand, north of Ladysmith. We were in our position at the proper time, and there sat for hours awaiting further orders and developments.

Just at the first break of dawn we heard the mausers of the Free Staters singing in the distance. There was no pause; it was continuous, and I knew that the brave Free Staters were carrying out their part of the program faithfully and well, because they had brave and dashing commandants and *veldtcornets*. Pretty soon we heard the mausers begin to sing right in front of us, and then we knew that the brave Pretoria Town boys were right at the English forts, yet it was not light enough for us to see them. Before we could see distinctly, the firing in front of us ceased, but with the Free Staters it continued as lively as ever.

Just before the sun peeped above the horizon, Long Tom on Bulwana, the guns on Lombard Kop, on Pepworth Hill and all the guns about Ladysmith sent shells whistling through the air. Everyone fired his gun when he pleased and where he pleased, although the night before it was ordered that the guns should be concentrated on someone point in due time to be named. The artillery boys were not to blame in the least, because they had not received any instructions. Now we saw about 150 of the Pretoria Town boys in a *sluit* about 100 yards from the English forts. They had tried to scale a high stone wall, and, failing, left four of their number dead at the foot of it and taken refuge in a *sluit* where we could now see them.

Only daring and fearless men would rush that fort and try to scale that twelve-foot wall. Our guns were now trained and turned loose on the forts just above the Pretoria boys. The English with five or six guns made a quick response, and for hours shells were flying back and forth with such rapidity that we were strongly reminded of our experience on Pepworth Hill. The Pretoria boys were in no danger, as long as we were firing, for the English had to keep themselves well protected. There was a Pretoria District Commando, about 700 strong, not more than 1,000 yards to our left. I mounted my horse and went to see them, for help was necessary. I found them lying under shade trees smoking their pipes and drinking coffee, as peacefully and unconcernedly as if there was no firing about Ladysmith. I told them of the position of the Pretoria Town boys, and tried to convince them that if they would turn out we would take the forts on the Rooirand. They simply answered that General Erasmus had told them that they would not be needed, and I rode back feeling disgusted.

General Erasmus had promised to support the Free Staters and the Pretoria Town boys, but instead of sending them any assistance, he went back about a mile out of danger, and left all to their fate. Some Transvaal Commandos had come up from the Tugela and partly taken the east side of the Platrand. They fought hard and bravely on the east, while the Free Staters who had captured some of the forts on the west side were still in possession, and almost engaged in a hand to hand fight with the English. They were constantly expecting re-enforcements promised by Erasmus, but none ever came. On our side we had simply an artillery duel, while on the east and west side of the Platrand the *burghers* continued hotly engaged in rifle fire at very close range for the whole day.

About four o'clock in the afternoon a terrific rain and hail storm fell upon us. We were ordered to pull down the guns and return to camp, regardless of the fact that the Pretoria Town boys were still held in the *sluit* by the English. The storm did not effect those on the Platrand, for the firing continued as heavy as ever. During this storm the Pretoria boys made a run for life and liberty, and although the English gave them a hot fire, all came out safely. It was not till late at night that the Free Staters and Transvaalers gave up all hope on the Platrand and returned to their camps. Everyone spent the next day in damning Erasmus, yet he was not dismissed, nor laid aside for reflection, because he was very wealthy, and belonged to one of the best families in the Transvaal. We had a heavy loss on that day, fifty being killed and 135 wounded. Of course the Free Staters were heavy losers. The English made a poor defence, and I feel sure that if Erasmus had sent his promised re-enforcements, the Platrand would have been taken, and of course that would have caused the immediate surrender of Ladysmith.

General White reported that he sent back eighty dead to the Boer lines. Another officer wrote that he counted 135 dead on the field. By just such official lying as this the British forces succeeded in killing off the entire Boer forces more than four times during the war, yet almost the entire Boer force was still alive at the end of the war. The military colleges of England must be special schools for turning out trained liars to command in the British army, otherwise the conduct of the British officer in his report of the battles, etc., of the Boer war is beyond my understanding. I have spoken very harshly of Erasmus, Meyer and Burger, but they eminently deserve all I have said. The bravest and the most daring of the Boer commanders will always find the rank and file ready to follow him, but not to lead him.

This statement will apply and prove equally true in all armies except the British, and it will not apply there, for the reason that there is such a wide chasm between the British officer and soldier, that the latter has neither respect for the former as an officer, nor confidence in him as such; consequently the British officer must drive the soldier into the fighting line. When once the British soldier has respect and confidence in his officer, he will follow him, without a murmur, into the very jaws of death. But I must here state one condition, and that is, that the British soldier who is ever ready to follow his respected officer must be either an Irishman or a Scotchman, for the Johnny proper, being degenerate, and no longer a warrior, does not believe in risking life for the off-chance of taking life.

Now I return to Buller and his army, and I see them making grand preparations to do something. I thought to myself that he had at last discovered the key, Längwani Hill, that alone would open the gates of the Boer lines, and lead him to Ladysmith, where many thousand starving people were praying for his coming. I was mistaken, for soon he and his whole army were seen coming around the bend of the Tugela towards Spion Kop. It was now evident to all that a big fight must take place to the west of Ladysmith, and in plain view of both besieger and besieged.

He pitched his camp behind what is known to the Boers as the *Bosch-rand*, a high, wooded mountain ridge that commanded all the hills on our side of the river. This river ran up to the very foot of the Bosch-rand, and then making a pretty sharp curve, wound its way back to the foot of the hills on our side. The river valley was perfectly flat and about 4,000 yards wide, and as the river wound its way through it, first touching the hills on one side and then on the other, it made a succession of U's. This was an ugly river, with steep, muddy banks, and as I looked at it and its beautiful valley, bounded by high hills, it reminded me of a great amphitheatre in which a few scattered Boers were to occupy the top seats, and a big English army the ring. Both the English and Boers were to be actors, and the gods above were alone to witness and judge one of the greatest, most exciting and destructive contests-at-arms of modern times, in which the Boers were destined to wear the crown of victory.

Buller's first attempt was to turn Botha's right, but after five days hard fighting he withdrew and fixed his attention on Spion Kop. General Botha had left only a guard of fifteen men on this *kop*, and in the very early morning of January 24th, a large force of Buller's men surprised them and drove them off. General Buller now had possession of the *kop*, and there was no valid reason why he and his big army should not march into Ladysmith with but little trouble or delay. But they didn't, and I will tell why they didn't.

General Buller had failed to get permission of a small band of Boer patriots who were near at hand. About ninety men of the Carolina Commando crawled up the kop, and, having reached the crest, immediately opened fire on the British force. Thus began the great battle, the bloody and disastrous Battle of Spion Kop. The ninety Boers were soon re-enforced by small detachments following each other up the *kop* until the total number reached about 250 men. The English held the *kop*, occupied the defences, and besides had at least fifteen men to every Boer.

Counting the Boers on the right and left sides of the *kop* who also took part in the fight, the total number of them engaged was about 600, but the actual number on the *kop*, who alone fought the big English force, was about 250 men. The Boers and the English were within easy point-blank range of each other, and at some points no more than fifty yards separated them. Here was the time, the place and the opportunity for the British to display that bold courage, that dash and fighting quality of which they have been boasting for centuries, for, with their overwhelming numbers, they would have easily swept that little handful of Boers off the *kop*. But they positively declined to take advantage of such conditions to display British pluck and courage, and, in the end, were themselves swept off. In their wars with the blacks, it had been their rule to hoist the Union Jack, boldly advance as at Khartoum, and when they discovered a horde of unarmed and defenceless negroes, make a mad rush, fall upon them and shoot them down; then apply the cold steel, and when they have murdered the last one and see him lying at their feet, with blood gurgling from his mouth, give three cheers for the Union Jack, and everyone at once apply for a Victoria Cross.

But on Spion Kop it was different, for no Union Jack was hoisted, no Union Jack brought to the battlefield, no rush was made, because a Boer was there, with a mauser in his hand—and that was a horse of another colour.—So the British halted and trembled, and then threw up the sponge and retreated as fast as their legs would take them, each hoping that he might escape the fatal bullet and receive his well deserved Victoria Cross. I may here add that when you find anyone so decorated with the Victoria Cross, you may generally put him down as a worthless son of a lord, or as a puny specimen of a puny, dissolute,

Good Englishmen after Spion Kop lying on the side hill.

diseased nobility, or the son of some moneyed, unscrupulous politician to whom the English Government must bow in obeisance. One in a thousand who has been decorated may deserve it, but I even have my doubts about that. Nearly all the officers and men of the British Army who have been given the Victoria Cross you will find in an English company's cigarette packages, and that is just where they belong. I shall not try to tell all that happened about Spion Kop, because every reader would cry out, "the same old story."

I must tell this, however; Buller's fifty or more cannon fairly tore the top off all our hills on both sides of Spion Kop, ploughed them up, pulverized them, and put them in perfect condition for sowing oats and planting mealies, but up to January 24th had killed only two Boers, an old man and his son, although more than 3000 lyddite shells had been fired. Joe Chamberlain and his pals made plenty of money that week, for tons of lyddite were consumed. The whole atmosphere was fairly laden with the yellow, sulphurous-looking lyddite fumes, and the Boers who finally emerged from their trenches looked like so many Chinamen. They were yellow about the eyes, nose, mouth and neck, and their clothes were yellow too; but when they washed their faces they were Boers again, and very lively ones at that.

The effect, and the only affect of Mr. Joe Chamberlain's lyddite fumes was to give the Carolina boys strength and courage enough to paralyze the Tommies as fast as they could show themselves on Spion Kop. This was a great blow to Mr. Chamberlain, because it meant a great future loss to him financially, for it disclosed the fact that lyddite in itself was very harmless; indeed, if any of Mr. Chamberlain's lyddite should, by accident, strike a Boer squarely in the chest, it is my honest opinion that that Boer would be put out of action; but, as is usually the case, if Mr. Chamberlain's lyddite shell should happen to miss the Boer by an inch or two, why, that Boer would be liable to drop more Tommies before that fight was over.

Louis Botha showed himself in great form, for he so placed his cannon and maxims that they could sweep the side hills and the Tugela Valley below Spion Kop, and, like a new broom, they made a clean sweep of everything. How that fight did rage during that whole day! It was heartrending to stand and watch the little band of heroic Boers face fifteen bullets for Everyone they could send; but bravely and unflinchingly they held their ground and won the admiration of the world. Spion Kop and the adjacent hills were in a shiver, convulsion after convulsion followed, as lyddite shell after lyddite shell penetrated and tore up the earth.

I must here mention that at one time during the struggle on the *kop*, the English felt that it was too hot for them, and naturally they hoisted three or four white flags. The Boers stopped firing at once, and four or five of them advanced to accept the surrender. Before reaching the defences, Colonel Thornycroft with re-enforcements arrived on the scene, hauled down the white flags and ordered the firing to recommence. The four or five Boers would have been shot down, had not the twenty-three English, who had already laid down their arms, accompanied them as they ran back to their lines. Fighting was now resumed and continued as if nothing had happened, until it grew too hot for the English again, and once more the white flags were hoisted. The Boers continued in their good work, regardless of the flags, and, as a result, the English are howling to this day about the Boers firing upon the white flags. If they hadn't fired upon them Everyone would have deserved being shot himself.

Time and time again during the war, the English would hoist the white flag for no other reason than to get the Boers to cease firing until they could get their own men in proper position, when they would declare that no one was authorized to hoist the white flag, and that the fighting must continue. The result was that after a time the Boer would not recognize the white flag, for he could no longer trust the English, and to surrender, the latter had to throw down their rifles, hold up their hands and advance towards the Boers. Although the English denounced this way of having to surrender as low, suspicious and cowardly, yet thousands upon thousands of them went through the formula before the war came to an end. It never occurred to them that the Boers were forced to adopt that precaution as a safeguard against treachery!

During the six days' fighting the Boers lost fifty killed and about 120 wounded. I don't know the British loss, but I hope that at some time during the twentieth century, the truth will leak out, and the number of the British killed and wounded become known. The top of the *kop* was covered with them; the sides of the *kop* and the Tugela Valley were also strewn with the dead and wounded, and the Boers were not curious enough to take the trouble to count them. The Boers requested the English to come and bury their dead, and the English, in reply, asked the Boers to bury them, and send them the bill. The gods might be able to make a comment to fit that bill, but earthly mortals would do well to hold their tongues. So I will pass on to General White and his inactivity.

More good Englishmen lying on the side hill.

CHAPTER 8

# White's Incapacity

Our investment circle was thirty-six miles in length, and at the time the Battle of Colenso was fought, was held by not more than 4,000 men. From Ladysmith to Colenso is about fifteen miles by the main road. By Colenso was General Buller with his army 35,000 strong. In Ladysmith was General White with his army 12,000 strong. Between these two armies was General Botha with his army less than 6,000 strong, including the investment forces south of Ladysmith. General Botha had, all told, ten guns. The two British forces had 150 guns. If, when Buller attacked at Colenso, December 15th, White had moved out with his whole forces to the south and attacked at the same time, the Boers would have been swamped in a few hours, and most of them would have been captured, for there was no way out of it except by Ladysmith, and, besides, they would have lost all their guns.

On January 24th, the same conditions prevailed, except that there were no mountains between Ladysmith and Spion Kop, and the intervening distance was about eighteen miles. Spion Kop is plainly visible from all parts around Ladysmith. The Boer force on the west side of Ladysmith was less than 1,000 strong. Had General White moved out with his entire force and fifty guns, he could have marched to Spion Kop almost without interruption. What did he do on both occasions when he should have been up and doing, if he wished to join Buller, see Ladysmith relieved, and the Boer forces captured and destroyed? Why, he and his 12,000 men simply lay in their holes and silently prayed for Buller's success.

When all the conditions are considered, it must be plain to the most simple minded that General White deserved to be forever buried in utter disgrace, but, instead, he was congratulated, promoted, and dined by his queen for his gallantry and success in nearly starving to death some 15,000 soldiers, women and children in Ladysmith. On both of these memorable days the Boers around Ladysmith were all on needles and pins, for they fully expected White and his army to move out, and they knew that if he did it would be impossible for them to prevent a union with Buller, and the consequent destruction of the Boer forces in Natal.

While General Botha was fighting the Battles of Colenso and Spion Kop, Commandant-General Joubert remained at his headquarters by Ladysmith, and on the first of these occasions I remember hearing him say:

> No, General White will not make any attempt to unite with General Buller, because he has been defeated so often, that both he and his men are thoroughly cowed and will be satisfied to remain concealed, and fervently hope for Buller's success.

As it turned out, he proved to be perfectly correct in his surmises.

About ten days after Spion Kop, February 5th, another attempt was made to break through our lines at Vaal Krantz, by about 3,500 men and several batteries. To oppose these was General Viljoen with less than 100 men. An exciting, hot fight ensued, and, wonderful to say, the English forces retired, recrossed the river, and made no further attempt to accomplish anything in the vicinity of Spion Kop. During the fight General Viljoen with two or three men took a desperate chance to save a pom-pom from capture. Under a terrific rifle fire, they hauled the pom-pom across a long flat, and then turned it on the English with great effect. Neither he, nor his men, nor any of the horses were touched, yet all passed through a perfect shower of bullets. In this fight at Vaal Krantz, the Irish Brigade lost three of its bravest, noblest and most patriotic men: Pat Fahey, Mat Brennen and Jim Lasso. They fell as the most advanced men, and they will ever be remembered most affectionately by the Irish boys.

Now I come to the final struggle at Ladysmith, when that awful hole was relieved, and the Boer forces retreated to the Biggarsberg Mountains, eighteen miles back on the road to Dundee.

To meet Buller, General Botha withdrew all his forces from Spion Kop and vicinity, and put them in their old positions in front of Colenso. As to whether General Buller really discovered that Langwani Hill was the key to our positions, or tumbled on to it by accident, I do not know, but, certain it was, that he was intent on getting

GENERAL BEN VILJOEN

possession of this hill, by making a flank attack on our extreme left. Langwani Hill was on Buller's side of the river, and once our left was turned, we could no longer hold it. It was not till February 18th that General Buller brought fifteen or sixteen batteries to play upon the Boer positions. It would prove tedious to describe the ten days of terrible fighting that preceded the relief of Ladysmith; so I will simply speak of it in a general way.

Buller finally succeeded in turning the Boers' left, and so Langwani Hill was abandoned, but not until the English had suffered severely. At Pieters Hill, Groblers Kloof, and the neighbouring hills where the Boers were well placed by General Botha, the hardest fighting took place. In the struggle to force the Boers from their positions, the English were driven back repeatedly to the river, although then numbers were about twenty-five to one against ours. Their dead and wounded ran well into the hundreds at each attempt, and on two or three occasions were allowed to remain as they had fallen on the open *veldt*, during the whole night, to suffer and die. The English have little or no regard for their dead and wounded, as I will in time to come show. In all these advances the English shells were constantly bursting among their own men and were directly responsible for many of their own dead and wounded.

Three Irish regiments were always placed in front, and these were supported by English regiments who kept safely in the background. As on previous occasions, some Irish regiments had surrendered after making a slight resistance. I believe, and hundreds of others believe, that the English deliberately and intentionally made the "mistake" of firing their shells into the Irish regiments, to drive them on and force them to take the entrenched positions from the Boers. This was not the first tune, nor was it the last tune that they made a mistake of this kind, and in every case it was the Irish who were chosen to suffer. Twice during these first five days of fighting, the good General Botha had granted an armistice to Buller to be used in caring for his dead and wounded, but these were woefully neglected and advantage taken to make better dispositions of his troops.

It is just as much of a latter-day Englishman's nature to be treacherous as it is for an American Indian to be suspicious. Every repulse was followed on the next day by another advance. The heavy lyddite shells kept continually pounding the hills, tearing off their very tops and filling the air with smoke and stones; yet the brave Boers remained unmoved in their positions, and kept up their deadly fire on the advancing Irish regiments. Each day's work was practically a repetition of the preceding one, until the 27th of February, when there was a great change. The Boers had now lain in the mud and water that half filled their trenches and, without relief and without food, fought incessantly for ten days till, being weary and worn and completely exhausted, they reluctantly left their positions and began their retreat.

The famous Krugersdorp Commando under Kemp held Pieter's Hill to the very last moment, and no one about Ladysmith, be he Boer or English, will ever forget the wonderful stand made by those 400 patriots against Buller's whole army and 100 guns. It is perfectly certain that every man of them accounted for at least one Tommie before the final retreat.

On the 28th, Ladysmith was relieved, and the Boers went back to the Biggarsberg Mountains. General White in Ladysmith could plainly see a line of wagons fifteen miles long, yet he made no move to delay or capture them. Worn out and exhausted as the Boers really were, I do not believe that Buller would have been successful in relieving Ladysmith had they not received the report of General Cronje's surrender at Paardeberg on the 27th. This news was deeply felt, and it so thoroughly discouraged the Boers that they lost heart and left positions without orders, which they could have easily continued to hold. To relieve General White and his 12,000 skeletons, General Buller had exploded hundreds of tons of Mr. Chamberlain's lyddite and lost as many men as he succeeded in relieving.

Mr. Chamberlain was a big winner, the English heavy losers, and the Tugela Valley is now renowned as an Irish graveyard. A few more wars like the South African would settle all of Ireland's many troubles, because the Irish would all be laid under the sod. How strange it is that a people who have fought against England's tyranny for centuries to secure their freedom, and are still fighting for the same end, will voluntarily join with their old and detested oppressor to deprive another people of their liberty, knowing, too, as they must, that in every instance they weaken themselves and strengthen their old enemy.

Yet, this is exactly what the Irish have done, and I have no sympathy for those who are today, (1903), sleeping in the Tugela Valley as a result of their own voluntary acts.

During a terrific rain storm on the night of the 27th, and in the very eyes of Buller's army on one side and White's on the other, our Irish boys were the chief instruments in pulling down Long Tom from the top of Bulwana Kop. It was fearful and exasperating work, and it was not until two o'clock in the morning that our large gun safely landed at the foot of the *kop* and started on its way to Elandslaagte. General Botha was near at hand with some 300 or 400 men, but he could have offered little or no resistance had an attempt been made to capture the gun.

Our hundreds of wagons, with all our cannon and maxims, were hauled through heavy mud and across an open flat for twenty miles, and safely landed in the Biggarsberg Mountains, and that, too, in the very presence and before the eyes of an English army of 45,000 trained officers and men, who never moved an inch in our direction.

Quite a cavalry force came out of Ladysmith, but when a few of the Irish boys opened fire on them, they all turned and fled back to town. The English should have captured all our wagons and cannon, and would have done it, too, had they known anything about their business. Buller and White together could have easily trained 150 cannon on us and forced us to abandon everything, but they seemed satisfied to stop just where they were, and, no doubt, congratulated themselves that the Boers had escaped without doing them further damage. Sometime before the relief of Ladysmith, the Free State Commandos had left and gone to meet Lord Roberts, who was advancing towards Bloemfontein; so it was only the Transvaal Commandos who took up positions in the Biggarsberg Mountain passes.

As the English had a big force on the Tugela River, about eighteen miles in front of Helpmakaar, the Irish Brigade was ordered to go to Helpmakaar and hold them back. Should the English get hold of this place, our positions in the Biggarsberg would no longer be tenable, for the line of retreat to Laing's Nek would then be seriously threatened. We found the Piet Retief Commando there, but about four miles behind the position it should have occupied. We learned, on questioning the officers, that it was too dangerous a place for Piet Retief men, and they would not risk a stand there. We then went and had a look for ourselves, and we decided that 200 men in the position could easily prove a match for any 5000 Englishmen who might come, so we were satisfied to try our luck. It was the strongest position for defence that I had yet seen, for it was impossible to flank it; and to take it, the attacking force had to come along one road, and the distance from the foot of this steep mountain to the top was at least two miles. The English knew that position and that mountain, and never made any effort to take it during our month's residence there.

In the month of April, I received word from Pretoria that about

1,000 Irish and Irish-Americans had arrived at Delagoa Bay, on their way to join my brigade. I was in great glee on receiving this long expected news, and lost no time in going to Pretoria, not only to meet them, but to prepare for them a red hot time with the English. I arranged with the President and Executive Council, to recall the brigade from Helpmakaar, bring it to Elandsfontein, where I would join it with something like a thousand Irish-Americans, and all proceed to Fourteen Streams, where I knew there would be some interesting fighting. Having done this, I at once took the train to Middleburg where I would meet the good boys from free America.

I was thoroughly convinced that the Irish and Irish-Americans were intent on doing something good for down-trodden Ireland by proving that England's difficulty was Ireland's opportunity. My hopes were high, and all sort of plans and schemes were passing through my mind when the steam whistle announced that I was in Middleburg. Here I found that the long expected boys would arrive on the following morning. The whole town learned of their coming, and all turned out to greet them. Finally came what I at first supposed to be the advance guard, the American Ambulance Corps of fifty-eight men from Chicago and Massachusetts. They were warmly received with the shouts and hurrahs of the assembled multitude.

When I found time to breathe I asked when the fighters would arrive. The answer was "We are the fighters! No more coming that we know off." Now I felt so thoroughly disappointed that I made up my mind to drop dead on the spot, but was saved from such a terrible ordeal by the idea suddenly occurring to me that possibly others would soon follow. I long lived in hope, but only to be disappointed in the end, for no more ever came.

Later on I will give the reasons, for I have since learned just what the trouble was. I was genuinely glad to see the Irish boys, and from them learned that it was through the efforts of my trusted old Arizona friend, Colonel John F. Finerty, of Chicago, and my new and most highly esteemed friend, Patrick J. Judge, of Holyoke, Mass., that sufficient money was raised by private subscriptions to equip thoroughly the Ambulance Corps of fifty-eight men and land them in the Transvaal.

It was not the fault of those two patriotic Irishmen that 100,000 Irish and Irish-Americans were not sent to South Africa to assist that little handful of Boer patriots in their struggle with the mighty British Empire for liberty and independence. In due time I will put the fault just where it belongs. The Boers had enough ambulance corps, so the Chicago and Massachusetts boys removed their red cross chevrons and, after being well equipped as fighting men, we all went to Johannesburg to join the boys of the old brigade who had just arrived from Helpmakaar. Having met, what a rollicking, joyful good time all these jolly Irish boys had!

CHAPTER 9

# The Fighting in the Free State

Our orders for Fourteen Streams were countermanded and we were instructed to proceed to Brandfort in the Free State. We took the train without delay and went on our way rejoicing. On reaching Smaldeel, a small station thirty miles from Brandfort, we were ordered to stop and wait for instructions; so we pitched our camp and put everything in readiness for a hot time, for we learned that Lord Roberts and his army of 90,000 men were advancing from Bloemfontein. Before our new arrivals receive their baptismal fire I will relate what had taken place in the Free State while we were engaged at Ladysmith.

During the month of November while we were in daily skirmishes with the English, who were trying to find a way of escape, there was heavy fighting south of Kimberley. Unfortunately we had there one thoroughly incompetent commander, General Prinsloo, of the Free State. General Prinsloo had most excellent *commandants* and *veldcornets*, anyone of whom would have made every fight a victory in those parts. General de la Rey was with Prinsloo, but the latter had higher rank, much to our regret. General de la Rey is a remarkable man and the Napoleon of the South African War. In due time I will give a short account of this great and good man and the deeds he accomplished.

Generals Prinsloo and de la Rey, with their combined force of some 2,000 men and, I think, two guns and two maxim Nordenfelts, were attacked on November 23rd by Lord Methuen with a force of 10,000 to 12,000 men and two or three batteries, together with several maxims. Of course Lord Methuen had an overwhelming force as compared to that of the Boers, yet, had Prinsloo acted with General de la Rey, the British would have suffered a severe defeat.

Prinsloo left his position just at the moment of victory, and, by so doing, came near getting General de la Rey and his men captured.

GENERAL LORD ROBERTS, F. M.
Notorious for destroying women and children and for helplessness when confronted with an armed foe.

They had actually to fight their way out. The republican forces fell back to Rooilaagte in the direction of Kimberley. Here the *burghers* to some extent fortified themselves, and awaited the arrival of Methuen. He, with his re-enforced army appeared and opened up their batteries on the Boer positions in the early morn of November 25th. A very hard and bloody battle was fought here, and it was Prinsloo again who gave way at the wrong moment and allowed Methuen to credit himself with another victory.

Prinsloo was always bent on giving way just at the wrong time, much to the disappointment and disgust of General de la Rey, and this, too, in the face of the fact that General de la Rey always took the brunt and did the hardest fighting. The world now has read Methuen's reports of these fights and the Boer reports too, so it is only necessary for me to say that the former's losses were exceedingly heavy, while those of the latter were exceedingly small. Judging by the losses, Methuen was badly defeated in both instances, but an English officer does not care how many men are shot dead so long as he does not lose a gun or have to retreat. To show the true character of this lordly Methuen, I will say that every low and beastly epithet his vulgar imagination could invent, he applied to the enemy, that he might excuse himself for shooting some twenty or thirty Boers, some of them wounded, whom he had captured. Of course he must add another lie, English-like, by claiming the abuse of the white

Now the time was ripe for the Boers to begin to shoot in retaliation the British officers and soldiers at Pretoria, who were spending their time playing football, etc. But the Boer is strictly governed by his religion, and the whole world could not induce him to resort to retaliation under any circumstances. I longed to be in chief command just for a few hours, but, fortunately for many British, I was not. The Boers were convinced that Lord Methuen would receive his punishment on the Day of Judgment, and I was just as thoroughly convinced that I did not believe in such long postponements in dealing with Englishmen.

The Boers fell back from Rooilaagte to Modder River, not many miles from Kimberley. Here Generals Prinsloo and de la Rey were re-enforced by the long expected General Piet Cronje, with about 500 men. He had come all the way from Mafeking on the western border of the Transvaal, but, tired as he and his men were, they were all ready and game for fight. Before Cronje's arrival, General de la Rey had practically assumed command over General Prinsloo, and placed the

Boer forces in position on the Modder River to give Methuen and his army another fight. On his arrival, General Cronje, being known to be the best fighter in the land, was given command over all the Boer forces. He looked over the ground and having thoroughly approved in every detail the dispositions of the men that General de la Rey had made, he calmly awaited the arrival of Methuen. Lord Methuen will never forget the Battle of Modder River, and hundreds of his men will never remember it.

The English were then and are now, (as at time of first publication), as afraid of General Cronje, as a baboon is of a snake, and I might say here, that if you bring a baboon in contact with a snake, dead or alive, and prevent him from running away, he will actually have a spasm. Methuen did not find out, however, until it was too late, that Cronje was there, for otherwise he would have asked for something like 20,000 men additional. Finally the 28th of November came, and there was Methuen and his army.

After carrying out his usual program of bombarding for several hours, Methuen advanced his lines, and the rifle firing began. After hours of terrific fighting, during which Cronje and de la Rey had unmercifully slaughtered, and in the end driven back the English, and during which time the Free Staters, too, had covered themselves with glory, and just at the moment when a great victory was really won, General Prinsloo suddenly withdrew his men and allowed the English to turn his flank. He seemed to be afraid to win a victory, and it is a marvel that General Cronje or General de la Rey did not shoot him or drive him to his home and put one of his thoroughly competent commandants in his place. The result of this sudden withdrawal was that the Boer forces had to fall back, and now we find them at Magersfontein.

> As Methuen had made but slow progress in killing Boers in honourable fight on the battlefield, he now gave way to his savage inclination and had some twenty or thirty wounded Boers whom he found in a farmhouse near the battlefield, deliberately shot in cold blood.

Of course Methuen had seen his men fall by the hundred, and no doubt he was highly enraged at the sight, but it requires a brute to deliberately take the lives of helpless, wounded men, and, in my experience with the brute creation, which is considerable, I am sure that there are exceedingly few brutes that would do such a thing. Even the sneaking hyena would refrain unless he were dying of hunger. Now Lord Methuen had learned that Cronje was on deck, and in the best of health, so he called for all the re-enforcements at hand and brought up his decimated force to something like 15,000 men and six batteries. Cronje was lucky too, and increased his force to something more than 4,000, but not much more. Methuen's were all trained and tried men, and, as the English would put it, invincible; Cronje had his ordinary farmers who knew nothing whatever about military training. No doubt Methuen did lots of thinking, but I do not believe he called any council of war, because he is too conceited and arrogant to do such a thing. He who deigns to make a suggestion to a lord is very liable to be sent away and told to attend to his own business.

Although he is supremely arrogant, I think he did some shaking in his boots because he knew that Cronje was in front. For several days after his terrible smash-up on Modder River, Methuen spent his time in recuperating and awaiting re-enforcements. Cronje and de la Rey spent their time in preparing for a fight at Magersfontein. In front of the ridge on which they concealed their small guns and maxims they put the Boers to work digging a trench. The trench being finished, it was so well concealed that the English could not see it. They knew that this scheme would work, because Methuen would not think of sending out any reconnoitring parties to find out just how the Boers were to make their fight. He would tell you that it was unnecessary because he had a balloon, and from that balloon he could see the Boers far behind their actual, but unknown to him position. The Boers were not in the trenches by day, but were far behind them. At night you could find everyone of them there, and in perfect readiness for battle.

CHAPTER 10

# Magersfontein and Paardeberg

At last the day came. It was Dec. 10th when Methuen and his big army came up and without delay began with their usual introduction, by turning six batteries upon the supposed position of the Boer force. For two days this formidable array of field and lyddite guns continued to roar and keep the very heavens filled with heavy steel shells that tore up the earth generally. No reply was sent back from any part of Cronje's lines, so Lord Methuen alone can lay claim to making all that deafening noise that so frightened birds and beasts during the 10th and 11th; but when you say noise, you have the sum total of the work accomplished by his vigorous display of fireworks.

It was in the very early morning of the 12th, that Lord Methuen decided that the fearful Cronje and his "dirty" Boers were either demolished or so terribly demoralized that they had fled for safety miles to their rear, because he had not heard a murmur from them for two days. Any man with a little grain of sense would, at least at this early hour in the morning, have sent in advance a well extended line of skirmishers to find out if the enemy were near at hand or had actually fled. No; this way of doing business would never meet with the approval of an English lord who had, by the accident of birth, inherited the brains of all past generations in his family line; so he moved his lines forward in close order.

When Methuen's lines arrived within about seventy-five yards of Cronje's trenches, the demolished or absconded "dirty" Boers sent a greeting in the form of a long, dazzling line of fire, which instantly died away, and with it General Wauchope and almost his entire Black Watch, the crack regiment of the English army. Never in all history was such a bloody and disastrous battle fought and won in such a short time. Methuen's men, one and all, regardless of orders or order, fled as fast as their legs could carry them, and the Boers did not fail to apply the whip and spur at every stride they made. Although the battle was now virtually over, yet some hard fighting took place during the day. Methuen could not reconcile himself to his most disastrous and disgraceful defeat at the hands of such a small force of Boers, so spent the greater part of the day in losing more before he finely concluded that he would have to return to his old camp on Modder River.

It is not my purpose to give long descriptions of battles in this narrative, for I know they are tiresome, but, painful to me as it may be, I must say something of that little band of Scandinavians who were with Cronje in that great victory. I knew personally almost Everyone of that band of sixty men. The Scandinavian is quiet, gentlemanly, and the most tractable soldier in camp, but the most daring, reckless and fearless soldier I have ever seen, when it comes to fighting. Not satisfied with the early morning's work, this little body moved out, on its own account, after the sun was well up, and deliberately attacked Methuen's army. They actually engaged a force of at least fifteen to one against them, and fought till they were practically exterminated as a body. Sure it is that each one of that reckless little band accounted for at least one Englishman before he forfeited his own life.

Having practically wiped them out, the English set to work to rob and strip them, and punch their bodies full of holes. General Cronje captured a small bunch of prisoners during the day, but sent them to Pretoria to play football. Early in the afternoon, Methuen, having satisfied himself that he had murdered enough of his own men, decided to retreat, and did so, but at a much more rapid pace than he had expected, for now Cronje's guns were turned upon him, and induced him to move more rapidly, and quickly vanish in the distance. Here was a fearful slaughter of English, the greatest so far during the war, but only because this great battle was fought just three days before that of Colenso, near Ladysmith, where General Louis Botha so terribly defeated General Buller and his fine army.

After Lord Methuen reached his old camp on Modder River, I have an idea that he did some really hard thinking, for he must make a report, and in that report he must show that his defeat was a victory, because a lord cannot be defeated. Unfortunately, I have never seen his report, but it is safe to conclude that he saw the Boers in overwhelming numbers and that some Colonial had proved traitor to him and led him into an ambush. I merely mention this as a guess, because it is the usual method adopted by the British officer to hide his incapacity. Methuen's soldiers are not through to this day damning him for his conduct in this battle, but we all know that soldiers' words are but naught in England when a lord speaks. It is an awful shame, but very true.

Methuen returned to his old camp fully convinced that he had had enough. He had no desire to try his luck again against Cronje and he never did. Cronje stopped just where he was for several weeks, looking for another advance of Methuen, or some other English army. He did not care how many came, for he was there to fight. I must say this about General Cronje that he may be thoroughly understood. He is stubbornness itself, will take advice from no one, is absolutely fearless, and constantly craves a fight with the English. I do not believe the world's history can show his equal as a commandant, but as a general he is an absolute failure. He must have someone over him, and under no circumstances must he be allowed to command. Order him to take a *kopje*, and he is sure to take it. Order him to hold a position, and he is sure to hold it. Order him to retreat, and he will do it. But put him in supreme command, and the combined influence of the immortal gods could not induce him to retreat, it matters not what the odds against him, or what the circumstances might be. Every drop of blood that courses through his body literally burns with patriotism, and of the whole Africander race I believe that General Piet Cronje would be the first to step forward and lay down his life for the freedom and independence of his people.

But I must say of General Cronje that he is a man wrapped up in his own conceit. He considered himself the only great fighter in South Africa, and, when captured, he is the very man to say that the Boers should surrender because the great Cronje can no longer lead them. In this respect he is a fool, but fools often become wise men by experience. If I should hear that General Cronje was condemning his fellow countrymen for prolonging the war after his capture, I should not be surprised, because he is so eaten up with his own importance.

Such is the man, General Piet Cronje, and may he live long, and have, as a commandant, one more crack at the British, and then I think all will be well for South Africa!

After the Battle of Magersfontein, General de la Rey was sent to Colesberg to take command of the forces against General French. General Piet De Wet and General Schoeman had been fighting French daily, and had been gradually driven back to their strong defensive position at Colesberg. The Boer forces were about 2,500 strong, but were divided into small commands in order to guard a wide extent of country. General French had only 15,000 men and thirty guns, so he made but small progress in his advance on Colesberg. The Boers hotly contested every inch of ground, and almost Everyone of the little commands did some daring work. Early in January, General de la Rey arrived and at once assumed command. Hot skirmishes were now the general order of the day all along the lines, and on January 25th, west of Colesberg, General de la Rey had made it so warm for him, that, instead of continuing to advance, General French[1] changed his mind and retreated. De la Rey followed him, but never came in touch with him again because he had left for Cape Town. It seems that after the Battle of Magersfontein, Lord Roberts became much frightened at the presence of Cronje and called for help.

French was ordered to report to him at once, and left early in January to help Roberts out of his troubles. General Clements took French's place, but could do no better than his predecessor against de la Rey. On February 11th, the Battle of Slingersfontein was fought. It lasted for many hours and was stubbornly contested by both sides, but in the end de la Rey proved too much for him, and General Clements fled to Arundel, forgetting to take his camp with him. The *burghers* were hungry and thirsty and this camp amply satisfied all their wants. General de la Rey was now directed to return to the Modder River and co-operate with General Cronje against General Roberts and his mighty army. During his short period of operating about Colesberg he had captured some 500 prisoners, driven French's army back and made good his record of never having been defeated.

In a few weeks after Magersfontein, General Cronje saw that the British were appearing in thousands in all directions, and he finally made up his mind to move his little command to Paardeberg. His very stubbornness prevented his moving earlier, but he was satisfied. He saw that he was being gradually but surely surrounded by an enormous army, yet he never quailed. He was begged by such patriots and great and competent generals as Christian De Wet, de la Rey, Phillip Botha and even Com.-Gen. Joubert, of the Transvaal, to get out of the ring nearly completed about him while he had an opportunity. He utterly ignored all of them, practically told them to go to Hades, and silenced them, for he was there to fight, and was going to fight. He did fight, and can history show anything to compare with it?

---

1. *French's Cavalry Campaign: a Special Corresponent's View of British Army Mounted Troops During the Boer War* by J. G. Maydon also published by Leonaur.

I am not going into the details of this nine days' fight, but will give the main features and the result. Here was a common, ordinary farmer, without any military training or education, in command of a little more than 4,000 equally untrained farmers, and four or five old Krupp guns. With him were a great number of refugee Boer women and children, who had come to him for protection against the insults and outrages of the British soldiery. Sad to relate, this is the actual truth, yet we still hear Anglo-Americans speaking of the civilized English. Opposed to him was the very flower of the English Empire. There were Lord Roberts, Lord Kitchener, General Kelly-Kenny, that able commander, Hector MacDonald, General French and many other stars of the British army. Altogether they had some 50,000 men around General Cronje. These men were all tried military men, trained and educated. Besides, Lord Roberts had 120 cannon, field guns and lyddite guns.

The British may tell you that there were mountains there higher than Mount Everest, but believe me, there are no mountains there whatever. General Cronje and his little band of patriots were on the banks of the Modder River, where infantry, cavalry and artillery could manoeuvre without any difficulty. It was, I think, on the 18th of February that Roberts began with all his guns to bombard Cronje. Almost continually for nine days, 120 cannon were busy trying to destroy that little band of patriots. Once Lord Kitchener thought he would play a Khartoum act. He recalled the time when he charged upon and murdered some 10,000 to 15,000 unarmed negroes at Khartoum, and saw no reason why he could not do the same thing with 4,000 Boers.

He forgot that the negroes were armed only with sticks, while the Boers had mausers. He advanced boldly, had hundreds and hundreds of his men slaughtered, and then fled as rapidly as he could. After the battle had been raging for two or three days, General Cronje asked for an armistice to bury his dead. Lord Roberts positively refused. During the whole war the Boers never once denied the English an armistice for that purpose, although they knew that the English, in every instance, took advantage of it to strengthen their position. There is a wide difference between a Boer savage and a civilized Englishman. Give me the former, but deliver me from the latter!

As Roberts had captured Cronje's ambulance wagons and would not allow any doctor to go and attend to his wounded, and as he was not permitted to bury his dead, of course, the condition of the camp became such that the women and children could not endure it; and

GENERAL LORD KITCHENER
One who believes that the only way to establish permanent peace in South Africa is to destroy the Boer women and children.

the Boers too were suffering on account of it, so Cronje's *commandants* and *veldcornets* forced him to hoist the white flag on February 27th. The battle was over and Lord Roberts had Cronje and his 4,000 men as prisoners of war. No doubt General Cronje would have been shot had there not been about 750 British officers and 4,000 soldiers as prisoners of war in Pretoria. This alone saved the old patriot's life, and we all know it.

On receiving the first news of the capture of the great Cronje and his army by the wonderful Lord Roberts, Commander-in-Chief, A. B. C. D. E., etc., all London took a holiday, went crazy mad, and the papers put out their posters showing that Cronje with 15,000 or 20,000 or 30,000 "dirty" Boers had been captured. When they finally learned that Cronje had only 4,000 men against Lord Robert's big army, all slunk their heads and retired to their homes. What Lord Roberts considered his greatest victory the world at large considered his greatest defeat.

What the English losses were we do not know, and I know that the English people do not know either, for Mr. Chamberlain says that the death lists are not yet completed. If the complete returns are ever made known, I think we shall see that Roberts had as many men put out of action as Cronje had in his command. General Cronje had about seventy men killed and about three times that number wounded.

I will now go to Stormberg and Aliwal North, the two really most important points on the Free State border, for here was the easy and natural way for the English to reach Bloemfontein.

At the beginning of the war the English occupied and well fortified Stormberg, and this was the only sensible thing they did. After a few weeks occupation, they, for some reason unknown to me, abandoned this position and fell back to Molteno. Of course the Boers lost no time in taking possession of the good work the English had done and abandoned. Generals Olivier and Grobler were there, and old General Hendrik Schoeman was near at hand. Schoeman was a fraud and afterwards joined the English to be blown up by a supposed empty lyddite shell in his home in Pretoria while engaged in a plot with others against his people.

That empty shell had a little lyddite caked in the bottom, and Schoeman, having struck a match and lighted his pipe, threw the still burning match into the empty shell. An explosion followed, tearing out the side of the building, killing Schoeman, another traitor by the name of Van Der Merwe, and Schoeman's daughter, and seriously wounding old man Viljoen. This proves that it is a good thing for traitors to make useful souvenirs of empty lyddite shells. It was a source of regret to all, however, that Miss Schoeman should have entered the room just as the explosion took place, and lost her life.

Both Grobler and Olivier were good officers and did good work. The total Boer force was less than a thousand with which they had to oppose General Gatacre and 3,000 men. Besides, Gatacre had six or eight cannon, as well as several maxims. Few shots were fired by either side until the 10th of December, when General Gatacre attacked. The fighting was very hot while it lasted, but it did not continue long before Gatacre saw his little army cut into pieces, and in a rapid and disorderly retreat to Molteno. In addition to his severe loss in dead and wounded, two cannon and over 600 of his men were taken. Before this battle all the English and Colonial papers were full of the wonderful deeds and the great capacity of this distinguished soldier, General Gatacre, and it was certain that he would make a skip to Stormberg and then a jump and land in Bloemfontein, leaving nothing but dead Boers behind him.

The British officer is a wonderful genius on paper, but a very weak sister on the battlefield. General Gatacre did a great deal in this district towards the ultimate independence of South Africa; for the number of men he arrested, charged as spies and then shot, is very great, and all their names are dearly cherished in the hearts of the Africanders. This battle finished the great Gatacre; at any rate, we never heard of him again during the war.

CHAPTER 11

# De Wet Looms Up

Now we will go to the western border of the Transvaal and see what has been done at Mafeking. No one ever displayed any interest in Mafeking, yet some skirmishing and letter writing was going on daily. General Snyman commanded the Boers and Baden-Powell the English. Mafeking is situated in an open flat dotted with a few small hills here and there. Baden-Powell dug holes and put his men and some women in them. They lived like prairie dogs. He had three or four years' supply of good ammunition, and there was no reason why he should not have been happy and contented. He laid big mines, but they never caught anyone. He loaded cars with dynamite and tried to explode them among the Boers, but he always failed. He would make bold attacks, lose a lot of men, then run back, crawl into his hole, and write a long letter complaining of ill-treatment. So it went on from day to day until the place was relieved. Captain Eloff had the place taken once, but old Snyman failed to come up with his 300 men, so the brave Eloff was left alone and captured. Snyman had given his solemn word to Eloff that he would not fail him.

Of all of the many utterly worthless generals the Boers had at the beginning of the war, I am sure that Snyman was the worst, and I am not certain that he would be a success at herding sheep. After Baden-Powell was released from Mafeking, we heard but little more about him as a fighting man. Judging by the volume of insane letters that he wrote while imprisoned, it is easy to conclude that he had at least two screws loose in his head. Many of the constabulary police we captured told us that although Baden-Powell was nominally in command, yet he never exercised any authority over them.

"Every little while," they said, "he would have to go home for private treatment because there was something wrong about his head."

GENERAL DE WET

I fully believe this, for the papers would announce his departure for London on account of sickness, and, after a three or four months' absence we would see him in some of the London illustrated papers togged up in great style, with a huge Texas *sombrero* on his head, the loose flowing cowboy shirt, trousers to match, and a very tall pair of top boots. Then it was that he intended to return. To be shot—with a camera—is his greatest delight, and to write foolish letters is his hobby.

After all, General Baden-Powell, there were worse specimens than you in the English Army during the war, and there are still many worse specimens in that same army today,(1903), many of whom hold higher rank than you. When I say that you have two screws loose in your head, I may be doing you a good service in the eyes of humanity, for you know that you armed several hundred *kaffirs* and had them with you in Mafeking, and that several hundred of the British-armed *kaffirs* outside of Mafeking murdered many old Boer men, women and children in their homes, who took no part in the war. No sane man, no honourable man, no true soldier would resort to such beastly methods to outdo his ten-fold weaker foe. In fact nobody but a Britisher would be guilty of such infamous conduct. Colonel Plumer with his mixed command of regulars and volunteers north of Mafeking and on the northern boundary of the Transvaal came so near doing nothing, that I will pass him by and give some of the reasons why the Boers laid siege to Ladysmith, Kimberley and Mafeking.

I admit that I cannot give a good one, for I don't believe there is one. However, the Boer officers generally thought it the best thing to do. Commandant-General Joubert told me that he thought that by holding Ladysmith closely invested, General White would soon consent to a surrender, and thereby save much bloodshed. The idea of killing people was repulsive to him, and, furthermore, he could see no reason for it. We could easily have gone to Maritzburg and then to Durban before Buller arrived, and at the same time held General White's line of communication.

This would actually have put General White in a worse predicament than he was in at Ladysmith. He could have done nothing, for all bridges and the railway behind would be destroyed and our total force was as large as his by the fifth of November. Once the Boers had seized Maritzburg, General White could have done nothing. It was all in our hands, and besides we would have received several thousand recruits from the Natal Boers. For no other reason except to save life was Ladysmith besieged.

Kimberley could have easily been taken, but here another factor came in. To take the place, all the Boers had to do was to destroy De Aar Junction, the supply depot there, and the branch line to Kimberley. Having done this, the next step was to proceed on the Cape Railway line and destroy it. The English could have done nothing without these lines, and Kimberley would have fallen without one shot being fired. But President Steyn prevented this because it put the Dutch Cape Ministry in a bad dilemma. This ministry was friendly to the Boers and no doubt wished them every success, but had the Boers proceeded as I have suggested, the British Government would have charged the ministry with treasonable conduct. So De Aar Junction and all the railway lines were allowed to remain in good order for the use of Lord Roberts and his army. The Boers in their every act were always swayed by their love of justice and humanity, and were always ready to sacrifice themselves in order to do good to others.

It was a vital mistake they made, and I repeatedly told them so, because they knew, and I knew, that the liberty and independence of their land were at stake. I used to beg General Joubert to throw the whole force of the Boers in the Free State into Cape Colony and destroy all bridges and railway lines, for I knew, if this was done, we would get 15,000 or 20,000 recruits in Cape Colony, and the English could never then push their way across the Orange River. But the good, humane General Joubert would never consent to do anything that might cause trouble for his friends in Cape Town. I respected him for the stand he took; in fact, I admired and loved him for it; but it was not business in dealing with such an unscrupulous enemy as Great Britain.

Ladysmith and Kimberley were practically relieved on the same day, February 27th, and a few days afterwards followed the relief of Mafeking. To lay siege to Mafeking was positively foolish, and had the Boers allowed General Baden-Powell to come out, why, they would have had him and all his men in Pretoria for their Christmas dinner at President Krüger's expense. Mafeking was of little or no importance to either party in the war, so long as the English were not permitted to cross the Orange River, and they never could have crossed or reached the Orange River if all the bridges and railways in Cape Colony had been destroyed. The Karoo, a wide desert, must first be crossed, and no large army would dare make the venture of crossing.

The way the English managed their transportation, and the food they furnished to the soldier, would have sufficed to kill half the army. Had the Boers of the Free State combined and entered Cape Colony, General Buller would have given up all hope of relieving Lady smith, and General White would have been a prisoner of war. What a fatal, fatal mistake it was to give so much consideration to the personal feelings of others, when the very life of the land was at stake! There were so many ways by which the Boers could have beaten the English and maintained the independence of the two little Republics, that it is positively painful for me to think or write about the incidents and outcome of the war.

I hope with all my heart that the Boers in the future will remember and never forget that it is absolutely impossible for religion and humanity to contend successfully against unscrupulousness and treachery in this civilized age of the twentieth century. If they will only remember this, and act accordingly, the day is not far distant when they will drive the British from South Africa's shores, and the Africander race will, for the first time in 250 years, breathe the air of permanent peace and be recognized by all the nations of the earth as a free and independent people, in a land over which will wave the Africander flag to the end of time.

In the last days of March General De Wet scored another victory against a far superior force under the command of General Broadwood. It was at Sanna's Post that General De Wet placed his 300 men in the bed of Koorn Spruit on both sides of the road crossing, and gave orders that not a shot was to be fired until he gave the command. The previous day he had directed Generals P. Cronje, J. B. Wessels, C. L. Froneman and Piet De Wet with some 1,100 *burghers* and four guns, to proceed to the east side of the Modder River, and bombard Sanna's Post as soon as it was light on the following morning. This would drive General Broadwood, his 2,000 men and nine guns, by him and his men concealed in the Koorn Spruit, for this was directly on their line of retreat to Bloemfontein. When General De Wet gave these orders, General Broadwood was at Thaba'Nchu but, to his surprise, he, General Broadwood, after it became dark moved his force to the Bloemfontein Water Works in the very presence of General De Wet and his men concealed in the Koorn Spruit.

At daylight General De Wet discovered this overwhelming force at close quarters, but he was not frightened for he felt that in his position he was equal to it. General Broadwood was breaking camp, and some of his teams and men were just starting on their way to Bloemfontein.

The Boers by strict orders, lay low and said nothing until the carts and wagons reached them, when, as fast as they arrived, they were made prisoners and concealed in the bed of the *spruit*, that is, a deep ravine. After nearly all the wagons and carts and some 200 Tommies had been made prisoners, General Broadwood discovered that there was something wrong about that *spruit*, and as he had five cannon very near to it he concluded to withdraw them and put them in a safer place. He was sorely disappointed for General De Wet had his eye on those five guns and besides the other generals with their 1,100 men opened fire on Broadwood's camp at the same time. Now was the time for confusion, and General Broadwood and his 2,000 men were so terribly confused that they lost no time in running for their lives, but they had sense enough to dodge the ford where General De Wet and his 300 men were concealed. On both sides of General De Wet, General Broadwood's brave 2,000 Britishers passed within easy rifle range and as fast as they could run.

As the 2,000 panic-stricken brave Britishers passed in review, General De Wet and his 300 patriots did not fail to make their mausers sing in unerring tones and give them a good send off. General Broadwood and two-thirds of his men escaped. He left behind 350 men killed and wounded, 480 prisoners, seven cannon and 117 wagons to the tender mercies of General De Wet. The total Boer loss was three killed and five wounded. The British Government and all London rejoiced over General Broadwood's escape. I must confess that he deserved a great deal of credit and merited the gratulations of his queen, for some other British general might have fared worse.

In the first days of April, after his great success at Sanna's Post, General De Wet collected more men and went to Reddersberg where he knew there were some English troops. On his arrival he found the English, but they did not make much resistance. They abused the white flag, and by so doing, killed one of his *veldcornets* and killed six of his men. The English having hoisted their white flag and all firing having ceased, General De Wet and his men advanced to receive their arms, ammunition, etc.

On arriving within close range the English suddenly began firing again although their white flag was still flying. General De Wet's men followed their example, and within five minutes several more white flags were flying, but so furious were the *burghers* at the English treachery that General De Wet was unable to restrain them till 100 English had been killed and wounded. Now the remaining 470 gladly and promptly laid down their arms. That one act of treachery caused the death of that brave and good *veldcornet*, Du Plessis, and General De Wet failed to appreciate the cause of humanity when he did not shoot down every officer among his 470 prisoners.

CHAPTER 12

# Paying an Instalment on the Irish Debt

I will now return to the Irish Boys whom I left at Smaldeel station, thirty miles north of Brandfort in the Free State. During the few days we spent here, every preparation was made for hot, lively work, for we knew that it was near the time when orders would come to advance and meet Lord Roberts and his great army of 90,000 men, with camion in proportion. On the afternoon of May 1st, 1900, we received instructions to proceed to Brandfort and join with General de la Rey, so, having packed all tents, baggage, etc., in a freight car—which we scarcely ever expected to see again,—we started on our way, and never a happier or more delighted lot of boys went to a holiday picnic than those that went to face English bullets and shells.

It was a long, cold ride, and late in the afternoon of the following day we were camped in the bush on the bank of the little creek at Brandfort. Rumours were soon going the rounds that the British were near at hand, but it was so dark that we could not have seen them had they been only twenty feet away. So we decided to go to sleep and get up before daylight in the morning, that we might be ready to meet trouble.

In the early morning we learned that the English had slept in the bush on the same creek, a few miles below us, and as soon as the sun came up we saw them. There before us was Roberts with his 90,000 men, by far the largest army that any of us had ever seen, and, as far as we knew, there was to oppose him a mouthful of Irishmen at Brandfort. The Russian *attaché*, Colonel Gourko, the French *attaché*, Captain Demange, and the American *attaché*, Captain Carl Reichmann, were there too. I think everyone of them came near being captured, for they were a plucky lot of fellows and were determined to see how the English would act in the face of a handful of Irishmen. I don't know how the spectacle struck the *attachés*, but the English reminded me of a lot of ants whose routine of action had been disturbed by some mischievous boy, for they seemed to be moving aimlessly in all directions. I really believe that Roberts and his 90,000 men were afraid that a few hundred Boers might lay an ambush for them at Brandfort. This idea is preposterous, but I tell you that Englishmen are terribly afraid of Boers, and when they see one, that one will appear as many as at least ten to them.

There is a line of *kopjes* running east and west. Several columns of cavalry were moving south of them and parallel to them. It was plain that they intended to attack that line of *kopjes*. There were no Boers in them at the time, but the English imagined they were full of them. Early in the morning the Heidelburg Commando, about 600 strong, joined with us at the tall hill by Brandfort. All then went at full speed to reach the *kopjes* before the English. We barely succeeded, for no sooner had we dismounted than the English began with both cannon and rifle to make it warm for us.

The new boys from Chicago and Massachusetts, although it was their first time under fire, were in great glee, and with the old men of the brigade began to fire. Although huge shells tore up the earth about them, and thousands of bullets were chipping stones and singing in the air, yet not one of them seemed to realise that he was in any danger whatever. They were all too intent on their own work to realise their danger. Between the Irish boys and the Heidelburg Commando there was a large and very high *kopje*, so that neither party could see the other. The Irish boys succeeded in driving the English right back and were much pleased with their work. About two p. m., a courier came near me and yelled out, "General Spruit says get your men away as quickly as possible."

In loud tones I asked, "What is the trouble?" But he was in too much of a hurry to give answer, and he was soon far on his way across the flat in our rear. I called to the boys and told them to come quickly, as there was imminent danger somewhere. Irish-like, they wanted to argue the case, for they saw no danger and besides they were having a really good time. I quickly told them to come, as there was no time for argument. I knew General Spruit well, and when he says "get out quickly," I know it is time to get out. We raced down the *kopje*, mounted our horses and started across the flat towards Brandfort.

Much to our surprise, we saw all the hills about Brandfort literally covered with English cavalry. I looked for the Heidelburg Commando and found that it must have retreated hours before, for not a man of it could be seen in any direction.

We were certainly in a serious position, for our line of retreat was cut off by thousands of English, and there were thousands in front of us. To get out at all, we had to march across an open flat and pass within 2,500 yards of the English, for there was only one pass through the mountains in our rear. We crossed the flat and, having reached the base of the mountains, I called the men and told them that it looked like a hopeless case for us. There really was not the slightest show for us because all the English had to do was to ride down 1,000 or 1,500 yards, and we were completely hemmed in.

I always swore that I would never be captured alive, and told the boys so. I also told them that I was going to make a run for the road that leads through the pass, and asked them what they wished to do. They said they would make the run with me. We started at once in single file along a path that wound its way through the bush. This led us to the left and front of the English. Every man had his eye pinned on the English, and a dead silence reigned. I was terribly worried and frightened too, for I fully expected to see the English move at every moment and interpose themselves between us and the road. On we rode until we were right in front of them and about 2000 yards distant. I felt a little better, for the English had not yet moved. I was constantly watching the hills on my left, in the hope that I might see a chance of climbing them.

Fortune favoured me, for I discovered a good path running up the hills, and I concluded that, as it was an emergency, we could go where the goats had gone, and so turned to the left on to this tiny little path. It was a hard climb, but we reached safe ground on top just as the British made up their minds to take us in. They were too late, as usual, and only advanced a small distance, when they turned about and went back. It was a very cold day, but the terrible strain the men and I had passed through, warmed all of us into a heavy perspiration. It was General Hutton who kindly allowed us to escape. He said in his report that he thought we had some English prisoners with us, and therefore did not dare to fire on us. The Chicago and Massachusetts boys had on khaki uniforms, and that is why Hutton was deceived. His excuse was a poor one, just the same, for he could easily have blocked our way without firing a shot, and besides any ordinary field glass at his distance would have shown him that every man carried a rifle. We owed our escape entirely to British stupidity.

As no Boers could be seen from the hills, we made up our minds that we were very far behind everybody. As it was now nearly sundown, we started out to put a few miles between us and the British. We had not gone far when we found ourselves in the camp lately occupied by the Heidelburg Commando. Here we found coffee, sugar, bread and meat, and as we had had nothing to eat all day, we stopped and had a good feast. Then our poor, tired horses enjoyed their feast too, and it gave me more pleasure to see them at their mealies than to eat myself.

It was dark before we saddled up and started on our way in search of the Boers. Finally we reached the main road and near by was a stack of oats at a farm house. I told the boys to help themselves, and every man piled on his horse all the oats he could well manage. We then went on our way until we reached a little farm in the open flat that I knew was about nine miles from Brandfort, so here we concluded to camp for the night. It was about ten o'clock when a courier rode into camp looking for me. He pointed out the direction of General de la Rey's camp and told me that the general wished to see me early in the morning. I was anxious to see the general too, for I did not like the idea of being alone in front of Lord Robert's army. Early on the following morning I took two men and started in search of General de la Rey. My directions carried me obliquely towards Brandfort and I concluded that the general must have camped very near the English.

We had gone about a mile when I saw seven men dressed as the Boers usually are, riding alongside a hill between us and Brandfort. The two Africander scouts with me declared they were Boers, and I declared they were English in Boer clothes. The way they held their legs and their position in the saddle had formed my opinion. An Englishman on a horse always reminds me of a wooden clothespin. We decided to go ahead, for our direction would not lead us into trouble, yet I did a lot of thinking about those seven men, for there was a very deep *kloof* near them, and the whole English army could be easily concealed in it. We had gone about another mile when we came upon one of General de la Rey's men on the look out. I knew him and asked him if he had seen the seven men. He said no, and then pointed out to me just where General de la Rey was encamped. I galloped all the way, because I thought there was danger in that *kloof*. I was so certain that I told Commandant Trichardt, of the artillery, that

GENERAL DE LA REY. WHO NEVER LOST A BATTLE

the English were near at hand, and that he would do well to inspan and prepare for business.

I did not get to see General de la Rey because he had gone to see his brother who had been seriously wounded the previous day. I must say that before reaching General de la Rey's camp I sent one of the men with me, Hendrik Slegkamp, after giving him my wire-cutters, back to the Irish camp with instructions to saddle up as quickly as possible and fall back to some *kopjes* about two miles in the rear. All the farms in that country are entirely surrounded by wire fences and one can't get through without wire-cutters. The last I saw of Hendrik, he was going at a full gallop. After chatting with Colonel Trichardt for about fifteen minutes, he ordered all mules and horses to be spanned in and saddled up, and then we started back towards my own camp. Knowing the exact direction, we took a short cut and, having reached the top of a ridge about one mile from General de la Rey's camp and about two miles from my own, we were fired upon from a mealie field. Across the flat I saw the Irish boys under fire and flying to the *kopjes* in the rear.

We could not get through the wire fences because I had let Hendrik have my cutters, and the English at long range were making it very warm for us. There was a little cottage about 400 yards away, and we put spurs to our horses and reached it as quickly as possible. A little Dutch woman showed us a sheep path which would lead us to the small gates that opened from one farm to the other. That was about the hottest path that we ever travelled, for the English had found our range and were making use of it. My boy's horse was slightly wounded; otherwise we were all right. I saw that the Irish were safe on the kopje, but we could not get to them on account of the wire fences. Just as General de la Rey's men had saddled up and all were ready to move, the English opened fire on him, but he managed to get his guns, wagons and everything out safely. The whole country seemed to be alive with English, and they all came out of that deep *kloof* where I had seen the seven men. I felt it in my very bones that the English were in that *kloof*, and acted accordingly. It was a lucky thing for all of us that I did.

During the evening I reached the Irish boys, and we crossed the Vet River and went into camp. Early next morning we met General de la Rey and his men, and there was general rejoicing. The general said he was going to give fight on the river, and put Roberts to a little trouble. With the Irish, he had about 2,500 men to fight Roberts and his 90,000.

The position was a good one, but of course the general knew that he could do no more than make the English do a lot of work, and possibly knock a few of them down before he had to retreat. Roberts finally showed up, and the deployment of that great body of men into fighting formation, with absolute mathematical precision, was really beautiful. I was so interested that I could scarcely take my eyes from such beautiful military figures. That awful man, that brave man, that gallant man, Major J. L. Pretorius, seemed to have no idea of the beautiful at all, for just before the military figure was completed in all its beauty, he fired a shell that fell right among them. That shell simply played the deuce and ruined a most artistic picture. Instead of order, precision and beauty, we now had to witness disorder and pandemonium generally, for the English soldiers broke away, some running one way and some another, not one seeming in the least inclined to take a chance on the next shell that might follow.

It was marvellous what havoc one tiny shell could raise in a military-trained and thoroughly disciplined army. Major Pretorius was nothing but a youngster, but then there was nothing in the British army that was anywhere near his equal. For a change, and as the Irish boys were the latest arrivals, General de la Rey said he would hold us as reserves. Major Pretorius started the fight with that shell, and soon 30,000 English with cannon and shell were trying to lay low General de la Rey and 2,500 patriots. When the fighting became really hot and close, the reserve, the Irish boys, were sent for and told to come as quickly as possible to the road crossing the river. We went, but to go into the firing line we had to pass through the belt especially shelled by the English guns. The boys did not murmur; they went out.

Strange to say, not one of them received a bullet. Now, they had a close range, and didn't they send the bullets to the right place? I think they did, and I know they did. There were a lot of British to our right and front in a *kopje* about 1,000 yards distant. I think they were Irish, for the English turned their maxims on them, killed many of them and kept them from firing on us. We did not fire on them because the English were doing the work for us.

That was really a pretty fight in which the Boers did not suffer, and about sundown General de la Rey ordered us to fall back. The Irish boys kept firing away until it was fairly dark, and I became frightened for fear they might be captured. The Boers had all left, and had those fool Englishmen known anything, they might have given us a run for our lives. We remained in order to see out of danger a few young Boers who were in an *arroya* very close to the English. When we did finally go back, mount our horses and start towards Smaldeel, we ran into the very boys that we had assisted to get out of the *arroya*, and by a mere piece of luck they didn't fire on us. I was calling to the men to hurry up and my voice was recognized, otherwise we would have received a volley. I had a very excellent pair of field glasses given to me by a Russian Count and I made good use of them when the English were arriving to engage us.

In Natal, the Transvaal and the Free State, from the day the war first began, I had tried to convince the Boers of the great importance of destroying the enemy's line of communication. I never succeeded in making any headway, however, for they could not be made to believe in the destruction of property. Here at Vet River I handed General de la Rey my glasses and told him to witness the trains on the opposite ridge from which thousands of infantry were tumbling to give us battle. The general realised now for the first time the strength of my argument, and was thereafter bent on destroying the railway lines. He succeeded in partially convincing General Louis Botha that the destruction of the lines was of the first importance.

Volunteers for the purpose were called for, and it was the Irish Brigade that promptly responded. In fact, I believe that the men of the Irish Brigade were the only ones that did, and I believe that they were the only ones among the Boers that understood the business. It having been decided by the Council of War that the bridges and railway lines were to be destroyed, I selected the men that I knew would do the work well. There were little Mike Halley, the ever to be remembered Joe Wade, Jim O'Keefe, Dick Barry, Tom Herlihy, Tom Tierney, and several others whom I selected for this most important work.

In blowing up the long and high bridge at Sand River, the Irish boys were exposed both to cannon and rifle fire, but not one flinched and their work was well done. It was while some Anglo-American engineers were trying to repair this bridge, that Majors Seymour and Clements, (both Americans) were killed by General De Wet and his men. I am sure that neither I nor the Irish boys would have shed a tear had the whole lot been killed. All were mercenaries in the strict sense of the word, and this class of men are not fit to live in any country.

Here I must mention a little incident in which Mike Halley was the principal actor. At the time that the bridges and railways had been blown up in good form and we had crossed Sand River and arrived at Riet Spruit very near the Sand River, General Botha had sent for Sergeant Joe Wade, Mike Halley and Dick Barry to give them further instructions. Strange to say, General Botha always waited until the last moment, in fact, to the moment when it was too late to do good work. The boys were always on the alert and sometimes acted without orders, blew up the bridges according to my instructions and felt much satisfaction. Now, when they were called up, General de la Rey happened to meet Mike Halley and bounced on him for too much enthusiasm. Mike did not know the general, and thinking he was an ordinary Boer, said "What in hell do you know about it, anyhow?" This settled the general and he replied, "Go ahead. You know your business, my boy."

When Mike was informed that he was addressing General de la Rey, he promptly went to him to offer his apology.

The boys were now given full swing and rails, ties and bridges were constantly flying in the air till we reached the Vaal River, the Transvaal border, where orders were received from General Louis Botha to destroy nothing more. What a puerile display of military knowledge! Lord Roberts moved along this long line across the flats of the Free State. He had three columns, each 30,000 strong. One followed the road along the railway line and the other two were on the right and left flanks. There were not over 2,500 Boers and three or four cannon to oppose him on these wide open flats, yet it took him twenty-three days to drive that little band of patriots a distance of 110 miles, and every foot of the distance was hotly contested.

When we reached Kroonstad all were very tired, but the Irish boys wished to do some more work before they left the town. The English, of course, were at our heels, but that did not concern them in the least. We rigged up a spring wagon with six mules, loaded it with provisions and ammunition and were ready to move out just after blowing up the bridge and thoroughly alarming the town, when it suddenly occurred to Mick Ryan to destroy the provision depot. It was an immense building filled with sufficient supplies to support an ordinary army for many days. I told Mick to go ahead and do his work well. He built a good fire against the building, and some Englishmen came up with water and put it out. Mick then warned them not to try to do it again. He kindled another fire, and when it blazed up, one of the same Englishmen dashed up with a bucket of water and put it out.

Mick struck him on the head with his rule, knocked him senseless and then warned the others that if any attempt was made to put out his fire again he would give them some bullets. He made up his fire again, and this time no one disturbed it. When the building was well on fire, someone yelled out that there were several cases of dynamite near the burning part of the building. Everybody fled for their lives, and Mick saw that immense supply depot burn to the ground. It was about eleven o'clock at night, and the great light was plainly visible to Lord Roberts and his army who were about three miles distant. The English are not yet through damning the Irish Brigade for their good piece of work.

The main part of the brigade went forward with the cannon, and it was just thirty of us that remained behind to finish up the good work.

After the supply depot was burned we left town and camped about three miles out on the Heilbron road. We had learned that the English had put themselves between us and the Boer forces, so we had to take this route. Early next morning we were just ready to move out when we saw about 400 cavalry coming for us. We hastened off and kept ourselves in safety although the English pursued us as rapidly as they dared. They did not give up the chase until we were near the little town of Heilbron.

Here we met President Steyn, and Judge Hertzog, and I can remember that the only subject discussed was the importance of playing on Lord Roberts' line of communication. I finally convinced them that it was the only way they could successfully fight such an immense army, and President Steyn telegraphed President Krüger for permission for the Irish Brigade to remain in the Free State. President Krüger wanted us in the Transvaal, so we said goodbye, and left for Rhenoster River at the railway crossing, where we learned that the Boers had taken up positions. General De Wet, however, went to work on Roberts' communications, and soon established for himself the greatest name of all the Boer officers in the field. Had we done in the Transvaal what De Wet did in the Free State, Roberts would have been driven into famine, and utterly disgraced himself in the eyes of the world; but this is not the place to explain, so we will wait until we reach Pretoria.

We left Heilbron early in the morning, and at night we were with General Botha and the Boer forces. We now learned that General Botha had officially reported us as captured in Kroonstad and he was very much surprised when I reported to him. Having told him what we had done in Kroonstad, and assured him that we had not been in any real danger, he instructed me to take position at the road crossing, on the river. These road crossings of rivers are always the warmest places when it comes to a fight, and as the English were then near at hand, I fully expected on the following day to have a most interesting time. On reaching our position, and having taken a good look at it, I was then convinced that the English would not attack, but would go around our flanks. I told General Botha that he would find that I was right, because this Rhenoster River is the best defensive position I had seen in the country. The banks were very deep and steep, and the river bed was caked sand, over which flowed a skim of water. We could gallop our horses for miles in that river without being seen or in any way exposed to artillery fire.

To attack the position, the English would have to advance over a grassy plain, gently sloping to the river, and 2,500 Boers in the river could easily have killed as many English without taking any risk whatever. I was certain that the English knew all about the strength of this river position and would therefore dodge it. It was about three o'clock on the following morning when we received orders to retreat, as the English had crossed the river on our left and right flanks. As it was very dark, we concluded to wait until daylight before retreating. Just as it was good light we moved away, and an English battery on a ridge some 2,500 yards distant, sent three shells at us, to move us along more lively. There was no more fighting of any consequence until we reached Klip River, near Johannesburg. The little band of patriots were always in touch with the big English army, and occasionally, some shots would be exchanged near the bridges which the Irish boys were charging with dynamite, but no damage was done.

I didn't understand then, nor do I understand now, why that great British army did not at least make an effort to capture that small band of Boers and all their cannon, while crossing the great open plain between Brandford and the Vaal River. For the operations of cavalry and artillery, there is no country in the world more favourable than those immense Free State prairies, and had Roberts made any use of his thousands of cavalry, he could have taken the Boer guns at any time, and the 2,500 Boers with them. He seemed frightened, and I believe he was, for he had not yet forgotten the slaughter at Magersfontein. We could never understand, either, why he followed the small Boer force, and left behind that daring man, General Christian De Wet, with 10,000 men. But more about this after we reach Pretoria. To the south of Johannesburg, General Botha had some short but lively fighting, and forced the English to move around to the west, where

General de la Rey warmed them up in good form.

The English also came in on the east, where there was a little skirmishing that did not amount to anything. We passed through Johannesburg, and went to within six miles of Pretoria. The Boers and British were actually camped side by side just north of Johannesburg, but the Boers were the first to find this out at daylight and so managed to escape being captured. General Botha is a pretty reckless man, and he did not get out any too quickly.

I urged the council of war at Vaal River to allow me to blow up certain mines in Johannesburg, but it was no use talking, not one of them would agree to it. They did not believe in the destruction of property. It was the mines of the very men who, with Chamberlain, Milner and Rhodes, had laboured so hard to bring on the war, that I was so anxious to blow up, and I regret to this day that we did not destroy them. All the immense stores of provisions in Johannesburg and Pretoria I wished so badly to destroy, that I fairly begged for permission to do it, but all in vain. With De Wet and 10,000 men behind Roberts, and on his line of communications, and all provisions in Johannesburg and Pretoria destroyed, Lord Roberts would have been a defeated man, for the reason that he had no food for his army. As it was, his men came nearly starving to death on half rations. I can never forgive the Boer generals for leaving such quantities of good supplies for the British.

The railway and telegraph lines between the Vaal River and Pretoria should have been completely destroyed, yet General Botha gave me strict orders not to disturb either. We were simply playing into the hands of the English, and doing more for them than they could possibly do for themselves. On the fifth of June we had to leave Pretoria, and, strange to say, we left the Pietersburg and Delagoa railway lines, all in good order with plenty of engines and cars for immediate use by the English. Why General Botha insisted on leaving all these lines intact, and well equipped for the English, I cannot understand. There was not a *burgher* in the field, that did not realise that the destruction of all railway facilities was a matter of grave importance.

Much as I admire General Botha, not only as a brave man, but as a first-class fighter and an able general, I must condemn him for his opposition to the destruction of the enemy's communications, and for his failure to destroy the enemy's supply stores. General De Wet had done his work so well that General Roberts was cut off from all communications with the Colony, and there was no food to be had in the country, except in the Boer supply stores.

Kootie Heystek, a Boer Belle, of Pretoria

Chapter 13

# General Buller Arrives in Transvaal

After the occupation of Pretoria, Lord Roberts issued his usual proclamation, to induce the *burghers* to lay down their arms. They were not to be sent away, their property was not to be molested, and they were to be allowed to peacefully occupy their farms. Thousands of the *burghers*, really believing that the war was over, took advantage of this proclamation and surrendered their rifles. Almost the entire Rustenburg district surrendered, and hundreds of men of the other districts did likewise.

As in the Free State, so in the Transvaal, as soon as Lord Roberts had the men and the guns in his possession, he at once violated his pledge, sent the men away, and afterwards destroyed all their property. The reason that the Boers did not make a stand at Pretoria, was that every shell the English might fire would land in the town, and kill women and children. Of course, this would please the English immensely, but the Boers never gave them the chance. As it was, they fired a few shells on the outskirts of the town, and wounded three Boer women. The English are bent on killing women, because they know that, so long as they are in the land, the Union Jack trembles with fear as it floats above them.

The Boers were in the greatest disorder when leaving Pretoria. There seemed to be no head, and *burghers* were going in all directions, north, east, south and west. General Botha ordered as many as he could reach, to proceed on the Delagoa railway line toward Middleburg. The English now made up their minds that there was no more fight in the Boers, and that the time was ripe to make a gallant display of dash and bravery on the fast retreating Boers. All titled persons of noble blood, were anxious to fill the London press with long accounts of their brave exploits, and Lord Roberts himself was not behind them in his desire for praise. The result was, that a large force was started in pursuit of the Boers, with Lord Roberts in command.

The fleeing Boers, on reaching Donkerhoek, about fifteen miles from Pretoria, were assembled by General Botha and General de la Rey, and all agreed not to run any further. There were about 7,000 of them, and they took up a position on a line about twenty miles long. It was on the 12th of June, that the British Army, and the lords, dukes, earls and so forth, appeared on the scene, and proceeded at once to wipe out what was left of the Boer forces. A very hot fight was the result, and the Boers wiped up the English, and gave them such a shock that they did not recover their nerve for months. Go to the graveyard in Pretoria, read some of the inscriptions on the head-boards, and you will find some missing earls, dukes and so forth, accounted for. Lord Roberts turned tail also and went back to Pretoria, to get out some more proclamations. He is a wonderful general, on paper, but on the battlefield he is a pitiful failure.

After this fight, General de la Rey, with 1,500 men, went to the Rustenburg district west of Pretoria, where all the *burghers* had laid down their arms. Lord Roberts had not had time yet to violate his pledge, so the men were still on their farms. General Botha now made Commandant Ben Viljoen a fighting general, and he proved a most excellent man. The Boers regained hope, and were as full of fight as ever. From Donkerhoek to Machadadorp is about 110 miles, a long stretch of beautiful, rolling prairie, well watered, dotted here and there with beautiful farms, and in all respects suited for cavalry, infantry and artillery to display great skill and excellent, work. General Botha is a nervy man, and he determined to contest every inch of ground to Machadadorp, and make it cost the English much time and many men to cross the fair prairie.

Every day General Botha and his small force fought the English army, and in all the engagements he was generally successful, as is shown by the fact that it required sixty days to drive him back to Dalmanutha, nine miles from Machadadorp. Here he took up a position to make a firm stand. He had to scatter his men along a line about twenty-four miles long, in order to prevent the English from turning his flanks. I think the position at Machadadorp was much better and stronger, but he did not think so. I believe now, however, if he had the opportunity again, he would try his luck at Machadadorp, for his line would not be over ten miles long, his flanks would be safe, and in case of defeat, he could retreat in good order.

I left General Buller and his army at Ladysmith on February 28th. Now he appears on the scene again. He had a most difficult task to fight his way through the mountains of Natal and cross into the Transvaal, but at last he had succeeded, and was on his way to join the army opposed to General Botha. It was about the middle of August that General Buller arrived. The entire British force now to attack the Boer forces was about 65,000 strong, while General Botha had less than 7,000 men. He did not have hills and mountains, as in Natal, but, instead, open, rolling prairies. It looked as if the English would ride right over us and kill or capture our whole force, but they didn't.

Lord Roberts sent about 600 women and children in open coal trucks to Belfast when it was midwinter and so cold that no one could keep warm. He did this, thinking that the Boers, rather than see their women and children suffer, and probably die, would come in and surrender. He was fooled, however, for General Botha put them all on the train and sent them to Barberton, where it was warm and where all had friends. Lord Roberts likes to fight women and children and takes as much pleasure in seeing them suffer as does Lord Kitchener. After General Buller arrived and took command, there was fighting daily on some part of the line for nine days before the final effort was made on the 27th of August. In the centre of our line were seventy-two of the Johannesburg police, who were on the ridge between Belfast and Dalmanutha. They had built for themselves stone breastworks about two feet high, but a shell would easily destroy any of them.

On the night of the 26th, General Buller changed his plans and concentrated his force on the centre, instead of on our left flank, and at six o'clock of the morning of the 27th he began with thirty-six guns to bombard the seventy-two Johannesburg police. As the railway line had been left in good order by General Botha's instructions, two huge siege guns came up on some flat cars. When they were fired, the whole earth seemed to tremble and the explosion of the shell was fairly deafening, yet they did no damage. I could see Everyone of the seventy-two police plainly, for I was with a Long Tom on a high point to then left. For seven hours without intermission, heavy lyddite shells were bursting on the ground about them and a dozen or so shrapnel were bursting over their heads at the same time. When at about two o'clock in the afternoon I saw a long line of cavalry put in readiness to charge their position, I felt sure that there was not one of them alive, for it did not seem possible for them with their little protection to escape.

Suddenly all the cannon ceased to roar and a dead stillness reigned for a moment, but only for a moment, for here comes the long line of cavalry at full gallop. It rapidly approaches and when within about 100 yards of the police there was a ring of musketry heard that positively filled me with an ecstasy of joy. The police were still alive, and with such rapidity did they use their rifles, and to such good effect, that saddles were emptied fast, and loose horses were running frantically across the *veldt*, some dragging wounded men whose feet were caught in the stirrups. They could not stand such a deadly fire, and turned and fled back, the police continuing to mow them down. They form line, are re-enforced, and again they charge, only to be driven back as before after a heavy loss. Four charges were made, and four times the charges were driven back, and no doubt a fifth charge would have followed had General Botha not ordered the police to retire. These brave men retired as coolly as they had passed through the seven hours' shell storm, and four times driven back that long line of cavalry.

Of the seventy-two men, nineteen were killed and wounded, among the killed being three officers.

Lord Roberts, who arrived at twenty minutes to one o'clock, according to his own report, pronounced this the severest bombardment of the war, and could not understand why the whole Boer force was not annihilated. Of course, Lord Roberts came up just as the battle was over, to save General Buller the trouble of making his report announcing a victory. There is no getting round the fact that Roberts is cute and smart and knows how to use the pen and steal the credit that belongs to others. He certainly deserves the title of Lord, or Earl, or any big-sounding name like that, with at least double the number of letters in the alphabet following it as a tail, for he has the gall to keep his title up to the high-water mark.

General Botha having ordered a retreat, of course Lord Roberts hastened back to Pretoria to issue another proclamation. He didn't say very much this time, for he was very tired sending cablegrams telling of his great victory, but he still had strength enough to proclaim the war at an end, annex the Transvaal to the British Empire, entreat the *burghers* to come in like good boys and lay down their arms, and forget his many dastardly deeds.

It was during this battle that that wonderful artillerist, Major J. L. Pretorius put Long Tom to the test that I had so strongly advocated at Ladysmith and other places. The Boer officers were all convinced that it would be dangerous to fire Long Tom except when fastened down to a heavy wooden platform. To build these platforms to stand the work a great deal of labour, at least twenty-four hours of time, and a great deal of strong material were required. My contention was that Long Tom could be used as an ordinary field gun, and would do good work without a platform as well as with one. To have so used this big gun at Ladysmith would have kept the British guessing, and the results would have been very different. At Dalmanutha, Major Pretorius did not have time to finish the platform, so he took the chances of firing Long Tom as he stood without one, and the result was excellent. He found his shooting was just as accurate, and that the recoil was never more than two or three yards.

Thereafter Long Tom was always used as an ordinary field gun, and Major Pretorius took him over the mountains by Lydenburg. With the exception of about twenty men, the Irish boys were all dismounted, having lost their horses near Pretoria. They were in position under Commandant Krüger , and when the English broke through our centre it looked as though they would be captured. They had to make about ten miles to reach Machadadorp, where they could take the train, and they barely made connection before the English arrived. The Boers scattered in all directions, some going towards Lydenburg, some to Neil Spruit, some to Devil's Kantoor, and others southward towards Ermelo and Carolina. President Krüger and the government were at Nell Spruit.

Chapter 14

# English Savagery

We now arrive at what I call the dark period of the war. For the first time I really felt that our situation was serious. The Boers were discouraged in spirit and much scattered, and several hundred of them deliberately rode into the English lines and surrendered. At one time it looked as if there would be a general surrender, but President Krüger was firm and said the war must go on.

President Steyn had arrived from the Free State. He, together with all the Transvaal officers and officials, concentrated their influence on President Krüger to persuade him to go to Holland, as he was very feeble and it required so many men to guard his safety. He positively refused to go, saying that he could not leave his people and that he would look after himself. His idea was to go to Pilgrims' Rest, but that little town was far away and it required many days of hard travel through the fever stricken bush-*veldt* to reach it. In the end President Krüger was practically forced to take the train for Delagoa Bay *en route* to Holland, and as the train moved off the staunch old patriot's eyes filled with tears and he sank down broken hearted.

He handed to General Botha 40,000 sovereigns, ($200,000) for the use of the *burghers*. This was his own money. He had no government money in his possession and the few thousand dollars that he carried to Holland belonged to him. All the *burghers* felt very sad at the good old man's departure and such was their love for him that they one and all resolved to fight harder than ever and bring back their great friend and patriot.

On hearing of the old hero's departure, Lord Roberts found a good opportunity to use his pen again. In effect he cabled the news that Ex-President Krüger had deserted his wife, his people and land, and gone to Holland, taking with him a very large amount of gold

Miss Annie Ollivier of Pretoria
a Typical Boer Girl

belonging to the people. He also had some abusive opinions to express about the good old man.

When Lord Roberts wrote and sent those cablegrams, he knew that he wilfully, maliciously and deliberately lied and I would be exceedingly happy to tell him so to his face.

Of course, Robert's idea in sending such a slanderous statement was to deceive the Boers throughout the land, and lead them to believe that President Krüger was really guilty of such infamous conduct; but the Boers had known the good old man too many years to be so deceived, and Lord Roberts only succeeded in making them love him still more. Roberts and Kitchener each issued many proclamations, all teeming with treachery and unscrupulousness, and if either had a grain of honour, and were forced to read his own proclamations to a public audience in any civilized country, I am sure that each would be stricken with a vomiting fit. I will have more on the subject of proclamations before I finish.

Now Lord Roberts had a most excellent opportunity to make an attack on the Boer women and children, who were helpless and in his hands, and one may be assured that he did not fail to take advantage of it. He notified General Botha that he would send all the women and children to him and that he must take care of them. General Botha replied that he would be pleased to receive all of them, as he wished to send them to Holland to remain during the continuance of the war, but that he must not rush them out all at one time, as it was very cold weather, in which all would suffer and many die. He wanted no more than a ship load sent at one time, so that he could properly care for them and send them at once to Holland.

This floored Roberts and he never answered. He could not stand the idea of the Boer women and children being sent to Holland, for in that case he could not fight them, nor could they be killed off in his concentration camps.

Before the President departed I discussed the position of the Irish Boys with him, and it was his opinion that all those who were dismounted should go at once to Koomati Poort and then, if hard pressed, go to Delagoa Bay and thence to America. All Boers who were dismounted were sent to the *poort*, so the Irish boys went also. Shortly after they reached Koomati Poort I telegraphed Captain O'Connor that I thought it best for them to go to America at once. I did this because I did not wish any of them to be captured. Should any be so unfortunate, I knew that it would go very hard for them, and probably cause them to suffer a slow death in some prison. Major McBride thought it best for them to go too, and he went.

General Botha soon put things in order now at Hector Spruit, and we started on our long, perilous journey through the bush *veldt*, our destination being, for some Pietersburg, for others Pilgrims' Rest and that vicinity. We left enough coffee, sugar, flour and so forth unharmed to last the whole British army for at least a month. How I did long apply the torch and destroy those great stacks of stores! There were about thirty Irish boys mounted, and determined as ever, with us, but distributed in small bunches with the different commandos.

I had joined with Major Pretorius of the artillery near Bronkhorst Spruit in July, but was now separated from him because the English cut in between us at Dalmanutha when he was with one Long Tom and I was with the other. My aim was to find Pretorius, and when near Pilgrims' Rest his brother-in-law, Gustave Preller, and myself set out to find him. Just before we reached the town of Pilgrims' Rest, we saw the English, about 15,000 strong, at the drift on the Sabi River, but we moved rapidly, reached the little town and heard that Major Pretorius with his guns, was about twenty miles ahead, near Aurichstad. We spent but little time at Pilgrims' Rest, because the English were very near us. Three days later we caught up with Major Pretorius near the Devil's Pulpit on the Olifant River. We had been separated from August 26th at Dalmanutha till this day, October 1st, so that we had plenty to talk about. He had saved all his guns and had fought the English at close range for more than three weeks.

We had a hard time getting the guns down the mountain to the river bank. He had six guns, including one Long Tom, and twenty-four artillery men with him. So steep and long was the open way to the river bank that we had to dismount the guns, put them on slides and turn them loose. Some would roll over, some would glide nicely, and then some would skip off into the rocks on the side. It meant a great deal of work, but every gun was landed safely without any damage whatever. We had a lookout, of course, and on the last day he reported several thousand English about six miles from us. They could certainly see the trail of the guns, and why they did not come over and take us we do not know, unless it was that they were afraid of an ambush. We now pushed on to Leydsdorp and finally reached Pietersburg on October 7th. Here we met President Steyn and his escort under command of a good soldier, Koos Boshof.

In two or three days two or three thousand *burghers* had assembled. General Botha cut through by Krüger's Post near Lydenburg and finally reached Botha'sberg near Middleburg. He had with him quite a good command. South of the railway the Ermelo, Carolina, Bethel, Wakkerstroom and in fact all the commandos on the high *veldt* had gotten themselves into fighting trim.

General de la Rey had assembled 6,000 men in the Western Transvaal who had surrendered their guns, armed them again, and put them in excellent fighting condition. General De Wet had put the whole Free State in perfect order, so that when we finished counting noses we found that we had about 30,000 fighting men in the field, while the English did not have over 250,000 men. Our chances were excellent, and the two little republics would have won their independence if the devil and all his angels had not been against them.

By the 15th of October General Botha had all his forces in the Eastern Transvaal along the railway line from Pretoria to Dalmanutha and on the Natal line from Heidleburg to Laing's Nek. General de la Rey was close to Johannesburg and Pretoria on the west. General Byers, a most excellent man and soldier, was north of Pretoria, and General De Wet was general traffic-manager for the railway line through the Free State. In fact, we were stronger and in better condition than we had ever been before, because we were concentrated. Of course, at one time during the war the Boer force was 35,000 strong, but it was too scattered and too much used for siege work to be of practical use.

During our six weeks' absence the English had busied themselves in building all sorts of forts along the railway lines. On a high commanding mountain a few miles north of Machadadorp they built eight forts at Helvetia and armed them with cannon, one being a 4.7 naval gun, bearing in large letters the name "Lady Roberts." English commands were moving about freely, believing that the Boer men were so scattered and demoralised that they would not dare to make a stand and fight. They were soon to be sorely disappointed for that able and most successful fighting general, Ben Viljoen, had gone to Rhinoster Kop, about fifteen miles north of Balmoral Station, to find out what the English were doing near Pretoria. Soon General Paget with 3,000 men, advanced, and attacked General Ben Viljoen and his 600 brave fighters of the Johannesburg Commando. Captain McCallum, Sergeant Joe Wade, Joe Kennedy, Mike Hannifin, Mike Halley, John McGlew and Jerry O'Leary, of the Irish Brigade were there too. General Viljoen took positions near the *kop*, and on the 29th of November General Paget boldly attacked. For hours his cannon roared, and thundered, and tore up the earth and rocks generally, but the Johannesburg boys were there and they were there to stay.

Having fired enough shells to have killed each man at least five times, then General Paget advanced his lines and the rifles came into play. Time and again these lines were driven back, and the last time they advanced to within fifty yards of the Irish boys. Didn't they keep the air filled with steel and didn't they do good work? Well, I guess they did. The English were driven back once more all along the line and did not try again. General Viljoen's men had used up almost all their ammunition and could not have repelled another advance. At night he retired a few miles back, in the hope of meeting his ammunition wagons, which were already due to arrive. General Paget was satisfied. He had had enough and made no further attempt to molest General Viljoen and the Johannesburg boys.

A board over one pit accounts for seventeen officers. The other pits bear no mark, so it is not yet known how many men were killed. However, the slaughter was so terrible, and General Paget so terribly thrashed, that he was relieved and sent home. Had he simply made a feint on General Viljoen's right flank the latter would have been forced to retreat without fighting, but it never occurred to General Paget for he was so sure that his frontal attack would be successful. General Viljoen lost three men killed and two wounded, and taught the English that the demoralized Boers were still able to defeat the disciplined English Army.

It was about this time that Lord Kitchener's proclamations and orders for the burning and destruction of Boer farms was given. The English visited, and destroyed in the end every farm, both in the Transvaal and in the Free State. All fences, crops, agricultural implements and so forth were destroyed. Even the towns of Dulstroom, Carolina, Ermelo, Bethel, Piet Retief, and many others were razed to the ground. Churches were torn down and the corner stones robbed of old church papers. Some of these papers were afterwards advertised for sale at fabulous prices. It was not until November, 1901, that this burning and destruction of property was completed, and the whole country left as a desert waste. On searching a farmhouse the officer in command would give the family ten minutes to get out what they could, but would at once spread the oil around and then apply the torch. All fowls, pigs, sheep and cows would either be shot down or

Dr. Nethling.     **GENERAL BEN VILJOEN**     Docks Young.
And some of his Commandants and Veldcornets.

driven off, and then without a mouthful of food, without shelter or clothing, the women and children would be left to starve to death on the *veldt*.

> I do not believe that in the history of the world, one could find more acts of barbarity and brutality committed by any people in any land than by the English in the two little republics of the Transvaal and the Free State.

There were about fifteen of us near Dulstroom watching the movements of the English in November, 1901. A column of about 500 strong rode up to a farmhouse occupied by a widow and eleven girls, her daughters. Soon we saw the girls pushing the organ out of the door and the smoke began to fill the windows and roof. Of course, one of the girls brought out the family bible too, for that is one of the most precious things in the household to them. The organ was pushed about forty yards away and placed by a stone cattle *kraal*. The mother sat down and began to play and her girls collected about her. The house was now enveloped in flames, the soldiers were killing fowl, etc., while the officers were cracking jokes at the poor mother and her children.

Of course, we thought that the old lady and her children were singing a hymn or psalm, because these are nearest to the Boer heart. The English, having completed their pleasant duty, rode off in search of other farms. We then went to the scene of destruction, because we knew that immediate help was necessary, as the sun would soon go down. On meeting them we asked the old lady how she could play and sing hymns while her home behind her back was burning and all her possessions were being destroyed? She replied, "We were not singing hymns or psalms, but our 'Boer War Song.'"

Here you have a fair sample of the Boer women. They are ready and willing to suffer from lack of food, to suffer from lack of clothing and bedding, to endure the cold of winter and the heat and fearful rainstorms of summer without any shelter over their heads, and, yes, they are ready and willing to face death itself, if the men will only stand and fight for the liberty of the people and the land. Yes, they are noble women, brave and patriotic women, the very women whom the English strove so hard to exterminate and whom they did murder by thousands in those prison camps.

So long as the Boer woman lives so long will there be a race of liberty-loving people in South Africa, so long will there be great

Boer generals and fighting patriots daily born, and sure it is that such fighting blood will assert its independence. No one is more certain of this than Roberts, Kitchener, Joe Chamberlain, Alfred Milner and the thousands of other women-fighters in England.

CHAPTER 15

# War Declared at an End By Roberts

But little was done by General Botha in the Eastern Transvaal; but General Chris. Botha, one of the best generals in the war, gave General French a great deal of trouble in the Ermelo district. French with his 11,000 men could make no headway and had to content himself with burning farms. In the Free State, during this month, General De Wet was having a very warm time. About 50,000 men were trying constantly to surround him, but he was too smart for them. He continued to capture and turn loose many men, and kept the English in a constant tremble. During the same month, the English left General de la Rey severely alone in order to concentrate their whole attention on General De Wet, who was fairly disgracing the English army and driving Roberts and Kitchener crazy.

Lord Roberts had declared the war at an end, and here was General De Wet daily tearing his army to pieces. He hates De Wet yet. During December—although the war was at an end,—there was some very warm and interesting fighting, Generals De Wet and de la Rey being the principal actors. In fact, there was so much fighting, and the Boers were so successful, that Lord Roberts pulled up stakes, fled for London and left Kitchener to continue his dirty work. I assure him that he could not have left a man more capable for such work than Kitchener, and he must have known his man pretty well. During this month General Louis Botha was inactive. General Ben Viljoen played havoc, however, with the English at Helvetia on top of the fortified mountain just north of Machadadorp. With 150 men General Viljoen made a night march and attack on Helvetia forts, took several of them, over a hundred prisoners and the 4.7 gun marked in big letters, "Lady Roberts." Many of the officers and men were killed or wounded and his night venture was a great success.

He did not lose any men killed or wounded, although on the following day the English in force pursued them. He brought "Lady Roberts" to his *laager* where she was greeted with shouts of joy, thoroughly inspected and admired by about 600 demoralised Boers. He kept her for a while then blew her up with dynamite. What a savage brutal act this was! It was just like the cowardly Boers! When all the ammunition was exhausted, we blew up our Long Toms, and Lord Kitchener, having found the remains of one of them, collected the pieces and shipped the whole to London to show what the English army was doing in South Africa.

We would have given him Lady Roberts' remains too, had he shown any desire to have them, but he didn't and they are wasting away on top of the Totausberg Mountain. The same Irish boys with one other, Dick Hunt, were in the attack on the Helvetia forts. Dick and Mike Halley were both barefooted and were looking for boots, yet they didn't have the heart to fit themselves out with the dead Tommies boots. Shortly afterwards, however, they threw aside modesty and were always well supplied.

On the return from Helvetia Mike Halley's horse gave out, so he stopped, unsaddled, and put him out to feed and rest while he himself lay down to take a nap. In a little while Veldtcornet Ceroni came along, found Mike and asked him why he did not go ahead, as the English were following up. Mike told him that his horse was played out and that he had stopped to give him some rest and grass. "Yes," replied the *veldtcornet*, "he will take plenty of rest now, for there he lies stone dead." Sure enough he was dead, and Mike's bare feet must now beat a long road. The *veldtcornet* took his saddle and so forth, and brave little Mike smiled and went on his way, and when he reached camp the *veldtcornet* gave him a present of a good horse.

I have forgotten the name of the captain who was in charge of "Lady Roberts" and who was captured with her, but remember that he was broken-hearted, felt disgraced and was disgusted generally because such a small force had attacked and taken those forts, the guns and so many prisoners. He was a terrible Englishman, and the sight of the Irish boys made him wild. He could not understand why an Irishman would fight against the queen and her forces. Had he asked any of those Irish boys he would have had their reasons in a very few sharp words.

In the Vryheid district near the Natal border, General Chris. Botha, a most lovable man, was firing away at the English, and putting them into shivers and doing good execution as well, yet Lord Roberts had declared that the war was over. In the Free State General De Wet was again in great trouble, for he was completely surrounded and it was impossible for him to escape, for Lord Roberts and Lord Kitchener had said so.

All England was ablaze with joy. The people of London were literally wild, so rejoiced were they, but when next day they learned that the wily De Wet had departed and taken their two guns with him, and several prisoners, a heavy gloom seemed to settle over that city. I will, for a change, go into the details, to a small extent, to show the difference between the British and the Boer officers. De Wet had his *laager* among some small *kopjes* where he put up a dozen or so tents. The English could just see the tops of the tents and knew that the dangerous De Wet was in one of them. They completely surrounded those tents and at daylight the following morning they were to make a determined attack and take not only those tents but all their occupants. General De Wet saw the English and determined they might have the tents, but that they would not get the occupants.

When night came, he left his tents standing, made a sly march and passed between the English commands. When daylight came he was in their rear, patiently watching for them to attack his abandoned tents. He was not disappointed, for they opened up all their cannon on those poor, unoffending tents, and kept up a merciless fire for hours before they resolved to go and accept General De Wet's surrender. When the cannon ceased to roar, all the English lines advanced and when they were well away General De Wet made a rear attack on the cannon. The English were at once convinced that General De Wet was in front of them and that some strong Boer commando was in the rear of them, and possibly that terrible man, General George Brand, was in command of them. They became utterly demoralised, hustled to escape and did escape, but De Wet captured two of their guns and rode off, satisfied with losing a few old empty tents,

With all their thousands the English were always outwitted by General De Wet who generally enjoyed a signal success. In anticipation, the English people would become overjoyed by the glowing reports of the English generals describing the little pen into which they had driven and confined General De Wet and his men and from which it was impossible for him to escape. But when the following day they learned that General De Wet had not only escaped but taken some prisoners with him, they would sneak home, remain quiet and anxiously await more glowing reports from the English generals. Isn't this a sure sign of degeneracy? Well I think so.

Now I will leave the Free State and stop in Cape Colony for a moment. Of course, all was peaceful there and the people were loyal British subjects, for the *London Times* said so. But Lord Kitchener felt that a strong British force in those parts might induce the people to be more loyal, and accordingly he kept one there. General Kritzinger with 600 or 600 men showed himself on the Boer side and at once made it very uncomfortable for the English in loyal Cape Colony. The war was over, because Lord Roberts had said so, yet here was hard fighting in Cape Colony as well as in the Free State and the Transvaal.

Now I will go into the Rustenburg district and see to what a mass of pulp the English have crushed General de la Rey and his patriots. The English had a strong force in the town of Rustenburg, and of course they must be fed, and to feed them long convoys heavily guarded were necessary. General de la Rey never denied food to the hungry in his life, but on this occasion, when a long convoy surrounded with numerous Tommies was slowly moving towards Rustenburg to feed the hungry, he could not resist the temptation of making an attack, for his own men might be hungry in a week or so. The result was that the convoy was taken, many Tommies buried on the roadside, and several of them taken prisoners, only to be disarmed and set free again. In the middle of the month General Clements, in conjunction with other generals and their commands, planned to surround and take in this old farmer, de la Rey. They planned well and their intentions were good enough, but the old farmer did not exactly like the idea and acted accordingly.

At the base of the Magaliesburg Mountains but a few miles from Hecpoort there are a long line of *kopjes* excellently situated for defensive work. The place is known by the Boers as Nooitgedacht, "never thought of," but I am sure that the Boers will never forget, and that General Clements will ever remember it.

General de la Rey realised that it was a very strong position and concluded to take it for his own use. He had an exceedingly strong and capable brother officer with him, in young General Beyers, who commanded the Waterburg commando. I do not believe that there was a better fighting general in the field than this brave and patriotic Beyers, and like those great generals, Celliers and Kemp, he was always ready for daring work. The English had planned to surround and take General de la Rey, but this Commandant-General of Western

Transvaal resolved to take in the English. So he told General Beyers to charge them from one side and he would charge them from the other. Of course, General Clements' force was much stronger than the combined forces of General de la Rey and General Beyers, but that made no difference so far as either de la Rey or Beyers was concerned.

About the middle of December, in the early morning, General Beyers, with his 350 men, charged over a half mile of open ground and came into close fighting quarters with Clements' force. *Kopje* after *kopje* was taken, and at times the Boers and English were within two yards of each other, yet the former continued to kill and drive till they completely routed the whole force and killed and captured nearly 800 men. The Boers did not know where Clements' cannon were, or they would have captured them, too. General Beyers' attack was a little previous, because General de la Rey had not had time enough to reach the charging point before Beyers had finished his work. Clements and his whole command, together with his cannon, would have been captured without doubt, had General Beyers delayed his charge for twenty minutes. But it was dark and very difficult for two forces to work in perfect unison. At any rate General de la Rey had the position he wished, and General Clements was in rapid retreat.

All this took place in the middle of December, yet the war was over, for Lord Roberts, the Mighty, the High, the Great Financier and Politician, had so declared nearly four months previously, and Conan Doyle had countersigned his declaration.

Before the end of December and the end of the year 1900, many Free Staters with General George Brand and General Hertzog, both able and determined officers, had crossed into the Colony, and other forces had entered Griqualand West, where some convoys were taken. So there was daily fighting in Cape Colony, the Free State and the Transvaal, and the Boers were successful in all the main engagements, this, too, in the face of the fact that the war was declared at an end both by Lord Roberts and Conan Doyle.

Eight Boer sisters of Wellington, Cape Colony

CHAPTER 16

# Boers Become Aggressive

The year 1901 began well, and the month of January was a very lively one, as there was hot fighting in every direction throughout the land and as far south as Cape Town. The English were alarmed; affairs in South Africa looked dubious and dark. The Boers were becoming more aggressive, Johannesburg was in a constant state of excitement, expecting every moment to be attacked and captured; the people were calling for protection, Kitchener was clamouring for reenforcements from England, and England was calling for help from Ireland, Scotland, Wales, Canada, India, New Zealand and Australia. At the same tune Lord Roberts was pulling the ropes for his earldom, and $500,000 for his proclamations annexing the Free State and the Transvaal, and declaring the war at an end. The English were short on horses and mules and these she must have at any cost, otherwise they were swamped.

There was but one country in the world from which she could hope to get them, and that was the last country in the world that should supply them.

The Government of the United States of America disgraced itself by violating the law and allowing British officers to establish recruiting camps for horses, mules and men on its sacred soil, thereby assisting the great monarchy of the British Empire to destroy two little republics in South Africa struggling so hard for their liberty and independence. One of these camps was in New Orleans, at Chalmette, a spot of ground sacred in the eyes and hearts of all true Americans.

The governor of the state protested against this camp. The mayor of the city protested against this camp, and the people of America protested against this camp, yet it was allowed to remain. The government in Washington City sent two officers clothed in the army uniform to visit and report on this camp. The two officers went there, shook hands with the British officers, had some wine, returned to Washington, reported that all was well, and the government established a police force to protect those British officers and that camp while recruiting horses, mules and men for the British Army in South Africa.

During the war of 1812 the English tried to lay waste our land, employed the Indian savages to murder our women and children, burnt our capitol, and the war closed with one of its greatest battles, in 1815, at Chalmette, in New Orleans. So our English Government in Washington waited some eighty-five years for the opportunity to apologize to the British Government for the terrible thrashing that the famous Andrew Jackson gave General Pakenham and his English Army at Chalmette, New Orleans.

It seems to me that this is enough to bring the blush of shame to the cheeks of every true American. If the people of the United States of America cannot find enough true Americans to fill the highest office in their gift, then the time has arrived when they should change their name and cease to call themselves Americans. Suffice it to say that just as the struggling Boers had all England alarmed and the English army pushed to hard straits, ship load after ship load of horses, mules and men from America began to arrive in Cape Town and Durban, and with them Lord Kitchener was soon able to put into the field ninety-one mobile columns. Many of these Americans were captured, and some of them said that the English forced them to enlist and fight, after they reached South Africa, while others declared that they were duly hired by the British in New Orleans to go with the horses and mules to South Africa and on arrival there take up arms against the Boers.

Little good it would do them, but all those who claim they were forced by the British to take up arms against the Boers, should at least vindicate themselves to the extent of laying their complaints with the proper officials in Washington City. Those who confess that they were duly hired by the English to take up arms against the Boers should be made to feel the stigma of their disgrace by being disfranchised and deprived of the rights of American citizenship.

I certainly feel that any republican who voluntarily assists a king or queen, or both, to kill or enslave other republicans, is not fit to live among republicans, for such a man in time of war is sure to commit treason if he gets an opportunity.

Strange as it may seem, it is yet true, the English never once attacked the Boers in the month of January. They were forced to fight on the defensive and the Boers made them do plenty of fighting. Without horses and mules what could the English do but spend their time in throwing up earthworks to defend themselves against Boer attacks, and I tell you the English were kept pretty busy from morn till night. The Boers were having a first class picnic with them, and had not the English Government in Washington, D. C., lent a helping hand, the British army in South Africa would have been hopelessly lost in the struggle. Now the reader can understand what I meant when I said some time back that the two little Republics would have won their independence had not the devil and his angels been against them. It is significant, and it means something when 35,000 Boers put an English army 250,000 strong strictly on the defensive, and the Government of the United States did not fail to come promptly to the British Army's rescue. But I must go ahead and tell what happened in the various and widely separated parts of South Africa during the month of January, 1901. It may not interest the reader, but it was a month of great worry and excitement both to the British army and the British Government.

Early in the month General Botha planned to attack Machadadorp, Dalmanutha, Belfast, Wonderfontein and Balmoral, all fortified stations of the Delagoa railway line. All the forts were well equipped both with men and guns, and the forts at each station were so placed that each could protect the other.

It was during the dark and rainy night of January 8th, that a simultaneous attack on all the stations on the line was to be made. For a distance of seventy-five miles the midnight hour was made hideous by the singing of rifle bullets, whizzing grape shot, and the roar of cannon.

The frightful noise could be heard for miles, and the Boers and English were face to face at the forts, some shooting and others using their rifles as clubs. The English lost heavily, but the attack was only partially successful. The Boers had tried to outdo ten to one against them in well fortified positions. The English at night always removed their guns at Belfast from the forts for safety and it was fortunate for them that they did, for General Viljoen with the Johannesburg boys took the big fort on Monument Hill with its maxims and men. He lost his bravest and best *veldtcornet* in the attack, Ceroni, who fell at the wall of the fort. Plucky Dick Hunt, of the Irish Brigade, was by his side, and he received three wounds, one in the lungs being a very severe one, from which he is suffering to this very day, (as at time of first publication). He, however, with his three wounds, was among the very first to scale the walls and capture the fort.

The fort at the coal mine was attacked by Major Wolmorans and about twenty-five artillery boys, including Sergeant Joe Wade, Sergeant Mike Halley, Joe Kennedy, John McGlew, Jim French, Captain McCallum and Jerry O'Leary, of the Irish Brigade. Here the Boers and the English were within two feet of each other, each trying to take the other's head off. Some of the Irish boys actually pulled the rifles out of the Tommies' hands. Finally the Tommies weakened and the boys jumped over the wall and took the fort. Lieutenant Cotzee showed remarkable bravery, was severely wounded and afterwards murdered by some *kaffirs* that had been armed by the British. The Boers held the two forts a few hours, helped to care for the dead and wounded English, and then with all their booty returned to camp. At all the other stations the Boers had to fall back because the English were too strong for them.

This affair put all the English to work next day along the line, strengthening existing forts, building others, digging trenches and so forth, to make their positions as strong for defence as possible. They were not only frightened, but astonishingly alarmed by the boldness and the aggressiveness of the Boers. We were camped about seven miles from Belfast, about 150 strong, could see everyone in the town, and the English, about 3,000 strong, could see us, yet they never dared to attack us. We had no defences whatever and were camped on the open prairie. "We were as safe as the people in Piccadilly."

General Chris. Botha near Blauwkop and not far from Standerton, attacked the English and had a good warm fight, and at the end the English thought it wise to pull themselves nearer Standerton. Shortly afterwards General Chris. Botha found the English between Ermelo and Carolina and again attacked and made it warm for them. In fact, he made the English commands that had sufficient horses hustle away lively, and they kept close to the railway lines for protection. General De Wet in the Free State was at all times next to the English, who now were not striving to corner him, but to keep shy of him. Near Lindley he attacked and had a fight with a column much stronger in men and guns than himself, but he was eminently successful, and before all could escape he made several prisoners. In Cape Colony, south of Kimberly and as far down as Cape Town, there was good fighting in many places. It required an English army 30,000 strong to protect the various towns, and yet the Boers had no trouble in accomplishing their ends. Judge Hertzog and General Brand were in one section, Commandant Fouche and General Kritzinger in another, while Commandant Wynand Malan and Commandant Scheepers were near to Cape Town.

All these generals and commandants were playing havoc with the English, and Commandant Malan, one of the most successful and daring young officers of the war, was within twenty miles of Cape Town when he captured a convoy. While he was here great excitement prevailed in Cape Town and the people were daily expecting the Boers to attack. Near Kimberly the other generals and commandants were attacking and driving the English, and once again Kimberly was in a great state of worry. So alarming were the conditions in Cape Colony that it became necessary to proclaim martial law in many districts, and re-enforcements were called for in order to try and suppress the invaders.

Now we will see what General de la Rey is doing in the Western Transvaal. The English are numerous everywhere and protected by forts in all parts. At Zeerust a large command is tied up by General de la Rey's men, not one of them shows his head above the wall. They cry for food and relief, but in vain. Only a small number of General de la Rey's men are there, but the number seems quite sufficient. The English are hard pushed and much worried, yet they do not dare to leave their walls and face the Boers.

For many miles along the Magaliesburg Mountains southwest of Pretoria, de la Rey is attacking and driving the English, and before the end of the month had cleared them all from the mountains and taken possession himself. Every advantage, both in men, guns and fortified positions were in the hands of the English, yet so fierce was General de la Rey's attack that they had to give way and abandon that mountain range. Near Ventersdorp and Lichtenburg some of de la Key's commandos attacked the entrenched and fortified English, and at Lichtenburg, where the general was in person, half the defences were taken and many English killed and wounded. Fighting continued here for several days, and had not re-enforcements arrived, General de la Rey would have captured or killed all the English commands.

**COMMANDANTS IN THE BOER SERVICE**
Colonel Blake, John Muller, Commandant Malan,
Lieutenant Malan, Commandant Conroy,
Commandant Lategan, Commandant Piet Moll.

In the Western Transvaal one of de la Rey's commandos attacked a convoy and its escort near Modderfontein, and a hard fight for several days, was the result. In the end, 250 men surrendered with two maxims, plenty of ammunition, loaded wagon train, and so forth. Having disarmed them and taken possession of the booty, the Boers sent the escort back to the English lines. It was during this month that General Beyers passed from the high veldt on the east to the Western Transvaal, crossing the railway line between Johannesburg and Pretoria. He did not forget to take a railway station as he passed. Some of his men made a raid to Johannesburg, upset the nerves of the whole population, took about two thousand cattle, a good number of goats and sheep and then returned to camp, satisfied with their day's work. Many other small fights occurred during the month, but not of sufficient importance to deserve mention. I think that I have given enough to show that Lord Roberts' war was at an end, and that he fully deserved his $500,000 and earldom for his proclamations. I have not heard yet what Conan Doyle received, but he is certain to have reaped a reward of some kind.

It was during the months of December and January that Lord Kitchener did some of his dirtiest paper work in the form of circulars praying the *burghers* to come in and surrender, and offering them all sorts of inducements to commit treason.

He made use of the *burghers* who had long since surrendered and whom he had not shipped out of the country because they were so loyal, to carry out these circulars and distribute them among the Boer commandos.

When they began to arrive they were at once sent back and told to warn all persons who should in the future appear in the Boer camps with such treasonable papers that they would be shot. Lord Kitchener prevailed upon them, however, and out they came again. Generals De Wet, de la Rey, Louis Botha, Chris. Botha and Viljoen all had some of them shot. Lord Kitchener protested against the shooting of his loyal subjects, but he was very careful not to send any more out. These Anglo-Africans who did this work correspond to what is known in the United States as Anglo-Americans or Anglo-Saxons, and just as much confidence can be put in the one in time of war as in the other. For it is this class of people who, in time of war, will be sure to ally themselves with that power which they believe most likely will be victorious in the end, regardless of their citizenship.

Any English lord or general, or any general who, to gain his end, puts a premium upon treason, will himself, under proper conditions commit treason, just as sure as he who offers a bribe is equally sure to accept one. An Anglo-African is a born or naturalized *burgher* of the Free State or the Transvaal who has an English heart, just as an Anglo-American is a born or naturalized citizen of the United States who has an English heart.

CHAPTER 17

# De Wet Alarms the English

Now I come to the month of February, 1901, and will give the reader a little idea of how the Boers conducted themselves during the twenty-eight days. The British Government had now granted Lord Kitchener's request, and started to South Africa 30,000 more men. England was so hard pressed for recruits that she had to send any and everything in the shape of a man, and most of her recruits were taken from bar-rooms, I imagine, for, of the 30,000 who came, Lord Kitchener had to send back some 10,000 as being utterly worthless for any use whatever. The remaining 20,000 were put in military training for six months, and in the end were unable to ride or fight, but he needed men so badly that he kept them to make a good display if for nothing else.

During the month before us General Louis Botha and his brother, General Chris. Botha, had a very lively tune. They were in the vicinity of Ermelo on the high *veldt*, in the Eastern Transvaal. They had made so much trouble that Lord Kitchener resolved to make a determined effort to corner and capture them. He collected all his available cavalry and having supplied them with plenty of maxims and guns he started them in six columns to bring in the two Bothas. General French was put in command of the English and was considered the best cavalry officer in the British service, so then there was no doubt but that he would present to Lord Kitchener the two ordinary farmer generals that had been causing so much trouble and alarm. The Bothas had with them about 1,000 men, and French was to corner and capture them with 15,000 men.

General French so placed his columns that when they all advanced they would enclose the Bothas within a circle from which it would be impossible to escape. The Bothas discovered French's object and

GENERAL JAN KEMP

before the columns could advance they attacked and put to flight one column and then moved off in the direction of Piet Retief. This was a surprise to General French, but he did not despair of capturing the farmer generals. He put all his columns in pursuit, and when the proper time came to cage them, the two farmers easily broke through the cordon and returned to the vicinity of Ermelo.

French was discouraged. He made no further attempt to capture the farmers, but was determined to do something before he returned, so he made war on the women and children and spread great distress and suffering among them. Some of these women were raped, others dragged out of their homes at night and made witness all their possessions consumed in flames. Many were driven on foot to concentration camps and kicked and cuffed about as so many beasts.

Having made the women suffer as much as possible, he gathered in several thousand cattle and sheep and returned to report what a successful expedition he had completed. At Lake Chrissi, between Ermelo and Carolina, General Botha had the nerve to attack an English camp 2,000 strong. It was a foggy morning, and the noise of the battle stampeded a band of wild horses and they ran into the Krugersdorpers' horses, stampeding them too.

This spoiled the whole affair, for General Botha had the English camp all but taken, but when the *burghers* saw their saddled horses running away they at once started in pursuit of them. Fortunately they had already captured several hundred horses from the English, for many of their own horses evaded them. Commandant Kemp, one of the most enthusiastic, one of the most energetic, pluckiest and best *commandants* in the Boer Army, was more than disgusted with his men for being so concerned about their horses, but he forgot for the moment that an infantryman is but of little practical use in war. The English, when the Boers retired, lost no time in fleeing to places of safety, and never again showed themselves on the high *veldt* until the horses, mules and men from America were put into fighting trim, and that was many weeks to come. The two Bothas had proved themselves equal to that almost, if not quite, unequalled De Wet, and such was the impression they made on Lord Kitchener that he requested General Louis Botha to meet and discuss with him some peace terms.

Before going elsewhere, I will tell what happened when last General Botha and Lord Kitchener met in Middleburg at the end of February. For the price of peace, Lord Kitchener told General Botha that after a time he would give the Boers civil government and give this, and that, and one million pounds to build up ten millions' worth of destroyed farms, and so forth. But Lord, or monacle-eyed Joe Chamberlain stepped in, and said "We will do nothing of the kind, and the Boers must make an unconditional surrender." Of course, General Botha smiled at both, and on his return to Ermelo told what had taken place at the conference, exhorted them to fight to the bitter end, and assured them that he would be with them heart, soul and body.

Now I will jump into the Free State and see what the wily De Wet is doing. De Wet, the Stonewall Jackson of South Africa, had all the English of the Free State on the run and, at the end of January, it looked as if he would sweep them from the country. Lord Kitchener resolved to corner and capture him, it mattered not what it might cost, for Lord Roberts and Conan Doyle had declared the war at an end, and if the English people should hear that De Wet was practically in control of the Free State, why, they would be inclined to think that both Roberts and Doyle were liars.

As a side remark, that might be expressing it mildly, but anyhow, Kitchener organized eight or ten columns, all he could get, because the English Government in Washington City had not yet succeeded in landing enough horses or mules for his needs, and sent them to surround and take in the troublesome De Wet. Now General De Wet was on the open *veldt* near Brandfort, where the English could see him from all directions, and all they had to do was to surround him and take or kill him. As De Wet had about 1500 men, of course it would be a very easy thing for 25,000 trained military men to gobble him in, in quick time. The several columns surrounded him, and despatch men were flying at full speed from column to column bearing instructions that would insure perfect unity of action. General De Wet, when he concluded that the several columns were in good readiness to bury him, saddled up, moved out and attacked the nearest column. He riddled it, put it to flight, and another column which came up quickly was also torn to pieces and scattered in all directions.

He took two of their guns, a maxim and a portion of their convoy, a few prisoners whom he released, and went on his way to Cape Colony without consulting with or asking permission of the other columns. I do not know what the officer in command reported on his return, but I suppose he made the usual one, that someone had betrayed him or that his horses and men were so fatigued that he could not make a successful pursuit of De Wet and his fresh horses and men. General De Wet did not stop to hear what kind of a report the English commander did make, because he was anxious to reach Cape Colony, find out what was being done there and replenish his command with horses, and so forth. He had to pass many English commands on the way, but he succeeded in sweeping them aside and reaching the Orange River, where the English had made every preparation not only to prevent his crossing, but also to capture him. Again he outwitted the English, crossed the river, entered Cape Colony, saw Judge Hertzog and other commanders, supplied himself with plenty of horses, had a tough fight with the English, abandoned some of his wagons, and then started back on his way to the Orange River where the English were sure to catch him this tune.

On arriving near the river he found the crossings in possession of the English commands, but he must cross, for he was anxious to go far to the north in the Free State, where he felt that his presence was necessary. He sent a detachment to a certain point up the river with instructions to show themselves, and in case the English advanced they were to retire, put spurs to their horses and overtake the command while crossing the river. The scheme worked beautifully, for as soon as the English saw the detachment they concluded that it was De Wet's advance guard and they prepared to attack him. The detachment played its part well, by going through the form of signalling to the rear.

The English made all possible haste to advance and attack De Wet and if possible hold him engaged until their other commands should come. As all were on the lookout for him, of course the different commands would lose no time in reaching the scene of action. The English completely abandoned the crossing in front of De Wet and made a hurried advance on the detachment. When 1200 yards away the detachment opened fire on the English and a short skirmish took place. At this moment De Wet rushed to the river, crossed it and put his men in fighting order to protect the detachment which he expected every moment. After firing a few shots, the detachment dropped behind the hill from which they had been firing, mounted their horses, put in the spurs and soon joined the wily De Wet across the river. Again the English were easily outwitted and De Wet was once more in the Free State. He had to fight his way all through the Free State, but the English were afraid of him, and he reached his destination at Heilbron without loss of time.

He had now made a round trip of about a thousand miles, had had many skirmishes, successfully fought two battles and landed home

Mrs Abraham Malan daughter of Commandant General Joubert and her young family

with but little loss. His trip had a great moral effect on the English army, the people of Cape Colony and Cape Town. The news of his invasion of Cape Colony had spread all over South Africa and had reached London. The English element in Cape Town and throughout the colony were crazy with fright, for all men were sure that De Wet would lay waste the country as the English had the Transvaal and Free State. The English forces in the colony were concentrated that they might make a successful defence when De Wet should attack.

Lord Kitchener and his numerous force of cricketers felt the cold chill running down their backs and were at their wit's end to make out a report that would so mislead the English papers that they would not express any regret at having presented Lord Roberts with $500,000 and an earldom for his proclamations, and for declaring that the war was at an end. All were so undone and such nervous wrecks that they did not remember that Conan Doyle had also declared that the war was over.

I think General De Wet made a great mistake in returning to the Free State so soon. With his energy, his ability, his prestige and men he should have gone to the De Aar Junction, destroyed that most important railway point and then followed the railway towards Cape Town, destroying it and all the bridges on his way. Such were the conditions in Cape Town at the time that had he gone ahead and penetrated as far as the Paarl, it is safe to conclude that he would have received at least 15,000 recruits, and these Colonial Boers cannot be surpassed for fighting qualities. Having done this, before retracing his steps he would have had an army 20,000 strong before he reached the Orange River. I always felt that the war should have been carried into Cape Colony and there finished, for the people were ripe for rebellion, and had Generals Botha, De Wet and de la Rey gone there with their commands it is certain that they would have risen, as one, and all joined the Boers. This would have meant the defeat and downfall of the English army and the independence of the Africander race throughout South Africa. But they didn't go there, and the Africander race has yet to free itself, (as at time of first publication).

During this month of February neither General de la Rey nor the English did anything worth recording. The English remained close in their forts, and General de la Rey was satisfied to rest his men and give his horses a chance to recuperate and fatten up.

CHAPTER 18

# An Exciting Trip

Now I come to the month of March, during which but little was done except in Cape Colony and de la Rey's district of the Western Transvaal. General Louis Botha was at Ermelo and the various commands were in their respective districts on the high *veldt*. The English did not come out because enough mules and horses had not yet arrived from America.

We all had a quiet but good time lying in *laager*, smoking our pipes and growing fat on mealie pap (ordinary corn meal mush) and fresh beef. In the Free State General De Wet had a few little skirmishes and a few of his commandos had a brush with the enemy, but little or no damage was done. It seemed that the peace confab between Lord Kitchener and General Botha in the latter part of February had a soothing and quieting effect on everybody. In Cape Colony, General Kritzinger, Commandants Malan, Fouche, Hertzog and George Brand were going at a lively pace in many of the districts. They seemed to continue to have their own way and keep the English on the constant jump, and captured many prisoners. All of them supplied themselves and men with at least two horses each, and the English were kind enough to give them plenty of ammunition. So the Boers in Cape Colony had no reason to complain.

In the western division of the Transvaal, General de la Rey's *commandos* had some pretty hard fights. The general attacked Lichtenburg and gave the English a good pounding. Had not reinforcements arrived just in time, he would have had the town and the English garrison. But as it was, he was forced to retire. One of his commandos near Klerksdorp attacked the English and forced them to retire. Near Kaffir Kraal General de la Rey had another fight, and although the English suffered severely, they were too many for him and captured his guns. The lieutenant in charge of the artillery was not to blame, however, for he was deceived by one of those Anglo-Africans who came to him and told him that General de la Rey wished the guns. Having obeyed he found himself and guns in the hands of the English. As this Anglo-African was evidently a *burgher*, the lieutenant thought nothing about it further than to obey instructions. Damn all Anglos, whether Americans, Boers, German, French or whatever their nationality.

Along the line of the Magaliesburg Mountains a few shots were daily exchanged between the English and the Boers, the English in the forts and the Boers in the foothills, but no actual fighting took place. General Beyers in the north was inactive, too, after he and General Plumer had had some hot fights, when the latter came to occupy the little town of Pietersburg, 180 miles north of Pretoria.

General Beyers had but a small command, but he kept General Plumer's force busy throwing up earthworks and preparing all sorts of defences. General Beyers placed his headquarters between Pietersburg and Pretoria and not far from the railway line, that he might continue to trouble the big force at Pietersburg.

Now I come to the month of April, when sufficient horses, mules and men had arrived from the United States of America for Lord Kitchener to put sixty-three mobile columns in the field, so the reader may be sure that the Boers had to make use of all of their natural wits to outwit the English. They did well, covered themselves with glory and again put the great English army to shame. The reader must remember at this time the actual fighting Boers numbered very nearly 30,000 men and no more. There were also on the farms several thousand women and old men, non-combatants, and children. I hope this will be remembered, for now comes the most interesting and marvellous part of the war.

During the next twelve months, the wonderful fighting qualities of the real fighting Boer came out and astonished the world, while the English army by its pitiful stupidity and unworthiness, becomes immortalized in the history of a fast declining and degenerated empire. General Ben Viljoen and "Fighting Bill," General Muller, learned that a large convoy was leaving Machadadorp on the Delagoa railway line for Lydenburg, where there was a large English command. They resolved to try to take it, and with nearly 500 fine soldiers and determined men they left their laager, marched about thirty miles and concealed themselves near the main road to Lydenburg. At last, after waiting a day and a night, the convoy with six or seven hundred escort came in sight, and all the boys gazed at it with eager eyes.

Nearer and nearer it came, till it came too near and the boys could not wait any longer. Off they went for it, fired a few shots, the escort fled, and the boys brought back about 100 loaded wagons with them. I tell you, the Tommies don't like the looks of the Boers when they come fast, and they put themselves out of danger as quickly as their horses can take them. Once again the English have supplied the Johannesburg commando with food, clothing and ammunition.

General Chris. Botha in the Vryheid district, like General Viljoen and General Muller, helps himself to a convoy that plentifully supplies him with all that is necessary in the way of food, clothing and ammunition, but the escort were all fortunate enough to escape.

Commandant Grobler ran against a large column of English five times his number, gave them a good short fight and then retreated as rapidly as he could. General Louis Botha and General Chris. Botha attacked a column 3,000 strong at Spitz Kop near Ermelo and kept these 3,000 Tommies moving lively all day. I really believe the English cavalry would do well if so many of them did not fall off when at a swift pace, and if they would not stampede and every man run for his life because a shell exploded near them. Here I saw over 600 cavalry put to flight by one shell from a French gun so directed by Major Pretorius that it struck and exploded in their midst. Major Pretorius had about twenty men with him, but the 600 Tommies had not lost any Boer guns and were not looking for any. As this body of 600 cavalry fled, several troopers fell off their horses and followed their fast flying comrades on foot. If the cavalry of other European countries is as bad as the English cavalry, my advice to them is to fight shy of the American cavalry—if it comes to a fight. This column intended to camp near Ermelo, but concluded that it was too warm for them and went several miles towards Carolina before going into camp.

Now there was a rest in this part of the world for about two weeks, and then, like a swarm of bees, the English columns fairly covered the whole high *veldt*, fifteen columns having shown up at one time. This was on the 29th of the month, so I will wait until the next month, May, to tell all that happened.

On this very day Major Pretorius, Gustave Preller and myself started on a round trip of 480 miles to the Western Transvaal with despatches for General de la Rey. We saw something, and before I forget it I must tell our experience. It was a perilous journey, but we felt confident that we would deliver the despatches and return to General

Louis Botha with the replies. With a cart and four mules driven by a Pondo *kaffir*, Kleinveld by name, two pack horses, and three riding horses, we started. On arriving at Olifantsfontein, about twenty miles from the Johannesburg-Pretoria railway line, we learned that it would be impossible to keep the cart with us because the English had every crossing so well guarded.

We decided to leave it, its *kaffir* driver and the young *burgher*, Van Rensberg, and go ahead with the two pack horses. Young Van Rensberg, a brave and noble boy, was instructed to await our return, but if the English should show up before we did, he was to use his own judgment and save himself, cart and mules. Off we went, and on reaching a ridge about nine miles from the railway line we stopped, brought out our field glasses and found that the English were numerous all along the line. But we must pass through, and that was all there was to it; so we decided to pass the line very near to Olifantsfontein, because the English wouldn't think for a moment that any Boers would dare to take such desperate chances. We waited till the sun was down. It was the 3rd of May and the full moon came up in all her glory just as the sun dropped below the horizon.

It seemed to us that it was as light as day, but go we must, and we did go. At about eight o'clock p. m. Major Pretorius said, "There is a line," and there it was. Cautiously we approached it, then crossed it and smiled a heavenly smile as we looked at the Tommies 600 yards away at the station, smoking, telling jokes and laughing by their camp fires. They had no guards out, and we passed by them without interruption, not seeing any trouble ahead. We rode on for a mile, stopped and rested our horses for fifteen minutes and then went on our way to the six-mile-*spruit* near Pretoria. We rode till one o'clock a. m. and we knew that we were near the Pretoria-Rustenberg main road, so we decided to stop, sleep until daylight and then hasten to Schurweburg, a farm settlement just twelve miles west of Pretoria. We hobbled our horses and went to sleep on the dry grass.

Just at daylight Major Pretorius stirred us up, and we caught, saddled and packed our horses and travelled at a gallop, because we were very near the English forts on the hill between us and Pretoria. Just as the sun rose we were crossing an *arroya* (a *spruit*), and Preller discovered a long canvas bag, well filled, by the roadside. It bore the name of one of Kitchener's scouts and had evidently fallen from a wagon during the night. The numerous horse and wagon tracks convinced us that we were very near an English command and therefore we must proceed very cautiously.

About one and a half miles to our right was the little farm settlement behind a ridge, and from the great column of black smoke that was rising in the air we concluded that the English must be there, engaged in a fight against the women and children and burning their homes. We turned to our right and went down the *arroya* and when at a distance of 400 yards, Major Pretorius, who was in front, leaped from his horse. Preller and I followed suit. About 500 yards to his left Major Pretorius discovered fifteen mounted English on a small ridge facing him. Near the *arroya* was a small clump of bush and in it we concealed our five horses as best we could. The Major and Preller crawled up a hill about sixty yards away to try and find out where the camp was, while I was to stay with the horses and keep an eye on the smoke. In a few moments I discovered between us and the smoking farm settlement, at a distance of about 800 yards, some 400 cavalrymen, all dismounted. The major had also discovered them and travelled back to tell me.

We now realised that we were in a bad box, and that it looked as if there was no hope to escape, for should we try to go back towards Pretoria we would be discovered and driven into that town and captured. In a few minutes the 400 cavalry mounted their horses and came up the *arroya* towards us, crossed it about 300 yards below us, passed about the same distance to our left and finally dismounted in the road just where a few minutes before we had picked up the bag. They were now about 400 yards from us and in plain view. Suddenly they mounted their horses, formed a semi-circle around us, in line of skirmishers, and began to fire, but in an opposite direction to us. Another 100 cavalry came up the *arroya* from the burning houses, driving some sheep, and passed behind us no more than seventy-five yards away. We heard distinctly all they said about burning and plundering the farmhouses. The firing became general all about us. Then we knew that some Boers had attacked the English, yet there was no possible chance for us to escape as far as we could see.

We all shook hands, and swore that we would not surrender, and having concealed the few valuables we had, we waited for the English to discover us. Should they kill us they would get nothing but our horses, and as a last resort we were going to mount our horses and run for our lives. The fight lasted till 10.30 a. m., about three and one half hours, and then the English formed columns, took their wagons and cannon and started for Pretoria. They had gone about 800 yards when they halted and dismounted. We did not like this, so we mounted our horses, rode down the *arroya* about 300 yards till we came to the wagon road that led to the farm settlement, and then put spurs and were away at full gallop. The English stood with their necks stretched like a flock of geese and gazed intently at us, but never fired a shot. We passed near five Boers in a *kopje* who were about firing on us, but seeing our pack horses they refrained. They could not understand how we could be Boers and come from the English lines, yet they knew that none but Boers had pack horses.

On reaching the farm settlement we found the houses were not burnt, but the barns and all food supplies were destroyed and hundreds of women and children left to starve. The object of this was to force the women and children to go to Pretoria and ask for supplies of food. Lord Kitchener would then send them to one of his prison camps for women and children, and cable to London that some 200 women and children from Schurweburg had come to him as refugees, seeking his protection, as all were in a starving condition. The Boers who had been fighting the English soon came in and reported their morning's work. We knew Everyone of them personally and were glad to see them again. When the fight began only six of the 110 men had horses, but when it ended they had nineteen more and six mules and one wagon loaded with supplies which they had captured from the English. With the mules they could now mount thirty-one of the 110 men.

During the fight a little fifteen-year-old boy by the name of Pretorius had walked about three miles to a point from which he could see if there were any more English coming from any quarter. He remained too long, and when he saw the English columns returning to Pretoria, it was too late for him to run and save himself. He had no idea that the English engaged in the fight intended to return to Pretoria so soon.

He followed the Boer instinct to save himself, and he crawled into an ant-bear hole about forty yards from the road and pulled his rifle with him. The whole column passed him by and when he could no longer hear the horses' feet beating the road, he ventured to peep out and see his position. He saw one man coming at a gallop about a half a mile away and he knew this man belonged to the column that had passed by, so he lay low and watched the lone trooper. When the trooper was about forty yards away little Pretorius jumped out of the hole, threw his rifle into position and called out, "Hands up!"

The trooper was an English sergeant and thought at first that the little boy was joking, but soon saw that he was in earnest, and at once surrendered. Little Pretorius made him lay down his rifle, ammunition, and so forth, and then started him on his way on foot. After the trooper had gone about 100 yards the little boy with two rifles, plenty of ammunition and a fine horse, bridle and saddle, went cantering away to the farm settlements. On his arrival he was the hero of the hour, and Everyone, men, women and children, congratulated him on his pluck and good soldier sense. Now thirty-two of the 110 men were mounted.

We stopped here for three days to rest ourselves and horses and to have new shoes put on the horses, for we had to pass through a very rocky country. We learned that the English forts were very numerous between us and General de la Rey, and that it would be difficult to pass them by without being captured, but we must take the chance. Here we first met the famous Boer Spy, Captain Naude, a young man about twenty-three years old. In due time I will tell all about him and his marvellous spy system in Pretoria and Johannesburg. While in this farm settlement he and a few boys went into Pretoria every night and brought out a good bunch of the officers' horses, bridles and saddles, so that by the time we said goodbye to all and started on our long journey, seventy of the 110 men were mounted. We arrived at this farm settlement on May 4th and left on the 7th, passed near Krugersdorp, saw the English camps about there and went down through Heckpoort.

We were now about three miles from Nooitgedacht where General de la Rey and General Beyers had taken General Clement's camp and killed, wounded and taken prisoners 800 of his men. Ahead of us we could see a long line of English forts, so we knew that there must be Boers in the Magaliesburg just opposite to them. We moved cautiously and kept our eyes on the forts. When nearly opposite to them and about 5,000 yards distant, we found some Boers, and I tell you we felt much relieved. The English had spent the previous day trying to shell them out, but had signally failed. We could not learn just where General de la Rey was, but they knew he was somewhere near Mafeking on the western border. We remained here for the night and learned that the English had forts everywhere in front, and that we must be very careful.

In the early morning we started to run the gauntlet and pass the forts. Each rode about two hundred yards behind the other for about

A TYPICAL BOER FAMILY OF FOURTEEN
S. W. Joubert and family

an hour an a half and then we found ourselves out of danger. Not a shot was fired at us, yet we were directly under them and not 3,000 yards away. We crossed a small mountain and were then in a great, wide rolling prairie, with Ventersdorp about five hours' ride to the left.

The many English graves we daily passed showed that heavy fighting had taken place along the whole line of the Magielesberg. On reaching a tall ridge we could see immense forts on all high prominences in our front, and we were much puzzled as to how we could safely pass them. We would stop and use our glasses frequently, because we were on risky ground. There was one large fort that was directly in our way, and we could not see how we could possibly pass it without going at full speed, and our horses were too tired to do this. We slowly approached till within a thousand yards of this place, when we dismounted, sat down to rest and made the best possible use of our glasses. We had excellent glasses, and for one hour there was not a second passed without at least one of us having the glasses nailed on that fort. It was about noon time, and to save us we could not see the slightest sign of life about the fort.

We concluded there was no one in it and we decided to take our chances and ride by it. We guessed right, and at a *kraal* near by the *kaffirs* told us that the English had left the fort the day before. This fort would accommodate about 1,000 men, so we knew that many English were prowling about somewhere and that we must keep a sharp lookout. We moved on rapidly, passed many of the forts, but were not delayed by any of them. Our horses were very tired and so were we, when we reached one of General de la Rey's commandos on May 10th. We felt relieved, for now we were sure that the despatches would be delivered and we could take a long rest. We were told that General de la Rey was at Mafeking, but would return in two or three days. In due time we learned that he had returned and that he was with his *laager* about six miles away.

We went to see him, and there we found with him one of his bravest and most dashing fighters, General Kemp. We delivered the despatches, he wrote his replies, and in one hour was gone to see one of his commandos twenty-five miles away, to get matters in readiness for a fight. He had one horse, worth about twenty dollars, a mackintosh, a revolver and a pair of glasses. With him was his son and Secretary Ferrera. He eats with his *burghers*, shares their blankets and carries practically no staff. He makes every man fight.

Within an hour after his departure a most important despatch arrived from General De Wet telling him that he must come at once and see him in the Free State, for it was on a serious matter that they must act. The despatch was forwarded to the general in haste. We remained here a few days with General Kemp to give our horses a good rest for the return journey. We had bread to eat and it was the first we had tasted for many months. At night, General de la Rey had the ground ploughed, the corn planted, and the wheat sowed, so that he always had plenty of everything to eat in the way of bread, mealie pap, pumpkins, sweet potatoes, Irish, etc.

On the 22nd of May we started back on the same route by which we had come. Two days after leaving General Kemp we heard heavy cannonading, as if someone had attacked somebody else. We were sure that General Kemp had a hand in it, because he was always looking for a fight and he was in that direction. We passed back through the English lines without any trouble whatever, and arrived at the farm settlements we had left on the 7th of May, on June 2nd. Seventy of the 110 men were mounted when we left and on our return the entire number was mounted and they had some forty horses to spare.

Veldtcornet Pretorius and Veldtcornet Jones were in command and both were brave, energetic and daring commanders. We remained here till June 7th to rest ourselves and horses and try to find out what had happened on the high *veldt* since we left. All we could learn was that it was covered with English camps and that Bapsfontein, just across the railway line, was still free of English. This was good news to us, for we left our cart and mules at Olifantsfontein, just six miles further on than Bapsfontein. Captain Naude, the famous spy, and six other men joined us to go to the high *veldt*. They had helped to rid all the stables at Pretoria of the English officers' horses, bridles, and saddles and now they are seeking new fields for adventure.

We started about three o'clock in the afternoon of June 7th, in order that we might be near the railway line before sundown. There was no moon now, and as it was cloudy, heavy weather, the night was sure to be very dark. Veldtcornet Jones went with us a part of the way to be sure that we would strike the line at the safest place to cross. Night came and we made for the line. It was so dark we had to keep in touch almost, or otherwise we would be separated and lose each other. To make bad matters worse, a slow rain set in and we could not tell whether we were going north, south, east or west.

I remember one laughable incident which I must tell about, for it will require only half a dozen words. We had been wading through

Captain J. J. Naude
The Great Boer Spy.

cornfields, reeds, muddy *spruits* and so forth for some time, but were getting along all right when we suddenly heard a most terrible splash. Oom Koos Bosch, horse and all, had suddenly disappeared in a deep pool of water that the rest of us had by mere luck escaped. We dragged him out, and after half an hour's hard work managed to get his horse out too. The banks were very steep and quite high. When La Blanche, his son-in-law, heard Oom Koos' voice, he rushed back to his assistance and in he went too, so we had to drag him out. It was a laughable affair, but both were so mad that one would have to take his life in his hand if he dared to give an audible smile.

We went on and rambled for hours trying to find the railway line. About nine o'clock all the large flash lights at various stations began to work. It was a sudden change from pitch darkness to almost broad daylight. We at once saw that we were very near the line and had the English opened their eyes they would have at once seen that we were near it. We had to hurry now, for the flash lights were playing all about us and we could see the entire line from Pretoria to Johannesburg. Soon we reached the line near Kalfontein Station, and cut some thirty or forty barbed wires, the field telegraph and main wires, then crossed some deep ditches, then the railway track, then some more deep ditches, and then cut thirty or forty more barbed wires and were free to go our way, and be assured that we lost no time in going, for we were within five hundred yards of a big camp at the station. Soon we were as "safe as the people in Piccadilly," but having passed over a ridge, we were enveloped in pitch darkness again and the rain was still falling.

We stopped and rested ourselves and horses for an hour, at one o'clock. in the morning. Then we started again, but had no light except that reflected on the clouds behind or by the numerous flash lights, so we rambled and rambled in search of Bapsfontein, where we would strike a big road that would lead us straight and right. Just at early dawn in the morning we saw several specks of fire and someone cried out, "Look out! there is something in front. Don't you see the fire in their pipes?" Some laughed at the remark and some of us didn't, and when we had ridden twenty yards further out rang the cry "Who comes there?" and it was "Who comes there?" along a very long line. It was no laughing matter now, and like a lightning flash we whirled about, put the spurs in and away we went at a full gallop regardless of the awful darkness.

We remained together, made a wide circuit, and having galloped for about a mile, we stopped on top of a ridge to await until there was more light. We did not know where we were, and we must find out. Sure we were that an English camp was near us, but where are we? When there was a little more light we saw a farm house about a half mile away, and two of the Boer boys rode to find out just where we were.

This was a "Hands-uppers" farm, and he was at home. He told them that we had just passed Bapsfontein, where there were camped about 2,000 English, and advised us to move rapidly for the reason that a detachment might be on the ridge in a few minutes. Fools we were, but we never thought about the fellow being a "Hands-upper," otherwise we would have taken him and his two good horses that were feeding near by us. At Bapsfontein we had actually passed between the main camp and the guards, and that is why they did not fire at us.

We now went on for three miles, for we knew now just where we were, and on reaching Kaffir Kraal, where there were plenty of mealies (corn) we stopped, unsaddled and bought a good feed for all our horses. While here we saw the English scouts on the ridge behind us and they saw us too, but made no move to disturb us. After an hour's rest, we saddled up and rode towards Olifantsfontein where we had left our cart and mules. When within a mile of this place we took up a gallop and when within a thousand yards we saw a lot of fellows preparing to fight. We came down to a walk, and the *burghers* who had prepared to fight saw that we were *burghers* too. We found here General Piet Viljoen, but not our cart and mules. Many and great changes had taken place along the scene since we had left it on May 3rd. No one had the slightest idea where General Botha or our cart and mules were, but all could tell us that the whole high *veldt* was fairly alive with English camps.

We remained here for the night and most of the following day, for our horses had been under the saddle for nineteen hours and necessarily they were exceedingly tired as well as ourselves. In the afternoon of the following day we boldly struck out on the high *veldt* to see what there was to be seen. On the 11th of June we came on some of the boys of the Bethel commando who told us that "Fighting Bill," General Muller, with 150 of the Johannesburg boys had just taken in an Australian camp about five miles away and captured over 300 men, two pom-poms, with 4,000 shells and some 400 horses. This was good news, and it was correct, too, and the Australians have not done much bragging since. They had not the slightest idea where General Botha was, but told us to look out, for the Englishmen were here, there, and so forth, pointing out to us the different directions of the English camps.

We went ahead towards Tritchardtfontein, which was near Bethel, and at night we came suddenly upon Commandant Hears and his men. Here was a spunky little commandant who had wrecked many trains and done his part towards worrying the English. He did not know where General Botha was, nor had he seen or heard of our cart and mules.

We camped with Mears for the night, and early next morning started out towards Bethel, but on seeing a lot of sheep that had just been killed, we changed our direction for Blauwkop, because the slaughtered sheep showed us that the English were in front. We reached the vicinity of Blauwkop just before sundown, and to our great surprise a Boer commando, too. A greater surprise was still in store for us, for on reaching the camp there was General Britz, another brave and capable officer, with his commando, President Steyn, General De Wet and General Hertzog, of the Free State, and our good old friend whom we had left some three weeks back, General de la Rey. It is unnecessary to say that we were delighted, yes, overjoyed, at our good luck, and as we all knew one another well, the reader may be assured that we spent a few hours most pleasantly.

I must here mention that General de la Rey and I each really first made out what the other was. During our short conversation three weeks back I had told him that certain conditions prevailed in another section and that to me matters looked serious. I went on and explained everything to him, but he could not but feel that I must be mistaken. Now we met again, and the first thing he said to me was "You were right, and we are here to correct and put things right." I had always distrusted the Acting President, Schalk Burger, and I had told General de la Rey so and given my reasons. I might as well finish up with this meeting before I take up the thread of happenings in April.

On the following day, June 19th, the Free State and Transvaal Governments were to meet at Waterfall, about twenty miles from Standerton and about six miles from a large English camp. Now we would see General Louis Botha, whom we had been seeking, and all the big bugs at one and the same time. It was just after sundown that all saddled up and started for Waterfall, where we arrived late at night and soundly slept.

About ten o'clock the next day we saw a long string of carts in the distance, and that was the approaching Transvaal Government. Soon they arrived and there was a general handshaking all around. Major Pretorius gave General de la Rey's replies to General Botha, although General de la Rey was there himself. In addition to these there were present, Acting President Schalk Burger, Secretary of State Reitz, General Ben Viljoen, General Smuts, President Steyn, General De Wet, General Hertzog, Commandant Ben Bouwers, a fine young officer, Major Pretorius and myself, and about 200 *burghers*. The burghers knew that something had gone wrong, otherwise President Steyn would not have taken the desperate chance of passing through so many English lines and crossing a well guarded railway line. In crossing this line the English poured a heavy fire into them and exploded a dynamite mine that had been carefully laid, but fortunately President Steyn and his men were clear of it by about thirty yards when the explosion took place.

Soon the council of war assembled and the secret leaked out. Acting President Schalk Burger and General Botha had written a state letter to President Steyn praying for a general surrender. That is the gist of the whole long letter. The council of war smashed that proposal into smithereens, and deprived all generals and acting presidents of the power to discuss peace terms with the English without the consent and presence of President Steyn, General De Wet and General de la Rey. I feel to this day that Acting President Schalk Burger was directly responsible for that state letter to President Steyn, yet I cannot understand General Botha giving his sanction to it by allowing his name to be coupled with that of Schalk Burger. Secretary Reitz in his official position had to sign it, but he was the most disgusted man I ever saw. Like President Steyn, General De Wet and General de la Rey, Secretary Reitz was as staunch a patriot as ever breathed, and one that would never say die, no matter what the conditions might be. He was game during the war, and as game as ever when the war came to an end.

Here were the two governments with no more than 200 men, in the very midst of thousands of English, holding a confab on the open prairie within six miles of a large English camp, and not one present in the least concerned, except Schalk Burger, who, I think, was pretty nervous. The English are wonderful soldiers, for they knew that the two governments were near them and they never made the slightest effort to take them in.

GENERAL SMUTZ
State Attorney General of the Transvaal.

All business having been finished and matters corrected and put right, President Steyn, General De Wet and General de la Rey started back to run the gauntlet and join their respective commands. Major Pretorius and I, on learning that General Smuts and Commandant Ben Bouwers were going with a good commando into Cape Colony, tried for permission to go with them, but were not allowed, much to our disappointment.

I will now return to my story of the April events in all parts. I have made quite a long side trip which may not prove to be of interest to the reader, but I assure him that had he been with us at the end of April he would have been equally interested with ourselves. As it was at the very end of April that the fifteen English columns suddenly invaded the high *veldt*, I will leave them till the first of May and go into the Free State. But little was done of any account, a little skirmishing here and a little there and not much more, for the English were making preparations for cornering and taking in the slippery De Wet once more.

In the Colony things were more than lively. General George Brand had captured a column and frightened two or three others half to death. General Kritzinger by his dash had made the English believe that there must be no less than 50,000 Boers in Cape Colony. Commandants Fouche, Scheepers, Malan and others were daily fighting in the different districts and captured several convoys. In fact, Cape Colony was truly in a state of war, and the Boers were in possession of the country. Lord Roberts was in possession of his $500,000 and his earldom, so he was not worrying, but General French was walking the floor day and night, for he realised that affairs in Cape Colony were very dark, and the position of the English in great jeopardy.

Not a day passed without fighting during the month, and it was certain that fighting would continue for many months to come, for the Boer officers were superior to the English commanders and could lead them a song-and-dance wherever they pleased. In the Western Transvaal the English had made several attempts to corner General de la Rey, but he was not to be cornered. Near Klerksdorp there was some fighting when a large force of English pounced on General Smuts and deprived him of one cannon.

The English reported this as a great victory, and I will tell you why. They think far more of losing one cannon than they do of losing 10,000 Tommies, for they consider Tommies as cheaply made in England as the Germans could manufacture them, while cannon are expensive in all countries.

Throughout the month troops were constantly shifting about in the Western Transvaal, but nothing really occurred worthy of note, as no change had taken place at Zeerust, where the English were still penned in. Far away in the north General Plumer at Pietersburg, and the English force in the East at Komati Poort by a combined action tried to clear the whole country between them of Boers. Their task was easy, because there were no Boers in those parts, except some women and children. Their homes and their possessions were burnt and destroyed and they themselves were sent to concentration camps.

The English spent considerable time in arming the *kaffirs* and giving them the necessary instructions for their murderous work. Chief Secockuni and his strong force, the worst *kaffirs* in the country, had already been armed by the English and were near Lydenburg on the one side and Rosenekal on the other. These very *kaffirs* murdered many men, women, and children with those English guns and ammunition, but further on I will go into the details of this dirtiest and most barbarous work of the English Army.

Now we come to the month of May, and a very lively one, too. General Ben Viljoen and General Muller crossed the railway line near Balmoral Station, and left the six pursuing columns all to themselves north of the railway line. They had simply left one large army to run up against another stronger still, for there were fifteen columns on the high veldt bent on capturing the government, General Botha and all the high *veldt burghers*. All these columns practically distinguished themselves by their puerile tactics. Not only did all the *burghers* easily evade them, but two or three *trek* wagons with women and children escaped being captured. Of course all the old men and women who remained in the few farmhouses still standing were captured and taken away. Then off to London would go a flaming report of so many *burghers*, horses and cattle being captured.

The English would enter all the good farmhouses, tear up the floors, and dig, dig, dig in search of money and jewelry that might be buried under the floor. Having satisfied themselves, they would then burn and destroy everything. At the end of this month there was not a farmhouse standing on the high *veldt*.

We had the great pleasure of seeing about 600 cavalry charge a farm house. We had never before seen such a daring, reckless charge, and there was not a man among that 600 that did not eminently win the V. C. We had read of the charge of the 600 at Balaclava, and in im-

General "Fighting Bill" Muller

And his assistant commandants and veldtcornets near Lydenburg, just before the general surrender

agination had often tried to draw the picture so glowingly painted by one of England's poet laureates; but this would sink into insignificance and pass into oblivion if only the charge of the 600 on the farm house filled with women and children could have been witnessed and depicted by some such realistic and blood-curdling poet as Alfred Austin or Rudyard Kipling. The one would never again have to describe in patriotic rhyme Jameson's raid, nor would the other have to live in "Bar-room" ballads, for so delightfully red would the words that each could have drawn from his imagination have been, that they could have painted in thrilling phrases a picture so bloody and hair raising as to immortalize them. I cannot describe this charge. It was too much for me, but we seemed to hear the command, "Charge!" and on they came, every horse with distended nostrils and wild, glaring eyes doing his best, not one man dropping from the pace, not one faltering, all surely determined to do or die. And in another moment the farm house is taken together with its occupants, women and children, who filled the doors and windows. In another minute all were driven from the house, the floors torn up, search for money and jewelry made, then the oil spread and the house consumed in flames.

But, you ask me where the blood is to come from? I will tell you. Those brave men set to work and killed over one hundred chickens, ducks and geese, several pigs, some calves and 2,000 sheep which they drove into the sheep *kraal* and killed with the bayonet. They were two and three deep, and that great mass of butchered sheep were rising and falling in different parts for many days, for many were still alive buried under others and slowly dying.

I had seen much of the bloody work of the Apache Indians far away in Arizona, but I had never seen anything that could possibly compare in down right cruelty to this piece of savagery on the part of the English soldiers. The prisoners of war in the way of women and children were now marched off and driven to the murderous concentration camps, and a stirring report of the daring charge made to London, the bloody end being omitted. This famous column now joined with the fourteen others and all began to chase the several Boer commandos who were scattered about the *veldt*. Remember that the high *veldt* is a high plateau without rocks or mountains, and it is practically impossible for any command to conceal itself from the English. General Louis Botha and the government were many times surrounded and cornered, but at picking up time, they were not present.

The various columns continued to follow them from place to place during the month, but no fighting men were lost. Quite a number of women and children were captured and sent to the concentration camps and invariably reported as so many *burghers*.

I now leave the English and Boers moving to and fro in all directions till the end of the month, and when all the high *veldt* is reported as swept clean of Boer commandos. Just before the end of the month General Ben Viljoen with Commandant Mears attacked General Plumer near Bethel and were prevented from taking in his column by the captured women and children being so placed that the Boers could not fire without killing some of them. This was a most cowardly piece of business, but it enabled General Plumer to rescue his men, with the exception of some thirty who were taken prisoners. These could not succeed in getting themselves behind the women and children without taking serious risk of being shot. General Plumer was satisfied to leave also a few horses and several thousand sheep which he had hoped to take with him to Standerton. No doubt some of those brave and chivalrous men who fought behind those Boer women and children were recommended for the V. C. and received it, such is the inclination of the British officer to report imaginary daring deeds in all engagements in which he may participate.

CHAPTER 19

# De Wet Cornered Again

In many parts of the Free State several skirmishes took place, but the English columns generally were occupied in trying to corner De Wet. A mighty army was brought to bear on him, for the English were convinced that, once he was cornered and captured, the war would come to a sudden end; but they did not reckon on the fact that a mighty army without a trace of military sense to guide its movements was a very harmless thing in the presence of such an able strategist as General De Wet. The Free State, with its broad, grassy, level plains, is a most beautiful country for cavalry and artillery operations, and although the English had thousands of cavalry, and guns without number, yet they seemed to be able to effect but little with either, or the two combined. They were so numerous that they fell over each other, and in the scramble General De Wet managed to pick up some of them.

In Cape Colony matters were daily growing worse for the British, and the Boers, ever increasing in numbers, were very active and aggressive in many districts. General Kritzinger captured a convoy, some prisoners and one or two fortified towns. General Brand had helped himself to one of the English supply trains, and Commandant Malan in the far south was fighting and accumulating war supplies. Commandants Fouche, Wessels, Latigan and other officers were doing good work in their respective districts.

In fact, there was daily fighting throughout the Cape, and the English were so upset and worried that they scarcely knew how to defend themselves. In the Western Transvaal General de la Rey's commandos had done some damage, and all were progressing nicely. Lord Methuen was active enough, but his columns were misguided and made suffer severely. Near the Mafeking railway line General de la Rey was much interested in several columns that were trying to corner and capture him. He had several skirmishes with them, took some prisoners, among them being three *burghers* who had deserted and taken up arms with the British. These were afterwards shot, and the English were convinced that General de la Rey had committed a great crime. A pity it is that all the other Boer generals did not commit many such great crimes in the beginning of the war.

When these numerous columns were about to make it very warm for him, General de la Rey doubled back between two of them and left for other parts. It was a week before Lord Methuen discovered that his bird had flown and was creating trouble elsewhere. It was on his return from his Mafeking expedition that Major Pretorius and myself met him and delivered our despatches. Some time ago I mentioned something about booming cannon in our rear a few days after leaving General Kemp, with whom we had spent a most pleasant week. It was this very General Kemp, who was always seeking a fight, that caused all that noise which so puzzled us.

Shortly after we left, General Kemp's scouts reported an English column moving about from farm to farm and destroying all of them. He had his men saddle their horses, and off they went in search of this column. They found it at Vlakfontein, where Major Pretorius and I had slept the day after leaving General Kemp. He set the grass on fire to conceal his men in smoke, advanced to within short range, surprised General Dixon and his 1,500 men, and in a short time put them to flight. General Kemp killed and wounded over 200, captured more than 100 men and horses, and took two cannon, which they turned on the fleeing column. This was a good piece of work accomplished by General Kemp and his 400 *burghers*. General Dixon and his men never stopped running till far away from all danger, for they supposed that Kemp must have had two or three thousand men.

No better men ever lived than those Krugersdorp men, and, taking the war from start to finish, I believe they did more and harder fighting than any other commando in the field. Like the Johannesburg boys they were brave, reckless, dashing patriots who defeated the English in many battlefields. General Beyers in the north troubled Pietersburg a great deal, but no fighting of any consequence took place. He had with him a most capable man, in the person of Captain Henry Dutoit, who commanded his scouts. Captain Dutoit was an artillery officer and was nearly torn to pieces at the Battle of Modderspruit on October 30, 1899. He was patched up by such able and competent surgeons as Dr. Max Mehliss, Dr. Lillepop, and Dr. Wepner, and in some way managed to survive.

A year afterwards some of his numerous wounds were still open, yet he was one of the most active and energetic officers in the field. He spurned all danger and fought like a very tiger to the end of the war.

Now I come to the month of June, a cold bleak month with piercing winds. We had but one blanket each, no overcoats, no tents, no shelter of any description, and how well I remember how near all came to freezing stiff every night. Still we had to keep on the alert, for the English were on all sides of us. They had burnt the entire high *veldt*, and but a little patch of grass could be found here and there. All houses were burned, all property was burned, all the grass was burned, and the scene was a most dreary, desolate one.

Before relating the events of this month I will try to tell in as few words as possible how we lived and managed so successfully to outwit the thousands of English about us and with whom we practically lived, because we were never out of each other's sight. The Boers were divided up into small bands 100, 200 or 300 strong, and each little band went as it pleased, and when it pleased, but generally confined itself to its own little district. These small commands were always in close touch with each other and could quickly come together if there was a chance of taking in some single English column that might be passing by. During the day, when not fighting, we would camp near some old ruins where we would find a little patch of grass that had escaped the fire. The English would generally see us and we were sure to see them at all times.

After sunset and darkness had set in, we would saddle up, dodge behind the English, find another little patch of grass, and then unsaddle, hobble our horses and try to get a little sleep. So cold it was that precious little any of us had during the night. We would put out no guards, but at four o'clock in the morning all would get their horses, saddle up and prepare for fight. We would then send out a man here and there, say about 1000 yards distance, to wait for daylight and to locate the English if possible. If none were to be seen at hand after the sun came up, we would unsaddle, hobble our horses again and try to get in some sleep under the warm sunshine. If the English were found near, we would probably have a short skirmish with them, knock a few from their horses, and then fly away to some other part of our district where we would be safe to get something to eat. We were sur-

CAPTAIN WILLIAMS
COMMANDING BOER SCOUTS.

rounded many times at daylight, but I will tell something about that later on.

As everything was destroyed on the high *veldt*, the reader will naturally ask how we got anything to eat, as we had no carts or wagons to carry food. I will tell him just how we managed to live and grow fat and strong on nothing. Before the rainy season set in, about October, the *burghers* would pull out their hidden ploughs, put the fields in good shape and then plant their mealies, (Indian corn). All this had to be done under the cover of darkness, and it meant a great deal of hard, tiresome work. In the following March and April we would have plenty of green mealies, and, later on, dry mealies. The English could not destroy these crops, though they tried and failed. If they turned their horses out to eat and trample it down, the green corn would kill them. When the corn ripened and became dry they tried to burn it, but failed because there was little or no grass in the fields. The result was that we had mealies on the stalk in all the districts. Many would be gathered, hidden in the high reeds along the small rivers, or buried in nice, dry pits. The English have often ridden over these without discovering them. Now, the reader may understand how we had mealies to eat ourselves, and some besides for our horses.

The English took all the *kaffirs* away and burnt their *kraals*. In these *kraals* there were large *kaffir* baskets, some that would hold fifty bags of mealies or *kaffir* corn. The English would set these on fire, but they would not burn. Then they would destroy the baskets and scatter the corn. In a pinch we would take this corn, wash and dry it and find it as good as ever with the exception of a little sand or gravel that might be in it. But a hungry soldier has little regard for sand and gravel under the circumstances. Now, we always had cattle near by, and generally two or three good fat bullocks with us. These we would drive along with us, until they were wanted. In every mess of two or three men, there was one ordinary coffee mill, but of course we had neither coffee nor sugar. We used these mills, however, to grind the corn into a rather coarse meal. It was hard, tedious work, but do it we must, if we were to have anything with our fresh meat.

Having ground sufficient meal for breakfast, a small tin pot filled with water would be brought to the boiling point, the meal carefully stirred in and constantly stirred for about forty minutes, when it would be cooked. Of course we had no salt; so our fresh meat would be thrown into the ashes, broiled to suit each one's taste, and then breakfast was ready. There is ammonia or some other kind of salts in the ashes, that help the meat out. For coffee, we had in each little mess another small tin bucket, which would be filled with water and boiled. Some meal would be burnt in a small pan, till black, and then put into the boiling water; this makes a very good drink, but I don't believe, reader, that you would like it.

When near the bush *veldt*, we often used acorns for the same purpose, and the coffee was very good. At times, during peach season, we dried some peaches, charred them and had a really delicious drink. Sweet potatoes prepared in the same way make a nice beverage, too. So you see that, after all, we lived very well. Live on mush and fresh meat, as we did, and you will never be sick.

We lived in this way for two long years, fighting all the time or trying to evade the English, and we lost but one man from sickness; this, too, in the face of the fact that we had nothing to protect us against the cold of winter, or the severe rain storms of summer.

Of course many English convoys were taken, and many railway trains, too, but the Boers have good sense, and will not eat any canned stuff. They would destroy all such, and only take what they could comfortably carry on their horses. To every man's saddle you would see tied either a small tin bucket, or a coffee mill, and these constituted our complete cooking outfit. On this high *veldt* there is practically no wood. So for fuel we would go about the *veldt* and collect dry cow dung, just as they did in Texas, New Mexico and Arizona in the early days.

Now, reader, you are sure to tell me that the English captured all our cattle, because you read it in the paper. Well, I confess they did; and let me tell you about it. When the war began, the number of cattle in the Transvaal and Free State together, was nearly 300,000. The English captured all these cattle, time and time again, and if you will take the trouble to look up their official reports, you will find that during the war they captured some 2,000,000 head from us, although we had less than 300,000 to begin with. Here is the explanation: the English would capture our cattle today, and make their report. Tomorrow, we would take the cattle back, but the English would make no report of it. They always reported the capture, but not the recapture, and that is how they captured some 2,000,000 head of cattle. The cattle were captured and recaptured so often that they grew to know the khaki's uniform as well as the Boer's rags: so when they saw a man or two coming, if he or they wore khaki uniforms, they would at once start toward the railway line. If the men were recognized by their rags as

Boers, they would all start for the high *veldt*, where the Boers always took them.

The poor, patient and willing cattle had hard times, and many and many miles they travelled during the war. At the end of it, the Boers still had nearly one-fifth the original number, and all were fat and in good eating condition.

Now, I will drop this subject for the present, and tell what was done during June. All the columns made another drive at General Louis Botha, east of Ermelo, and they had him cornered this time sure; "there was no possible chance for his escape," and all that remained to be done was to go through the formal ceremony of surrender of the Commandant General of the Boer forces. True it is they gave him a lively dance, in double quick time, too, but when they closed they found that General Botha and his men were missing, and had left them nothing but the corner. This was too bad, for the English felt much disappointed at the idea of having to correct all previous reports. To add to their misery, General Chris. Botha slipped up behind them, fired a volley into their rear, and nearly shattered the nervous system of the whole English force.

It was simply a joke on the part of General Chris. Botha, and having played it, he and his men rode away to some warm spot where they could rest and eat their mealie pap and fresh meat. One of these English "drives" is a wonderful tactical success when the number of telegrams, and the quantity of paper required in the execution, are considered. However, as long as there were any women and children on the *veldt* they managed to get some of them, and these they could kill in the concentration camps, if they couldn't kill their men on the battlefield.

CHAPTER 20

# An Irish Boy's Strategy

In another part of the high *veldt*, about 300 Australians ventured out on a little side trip from the column. I think a Colonel Beaston was in command of them, though I am not sure about it; but it makes no difference, for the Australians were there, and ready for business.

"Fighting Bill," General Muller, was near by also. He took 150 of the Johannesburg boys, among them being Sergeant Mike Halley, Jim French, Sergeant Joe Wade, Mike Hanafin, Joe Kennedy, John McGlew, Dick Hunt, Jerry O'Leary and Captain McCullum, of the Irish Brigade. With these he made a night ride, slipped up to the Australians as they were sitting and telling stories about their camp fires, and took them all in before they could realise what had happened. With them he took two pom-poms also, and some 300 horses, saddles, bridles, and as many rifles and plenty of ammunition. The last I saw of the Australians they were still trying to explain just how it happened. General Muller was very kind to them, and having taken possession of all they had, turned them loose and advised them to go home to their mothers.

A little incident happened just at the right moment to save many lives, and good little Mike Hanafin was the hero. The Boers having charged into the midst of the Australians, of course all were pretty well mixed. Mike Hanafin, it so happened, ran upon the Australian bugler, and an idea struck him at once which when brought into play made him a little hero. He threw his rifle into the bugler's face, and told him to sound "*Cease Firing*," or he would blow his head off. The bugler promptly obeyed, and, of course, all the Australians ceased firing at once. The major in command ran up to the bugler, swore at him, and ordered him to sound, at once, the "*Commence Firing*," not knowing that Mike Hanafin had relieved the bugler of his bugle as soon as the

"*Cease Firing*" had been sounded. While the major was swearing at the bugler, Joe Wade or Mike Halley, I have forgotten which, rammed the muzzle of his rifle against the major's stomach, and told him that he could have all the fight he wished. The major, in an awful tremble, threw up his hands and said "No, no, no, I don't want to fight any more."

General Ben Viljoen on joining General Muller and the Johannesburg Commando, decided to recross the railway line near Balmoral, and operate north of Middleburg. He approached the line in the evening, and decided to capture some blockhouses in order that he might be able to take over his cannon and wagons. He took the two blockhouses, and about half his commando crossed, but the wagons and cannon were stopped by re-enforcements arriving from Balmoral. It was within ten feet of one of these blockhouses that the brave and reckless little Mike Hanafin lost his life. From a hole in the ground under the blockhouse a Tommie fired and killed Mike, who fell within four feet of the muzzle of the Tommie's rifle. Plucky Dick Hunt, on seeing Mike on the ground, went to his assistance, believing that he had been wounded.

On reaching Mike he spoke to him but received no answer, so he knew that little Mike was dead. Hunt stooped down to pick him up, and as he did so, the Tommie fired up from the hole and the flash caught Dick in the face. The bullet grazed his forehead and pierced his hat. Joe Wade and Joe Kennedy, who were near by, came to Dick's relief, and the three carried Mike's body a few yards away, and then returned to the blockhouse. They now knew about these holes, and they crept up to one of them, slipped the muzzle of their rifles just over the edge of the hole, without the Tommie knowing it; they fired and the Tommie fell dead.

This frightened the other Tommies who were watching at other holes, and the blockhouse was surrendered. The brave little Mike was dead, however, and those Irish boys today, (as at time of first publication), mourn his death. Mike, after the war had begun, walked from Beira, over 500 miles distance, to Delagoa Bay, and then worked his way into the Transvaal, and joined the Irish Brigade. He was very modest and quiet, but a reckless little enthusiast when it came to a fight with the English. A tenor drum that he had captured months previously, and the bugle, are in the hands of the Irish boys, but they have not yet decided what they will do with them. Hallowed is the little plot of ground where he lies buried, for there lies the remains of

CAPTAIN JACK HINDON
The famous train-wrecker

a true Irish patriot and lover of liberty.

A week after this first attempt to cross, another was made, but this time General Viljoen called Captain Jack Hindon, the great train wrecker, to his assistance. Jack laid his mines along the railway line, and when all was ready the commando, guns and wagons advanced. On nearing the line they were discovered from the blockhouses, and firing began. This brought the armoured train down upon them. This on reaching Jack Hindon's dynamite mines, was blown sky high and completely destroyed. General Viljoen, his guns and commando now easily crossed, and Captain Jack returned to his little commando near Middleburg. General Spruit, that good man who was afterwards killed, and who saved the Irish Brigade at Brandfort, tried to have a fight with an English column near Heidleburg, but his horses proved to be too slow, and the English, after a hot race, succeeded in escaping and reaching the protection of that well fortified little town.

Many other early morning skirmishes took place, but we always hurried away as soon as we emptied a few of the English saddles. Our force was so small, as compared to the English, that we had to run; but we always put in some effective bullets before we put in our spurs.

Right here, before I forget it, I must answer the charge that the English constantly made against us, that Boers would never stand, but fire a few shots and run away. General De Wet answered, and to the point, "Yes," he says, "we shoot and run away, and that is the reason why so many English are killed, and so few Boers." The fact is, that if ten Englishmen happen to fall upon one poor Boer, such is their courage, that they will never let up till they have beaten him almost to death; whereas, if three Boers fall upon ten Englishmen, and take them in, (as they invariably will) the Englishmen will say, "You acted basely in attacking us in overwhelming numbers."

This just about explains the difference between an Englishman and a Boer in an open fight, and this great difference is just what is going to free South Africa of English rule in the near future.

When I think of this and Chamberlain's visit to South Africa, I often wonder if he does not sleep with that eyeglass well fastened in his eye, that he may see what is going on about him in hours of danger. He is scared, all right.

In the Free State, General De Wet has been in trouble again, but he was not worrying about it. Near Reitz, a little town not far from the Vaal River, a huge column fell upon him, and a fight was the result. He was punched about considerably but he can well say, "You should see the other fellow." The huge column was knocked out, put to flight, its wagons, thousands of sheep and cattle captured, and, besides, General De Wet had the pleasure of disarming a lot of prisoners and telling them to go home and learn how to play soldier. There was also some fighting south of Bloemfontein, with little damage to either side, but in Cape Colony all was ablaze. General Kritzinger captured two toy: is, some wagons, prisoners and a large quantity of ammunition. Commandant Malan had been equally as energetic on the southern part, while Commandants Lotter, Latigan, Fouche, Wessels and others were creating much trouble and excitement in their districts.

There was more actual fighting in Cape Colony than in any other place. Had the commandant generals of the Transvaal and Free State been there with their commandos, it is almost certain that the whole Cape would have rebelled.

In the Western Transvaal, General de la Rey took advantage of the cold weather to recuperate his horses. In the north General Beyers likewise remained quiet. During the winter season, the Boers in the Free State and Transvaal must keep passive if possible, otherwise they would lose all their horses and thereby be unable to carry on the war. Infantry is of little or no use in war, when opposed to cavalry. All other things being equal, that army which is strongest in cavalry should carry off all the honours of battle. Modern guns and arms make it imperative that an army be able to move quickly and change position with such rapidity as to cover a mile in five minutes. Infantry can't do this. Even in a mountainous country, cavalry will, man for man, easily defeat infantry. No one realises this more than the Boers, and that is the reason why they always look after their horses first and then themselves.

During July, the Boers remained inactive, and were but little annoyed by the English. It was frightfully cold at night, and of course one had to be on the move every night, but the English, who were all about us, seemed to dread the cold as much as ourselves. General Smuts[1] and Commandant Ben Bouwers had now entered Cape Colony and joined with General Kritzinger and his excellent staff of commandants. General Kritzinger took in a few trains and captured some provisions, while his *commandants* amused themselves in daily skirmishes with the English.

---

1. *With Botha and Smuts in Africa: No 1 Squadron of the Royal Naval Armoured Car Division* by W. Whittall also published by Leonaur.

CHAPTER 21

# English Surprise the Boers and Are Routed

It was during the month of August that Lord Kitchener issued his proclamation warning all *commandants, veldtcornets*, etc., that if they did not come in and surrender by September 15th, they would all be permanently banished from the country. I wished at the time that Lord Kitchener could see the Boers as they read his proclamation. They threw their hats in the air, and gave three cheers for "Kitch, the woman butcher," three cheers for "Kitchener, the wind-bag," three cheers for "Kitchener, the scared butcher." I witnessed all this, and felt proud of the Boers for so pouring out their hearts.

That proclamation created new life, and the Boers were determined to show Lord Kitchener what they thought of it and him, by September 15th, although they were so hemmed in that they could scarcely move. Lord Kitchener heard that the Boers made much sport of him and his proclamation, and evened up with them by slaughtering thousands more of their women and children in the concentration camps. In this line of business, I don't believe that Lord Kitchener has an equal in the history of the whole world. He is a good one.

General Louis Botha at once made up his mind to go into Natal and find out what was going on in the enemy's land, and called for a few men from each command. He assembled 1,500 men, and with him went General Chris. Botha and Commandant Opperman, two of the best officers in the field. However, this command did not go until September, so I leave it for the time being.

Far away in the bush *veldt*, east of Lydenburg, was a strong fort manned by Steinaker's Horse, and a lot of his allied armed *kaffirs*. General Ben Viljoen made up his mind to take them in, and with that fighting *commandant*, Piet Moll, the brave Captain Malan, and the gallant Veldtcornet Schoeman and 100 men, he set out at sunset to accomplish his object. The fort, Pisana, was reached in the very early morning, and Commandant Moll and Veldcornet Schoeman at once rushed upon it. The defenders poured in volley after volley on them, but they went ahead, scaled the high wall and captured the whole affair. Six men were killed, and good Piet Moll was severely wounded, but I am happy to say that he recovered and is ready to do battle again. Captain Francis, who commanded the fort, and one white man was killed, besides a number of armed *kaffirs* in khaki uniform. The *kaffirs* fought bravely, but the white men hid themselves in holes.

General Viljoen thought these white men, about thirty, were all freebooters, who had employed some seventy *kaffirs* to fight with them. Lord Kitchener, who had always sworn that the British had not armed any of the 30,000 or 40,000 *kaffirs* now fighting the Boers, had to acknowledge that both the whites and *kaffirs* were a part of his military force. He saved the whites, but not the *kaffirs*. I will have much to say about this *kaffir* business, before I am through, but not just now.

The fort had scarcely been taken before Chief Pisana with about 500 of his armed *kaffirs* came to Captain Francis' rescue, but General Ben Viljoen and his men soon put him to flight. The fort had been taken so quickly that Chief Pisana could not reach his friends in time. It was a shame that every white man in that fort was not shot down, for not one of them was fit to live. Each one had two or three *kaffir* girls with him, whom they called their wives, and all were living, not as human beings, but as the lowest of beasts. The vile Steinaker and his brutes never again showed up in those parts.

On the high *veldt* near Olifantsfontein, and just at sunrise, the English opened a hot fire on about 100 of us at a distance of no more than 300 yards. Major Wolmorans, of the artillery, was in command. He had put no guards out and we were caught, most of us, sound asleep. The rapid firing aroused us quickly, and when Major Pretorius and I (we always bunked together) jumped up, we saw twelve Tommies trying to drop us. All the horses stampeded, with the exception of six, and it certainly looked as if we were at last captured. Commandant Prinsloo, a most level-headed and dashing young officer, with about 100 men, was about a quarter of a mile from us, and he was attacked at the same time.

I had a fine horse that Major Pretorius had given me, but he was the craziest animal under fire I ever saw. He was one of the six horses

YOUNG WOHLITER
Who would not have his hair cut during the war.

that were tied and couldn't run away. The other five were quiet, and easily saddled, but no dozen men could put a saddle on mine, because he was standing on his hind feet and fighting with his forefeet. As the English had the small sum of $25,000 on my head, I was determined not to be taken in, if I could help it, so I jumped on him, he leaped into the air, went over a stone wall and seemed to be trying to break his neck. Having gone about 800 yards, I got control of him, hauled him in and turned about to see what was going on. I could see no more than thirty or forty English, so went back at once. I could see our stampeded horses about three miles away, and half of the artillery boys in hot pursuit.

The English broke and fled, and Major Pretorius with four mounted men, went after them in hot haste. It looked foolish, but it turned out otherwise. Those five men chased those forty scouts and Captain Wood and Captain Morley for nine miles, killing four and wounding seven, and capturing some horses. Captain Morley was severely wounded by Major Pretorius, who charged upon him with his mauser revolver. We missed being captured by the main column passing about one mile from us. Had all of them been present, I think that not one of us would have escaped being killed or captured.

A few days afterwards, we read Captain Wood's report, and in it he said that he and forty of his scouts were ambushed by about 700 Boers in the early morning, a fight ensued in which he counted twenty-three Boers killed, but did not know the number of wounded. We all exclaimed, "What a liar!" We had just one man slightly wounded, and Captain Wood's scouts, who were prisoners in our camp, will tell him so, too. Speaking of his own loss, Captain Wood said that Captain Morley was severely wounded in the stomach, four men killed, seven wounded and fourteen missing. We knew nothing about the fourteen missing, for we only saw the four killed, and the seven wounded.

Every day for the rest of the month we were attacked by the English, and a short hot skirmish would ensue. In the end, of course, we had to fly, for the English were always fifteen or twenty to one against us. It was very trying work, and the nights were still severely cold, yet the boys were always in good spirits, and ready for business.

In the Free State some blockhouses were blown up, some taken, and one or two trains fell into General De Wet's hands, but otherwise there was little done. In Cape Colony, both General Smuts and General Kritzinger were very lively. More towns had been taken, several convoys and many prisoners had been captured, and, on the whole, the English had been badly worsted throughout the Colony.

September is the month in which Kitchener's proclamation of banishment is to take effect, and the Boers came in to surrender in this way. General Louis Botha was near the Natal Border and found English and fortified camps plentiful. Forts Prospect and Itala, both fortified places, were attacked and after very severe fighting for many hours, General Botha's men proved too much for the English behind the walls, and gained two victories. He had one more short fight, and when ready to start back to the high *veldt* he found that he had taken three guns, over 300 prisoners and 130 heavily loaded wagons; this, too, on the very day that he and his officers were to be banished if they did not come in and surrender.

Matters were quiet in the Free State, so we pass on to Cape Colony. On September 15th, the day of banishment, General Kritzinger attacked and put to flight one column, while General Smuts smashed another and took two extra guns with him. This day was celebrated all over Cape Colony by the *commandants*, but I regret to say that two of the very best of them were very unfortunate. Commandant Lotter and over a hundred men were surrounded and captured after a most desperate fight. Because he made such a brave showing and because he wrought so much havoc with English columns, he was promptly hanged. Young Scheepers, who was so ill with fever that he could not ride, was also captured, tied in a chair and shot, as well as his two lieutenants, Wolvarts and Schoeman. These brave men had fought many successful battles and laid low many English officers and men, therefore, they must die. After a while I will have something more to say about these good men, young Louw and other martyrs.

In the Western Transvaal, General de la Rey also celebrated the 15th of September by taking 200 men and attacking Colonel Kekewich and 1200 at Selons River. Colonel Kekewich lost all his horses, his wagons, had a narrow escape, and he with his men fled as fast as their legs could take them, while General de la Rey continued to harass them. Had General de la Rey had a few more men, he would have taken the whole column, but he had to content himself with all the horses.

All this went to show Lord Kitchener how much the Boers thought of his threats and proclamation. If there were 10,000 Boers in the field, and no more than 50,000 English, and the Boers should issue such a proclamation, why, the English would fairly break their necks, such would be their haste to lay down their guns. But the Boers are soldiers who love liberty and their country, and therefore are not men to run and lay down their guns because some high butcher at the head of 300,000 men threatens to banish them forever from their country If they do not.

CHAPTER 22

# The Only Naval Battle of the War

In October, Major Wolmorans, Major Pretorius, myself, Lieutenant Johannes Malan, sixty-three artillery boys and one Irish boy, Mike Ryan, started for the Pietersburg railway line to take in a train. To get there we had to pass through the blockhouses on the Pretoria-Delagoa railway line. We camped about six miles from this line, and when it was dark we saddled up and went on our way. The blockhouses were so numerous that we would have to pass close by them, but as they were not dangerous institutions, we thought little about them. The armoured trains by Balmoral Station were our great danger, for they were equipped with men, cannon, maxims, and large search-lights.

At a point about 1000 yards from the line, we halted and Major Pretorius rode ahead to investigate. We were just about one and one-half miles from Balmoral, and great caution was necessary. Major Pretorius, when nearly 100 yards from the line, discovered the armoured train, all in darkness, just where we were to cross. He quietly slipped back to report and all had to turn back to the camp we had left. The moon was nearly full, and this bothered us, for we wished to cross early in the evening, and as the moon came so soon, we were liable to be discovered. We remained in our old camp that night, and went to another burnt farm house, about a mile distant, where we stayed during the following night. It was well that we did so, for on the morning afterwards, our old camp was surrounded, and the English maxims cut down nearly all the trees about the ruins. On hearing the maxims, we mounted our horses and rode to the top of a ridge to find out the trouble. The English, on seeing us, fled in haste to Balmoral Station, whence they had come.

We waited about for two more nights, and then decided to move out and cross the line right by the station. We started very early, in order to be ahead of the moon. We reached the line and just as we were crossing it, the moon begun to peep above the horizon. We could plainly see the Tommies sitting by their fires, smoking their pipes and enjoying themselves. We were not out of danger, by any means, for should we be discovered, the armoured train would run up and easily sweep us off with the maxims.

Half a mile in front of us was a bad creek to cross, and there we expected trouble. On reaching it, we found it well protected with barbed wire, but this was soon cut, and we were safe on the north side of the line. We did not go far before we unsaddled, slept a few hours, and then rode on towards Rhinoster Kop. On the night of the second day, we camped in the bush about twenty miles northeast of Pretoria, and not far from the Pietersburg railway line. On reconnoitring, the line was found so well guarded with armed *kaffirs* that it was thought unwise to try to take in a train.

Major Wolmorans then turned his attention to some cattle near the Hatherly Distillery, which is on the Pretoria-Delagoa railway line. He went in with about thirty men, spent the night in rain, and received a sweeping fire from an armoured train which was near at hand. No one knows how anyone escaped, but not one was touched. On their return next morning, they presented a very sorry looking appearance. We went back a few miles and camped at Zusters Hoek.

This little escapade stirred up the English and three columns promptly showed up. Commandant Groenewald with 200 men, and Jack Hindon with sixty men joined with us and drove one of the columns back close to Pretoria. They then returned to their camps near Rhinoster Kop and we were again alone and camped at Zusters Hoek. The other two English columns were still near Balmoral.

On the following day, we could see the English scouts on a hill about five miles away, between us and Pretoria. Major Pretorius and I were sure that an attack was intended that night, and we tried to get Major Wolmorans to move away. But he wouldn't. We told him that we were going to a good *kopje* a short distance off, in the early morning, because we did not care to be surrounded and captured. He said all right; so at daylight we went to the *kopje*, but the English did not come. They were still on that same hill.

We remained where we were during the day, and Major Wolmorans remained where he was. Night came and the men went to Major Wolmorans and asked him to move to the *kopje* where Major Pretorius and I were. He told them that there was no danger, and that he would stay where he was.

At daylight the following morning we were aroused by the singing of maxims in the direction of Major Wolmoran's camp. About 700 cavalry had him three-quarters surrounded, all firing, as well as four maxims which clattered continually. The artillery boys ran for their horses, some saddled, others had no time, and some couldn't get their horses at all. Here they came towards us in the wildest disorder, Major Wolmorans with them. The English, whooping and yelling, followed in hot pursuit, and a race under whip and spur for four miles followed. The English lost, and all the artillery boys escaped except twenty-six, who were captured in the camp. This long race caused the remaining thirty-seven men to scatter so that it was a week before they all got together. Half of them were without blankets, saddles and cooking utensils, and be assured they were a dilapidated, disgusted looking lot of men. Major Wolmorans, too, had lost all he had, and Major Pretorius and I had lost nothing.

We now set out to return to the high *veldt*, where we arrived early in November, because we had no trouble whatever passing blockhouses and railway lines. Among our captured was Mick Ryan and a little Frenchman by the name of Regal, and I felt sure they would be shot. Strange to say, two men, supposed to be Ryan and Regal, were shot on October 29th, three days after the capture. The two unfortunates were young *burghers* who talked English. I must here state that towards the end of the war, all those who spoke English and were captured were almost sure to be shot.

The Australians and Canadians murdered many men after they had surrendered, and I have heard them boast about it in Pretoria after peace was made. They were the most thorough bred ruffians that ever put their feet on South African soil, and had the Boers known during the war what they learned after the war, about the many innocent men murdered in cold blood, I am sure that at least half of the Canadian and Australian contingents would have been shot, for at least that many had been captured. The Boers always treated them as soldiers and gentlemen, and on releasing them would always wish them better luck next time.

Near Pietersburg lived some Boers, two or three, and they were supposed to have money. Of course, they were "Hands-uppers," having voluntarily gone in and surrendered their guns. With them was a German missionary and one English soldier, a visitor. Major Morand and Lieutenant Hancock, two Australian officers, went to this farm with the intent of robbing the Boers, not knowing that there was an English soldier there. On making their demand, the Boers protested and were at once shot down. The German missionary showed himself, and of course Major Morand had to shoot him, too. In the house was also this English soldier, and to close his mouth they shot him, too. A *kaffir* was at the place, and told the officers at Pietersburg. Major Morand and Lieutenant Hancock knew nothing about the *kaffir*, for they had not seen him, so they proceeded to rob the house and their dead victims.

On returning to Pietersburg, both were arrested and charged with murder. They were tried and shot "for murdering Boers," nothing being said about a German missionary and English soldier. The fact is, they were both shot for murdering the English soldier, and for no other reason. Had not the proper authorities shot them, the soldiers would have taken the law in their hands and done the work. It does seem that the English can do nothing without resorting to deception or lying, and in this they easily excel the whole civilized world. Any British officer or soldier who could prove that he had murdered more Boers than any other man in the army, would be certain to receive the Victoria Cross.

In the Free State everything was very quiet, so I will pass into the Colony. October is a particularly conspicuous month, because it witnessed the only naval battle of the war. This took place at Saldanha Bay, a few miles above Cape Town, on the east coast. The Boers had passed through Cape Colony and landed at this beautiful bay, where they took seven English officers prisoners. Not far out in the bay an English boat was anchored, and the Boers thought they would seize it. They collected all the row-boats about the place, took their rifles and in one long line advanced to make the capture. When near enough, they demanded its surrender. The captain refused, and the Boers opened fire. The captain became frightened, and put up the white flag.

Just as the victorious Boer sailors were about to take possession, they discovered an English gun-boat coming to the rescue, so they had to paddle for all they were worth to reach the shore again before this gun-boat could get within range. They succeeded and were safe, but the gun-boat stopped short of rifle range, so the battle was over. The Boers remained here for a day, then released the seven officers, and went prowling about the Colony as they pleased. The inhabitants supplied them with food, horses, clothing and everything they could

Acting Treasurer with the Boer Forces.

possibly wish.

When the news of the naval battle reached Cape Town, of course the English went crazy with excitement, for they fully expected to see the Boers in their midst every moment. Lord Kitchener became alarmed, too, and proclaimed all Cape Colony under martial law. That naval battle caused much trouble, for now martial law was supreme throughout the Colony, and young men and women were everywhere arrested and imprisoned from one to six months for assisting the Boers, while the inhabitants of the Colony had to submit to having their horses forcibly taken from them, or to witness then: being shot by the English troops. All their food stuffs, sheep, cattle, etc., were taken from them, and they were all left high and dry with seven days' food in the house. All their forage and grain was carried away or burnt, and had it been possible, their crops would have been destroyed, too.

Yes, that naval battle put things in an awful mess in Cape Colony, and had Generals Botha, De Wet and de la Rey been there with their forces, 75,000 rebels would have joined them and their two little Republics, and Cape Colony would today, (1903), be free and independent. Generals Smuts and Kritzinger and all their *commandants* were daily fighting in some of the districts, and the very fact that martial law was now made to cover the entire Colony, showed conclusively that Lord Kitchener and the British Government were both much alarmed, and looked upon the situation as so critical as to demand every attention.

In the Western Transvaal, General de la Rey found Colonel Van Donlop and his column in his way, so he attacked them, put them to rout, took fifteen of their wagons heavily loaded, and went on his way to the Magielesberg, where several columns had lately tried to corner the cute General Kemp. This Colonel Van Donlop was not out to fight men, but to maltreat women and children. He was burning their homes, and all their possessions, and leaving them to starve to death on the *veldt* because they would not make their men come in and surrender.

CHAPTER 23

# General De Wet's Daring Work

In the month of November, although on the high *veldt* there was daily skirmishing with the English, there was but one really good fight, and that was one of the most brilliant and dashing of the war. In the eastern part of the high *veldt,* many of the English columns were at their same old game, trying to corner General Louis Botha. For the tenth time, he had outwitted them and escaped from their clutches. He at once left those parts, and came to our section in the west. At Brakenlaagte, not far from the little town of Bethel, he discovered an English column. He collected some of the small commandos near and found he had 470 men. This he considered sufficient for his work.

Brakenlaagte is a beautiful grassy plain, very tempting for a cavalry charge. About a mile behind the main column, the English commander, Colonel Benson, left a strong rear guard and two guns. General Botha decided to charge first the rear guard and then the main column, which was about 1,500 strong. He gave the word, and off the Boers went at high speed, whooping and yelling and crying, "Look out, Khakies, we are coming." The rear guard mounted and fled, leaving two guns behind them, but the most of the *burghers* passed the guns and continued the chase. So demoralised were the English, that many of them threw away helmets, rifles, belts, etc., and ran in all directions in hope of escaping. A part of the column, however, stood its ground well and poured in a hot fire on the Boers near the two captured guns. Finally the whole column, with its four remaining guns, fled, leaving wagons, carts, etc., in the hands of the Boers.

General Botha with 470 had, by a dashing charge, won a most brilliant victory. Over 300 English were killed and wounded, and nearly 400 taken prisoners. These men were released. This column never again took part in the war, and was for months laid up for repairs. Its

WILL BARTER, JOHN HYGELSEN KLOPPER.
The Treasury Department in the Field.
Win. Barter, chief of the Money Printing Division, on the left.

brave commander, Colonel Benson, was mortally wounded and soon died.

Among the first captured was one Tommie, with whom a young *burgher* had exchanged clothes, and by accident General Botha saw this Tommie and, taking him for one of his *burghers* who was lagging behind, struck him with his whip and ordered him into the fight.

The poor fellow was scared half to death, but found words enough to murmur, "I am an English prisoner." General Botha then saw what had happened to the young fellow, and he immediately apologised. The young fellow said in reply "That he was proud that he could say that he had been struck with a whip by such a brave man, and the *commandant* general of the Boer Army."

Among Colonel Benson's letters was one written that day to his wife, and in it he stated that he had been searching for the Boers all day and had been much disappointed in not finding them, for he was longing for a fight. The letter was returned to be forwarded. Colonel Benson had a great reputation as an artillerist, and was undoubtedly one of the bravest and most dashing officers in the English Army.

General De Wet and some of his *commandants* had a few small fights in the Free State, but none of any importance. General Smuts was creating considerable excitement in Cape Colony, and some of the commandants were doing likewise. One of Smuts' commandos captured about 200 men in one fight. The English press claim that these men deliberately refused to fight, and laid down their arms on a preconcerted agreement. I do not know how much truth there is in this, but I do know that the Tommies were getting tired of being shot down. Many hundreds of prisoners taken on the high *veldt* would fairly beg not to be released, and said they would be glad to live on mush and meat. They were so utterly disgusted with the war that many, after being released, would follow up the Boer commandos, and then beg not to be sent away.

Sometimes they had to be sent in with an escort. We could have put many in the bush *veldt* where there was food, but had any of them died of sickness, the English would have sent the news broadcast that they had been murdered. Evidently they preferred to be so murdered by the Boers rather than be actually murdered by their incompetent English officers.

With few exceptions, certain it is that the British soldier had but little respect for the British officer. Many times Lord Kitchener sent his cablegrams charging the Boers with maltreating or murdering some of the English prisoners, and after peace was made some British officers took pleasure in throwing this libellous charge into my face. In every instance I replied "Yes, you make this charge against the Boers; but call up some of the men who were taken prisoners at the same time, and let me hear what they have to say about it." Not one of them would think of doing this, because they said that an English officer's word was as good as his bond. No English officer would dare to submit the case to such a test, because he knows that the first man questioned would prove him a liar.

I came near getting into trouble with some of them on this subject, for at times my retorts were very warm and to the point, considering that I had just surrendered my rifle, and was being closely watched by a lot of hounds. The very fact that Everyone took particular pains to bring up this subject was proof in itself that they were lying, and trying to find someone who might say that possibly he had seen one man unfairly shot. I have seen and talked with hundreds of English prisoners, but never heard one make any such a charge. In fact, everyone will tell you that the Boers treated him as a soldier and a man, wounded or not wounded. In other parts of the land, there was no fighting of any consequence.

In December, although we had the usual daily attacks on the high *veldt*, there is but one that I will mention, because I read General Bruce Hamilton's report of it. At Wilkrans, a high ridge about nine miles from Ermelo, there were about 300 of us camped, with General Piet Viljoen in command. From this position, our scouts reported that there were twenty-eight English camps in striking distance and well around us. Our chances for escape were none too good. Yet General Piet Viljoen did not consider that we were in any danger.

Without going into details, I will simply say that at daylight the following morning, we were surrounded by 4,000 cavalry, and it was a case of run for your life or surrender. All escaped but sixty-nine men, and our one cannon. Not a man was killed on our side, that is certain, and if any were wounded, they were taken prisoners. We escaped under a hot fire, and this was kept up on us for about three miles. In his report, General Bruce Hamilton had sixteen killed, many wounded, whom he left at the farm ruins, and one gun taken, as well as sixty-nine prisoners. How an English general can report such a monstrous lie is beyond me, for he knows that his men know, and that we know that no one was killed on the Boer side. Within half an hour after the English left, some of the boys rode back to look over the place. There was but one man killed in that fight, and he was a Scotchman whom the English half buried before they left. Bruce Hamilton is generally known as "Brute" Hamilton, and while this name fits him as far as it goes, yet "Brute Hamilton the liar" would fit him still better.

It was during this month, too, that I suffered the loss of my old friend and companion, Major J. L. Pretorius. During my absence he and thirty-three artillery boys were surrounded by about 300 cavalry near Balmoral Station, and captured. Be it said to his credit that he and his men never surrendered. Every cartridge they had they fired, and when they had no more, the English simply came and took them. I was sure he would never hoist the white flag, and I was sure, too, that he would never surrender as long as he had a cartridge left. He was a dashing fellow, thirty years old, and did not know what fear was. He is one of the great Pretorius family of South Africa, and he made the name good. Had he not been so reckless, I think he would have been appointed a general, and I am sure he would have proved himself a most brilliant one.

To show what a reckless devil he was, I will tell you that one day I was about 1,500 yards from him and another reckless fellow, Lieutenant Roos, of the artillery. They wished to attract my attention and have me come where they were. To do this he and Roos loaded their rifles, took deliberate aim, and fired at us. The bullets went just over our heads, and struck not twenty feet from us. We concluded they were English, and prepared to return the fire, when off they galloped. We went after them and found them at a house that had only been partially destroyed. We recognized their horses tied to a tree, and rode up to them. I gave him blazes, but he simply smiled, and said, "Can't you take a joke?"

Now that he had been captured, I felt very lonely, and took but little pleasure in every-day life. The English were continually after us, however, and surrounded about eighty of us at daylight in the morning. Firing seemed to come from all directions but one, and in that direction we looked for safety. We went at full speed and had gone but a few hundred yards when we saw some cavalry just coming up in front of us. We thought we were gone, and this cavalry thought we were charging them, so off they went at the top of their speed. We were brave now and went right after them, scattered them and chased them three miles, when we stopped, having captured in the race sixty-three of them with as many fine horses. That is what we considered great luck.

The Government Veldt Mint in the last ditch

Now I will go into the Free State, and say a few words about one of General De Wet's most daring deeds.

It was at Groenkop, a high hill on the farm Tweefontein, near the little town of Bethlehem. It was Christmas eve and all wanted a Christmas pie. This was a high hill with three very steep, abrupt sides, while the other was a gentle slope leading to the plain below. On the top of this hill were about 380 men well protected in about twelve forts. General De Wet, when it was dark, took 500 men and approached the steep side opposite the one of easy ascent, because he knew that the English would all prepare for attack from the easiest way. He and his men crawled up that hill, and when first challenged by the English sentry they rushed forward, and after a hot face to face fight, captured all the force, forts and stores. According to General De Wet's own report, he lost fourteen killed and thirty wounded, while the English lost 116 dead and wounded, and 240 prisoners. He took one cannon, one pom-pom, twenty wagons, a great quantity of ammunition and rifles, 500 horses and mules, and a load of whiskey, so he and his men were well supplied for a fine Christmas dinner.

Strange to say, the Boers nearly always took from the English their Christmas dinners. The first Christmas they took nearly all the queen's chocolates, the second Christmas, all the plum puddings, and now General De Wet, a third Christmas, has taken the poor devils' Christmas dinner from them again. I heard some prisoners once say that they wished their friends at home would secretly send them Christmas dinners three months ahead, so that they could get them and eat them before the Boers found it out.

Generals Smuts and Kritzinger continued to make things merry in Cape Colony, and their *commandants* helped themselves to several convoys, much to the regret of the English, but with great pleasure to themselves. Before the month closed, however, General Kritzinger was severely wounded while trying to rescue one of his wounded men near a blockhouse, and was in consequence captured. In this was a severe loss, for he was a dashing and persistent fighter.

Many other small fights took place, and the Boer *commandants* were generally successful in taking a few prisoners and wagons.

CHAPTER 24

# General De Wet Completely Cornered

The year 1901 came to an end and the Boers were still in excellent spirits, and good fighting trim. Our little command was twenty-five miles from Pretoria, and in addition to our dinner of mealie pap and fresh meat, we received through our famous spy, Captain Naude, our weekly mail from Pretoria. Letters informed us that Lord Kitchener wanted reinforcements to bring the war to a speedy end, and that the application of martial law in Cape Colony was making trouble among the British subjects. With all this the *burghers* were highly pleased, but the further news, that their women and children were daily dying by the hundreds in the prison camps, cast a gloom over all, and they spent most of the afternoon and evening in prayer.

Lord Roberts, Lord Kitchener, Joe Chamberlain and Milner, all fully realised that the only way to bring the war to a speedy end was to destroy the Boer women and children as quickly as possible. They all worked to the same diabolical end, and within eighteen months their death lists contained the names of 22,000 defenceless Boer women and children.

The new year begins well, for the *burghers* are determined to fight. They did not generally know, however, that their women and children were being murdered by wholesale, otherwise I am sure they would have stopped the war at once. The English columns made a desperate effort on the high *veldt* during January, and it was fighting here and there and everywhere every day. There was no rest for anyone, and I think that General Botha was cornered every day, but he was never found in the corner. I was with Commandant Joacham Prinsloo and 120 men early in this month of January, and we camped by the

Klip-Kopjes about six miles from Bronkhorst Spruit, a station on the Delagoa railway line. It was very warm and we were trying to shelter ourselves from the sun by hanging blankets on our rifles, when suddenly, about ten a. m., the English began to fire on us from some *kaffir kraals* about 800 yards distant. Our horses were out grazing, but within five minutes all had caught their horses, saddled them, and were striking for the English.

The English scouts left the *kraals* when they saw the Boers coming in a gallop. On reaching the *kraals* and *kopjes* near by, we discovered about 700 advancing. They tried at first to surround us, but grew frightened, because they saw the Boers were too determined, and all began to retreat. The Boers charged and the English fled with the Boers hot after them. This regiment of 700 men was the Scots Greys, and all were panic stricken. They were scattered in every direction, and making for the forts on the railway line. Before they found safety, however, the Boers had killed seven, wounded eighteen, captured twenty-three men and nearly sixty horses, bridles and saddles. The enemy really put up no fight at all, and when asked the reason, they said, "Our time is up in March, and we are not going to fight any more, for we are tired of it, and the English always manage to keep out of the fight."

I merely mention this to show the feelings of some of the so-called Scotch regiments at this stage of the war.

In the Free State they were constantly cornering General De Wet, and, although he was many tunes cornered, yet he was never captured. In Cape Colony the Boer *commandants* kept all the districts in great turmoil, and General French and his big army seemed helpless to do anything. Besides, the blockhouses were giving the English trouble too, for Commandant Alex Boshof was slipping up nightly and blowing them up with dynamite. This perfect little dare devil, with his equal, Captain John Shea, blew up fifty or sixty of them, and so terrorised the Tommies that they would not take chances in them at night. Now, the commandos could cross the lines easily, for the Tommies would lie in trenches and not shoot if the Boers let them alone.

In the Western Transvaal, some of General de la Rey's commandos were sent after cattle to the Mafeking border. They were successful and returned with some 20,000 head. Little else was done in this part of the world. In the North, General Beyers attacked Pietersburg and after a very hot fight, released 160 Boers whom the English had in a camp near the town. Fortunately, he was able to take them out all mounted and well armed.

Now I come to February, when there is not nearly as much rain as in January. During the month of January, heavy rains fall daily, and as the Boers were without shelter or overcoats and constantly wet, they were not inclined to be active. In February, they are dry at least half the time, so one may expect them to do something.

I forgot to say that late in January, in company with Walter Trichardt, a young Colonial, and four young Boers, I decided to cross the railway line, and visit Commandant Trichardt and Captain Jack Hindon, both old friends of mine. We foresaw much trouble, so we concluded to make a careful survey of the situation before trying our luck. Walter and myself rode directly towards Balmoral Station, on the main road, and when within about two miles of the numerous forts and blockhouses, we halted and used our glasses. We could see no one about the forts or blockhouses, so we rode on till within 600 yards of one of the largest forts. Now we were close to Balmoral, could see the poor women and children cramped up in the beastly concentration camp, and about 200 Tommies. In the forts and blockhouses we could discover no life whatever, so we knew that all available men were out trying to corner General Botha.

We came back, joined the four young Boers, returned to the line within a mile of Balmoral, cut twelve barbed wires, and went on our way. The English had put up dummy soldiers at the blockhouses, and dummy cannon on high points near them, but we were not frightened by them in the least. I mention this, because we soon had trouble, and I witnessed something that will give Joe Chamberlain, Lord Kitchener and Lord Milner the direct lie. We are now in February, and about twenty-five miles north of Middleburg. We are with Commandant Trichardt, of the Artillery, Captain Jack Hindon and Captain Karl Trichardt. The entire command is 213 strong. It is rolling prairie where we are camped, and on the Middleburg side are several thousand cavalry, and on the north side about five miles distant, some 4,000 *kaffirs* who had been armed by the English.

We kept a good look out both ways. Yet before the month came to an end, we were surrounded at daylight and suffered severely. Colonel Park with about 4,000 cavalry and 600 armed *kaffirs*, made a night march and attacked us just at sunrise. They were on three sides of us, and the 4,000 armed *kaffirs* were on the fourth side. They began to fire on us at a range of six or seven hundred yards, and as our horses were not saddled, but out grazing, one can well imagine that we were in a hot corner. Every man ran for his horse and pack horse, and under heavy fire saddled and packed. Then it was time that every man should make a dash for liberty. We put in the spurs and all made the dash, but unfortunately only thirty-nine of us succeeded in escaping. My pack mule always followed me, and although she fell far behind and the English hurled a storm of bullets at her, yet she came through all right, and joined me. These 600 armed *kaffirs* were on the English left flank and fought in line with the Tommies; yet Chamberlain, Kitchener, Roberts, and Milner all swore that they had no armed *kaffirs* with them in the war. Now, when any man tells me that such Englishmen as these are capable of telling the truth, I know at once that man is either an Englishman himself or an Anglo-American.

On the high *veldt* the English columns were still very numerous, and there was daily fighting, but the Boers held their own and suffered but little. Commandant Alberts and Veldtcornet Tromp attacked the Scots Greys, who had shown up again, and utterly routed them near Springs, killing and capturing a few, and several horses. These Scots evidently meant it when they told us in January that they would not fight any more. In the Free State there was an army 60,000 strong in the field, bent on cornering and capturing General De Wet. They had him and his *burghers* with 500 cattle in a triangle, two sides of which were lines of blockhouses and networks of barbed wire. On both sides the blockhouses were very near to each other, and all well manned. It would seem almost impossible for any Boer force less than a thousand strong to pass through.

On the third side were about 40,000 English, and their plan was to drive General De Wet into the angle formed by the blockhouse lines. They were advancing rapidly, and General De Wet knew that he must decide and act quickly, so he made up his mind to cross the Lindley-Kroonstad line of blockhouses. It was a very dark night and he had lost sight of his cattle, but there was no time to lose in trying to recover them. On reaching the line, he cut out a passage in the net work of barbed wire within a hundred yards of the blockhouses on either side, and passed through without a shot being fired. He went on for a few miles and unsaddled for the night. He had not been in camp very long before he heard shouting in the darkness, and much to his surprise here came four young *burghers* with the 500 cattle which he had given up as lost. These youngsters had cut away the wires and driven all these cattle between the blockhouses without the English firing a shot. The blockhouse system may be a great invention, but it is of no earthly use when fighting such an enemy as the Boers. I am sure that we crossed the blockhouse lines on the high *veldt* at least fifty times, yet I never heard a shot from one of them.

I remember one occasion when 300 Boers, about 100 trek wagons loaded with women and children, and nearly 10,000 head of cattle, passed through a line of blockhouses, and not one shot was fired. We were well surrounded, and on the following morning, the English spent hours hunting us within the circle, while we were at least ten miles away. The English officer is certainly a brilliant soldier.

It was only a few days after this that the English suddenly came upon these wagons, women and children, and, of course, captured them. About an hour afterwards, a small Boer commando with a French gun discovered the wagons moving along with an escort of about fifty Tommies. The Boers could not attack, on account of the women and children, but one of the artillery boys thought he would see what effect a shell would have on the escort. He sighted the gun so that the shell would be sure to fall well to one side. The shell struck and exploded, about 200 yards from the escort, and every man fled as fast as his horse could take him. Then the women turned their wagons about and returned to the Boers. To each wagon was yoked from twelve to sixteen bullocks, and the women had to drive them. It was a sad sight to see those young and old ladies, and even children, working like slaves to escape capture by the English. They preferred to take the chance of being shot or of dying in open field, to sure death in the English prison camp.

The bird having escaped for the hundredth time, the English columns went back to their respective stations, and then General De Wet, too, returned to his old corner.

After a week's rest, out came the English, more numerous than ever, and the general could see columns of them in every direction. It was plain to him that they did not intend to make use of the blockhouse lines, but to form a continuous circle around him. They succeeded, and General De Wet was again rounded up. When night came, he started out for freedom or death, and as soon as his scouts came in contact with the English, lively firing began. He ordered his men to charge, and they broke through, but lost eleven men killed. Some of his *commandants* became confused, and did not get through, but on the following night, all broke the same circle, with the exception of two that were captured. Although there were 60,000 men in that circle, yet they dug trenches, so fearful they were of General De Wet and his men. Maxims and rifles were concentrated on the band of patriots, but it faced the storm of bullets, charged over the English trenches, and De Wet was free for the one hundredth and first time; and that is why you will still hear the real Englishmen talking about the cowardly De Wet and his *burghers*. Every word that falls from your lips, Mr. Englishman, is an unmistakable sign of your degeneracy.

In Cape Colony, General Smuts and his numerous *commandants* were so active that an alarming state of affairs continued to prevail, and the English shot down, without trial, many suspected rebels in the various districts. In the Western Transvaal, General de la Rey had been busy in many parts, but especially at Yzerspruit, where he again fell upon Colonel Van Donop, captured 600 prisoners, killed and wounded 200, took three cannon, a convoy of 150 wagons and 1500 mules. This was a good afternoon's work, and General de la Rey ascribes its great success to the personal bravery and daring of General Celliers, one of the very best fighting generals in the war. General Celliers, with less than 500 *burghers*, proved too much for Colonel Von Donop and his 1000 English; yet the colonel came out all right, for he reported that he had been attacked by an overwhelming number of Boers; this, too, in the face of the fact that Lord Methuen had just swept all the Boers out of this part of the country.

To read a British commander's glowing report, describing how thoroughly he has swept the Boers from a certain district, one is not apt to be much amused, but following on his heels is another British commander, and to read his report, relating how thoroughly he has been wiped up by an overwhelming force of Boers, one feels very much inclined to laugh. Not a week passes but that some of the English commanders are guilty of just such amusing contradictions. The English officers, with very few exceptions, excuse all these blunders and acts of stupidity by that one phrase, "Attacked by an overwhelming force of Boers," notwithstanding the fact that the officer who has just preceded him reported the same ground as swept clean of the Boers. Lord Kitchener cables these contradictory reports regularly to London, and the people, with their eyes bulging out of their heads, read every word of them, but not one ever sees the joke.

During the month of March, there were plenty of small fights on the high *veldt* in the Free State and in Cape Colony, but none of them were of much importance. In the Colony, General Smuts captured a few towns, some prisoners and drove some of the English commands to the sea, but no heavy fighting took place. In the Western Transvaal

COMMANDANT PIET MOLL (SECOND FROM THE RIGHT)
His trek wagon and staff

was fought the most brilliant battle of the war, at Klipdrift (Tweebosch) on the seventh day of March. For more than two years, Lord Methuen with an army ten times as strong in numbers as that which General de la Rey had, struggled in vain to capture or destroy this Boer leader and his little army of patriots. They had fought over thirty battles, yet Lord Methuen could not lay claim to one real victory over General de la Rey. On this seventh of March, 1902, Lord Methuen with four cannon, 1,600 men and 134 wagons, arrived at Klipdrift, a beautiful place for a fight or a good horse race. General de la Rey, with 740 men, made up his mind to take in Methuen and show his *burghers* a real earthly Lord. He could see that Lord Methuen was well prepared to fight, and that if he were to win he must win quickly.

He went to each of his 740 men, and told them that at the command, "*Charge*," all must use their spurs and lose no time in taking in the cavalry rear guard. All being in readiness, the old war-horse gave his signal, and his 740 patriots responded. Away they went, with the old war horse in the lead. It was a charge, a real cavalry charge, and with such force did those 740 patriots go over that broad beautiful plain, that the 500 English cavalry rear guard fled at the very sight of them. A few followed the fleeing cavalry, and the main body went for the infantry. So frightened were they that most of the infantry threw their rifles down and their hands up, while the rest took quarter in a *kraal* with Lord Methuen. The cavalry was still running and the *burghers* still pursuing, but the latter's horses were not fast enough, and they finally had to abandon the chase. Lord Methuen made a short stand in the kraal and then hoisted his white flag.

All was over. Lord Methuen and 900 of his men were prisoners, nearly 200 of his men were killed, and 163 wounded. In addition to Lord Methuen and his men, General de la Rey also captured four cannon, 134 loaded wagons, 500 horses, and nearly 1,000 mules. At best, little de la Rey, the farmer, the Boer general, had taken in Lord Methuen, the second in command in South Africa, a trained soldier with a trained force more than double that of the untrained farmer. Lord Methuen was shot in the thigh, and the bone was broken, therefore he was severely wounded and must receive every care and attention.

Some five months before this fight, Lord Methuen was fortunate enough to capture Mrs. de la Rey and her children, during the general's absence. Her wagons, her food, clothing and every bit of bedding were set aflame, and burnt up, and she and her children were left on the bare *veldt* to starve or die, because General de la Rey had so often defeated Lord Methuen in honourable battle. Mrs. de la Rey took refuge in an old hut, after walking several miles in search of some Boers who might be near by. She had to suffer the pangs of hunger, expose herself to beating rains, and with sore feet cross the barren *veldt* in search of some of her people. When almost exhausted from hunger, fatigue and pain, she and her little ones were found by the Boers and immediately cared for.

Now I return to Tweebosch, where Lord Methuen lies prostrate and suffering great pain. It was Mrs. de la Rey that came to help comfort him, to prepare his food, and pray for his recovery. I have often wondered if Lord Methuen, as he lay on his sick bed, ever recalled the good time he had, when with fire and dynamite he destroyed General de la Rey's beautiful home and all his property. I think not. General de la Rey showed his savage instinct by sending Lord Methuen and all his wounded men and prisoners back to their own people, where they could receive more comfort and better surgical treatment.

Some time after Lord Methuen's return, General de la Rey was summoned to the Peace Conference, and as his path led him near by, he stopped to see how Lord Methuen was progressing. After a short conversation, so it is related, Lord Methuen said: "You know, general, that that was not my own column you captured."

"Yes, that is true," replied the general, "I remember that I took in your own column some months ago."

Before the month closed, General de la Rey found an opportunity to test the Kitchener blood, and took advantage of it. It was on March 31st that General de la Rey attacked General Walter Kitchener and his convoy. Although he failed to capture the convoy, which only narrowly escaped, so disastrous was this fight in the loss of men killed and wounded, that it was generally believed that General Kitchener would be sent home in disgrace. But being a brother of Lord Kitchener, he was probably decorated with the V. C. for his rapid flight and escape from General de la Rey. When the English run up against three such old farmers as Oom Koos de la Rey, Chris de Wet and Louis Botha, many are liable to find a grave, while he who reaps honours must have shown his running ability to be most excellent. With their numerous maxims and guns and their great preponderance in men, all thoroughly trained, the English should have easily won all the important fights of the war, but, thanks to British stupidity and incompetency, the Boers were almost invariably the victors.

The last fight of the war was fought in the first part of April, near

Desperate prisoners of war in Bermuda, from seven years upwards

Heidelburg. Commandant Joacham Prinsloo, a young and energetic Boer, a most gracious and lovable man, one of the best officers I ever saw, here made his last charge. Preceding the charge, a very hot fight took place, and Commandant Prinsloo received two bad wounds, but he nerved himself up, ordered and led his last charge, saw the last battle of the war a victory, and the last shot fired in that last battle gave the commandant a third wound, a fatal one, and he rolled from his horse and died a contented patriot.

The brave Veldtcornet Vander Walt, badly wounded himself, felt sorely grieved as he gazed upon the lifeless remains of his beloved commander, but consoled himself in the knowledge that Commandant Prinsloo had lived to see his enemy utterly routed.

Chapter 25

# Peace Terms

It was about the beginning of April, that Acting President Burger received from Lord Kitchener a copy of the correspondence that had passed between the British and Netherlands Governments. As this related to peace in South Africa, Schalk Burger, so he said, took this act of Lord Kitchener as an invitation to discuss terms and the termination of the war. All knew that Schalk Burgher, Lucas Meyer and J. B. Krogh were always anxious to surrender or make peace at any price, and for this reason Everyone of them should have been removed, and patriotic men put in their places.

It was just a year ago that Schalk Burger sent that letter to President Steyn begging him to surrender, as the people were starving and it was impossible to fight any longer. Yet the *burghers* had fought another year, had been more successful than at any other time during the war, and all were still fat, saucy and in high spirits. However, he managed again to get a meeting of the two governments, which was authorized by Lord Kitchener. As Lord Kitchener, Lord Roberts, Joe Chamberlain and Milner were continually telling the English public that it was the officers, and not the *burghers*, who were carrying on the war, it was decided to have a conference of delegates, duly elected and instructed by the *burghers* themselves. For this purpose, all military operations were suspended and the different commandos in their respective districts came together to make known their feelings and elect a delegate.

I was then with the Johannesburg Commando, on the Sabi River, near Lydenburg. Lucas Meyer and J. B. Krogh arrived with the necessary instructions, and explained everything to the *burghers*. They tried in every way to deceive the *burghers* into voting for surrender and peace, but utterly failed. Every man in the commando declared for independence or war, and the men of the Lydenburg Commando did

BOER PRISONERS WITH THEIR NURSE AT BERMUDA

the same.

Commandant W. J. Viljoen was elected as delegate by his men, the Johannesburg Commando, and Commandant David Schoeman was elected as delegate by his men, the Lydenburg Commando. I heard both of these *commandants* pledge their words to do as their *burghers* wished, and stand for independence or war. Both of these commandants at the Conference stood for discontinuing the war and accepting the British proposals. With the exception of two or three small districts, all the *burghers* of the land were unanimous in declaring for war or independence. I must here state, however, that the *burghers* did not know at the time that 22,000 of their women and children had been murdered in the English prison camps, and that probably in another year all the rest would meet the same fate.

The delegates all being elected, they met, sixty in number, on May 15th, at Vereeninging, on the Vaal River. On the 31st of May, they agreed to accept the English proposals, as follows:

PEACE TERMS.

General Lord Kitchener of Khartoum, Commander-in-Chief, and His Excellency Lord Milner, High Commissioner, on behalf of the British Government;

Messrs. S. W. Burger, F. W. Reitz, Louis Botha, J. H. de la Rey, L. J. Meijers, and J. B. Krogh, on behalf of the Government of the South African Republic and its *burghers*;

Messrs. M. T. Steyn, W. J. C. Brebner, C. R. de Wet, J. B. M. Hertzog, and C. H. Olivier, on behalf of the Government of the Orange Free State and its *burghers*, being anxious to put an end to the existing hostilities, agree on the following points:

*Firstly*: The *burgher* forces now in the *veldt* shall at once lay down their arms, and surrender all the guns, small arms, and war stores in their actual possession, or of which they have cognizance, and shall abstain from any further opposition to the authority of His Majesty, King Edward VII., whom they acknowledge as their lawful sovereign. The manner and details of this surrender shall be arranged by Lord Kitchener, Commandant-General Botha, Assistant-Commandant General J. H. de la Rey, and Commander-in-Chief De Wet.

*Secondly*: Burghers in the *veldt* beyond the frontiers of the Transvaal and of the Orange River Colony, and all prisoners of war who are out of South Africa, who are *burghers*, shall, on their declaration that they accept the status of subjects of His Majesty King Edward VII., be brought back to their homes, as soon as transport and means of subsistence can be assured.

*Thirdly*: The *burghers* who thus surrender, or who thus return, shall lose neither their personal freedom nor their property.

*Fourthly*: No judicial proceedings, civil or criminal, shall be taken against any of the *burghers* who thus return, for any action in connection with the carrying on of the war. The benefit of this clause, shall, however, not extend to certain deeds antagonistic to the usages of warfare, which have been communicated by the commander-in-chief to the Boer generals, and which shall be heard before a court-martial immediately after the cessation of hostilities.

*Fifthly*: The Dutch language shall be taught in the public schools of the Transvaal and of the Orange River Colony when the parents of children demand it; and shall be admitted in the Courts of Justice, whenever this is required for the better and more effective administration of justice.

*Sixthly*: The possession of rifles shall, on taking out a license in accordance with the law, be permitted in the Transvaal and the Orange River Colony to persons who require them for their protection.

*Seventhly*: Military administration in the Transvaal and in the Orange River Colony shall, as soon as it is possible, be followed by civil government; and as soon as circumstances permit it a representative system tending towards autonomy shall be introduced.

*Eighthly*: The question of granting a franchise to the native shall not be decided until a representative constitution has been granted.

*Ninthly*: No special tax shall be laid on landed property in the Transvaal and the Orange River Colony, to meet the expenses of the war.

*Tenthly*: As soon as circumstances permit, there shall be appointed in each district in the Transvaal and the Orange River Colony a Commission, in which the inhabitants of that district shall be represented, under the chairmanship of a magistrate or other official, with the view to assist in the bringing back of the people to their farms, and in procuring for those who, on account of losses in the war, are unable to provide for themselves, food, shelter, and such quantities of seed, cattle, implements, etc., as are necessary for the resuming of their previous callings.

His Majesty's Government shall place at the disposal of these Commissions the sum of £3,000,000 for the above mentioned purposes, and shall allow that all notes issued in conformity with Law No. 1, 1900, of the Government of the South African Republic, and all receipts given by the officers in the *veldt* of the late Republics, or by their order, may be presented to a judicial commission by the government, and in case such notes and receipts when found by this commission to have been duly issued for consideration in value, then they shall be accepted by the said Commission as proof of war losses, suffered by the persons to whom they had originally been given. In addition to the above-named free gift of £3,000,000, His Majesty's Government will be prepared to grant advances, in the shape of loans, for the same ends, free of interest for two years, and afterwards payable over a period of years with three *per cent*, interest. No foreigner or rebel shall be entitled to benefit by this clause.

The war was now over and temporary peace once more reigned over the land. The *burghers* on hearing the news that peace was declared were wild with delight, and great was their rejoicing, for they were sure that independence had been granted. But when they heard, two days afterwards, that it was practically an unconditional surrender, they were frantic with rage, and some even threatened to kill their delegates. When they again heard that 22,000 of their women and children had been murdered in the English camps, and that to continue the war for another year would probably mean the extinction of their race, all were silent, and are silent yet, (as at time of first publication), but doing much thinking.

Some families became totally extinct during the war, and there is not one in the land today that is not in mourning for the loss of one or more relatives. Anyone of the so-called great civilized nations of the world may send an overwhelming army to a distant land and murder and enslave a humane, God-fearing and noble race of people, and not one murmur of disapproval will be heard from the others. But let some interfering missionary go to China, stick his nose in other people's religious affairs, and render himself so obnoxious as to lose his head, then all the civilized nations will rise as one, denounce the act and demand the immediate execution of the party who had probably done a good service for his state and mankind. Yes, all civilized nations might be sublimely humane if they were not so beastly savage.

### Peace and Result.—Coronation

The Peace Terms being duly signed, all the commandos went to certain specified places in their respective districts and surrendered their arms. Of course, no one had any ammunition, but each one turned in a gun of some kind, and some of the most antiquated guns I ever saw were tendered, but they had a hole in them, and at some distant time in the past had been fired; so no complaint was made by the receiving officer.

In General de la Rey's districts there were many who would not give their guns in person to the English, but piled them up on the *veldt* and told General de la Rey to do with them as he pleased. The receiving officers, on arrival, asked where the *burghers* were, and on being informed that they had gone, seemed very much put out because they were most anxious to get every man's full name, his district, etc. Then again, there are several who never surrendered any rifle at all, but the English do not know who they are, and probably never will. Together with the Johannesburg Commando, I surrendered my rifle at Potlood Spruit, a short distance from Lydenburg.

After all was over, the English intended to put the boys of the Irish Brigade over the border. I told the boys to tell them that they would have to put a rifle at each one's back, to get him to obey. They did as directed, and the English officers thought it best to drop the matter.

It was fifty miles to Machadadorp, the nearest railway station, and having received our permits, Commandant Pinaar, Veldtcornet Young, Captain Blignault, Lieutenant Malan and myself mounted our horses and started for Pretoria. We camped at Klip River where there was a small number of men in a fort commanded by a major.

The Tommies were very civil to us, and many of them, together with a young 2nd lieutenant gathered about us. In the course of the conversation, a sergeant said, to us, "Why did you surrender?"

We answered that we supposed we had to, and asked him if he were not pleased.

"Yes," he replied; but he said: "Do you see that major standing under that willow tree by the forts?"

"Yes," we answered, "we see him."

"Well," he continued, "we just wanted one more fight, so that we could knock him over, too."

We were naturally very much surprised that an English sergeant should make such a remark in the presence of an English officer, but the latter seemed to take no exception to it.

More than 2500 English officers were killed during the war, and the English press explain it by charging that the Boers deliberately picked them out and shot them. The fact is that at a distance of 200 yards, no one could distinguish between an English officer and an English soldier, because in appearance they were identically the same. When in our presence, we could distinguish the difference, because the officer's uniform was of a much finer quality of goods. The English prisoners used to tell us that they had evened up with this officer, and that one, and that many more were doomed before the war came to an end.

It is almost certain that the English killed more than half the number of officers who fell, because they so utterly despised them. Being so neglected, and treated worse than dogs, the English soldiers take advantage of the first favourable opportunity for their revenge. Those English officers who look after their men and treat them as human beings will never fail to find the English soldier respectful, obedient and faithful.

It was about June 20th when we reached Pretoria, and here we found hundreds of the *burghers* who had already surrendered near by Pretoria. Without exception I found Everyone disgusted with the Peace Conference, and as they explained why they thought peace was made, I wondered if Schalk Burger, Lucas Meyer, and J. B. Krogh did not each feel as if his ears were on fire.

Although we had not seen Pretoria for two years, yet we could observe no change except in the new faces we met on the streets. Once we knew every face, but now we scarcely saw one that we had known before. The Boer element of the town remained away from the frequented streets, because they did not wish to mingle with the English. When the Peace Terms were signed, it was distinctly agreed between Lord Kitchener and Lord Milner, and the two governments, that no *burgher* was to be required to take the oath of allegiance to the king, and the *burghers* in the field before the surrender were so informed.

Now, to show what dependence can be put upon an English officer's word, I will tell you just what happened. Married men were most anxious to remove from the concentration camps what was left of their families. They purchased food, supplies, bedding, clothing, etc., put all together with their families in open car trucks to be carried

DAUGHTERS OF LANDROST SCHUTTE OF PRETORIA.

to the railway station nearest their farms, and there deposited. Others loaded their provisions, etc., and their families in bullock wagons. No one could go any where without a permit, and now that these farmers were ready with their families to go to their burnt farms, they applied for their permits. All were informed that permits would be granted as soon as they took the oath of allegiance to the king, and not before. With one or two exceptions, all refused to take the oath, and I saw one *burgher* remove everything from his car truck, and go into camp on the hill side. This created plenty of trouble, and the *burghers* were highly incensed. The Boer generals told Lord Milner that if he did not make his word good in regard to his agreement about the oath of allegiance, they would not be responsible for the result. Lord Milner then granted the permits, and the *burghers* went to their farms.

Now another scheme was tried, and a few of the *burghers* were caught in the trap. Of course all the Boer families were much scattered, some being in Natal, others in Cape Colony, others in the Free State and others still in the Transvaal. Suppose my farm and home were in the Transvaal and my family were in the Free State or Cape Colony, and I should ask for a permit to go and bring it. The permit would be granted at once, and I would take the train for the Free State or Colony, as the case might be. I meet my family, make all arrangements to return and then apply for my permit for myself and family to return to our home in the Transvaal. We are promptly informed that the permit will be granted as soon as I take the oath of allegiance to the king. I was surprised that the women and children were not called upon to take the oath too. I must now either stay in the Free State or Colony, or take the oath, as there is no way by which I can communicate with the Boer generals.

Every letter was opened and censored and forwarded or not, as the English officer might decide. Secret instructions had been sent to all officials in South Africa, that no return permits must be given unless the applicants first took the oath of allegiance. About a dozen *burghers* were caught in this trap before it was exposed. Again there was much trouble, but the *burghers* could get no satisfaction, so they would write to their families to come to them, and the English could not refuse them permits, because they were not required to take the oath.

The Peace Terms required that all *burghers* should lay down their guns and acknowledge King Edward VII. as their lawful sovereign, and no more. This applied to prisoners of war in the same way as to the *burghers* in the field. Here I insert a private document giving private

PREDICANT BOSSMAN OF PRETORIA
Threatened with imprisonment for his free speech.

instructions, and it shows plainly what an unscrupulous thing an English official or officer is.

## Procedure to be Adopted in Selecting Prisoners of War for Return to South Africa.

### 1. Classification of Prisoners in Order of Return.

The selection of prisoners of war for return to South Africa should be made in the following order:

1. Those who have volunteered for active service, and are considered likely to become loyal subjects and useful settlers; and those who appear willing to accept the new order of things cheerfully.
2. Those who have shown no particular bias.
3. Irreconcilables, and men who have given trouble in the camps.

Lists of all prisoners of war have been prepared by the D. M. I., S. A., in conjunction with the local authorities of each district, divided into three categories, and it is desirable that this order should be maintained, as far as possible, and the lists made out by *commandants* of oversea camps, combined with the lists forwarded from South Africa, the corresponding classes being merged together.

It is to be understood that the lists supplied from South Africa are merely a general guide, and *commandants* of camps are invited to use their discretion in modifying the order, where their experience of the individual convinces them that an alteration is necessary.

No shipload of prisoners of war should include more than 100 men belonging to anyone district.

### 2. Oath of Allegiance.

No prisoner of war should be embarked without taking the Oath of Allegiance, or the approved equivalent declaration. The oath or declaration must be signed in triplicate, and it is of the greatest importance that the prisoner should retain one copy of the form, for purposes of identification, and that one copy should be forwarded to the Colonial Secretary of the prisoner's Colony for record.

### 3. Nominal Rolls to be Sent in Advance of Prisoners.

To facilitate the work of repatriation in South Africa, a nominal

MRS. BOSSMAN, WIFE OF THE PREDICANT

roll of all prisoners should be posted to the Military Secretary to the High Commissioner, at least a fortnight before embarkation.

This nominal roll should give the prisoner-of-war's number, and the farm, district and colony to which he belongs.

### 4. Special Lists.

Special lists will be forwarded from time to time, of men whose early release is approved by the High Commissioner, and these men should have precedence of all others; similarly, names may be sent of men whose early return is not considered advisable, and such men should in each case remain till the last.

### 5. Prisoners Allowed to Go at Own Expense.

Prisoners of war who take the Oath of Allegiance, and who belong to Class L, may be permitted to proceed forthwith
(a) To South Africa, (provided they have the means of supporting themselves on arrival.)
(b) Elsewhere. In each case at their own expense.

The names of prisoners released under this clause, and the ships by which they sail, should be communicated to the Military Secretary to the High Commissioner, by telegraph, in the case of persons returning to South Africa, and by post in other cases.

### 6. Preference to be Given to Men With Families in South Africa and to Farm Owners.

It will be advisable in compiling the lists mentioned in par. L, to include only a small percentage of unmarried men without farms or means of livelihood, and to push forward as much as possible, men having families who need their support, and farms to which they can go immediately on arrival in South Africa, as it is this class who provide the work for the *bijwoner* class, whose return for this reason, it is necessary to retard.

### 7. Foreigners.

Foreigners will not be allowed to return to South Africa.

### 8. Procedure on Arrival in South Africa.

On arrival of prisoners in South Africa, the S. O. Prisoners of War at the port of disembarkation will take over the prisoners of war, classify them according to districts, and arrange with the Repatriation Board in the two colonies for their distribution.

The Repatriation Board will then make all necessary arrangements at the district concentration camp for the accommodation of the *burghers*, and for returning them to their homes as soon as transport is available.

In the case of prisoners of war released in accordance with par. V. of these instructions, the S. O. Prisoners of War at port of disembarkation will arrange to meet them and take the particulars necessary for keeping all complete records.

W. Lambton, Lieut.-Colonel,
Military Secretary,
South Africa. Pretoria,

Fourth of July, 1902.

By the Peace Terms all prisoners of war were to be returned as promptly as possible, yet there are still prisoners of war on some of the islands today,(1903), ten months after the Peace was made. The above document shows plainly how determined an Englishman is to violate his sacred pledge. When I say that no Boer now would believe on oath either Lord Roberts, Lord Kitchener, Lord Milner, Joe Chamberlain, or any other English official, I mean just what I say, and I am sure the Boers are justified. On the day that the Coronation services were to be held, all Dutch churches were to sing "God Save the King" at the conclusion of the services. In Cape Colony armed men were actually present in some instances. In not one Dutch church in the land was the order obeyed, and English bayonets could not have made the people sing it, so repulsive is it to them. Even inscriptions on corner stones of public buildings were chiselled off, that something in English might be put in their places.

The English had shown so much meanness and treachery, that on the day for the Coronation services to be held, all of the 800 or 1,000 *burghers* in town pinned on their coats the Transvaal colours, and decorated all the Boer children with them. I didn't like to be behind, so I pinned mine on, too. As the English had no love for me and were actually thirsting for my blood, I stayed with my friends, the Boers. Six times that morning I was ordered to remove my colours, and six times refused, telling them that it was impossible for me to do so, and that they would have to do it. In every instance they took a look at my associates, and walked away. When the hour arrived for the services to begin, there were less than 200 white people, exclusive of soldiers, assembled in front of the government building.

Next to these were about 200 *kaffir* women, mistresses of the English officers, and men. Next to these men, about 300 *kaffir* boys who had fought side by side with the English against the Boers. Next to these was an open space of ground about eighty yards wide. Next to this open space were about 800 of the Boers who had so lately surrendered. The band played, then there was a prayer, followed by some talk, and the services were over. Again the band began to play, and when the first notes reached the Boers, they discovered that it was "*God Save the King*," so all turned their backs and walked down Church Street.

Both Boer and Englishman will admit that I have given a very short but accurate description of the Coronation services and the people assembled to witness them. But to read the English press on the following day, one could easily believe that all the Boers in the land were present to show their great love of their new Sovereign King Edward VII.

In the afternoon it was rumoured about town that in the evening during the parade and displaying of fireworks, all Boer houses not lighted up and displaying the English flag would have the windows and doors smashed. The Boers prepared themselves, Everyone being armed with a good stick, and when night came Everyone was ready for business. All Boer houses were in total darkness. No flags were flying, but not one was interfered with. The English had met these Boer boys before and they had no desire to meet them again. Had the doors and windows of one house been smashed, I firmly believe the Boers would have taken the town. The Boers had surrendered, but they were determined that no Englishman would spit upon them with impunity. Through the English soldier, and through the officers' reports, and by witnessing many barbarous acts in the field, I learned a great deal about the English officer, but in Pretoria I learned enough more to sicken even the most rabid Anglo-American, and now I am going to recall to him a little that he has done to make him well known.

CHAPTER 26

# Poisoning of Boer Prisoners at St. Helena

In some of the towns occupied by the English, and therefore not burnt down, the English commanders sent away such women as they felt sure the English officer could not make bend to his wishes, it mattered not what kind of a threat was made. All doubtful women were allowed to remain, and the great majority of the doubtful ones proved as loyal to themselves and people as those sent away. But in every town, so occupied, naturally there were many weak women who, under threat of being sent to some abominable camp where they would surely die, would consent to submit, if allowed to remain.

Even officers with the rank of general were in this damnable business, and I can prove it to their full satisfaction. In Rustenburg, for instance, Mr. English General, officers would appear at the back door late at night, rap hard and alarm the young women. Of course no men were near, for all were in the field. On being asked what was wanted, they were told to open the door and let them in. On being refused, these English ruffians in officers' uniform would make all kinds of threats, such as "we will break in the door," "withdraw food," " we will load you on a wagon and send you far away where the suffering is terrible, and the people are dying fast," etc., etc.

In a few cases these ruffians carried their point, be it said to their eternal shame and disgrace. Hundreds of just such acts of infamy on the part of the English officers, can be proved in every town occupied by the English troops. In many instances even the English soldiers following the example, would try the same tactics, but they were easily frightened away. On meeting a young Boer woman, the first idea that enters the English officer's head, is to seduce her by flattery and promises, but, failing in this way, he resorts to threats to frighten her into submission.

In Pretoria, Johannesburg, Bloemfontein or any of the Boer towns, any woman seen walking or riding with an English officer, was marked at once as a mistress or common prostitute. The married officer who had his wife with him, would suffer from this, unless the people knew that the woman was really his lawful wife. In Pretoria, on Skinner Street, several of us were amused late one Sunday afternoon, on seeing an English officer with the rank of captain walking with two Hottentot *kaffir* girls, one on each side, and both dressed in white linen and wearing pink stockings and high heeled slippers. These *kaffir* girls were about sixteen years old, and he looked supremely happy as he braced his shoulders and passed us by.

Just on the border of the Pretoria township was a very neat *kaffir* hut, and one day when we were near it, two of the artillery boys ventured that far, but before reaching the hut, they saw a man in khaki uniform mount a horse and fly. The boys went to the hut, found two *kaffir* girls, and the rendezvous of an English officer. They took all his clothing, his top boots, some fine blankets, a revolver and some trifles, and returned to camp. The uniform disclosed that the keeper of the hut and women was a 1st lieutenant. The *kaffir* girls told the boys that their master would get the soldiers and come after them, if they did not leave his clothes, etc. Sure enough, next day there came a column, and after a short skirmish it wheeled about and returned to Pretoria.

When the columns were raiding and burning farms in the bush veldt, in many instances they would drag the Boer girls, from sixteen to twenty-three years old, out of the houses, put them on wagons and cart them away, leaving the mother and little children to watch their home burn down and grieve over the fate of the girls. I can prove this to the very hilt, and without any trouble, too. The intention of the officers was to seduce these girls if they could, and if they couldn't, why then to use them anyhow, and I firmly believe that many of those innocent girls were forcibly violated. Where there were no young women, the little boys from seven to ten years old would be dragged from their homes and put in the camps. Many little boys of this age have walked and run miles to get with a commando, to escape being dragged away from their mothers, and many of them, too, have been shot down while trying to fly from English barbarity.

Along the railway lines, wherever you find an English camp, there, too, will you find a *kaffir* camp. These *kaffirs* were forcibly taken from their *kraals* on the Boer farms and put near the English camp. The reason given was that they wanted the men to work in the mines, and prevent them from giving information to the Boers. This was merely rot, for the Boers needed no information, as the English were always in plain sight. The truth is that they wanted the *kaffir* women for the use of the English soldiers and officers, and today, (1903), you can see half-caste kids by the score about those *kaffir* camps.

The *kaffirs* are a very chaste people, immorality with them being punished by death, and now the *kaffir* men who were forcibly taken from their *kraals*, and have seen their women debauched, hate the English with a bitterness that no pen can adequately describe. Yes, the English officer in the eyes of civilization is a typical gentleman, but as known and believed by the savage *kaffir*, he is a brute. English officers, sick in hospital, and those not in hospital, plied their art with the English Red Cross nurses, and over eighty of these had to be sent back to England.

So notorious were the relations between these nurses and the English officers, that the former were known among the enlisted men and the people generally, by a name borrowed from the Veterinary Department, and too utterly vile to be printed.

In reading a little book some tune ago, I came upon a passage that reminded me so forcibly both of the English and the ships' officers, that I here quote it. "Oh! if hell has a pit hotter and more intolerable than all the rest, a just God must surely reserve it for the lurking foe, the English officer, the seducer dammed." Of course the words, "the English officer," are my insertion, and the space they occupy is most appropriate for them.

So much has been said and written about the English concentration camps, that I will not dwell upon this subject to a great extent, yet I must say something, because I fear that all are not acquainted with these diabolical institutions.

In the first place, I must tell what a concentration camp is. It is a lot of tents, 100 or 200, or possibly 600, all pitched close together on a piece of exposed *veldt* on the railway line, and surrounded by a network of barbed wire. On each of the four sides of the camp is a gate, and at each gate there are two armed men to see that no one escapes. In every tent there is a family. That is, a mother and her children. It matters not what the number of the family may be, that family must live, or rather try to exist, in that one tent. All are closely confined within that network of barbed wire, and there they must remain, and

ONE OF MILNER'S VICTIMS
A Boer child in the first stage of death from starvation or poison in an English prison-camp. Taken by a young Boer spy in the English prison-camp at Irene, near Pretoria.

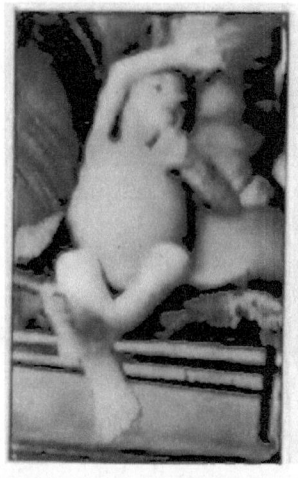

ONE OF KITCHENER'S VICTIMS
A Boer child dying either of starvation or of poison in one of the English prison-camps. Taken by a young Boer spy in the English prison-camp at Irene near Pretoria.

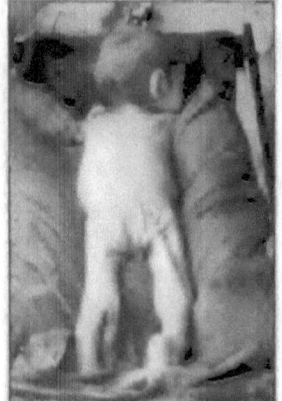

ONE OF CHAMBERLAIN'S VICTIMS
A Boer child that has just died from starvation or poison in an English prison-camp. Taken by a young Boer spy in the English prison-camp at Irene, near Pretoria

subsist on such food as the English officers wish to serve them. To each family is given about one-fourth as much fuel as is necessary, so at least four must club together and cook together, if they do not wish to eat their food in the raw state. Every family is limited in the amount of water to be used, and must take what is given.

Now the reader has a typical concentration camp, in which the women and children are packed like sardines, the very women and children that the English once told the world were refugees, but now acknowledge as their prisoners. Once one of these camps was established and filled with women and children, but a few days passed before they began to die, and such was the death rate, that special details of men were employed daily to dig graves for the burial of the dead. When one considers, that within a period of six months, more than 12,000 of these women and children died, he must begin to think that something is wrong. In the camp at Irene, near Pretoria, I know of one mother and six children, all healthy and strong, who were all dead within seven days after being confined there.

The children were not sick, but would refuse food, their feet would swell, their stomachs bloat, and in a few days they would pass away. This looks very much like poison of some kind; and the Boer women who were not in the camp, assured me that poison was discovered in their food. I believe this, because I have heard the English say that they could never hope to hold the country as long as there were Boer women and children. The Boer women in Pretoria, begged for permission to take food which they had cooked themselves, to the sick women and children in the camp, and in every instance they were refused, and told that the authorities would furnish the food.

As surely as I live this moment, I firmly believe that the English made use of poison in the food to destroy those women and children, and many Englishmen are as convinced as I am, only they have not the nerve to say so.

I know the Apache Indians, and particularly one of their great war chiefs, the notorious old Geronimo.[1] He was an Apache general, without education, without training, utterly unacquainted with all ideas of civilization, but shrewd and cunning, and, when on the war-path, would murder every man, woman and child he could lay hands on. I have travelled with him hundreds of miles, and followed the path along which lay his many victims, and therefore am acquainted with

---

1. *Geronimo: the Life of the Famous Apache Warrior in His Own Words* by Geronimo also published by Leonaur.

his method of doing away with his enemy in time of war. I know of Lord Roberts and Lord Kitchener, and their orders and proclamations. I know that both are highly educated, trained soldiers who are thoroughly acquainted with all the teachings of civilization and humanity, both in peace and in war. I have fought against them in South Africa, and I therefore am thoroughly acquainted with their method of fighting their enemy, and of doing away with men, women and children.

Those who were unfortunate enough to fall into Geronimo's hands, were killed outright, and without any ceremony or excuse, and his victims are numbered by the hundreds. Those unfortunate Boer women and children, who fell into the hands of Lord Roberts and Lord Kitchener, were doomed to slow death by torture, and the victims are numbered by the thousands.

The old savage chief showed far more humanity in his way of waging war than was shown by the two civilized lords. The one was open in his every act, while the others strove to keep all in the dark, by false reports and deliberate misrepresentations.

Had the war lasted another twelve months, I firmly believe that every Boer woman and child confined in the English prison camps of the Transvaal and Free State, would have died a slow death, and the Boers so believed when they consented to surrender. Three or four hundred Jews are deliberately murdered in Russia, and the civilized world is struck with horror. The Government of the United States sends in a petition of protests and is snubbed.

Thousands of women and children are murdered in South Africa, and the civilized world is undisturbed. The Government of the United States refuses to send in a huge petition of protests, and receives English thanks. I don't know who is Secretary of State for the United States, but I am sure it is either John Hay or Joe Chamberlain, or possibly both.

I will now drop the subject of the suffering Boer women and children, and take the reader to other parts, that he may see how the prisoners of war were treated on some of the English Islands.

I can prove that ground glass was used on the Island of St. Helena to kill the prisoners—and I would like the opportunity of doing it.

The English will fight shy, for they know that I know what I am talking about. Here were confined officers as well as men, and when they saw that some of their people were beginning to run down, and continued to run down until they were put in the grave, they began to think, and recall the fact that the English were supplying the food. Vegetables they suspected, but they did not come often and plentifully. Finally they decided when they did come they would not eat them, but put them to the test, and find out if there were any contamination. Nearly Everyone found ground and broken glass in the vegetables, but not at every inspection. Sometimes several vegetable days would pass by without any glass being found, but then a day would come when all or nearly all were rewarded.

This is a terrible charge to make, and I would not dare make it, did I not know that it can be proven to the complete satisfaction of any judge and jury. Many of the prisoners kept what they found as a souvenir, and every time they think of it they congratulate themselves for having sense enough to mistrust the English and the food they furnished.

To return to the concentration camps, the tents were sometimes 16 x 16 square, and in that tent there might be a family of four, or six, or a dozen. If there was a *kaffir* girl servant, she must sleep in the tent, too, but was not allowed to draw rations. No visitors were allowed, because they might tell tales out of school. After peace was made, the mother of any family wishing to be released to return home, had to sign a declaration to the effect that she had at least $500 in cash, that she would not apply to the government for help in any form, and that she would relinquish all claims for damages to her home and property. In addition to this she had to take an oath that she did not know of any arms or ammunition being concealed about her place, or in any other place. Those who could not or would not sign the above declaration, and take the oath, were held as prisoners of war in the camp.

After all the farms had been burnt, all property destroyed and there was no food to be had, and after more than 15,000 women and children had been buried, Lord Kitchener made a very generous and English-like offer to General Louis Botha. He said that he would return all the Boer women and children to their farms and give them three months' rations if Botha wished to have them. General Botha replied that he would be pleased to receive them, but six months' ration must be furnished so that they would have time to grow a crop, as he had no food for them. Lord Kitchener declined to accept General Botha's amendment, for it plainly meant that the women and children would not starve to death and that the Boers would not have to surrender to save them.

CHAPTER 27

# A Perfect Spy System

During the last two years of the war, the Boers had a perfect system of communication with Pretoria and Johannesburg. Captain J. J. Naude, a young Boer about twenty-three years old, was chief spy, and it was he who organized the force that did the work. In Pretoria he had seven Boer ladies, all smart and daring, and all prominent in Pretoria society. Their duty was to collect all information, official and otherwise, about what the English were doing in Pretoria, and what their intentions might be, have it typewritten and ready for delivery every Wednesday evening.

Every Monday, dressed in an English officer's uniform, Captain Naude would work his way through wire fences, forts, blockhouses and three lines of guards, into the town and stop at the home of a Mrs. Van W———. Sometimes he would stop with one of his other spies, at the home of a Mrs. M———. Another one of his spies, a Mrs. H———, often drove with him in a carriage through the streets during the day, and visited certain important places. The English soldiers invariably saluted Captain Naude as he passed by them. In the evening, at the house where he was staying, Miss M———, known as "Little Megs," Mrs. A———, possibly Mrs. J———, Mrs. M———, and Mrs. H———, would assemble to talk over the situation, put everything in proper form for Captain Naude, and then quietly return to their homes.

These ladies would in person deliver all letters brought in by Captain Naude from the *burghers* in the field, and he would take back the answers. He conducted his affairs in Johannesburg in the same way, but here his assistants brought out a typewritten paper every week, telling the people what had happened in the field, which the English tried to keep concealed. These typewritten papers would be posted up early in the morning, and before the English authorities could find and tear them down, hundreds of people had read them.

Little Megs, who since the surrender has changed her name to Mrs. Jan—, took desperate chances on many occasions, and actually supplied the Boers near Pretoria with ammunition, clothing, boots, etc. Her father's farm was a few miles out of town, and she would get a permit to go there and back and bring in vegetables. She always drove out with four horses to her cart, and came back with two, leaving the others with the commando. Sometimes, English officers would accompany her, and often she felt much alarmed, but her coolness and nerve always brought her out all right. Several times she was under heavy fire, being caught between the Boer and English lines. Many shot and shell passed over her head and many came near catching her, but never did she waver.

When all was over, she would pursue her way and deliver her contraband goods. She was in constant communication with a young lady, a cousin of hers, in far away Cape Colony. This cousin was a Miss Maggie Joubert, about twenty-three years old, and one of the pluckiest and most daring young ladies in the world. Her people are wealthy, but are Africanders to the backbone, and took the desperate chance of losing their property in order to help the cause of freedom. Most of our information as to what was going on in Cape Colony came from letters written by Miss Maggie Joubert to her little cousin Megs in Pretoria. Little Megs would give this information to Captain Naude, and he, in turn, would bring it out to the commandos, so our lines of communication were complete and our information genuine.

Miss Joubert would write on one side of the paper an ordinary family letter, and leave the opposite side blank. On the blank side she would write with lemon juice for her ink, and tell all about the English, where they were, what they were doing, the location of forts, etc. She would also tell all about the Boer forces, where they were and what they were doing. She also sent these letters to prisoners in the far away Islands, and kept them well informed. She knew at least one in every place who knew her method.

For two years she kept this up, but about six months before peace was made, the English began to suspect her, because she wrote so many letters. To one of her letters to little Meg in Pretoria they applied the hot iron, and out came the lemon juice as black as ink. This exposed her, for the English now read all about the movements of their troops in the Colony, their location, etc. Two police were sent to arrest her at once. She was carried away to Wellington, and locked up in a cell. After remaining there for a week, she was taken to the Paarl and imprisoned. Neither her people or anyone else was allowed to see her.

After a few weeks she was tried by a military court. This court tried to find out from her whether she had given any information to the enemy outside their lines. She always answered: "You have my letters, and must find out for yourselves." Little Megs was inside the English lines, and she was never in any way suspected of being a spy. The court found Miss Joubert guilty of treason, and sentenced her to five years' hard labour. She told the court that she could stand just as much as they could give her. She was returned to her cell and very closely confined.

Lord Kitchener commuted the sentence to six months' imprisonment without hard labour. The matron of the prison secured her some silks and she spent her time making fancy articles. In the evening she would sing the *Volksleid* (National Anthem) and then say the Boer prisoner's prayer, one verse of which is as follows:

*When shall I be, shall I be returning*
*To my dear old plaats, to my good old home*
*Where the duiker, spring-bok, and Koedoe roam*
*And the hot fire of freedom is burning?*

Miss Joubert's daily rations consisted of one bottle of milk, one pound of bread, and one pound of meat. This food without change for six months, proved too much for her. She fell very ill, and how she lived to the end of the time, she cannot explain. She was considered a dangerous character, and a close damp cell must be her home, and in that home she was doomed to live or die on food that would probably kill a *kaffir*.

Major Benson of the Intelligence Department, by way of consolation, told her that after enjoying the blessings of English liberty for two years, she had acted like a cur, and therefore deserved to suffer. She replied that she was proud of all her acts, and she was ready to suffer for them.

Several other ladies are lying in prison cells today, (1903), charged with giving the Boers information, and probably will remain there until death comes to their rescue and frees them. Miss Joubert and her comrades who have been locked within prison cells all know what it is to be grossly insulted by the English officer, and all have suffered. Little Megs and her associates in Pretoria, and Miss Joubert

MISS MAGGIE JOUBERT
The beautiful Boer Spy who was imprisoned in an
English cell for six months.

and her companions in Cape Colony are all noble and grand women. The flame of patriotism glowed in their hearts. All were ready to be sacrificed to save the Africander people from being shackled with the chains of the slave. All spurned danger and faced death itself. They are patriots, and their names will endure.

Captain Naude, the commander of the lady spies in Pretoria, was well known in the town, and his young wife and his people resided there. The English knew him, too, and they were aware of the fact that he was coming in and going out. They had a standing reward of $10,000 for him, dead or alive. Every few days every house in Pretoria would be carefully searched, and the three lines of guards put on the lookout for him.

Nothing was left undone to catch or kill him, yet he went in every Monday evening and came out every Wednesday evening. He is the coolest, most determined and daring young man I ever saw, and I believe he is the most wonderful spy known, when all the circumstances are considered. He wore a slight moustache, an English officer's uniform, could talk but little English and would drive in an open carriage through the principal streets of the town in open daylight; yet he was never caught, though hundreds of detectives were watching for him. Many letters has he taken in for me, and he never failed to bring me back the answer. In my eyes he is a marvel, and the Africander people are heavily indebted to him for the services he rendered to them and their country. Long may he live.

I must say a few words about the American consuls in South Africa. I was in that country eight years, and during this time I naturally became acquainted with some of them. In the first place, I must say that their pay is so small that it is almost impossible for them to make both ends meet, it matters not how economically they live. Good men and smart men will naturally refuse such an appointment, unless they have spare money of their own to spend. The first consul who was sent to Pretoria was C. E. Macrum, and he was a good and smart man, and an excellent one for the place, as well as a genuine American. He was perfectly conversant with all the causes that led up to the war, and he knew that the English forced the Boers into it for no other reason than to take the Johannesburg gold fields; therefore, a few months after the war began, he was recalled. Young Adelbert Hay, son of John Hay, Secretary of State, was appointed in his place. When he arrived in Pretoria it was plain that he was an Englishman, both in heart and soul. I have an idea that he was so educated before he left Washington

City, judging him by his conversation.

He had not been there more than two months before he changed, and became pro-Boer both in heart and soul, and so remained till death. He was thrown in close contact with the English in Pretoria, soon learned what an Englishman really was, why he was fighting the Boer, his methods of fighting, etc., and he became thoroughly convinced that all he had been taught to believe about the English, and the war, was utterly false. He learned of their barbarity in war, their treachery and unscrupulousness, and he saw their treatment of the Boer women and children in the prison camps, which he declared to be sickening. I don't know but if the whole truth were known, I think it would be found that the powers that be in America came to the conclusion that young Mr. Hay was not the proper man for his position in Pretoria, and he therefore resigned. When the news of his sudden death reached South Africa, the Africander people felt deeply grieved, and at several of their evening services his name was affectionately mentioned in their prayers.

W. D. Gordon, the Consular Agent in Johannesburg, is unquestionably the ablest and strongest representative that the United States has ever had in South Africa. He is a genuine American, a successful business man, and as Consular Agent he carefully guards American interests and American citizens, while by his honesty, uprightness and openness, he commands the respect of the whole people. The English respect him because they are afraid of him, and know that they can neither deceive him nor win him by flattery. He receives no salary as Consular Agent, yet the position costs him much time and trouble. No act of his will ever bring discredit to the American people or his Country.

It was but a few weeks before war was declared that I met Consul General Stowe of Cape Town, and although I was convinced that he was American, yet I could not make out whether he was an Anglo-American or a genuine Englishman. In a conversation with him in Johannesburg, he told me that on hostilities breaking out, he intended to come to Johannesburg and hoist the Stars and Stripes over Heath's Hotel as his headquarters. Now, Heath's Hotel was the chief rendezvous of the most rabid Englishmen, and it was very much feared that when war once began, the Boers would destroy the building. Consul Stowe was determined to prevent this, if possible, by placing his august person in the door, and waving the Stars and Stripes above his head. Of course, the Boers never had any idea of destroying this hotel, or any other property, but the English press tried to make the world believe otherwise. By way of retort, I told Consul Stowe that if he hoisted the American flag over that hot bed of rebellion, we would set fire to the other and adjoining buildings, and that if he were unfortunate enough to be caught in the general conflagration, he would have no one to blame but himself. He changed his mind then, and said that, after all, he thought he could be of more service in Cape Town than in Johannesburg.

During the war, Consul Stowe was very prominent in English circles, and no doubt he served them well. On one occasion, on the 4th of July, an American lady intended to give a dinner to some Americans, and she thought of inviting some English also. As some of the latter were sure to come, she thought it would show courtesy if she put up a British flag as well as the American flag. She spoke to Consul Stowe on the subject, and he told her that most certainly she must hoist the British flag. He further told her, that she must float the British flag on top of the pole, and the American flag below it on the same pole. This will give the American people a slight insight into the character of the American Consul-General at Cape Town.

On another occasion, he concluded to visit Pretoria for reasons best known to himself. Above the finest carriage in the long train, he hoisted the American flag, and then he, etc., etc., were ready to move out. All was smooth sailing until far into the Free State. Suddenly the train stopped, firing was heard, and the Boers were all around the unfortunates. Soon the white flag was hoisted and the train captured. Captain Daanie Theron, the famous Boer scout, the little man so dearly loved by the whole Africander race, with his hundred daring patriots had committed the terrible offence of firing upon a train floating the Stars and Stripes, and capturing the American Consul-General of Cape Town, the great Colonel Stowe.

He captured something else, too, for there were on that train about seventy-five English soldiers, and they fell into his hands, together with their rifles and ammunition. In Colonel Stowe's carriage there were some lordly looking individuals, too, but as all were Colonel Stowe's private secretaries, Captain Theron did not disturb them. He allowed the carriage floating the Stars and Stripes to proceed on its journey to Pretoria. I never heard, but it is safe to say, that he landed his secretaries in Pretoria, and that at a swell banquet many stirring and patriotic' speeches were made.

Of course, the English press was full of glowing accounts of the way in which the savage Boers had insulted the American flag, but not one of them thought to mention anything about English prisoners and private secretaries. No doubt Colonel Stowe was a great credit to the American Government, but I would not like to add "and also to the American people," because I am not seeking trouble.

Chapter 28

# The English Arm Kaffirs

Now I wish to say, and will say, a few words about English war correspondents. I never met but two personally, and they were prisoners of war in Pretoria, having a few days previously been captured by the Irish Brigade at Elandsfontein near Johannesburg, at the time of the British occupation of this city. The two gentlemen were Lord Cecil Manners and Lord Roslyn. They were given comfortable quarters in the Grand Hotel, and both seemed contented, although they were anxious to be released, that they might see what the English and Boers were doing just outside of Pretoria. They were not prejudiced and thick-headed, as you generally find Englishmen of their class, and both impressed me as being honest, reasonable and desirous of the whole truth.

Lord Roslyn showed one of his reports to me, made while Buller was trying to relieve Ladysmith, and Lord Cecil Manners gave me his views, too. Both of course were Englishmen, and very handsome and fine looking ones, too. Naturally they viewed matters from an English stand point, still I was surprised at their fairness, and I do not believe that either would intentionally twist a fact in order to conceal British blunders. Now this brings me to one that I did not meet, but one I wanted to meet. His name is Bennet Burleigh, and he was war correspondent of the London *Daily Telegraph*.

In Johannesburg there is a house known as the American Hotel, and the proprietor of that house was Dave Norris, an American, and one of the worthiest of the race in South Africa. He despised the English, loved liberty and longed to see the Boers free and independent. All the Irish boys knew him, and all loved him, and he in his turn was as warmly devoted to them, so, naturally, when any of them were in Johannesburg, they were always to be found with good' Dave Norris

Miss Minnie Kingsman a Boer *belle* of Johannesburg

in the American Hotel; and wherever the Irish boys were, there I, too, would be.

Now I will return to Mr. Bennet Burleigh. As soon as the English occupied Johannesburg, they heard that I was still in the city. All wanted me and they wanted me badly, because it meant quite a neat sum of money to the fortunate man. Bennet Burleigh was not a combatant; he was a war correspondent, and was not supposed to take any active part.

Late one night, Dave Norris was aroused and, on opening the door, in walked Bennet Burleigh with a revolver in his hand. In the adjoining room there was a man named Wilson, and to Wilson's ear he placed his revolver, and said, "I have you at last, Blake, and you are good meat."

"Butch" Wilson replied: "Fooled again, old man! Colonel Blake is not here."

"Butch" having proven his identity, was released. After a few nights, Bennet Burleigh was again in the American Hotel, but this time put his revolver in old John Langtry's ear, and said: "I know I am right this time, come on here, sir, and be quick about it."

Old John asked him what he wanted him for. "I know Blake by his photo, and you are the man, so get out."

Again Mr. Bennet Burleigh, the war correspondent, *the non-combatant*, was sorely disappointed. Had this thing, Bennet Burleigh, been captured by the Boers, he would have whined and cried and begged to be released, because he had nothing to do with fighting and only acted as a correspondent.

After the general surrender, one of the English majors whom I knew quite well, told me that Mr. Bennet Burleigh was very anxious to meet me, and would like an appointment. I was highly pleased and told the major that I would be glad to meet Mr. Burleigh at the Grand, in the evening, and that if he presented him to me I would make him a beautiful present, or give anyone $25.00 who would bring the man face to face with me. Mr. Burleigh never showed up, and I inquired after him, but he had gone to Johannesburg. He soon left for England, so I never had the opportunity I so longed for.

Bennet Burleigh is a cowardly thing, and such a thing cannot possibly make a truthful report. Take all his writings during the war, and I very much doubt whether one grain of truth could be found in anyone of his reports. We read many of his detailed descriptions, and they were so ridiculously false that we could not help laughing. Mr. Bennet

Burleigh, you are a thorough-bred Englishman, typical of a degenerate race, and I now drop you as I picked you up, a dirty thing.

Now I come to the subject of armed *kaffirs*. On the English side of the western border of the Transvaal, the English armed several thousand *kaffirs*, and instructed them to make raids on the Boer farms across the border, and take all cattle, sheep, horses, etc., they could find. The *kaffirs* were delighted and lost no tune in carrying out their instructions. They crossed, and on the first raid murdered more than fifty old men, women and children, and destroyed their property. They came again, and nearly all the Boers were withdrawn from Mafeking in order to fight them, and drive them out. They slaughtered the *kaffirs* by the hundreds and drove them back to their English allies for protection.

While the troops were absent, Baden-Powell did not leave his prairie-dog-holes and come out, because he was afraid the Boers might catch him out, and that would be the end of Baden-Powell and his letter writing. A Boer commando had to be formed and kept near the border to protect the women and children from these savages armed by the English. All of the many thousands of *kaffirs* in the Rustenburg district were so armed, and at times General de la Rey would have to abandon all operations against the English and go and fight them, to drive them far from the women and children. All the thousands of *kaffirs* between Pretoria and Pietersburg and those to the north of Pietersburg were also armed by the English, and General Beyers had to fight them much more than he did the latter, in order to save the women and children from being outraged and murdered.

Armed *kaffirs* were stationed all along the Pretoria-Pietersburg railway line and did all the work that Joe Chamberlain told the British Parliament the English soldiers were doing.

Northeast of Pretoria, north of Middleburg and all about Lydenburg and Pilgrims' Rest, were thousands of England's savage allies who murdered hundreds of men, women and children. In the east, about Komati Poort and along the Swazieland border, the same conditions prevailed and the outrages committed are too sickening to put in print. Nearly sixty men were attacked, murdered and cut into pieces at one place.

All the blockhouses along the eastern border were manned with armed *kaffirs*. About thirty women and children who had their homes burnt on the Piet-Retief border by the English and were left to starve to death, started out on foot to find some Boer commando, and get food and relief. They had to pass through this line of blockhouses manned by the armed *kaffirs*. The savages seized and outraged all of them, and then drove them into the high *veldt*, where they were abandoned. They were found by the Boers, and a more sickening sight or characteristic picture of English brutality and savage outrage could not be imagined. In the face of all this, Lord Kitchener, Lord Milner and Joe Chamberlain swore to the world that no armed *kaffirs* were employed by the English troops!

There were between 30,000 and 40,000 *kaffirs* armed by the English, and instructed to kill off the Boers. The *kaffirs* had always been friendly to the Boers but the English went to them, and told them that if they did not take up arms against the Boers, they would destroy all their food and not allow them to grow any more as long as the war lasted. The *kaffirs* in the mountains near Lydenburg were not to be so threatened because the English knew them and were afraid of them. In order to get them to fight the Boers, the English promised to give them all the Boer farms in their section at the end of the war. Many of my good friends were murdered in cold blood by these same *kaffirs*.

At the town of Lydenburg, the English had more than 1000 armed *kaffirs* side by side with them. At Middleburg they had about 600. In all the blockhouses and forts along the railway lines there were armed *kaffirs*, with the English soldiers, and the *kaffirs* were generally in the majority.

After the war came to an end, the English sent wagons and carts out to bring in the rifles, but the *kaffirs* refused to give them up until the English had made good their agreement. The *kaffirs* fairly drove out the English, who then came to the Boers and asked them to join with them and help them disarm the *kaffirs*. The Boers refused to a man, and told them since they had armed the blacks, they must now disarm them. The *kaffirs* took possession of the Boer farms which the English had promised to give them, and would not let the Boers return.

At this time, I do not know how the affairs were settled, but I think all *kaffir* claims were paid for, but the rifles were not given up.

Now that the war is over and hundreds of men, women and children have been murdered by these savages, Lord Kitchener, Lord Milner and Joe Chamberlain are ready to admit that they armed thousands of *kaffirs* and used them against the Boers. They now admit it because they have to, for if there was any possible way to lie out of it, it is certain they would take advantage of it.

The English officers, English soldiers and *kaffirs* all tell you now that they were armed by the English, to fight the Boers, and the savages do not hesitate to tell why they turned against the Boers. It is hard for Joe Chamberlain, and Milner and Kitchener to lie out of it. They can't do it, and they are too smart to try it.

For eighteen months we had the *kaffirs* on one side and the English on the other, and the narrow belt between was not more than twenty-five to thirty-five miles wide, and here it was that we must live and fight and try to protect ourselves. Sometimes we were fighting the English, and sometimes the *kaffirs*, and sometimes both at once. How we managed to hold our own and escape what the English call sure death, I can not explain, but I do know that nearly all escaped.

I have heard much about Geneva Conventions, Hague Conferences, and have had to know something about International Law, and I am forced to come to the conclusion that all these peace and humanity posters are only intended for times of peace. Great men meet at Geneva; great men meet at the Hague; great men meet to discuss questions of International Law; all are lovers of peace, all love humanity, all are determined to reduce the sufferings of mankind to a minimum in times of war.

> But lay at their feet the lifeless form of a child mutilated by an English shell, or a savage armed with an English rifle, and all will throw up their hands in horror, and cry out "what a pity! But the English are a civilized people, and we must support them."

When I hear learned and humane men discussing the sufferings of man, Geneva Conventions, Hague Conferences and International Law, I feel like crying out "Rot, rot, rot! and three times Rot, rot, rot!" because that is all there is in the whole business. The savage fights to kill; he asks no quarter, and he gives none in times of war; he has no Geneva Conventions to conceal him while murdering the wounded; he has no Hague Conferences, no International Law; but he is not a hypocrite, because he proclaims just what he is, and will not appeal to long-faced humanity to make screens to hide his acts.

I know the savages, because I have lived with them. I know the civilized, because I have lived with him! and when it comes to decide on questions of honour, humanity and justice, give me the savage every time. The great savage nation a are better governed, are infinitely more moral, more humane and just, than any of the so-called civilized nations.

The Great Indian tribes, before they were corrupted and polluted by the presence of white men, were proud, high-spirited, well governed, happy and contented, but now they are low, degenerate, immoral and miserable. The great *kaffir* nations of South Africa, the Zulus, the Basutos, and the Swazies, probably the finest races of people in the world, are far more free and independent, better governed, more moral and contented than the people of the so-called civilized nations on the globe. Both men and women are pictures of physical perfection; they are proud, but not boastful; they are honourable and truthful to each other; immorality with them is punished by death; and they live at peace with each other, and with the world, so long as greedy, unmoral white man does not interfere.

Now I will pass on to what is in the world known as "hands-uppers," that is, those *burghers* who for various reasons voluntarily went into the English lines and surrendered their rifles. On the occupation of Bloemfonteim, Johannesburg and Pretoria, thousands of this name really thought the war was over, and acted accordingly. All Boer officers totally condemn them, and declare there was no excuse for them. Here I differ with the Boer officers, and say that they themselves were entirely responsible for nearly everyone who voluntarily surrendered his rifle. Thousands upon thousands surrendered on the occupation of Johannesburg and Pretoria, believing that the war was at an end. Under Lord Robert's proclamation, setting forth that the war was practically over, and assuring all *burghers* who came in and surrendered their rifles, that neither they nor their property would be in any way molested, thousands of others surrendered.

Not a Boer officer in the field opened his mouth and told the *burghers* anything. When they did assemble the *burghers*, and talked to them, their theme was Christ and His teachings, and that all must follow the narrow path, because the broad one led to hell. Not in a single instance did any Boer officer tell the *burghers* what their duty to their country was; not a word about patriotism was ever mentioned, not a hint given that the war would proceed more vigorously than ever after the fall and occupation of Pretoria. No, the *burghers* were absolutely ignored, and while I deplored the fact that so many thousands of them surrendered, yet I felt that the Boer officers deserved infinitely more censure than the *burghers* themselves.

For instance, General de la Rey, the noble and patriotic defender of his Country, called upon the *burghers* in the Rustenburg district to take up arms again and fight for their Country. All responded, and General de la Rey had to send hundreds of miles for rifles and ammunition with which to equip them. I, at least, do not censure this class of "hands-uppers," but I do censure the Boer officers, all of whom were guilty and strictly responsible for their conduct. Had there been no surrenders, the Boers would have beaten the English.

In Ermelo, in 1901, I heard General Louis Botha make a speech to the *burghers*. I did not like what he said, and thereupon did not agree with him. He told them they could go and surrender if they pleased, but if they did go, it would be without his permission. This was really an inducement for them to go and surrender. Idleness always creates discontent, and from this all the *burghers* were suffering. They could see no reason why they should lie in *laager* and do nothing, and if that was what General Botha wished them to do, why, they said, it is better to go and surrender, and be through with the business.

I certainly blame General Botha for the surrender of hundreds of men, and while I like him and know that he is a great fighter when pushed to it, yet I must be honest and tell him the great mistake he made, in not keeping the *burghers* in hand, and giving them plenty of fighting, for they were always ready to fight when there was anything to be accomplished. I used to wish to say to him:

> General Botha, you know what the Governor of North Carolina said to the Governor of South Carolina, "It is a long time," not "between drinks," but between fights.

The English columns had not then swarmed over the high *veldt*, and both the Delagoa and Natal railway lines were easy to destroy, and many trains could have been taken, yet he would not allow the *burghers* to molest them. I did not understand him then, and I don't understand him now. Captain Jack Hindon and that most reckless officer, Lieutenant Hendrik Slegkamp, were destroying armoured trains and freight trains, near Balmoral, and they captured enough supplies and ammunition to support the whole Boer army, yet the *burghers* were not there to help themselves and make provision for the future.

Captain Hindon and Lieutenant Slegkamp had only about 100 men, yet they were in every way successful. Captain Karl Trichardt, a son of the patriotic Commandant Trichardt, of the State Artillery, joined with Captain Hindon and Lieutenant Slegkamp *and together they took in more than 100 trains in two months.* The *burghers* were most anxious to have a hand in this business; but General Botha discouraged them, and in every instance, when they requested him, they were refused. I do not like to criticise General Botha, because he is a most excellent fighter, but I feel that in telling him his weaknesses, he may, at some time in the future, remember what I say, and benefit by it. I know that he is loyal and true, but he must feel the prick of the spur in order to develop the high speed that is really in him.

I say all this with the best intentions, General Botha, for you are a young man, and in the future possibly your services will be needed. To your tact, courage and generalship, add energy and foresight, and I assure you that you will prove yourself a star of the first magnitude in the eyes of the military world; but remember that you can not ignore and allow to remain undestroyed the enemy's line of communications, when all is in your own hands. Make your plans to win, but also prepare for disaster, and your name will go down in history as a great general. Of General de lay Rey and De Wet, I have but one criticism to make, and that is they must tell their *burghers* less of religion and more of the duties they owe to their Country.

The *burghers* know their bibles as well as the officers, can pray as well and preach as well; then why should their officers keep trying to drive more bible into the *burghers*? When the officers tell them that God has ordained that all men shall be free, and that all *burghers* who submit to live as slaves to an English Sovereign can never hope to pass St. Peter and enter the gates of heaven, they have said enough on the bible question. In contending with such an unscrupulous and God-banished government as the British, they must remember that their rifles and artillery must take first place. The Boers are by nature intensely humane and religious, and command the respect and admiration of all who know them, but they must remember that when at war with the English, they are fighting a lot of savages, and that by way of retaliation they must play the savage, too.

The civilized Christian preaches of humane war, but has anyone ever taken part in or witnessed a humane war, or can anyone mention a humane war since the world was created? When two civilized nations go to war, each strains every nerve to mow the other down, to cut his throat, to mutilate and kill him,—by fair means or foul,—and when the battle is lost and won, they commiserate and sympathize with them, and grieve to see so many hundreds of their fellowmen writhing in agony on the battlefield. This is what they call humane war in modern times. If the greedy, ambitious and unscrupulous politicians who draw the people into war were forced to shoulder the rule and take position in the front line of battle, then we would have a truly humane war, because they would then find a way to settle all differences without resorting to force of arms.

Had the English law required Joe Chamberlain, Alfred Milner and C. J. Rhodes, to go into the front line of battle as proof of their earnestness and sincerity and of their love for their country, it is certain that the pages of history would never have been stained by the account of the bloody war in South Africa.

Now a few words on the Anglo-Boer, a class of men in my opinion far more contemptible than such men as Roberts, Kitchener, Milner and Chamberlain who had burned down the Boer homes and left the Boer women to starve to death, because they did not make their men come in and surrender. The Anglo-Boers deserted their people, took up arms with the British and materially helped them to destroy their own people's farms and make the women and children suffer death, if possible. These Anglo-Boers were organized into a military force and christened by Lord Kitchener as National Scouts. To show their great loyalty to the British Crown they endeavoured to prove themselves more cruel to the Boer women and children than the English ever were, and they made thousands of them suffer. The Boers were fortunate enough to capture a few of them and they were promptly shot. All of them would have been shot had they been captured.

After the general surrender anyone of those National Scouts who dared to go back to his own farm would promptly meet his just doom. The English would bury him and ask no questions. Within the first two months after the surrender, twenty-two of them were buried, and I learn that occasionally one or two of them are buried now, (as at time of first publication). They have to live under the protection of the British troops to avoid being killed. It is hoped that in time the entire 3000 will have died unnatural deaths. In hundreds of instances their own wives and children deserted them and would not allow them to come near them. Many of them wanted to go to Somaliland and help the English fight the Mad Mullah and his negroes, but the English Government felt that they could not be trusted. They are now ignored and despised both by the English and the Boers, and the most commendable act they could do would be for each to cut his own throat and thus earn the thanks and approval of present and coming generations.

The traitor is the most despicable of all the animal creation, and of the National Scouts I say with Tom Moore:

"May the blood that courses through their dastardly veins and recoils at the very sound of Freedom's call, stagnate in chains!"

I will now sum up the reasons why the Boers lost their independence and country, and then throw in a few scraps which are worth recording. In the first place, the Boers lost because they made the fatal mistake of laying siege to Ladysmith, Kimberly and Mafeking. Had they driven ahead and take possession of the capitals of Natal and Cape Colony, all three of these depots of supplies and ammunition would have fallen into their hands without a shot being fired; and besides they would have received at least 75,000 recruits from the Colonies. Mafeking was absolutely of no importance to them.

Of course, Baden-Powell was there and thousands of dum-dum bullets, and three or four years' supply of food, but all this in the beginning was not wanted. Baden-Powell would never have ventured a day's march from his prairie-dog-holes had there been Boers present, because he did not wish to take any chances of being captured. In the second place, the Boers lost because so many thousands of them surrendered voluntarily on the occupation of Bloemfontein and Pretoria. The Boer generals I hold entirely responsible for this. Had they met and talked to them and explained Roberts' proclamations, they would have prevented at least 35,000 men from surrendering.

In the third place even after the voluntary surrender of so many thousands of men, had the three generals, Chris De Wet, de la Rey and Louis Botha, concentrated their forces and carried the war into Cape Colony, they would have won, because they would have received as many thousand recruits as they had lost in men who had voluntarily surrendered, and more, too. They could have taken complete possession of the English lines of communication, and this would have forced the English to abandon both the Free State and the Transvaal. But with a hammer and a spike one could not drive into a Boer general's head the real importance of his enemy's line of communication and the necessity of its destruction.

In the fourth place, the Boers lost because the English Government in Washington, D. C., allied itself with the English Government in London, England, and allowed British officers to establish a military camp at Chalmette, New Orleans, for recruiting horses, mules and men for the British army in South Africa. This was a most damnable piece of business. More than 200,000 horses and mules were sent, and I don't know how many thousand men.

So anxious was the English Government in Washington, D. C., to

SOME OF THE IRISH BOYS JUST AFTER THE GENERAL SURRENDER

Mike Halley, Sidney Blake, Jerry O'Leary, Dr. Worthington, Jack McGlew, Dick Hunt, Jim French, John Langtry, Pete O'Hare, Joe Kennedy, George Waldeck, Dave Norris, Colonel Blake, Lieutenant Malan, Joe Wade.

supply, the British Army in South Africa with horses and mules that today, May, 1903, there is a deficiency of them in the United States and our own cavalry regiments can not be mounted.

On reading all this in the newspapers, the Boers would come to me and ask me to explain the conduct of the government. I recalled to them the fact that Mr. Hay, Secretary of State, had been ambassador for a month or so in London, and that the English had so stuffed him with flattery that he had forgotten that he was a republican and a citizen of a republic, and that they must expect him to be English in his every act.

Strange to say, practically all American ambassadors to England return to America as Englishmen. They cannot stand against English flattery. Read the papers and you will see that at every private dinner or reception of the king the American ambassador is the only foreign representative honoured with an invitation. He accepts, the king lets him sit for five minutes in his own chair, allows him to recline on the couch where Queen Victoria once took a nap after returning from her drive in Hyde Park, and that settles him, he is denationalized. Kings, queens, earls, lords and so forth, are trained flatterers, and there is certainly much power in these titles, too, for let a dissolute, caddish earl who thinks nothing of his mother, but is devoted to his mistress, come to America, there are many rich girls who are ready at once to vend their souls and bodies and give their fortunes for the title of princess.

All learn what there is in such a title when it is too late. I lived in London fifteen months and I saw a great deal. The nobility or upper set, and the lower class of Englishmen, are dissolute and immoral to an extreme, while the middle class is perfection. In this class one will find the moral, refined, upright, and honest Englishmen, and no where in the world can be found a better class of men and women than in this middle class. Unfortunately they are but few, as compared to the whole, and being sandwiched in between the mighty upper and lower classes, or immoral and dissolute classes, it is inevitable that in the end they will be squeezed to death. And then it is that the remains of a once glorious and proud old England will be laid away in the same vault with those of Rome and Spain.

There is not an Englishman living that does not at heart despise every American, yet he must look to the American for his food. All talk of their cousins across the sea, for all now know that their very existence as a nation depends upon the good will of America. I have talked with many business men in London, and all, in speaking of American merchants, say, "He is smart, but not a good business man." They mean by this that all Americans are rascals, and so they believe.

In 1895 I was amused one morning when I read in one of the Cape Town newspapers that:

> It was strange to see on Adelaide Street, this morning, the American Consul in a sober condition.

I was also amused in London during the Spanish War to witness such men as Dewey, Schley and Sampson hissed in the theatres on the very mention of their names. One picture of the battle-ship *Maine* leaving New York, was hissed by the whole house. Another of its destruction was applauded, yet there are thousands of Anglo-Americans to be seen walking the streets every day. For more than a hundred years the British Government has laboured to disunite our Union or in some way to destroy our Republic, yet we still have Anglo-Americans, and, be it said to our shame, an English Government in Washington, D. C. Let a crown prince or some great lord come to the United States, and then something is sure to happen. Such personages come to flatter and arrange matters in Washington for a slap at the United States. The Venezuelan disgrace was the outcome of Prince Henry's visit.

Lord Charles Beresford comes to tell us how much England loves us and the Monroe Doctrine, and we are then ready to give up our rights to Alaska. It is time for the American people to see to it that no one but true Americans shall hold the highest offices in their gift. Plain it is that we are drifting towards imperialism, that is, corruption and crime. The records of our action towards the Philippines and of the conduct of our army towards the Filipinos will mark the darkest pages in our history and prove loathsome to posterity. The Filipinos long to be free, and our motto seems to be to kill or enslave them. It is unnecessary to give reasons, for the daily papers fairly teem with accounts of barbarous and murderous acts on the part of several army officers towards the people, black and white, of those far away and sorely afflicted islands.

Strange to say, our Secretary of War brings down heavily the stamp of his approval on all these outrages and endeavours to keep the people in the dark as far as it is within his power. The very people who declared for liberty for all, and fought to free the blacks of the Southern States, are now fighting to enslave the blacks and whites of the far-away Philippines. I admire nerve, but despise hypocrisy. Now I must say a word about the Irish and Irish-Americans on their conduct in America during the South African War. There are many millions of Irish in America and there is one organization, the Clan-na-Gael, known as the Physical Force Element. For nearly half a century this organization has been crying and preaching that "England's difficulty was Ireland's opportunity."

They have blown up a few barns and woodsheds in the rear of some lord's residence, managed to get some good patriotic Irishmen behind the bars of English prisons for life, and tried to turn the course of the Gulf Stream in order to frighten or freeze England. But when an English military camp was established in New Orleans to recruit horses, mules and men, they did nothing but prohibit every member of the society from doing anything towards its destruction. Every man of the rank and file wanted to destroy that camp, and stop the shipment of the horses, mules and men to the British army in South Africa, and were ready to volunteer for the service. They saw England's difficulty and wished to take advantage of it. But their leaders said NO, and not one man was allowed to open his mouth or do anything.

Lord Salisbury and Chamberlain must have known all about the stand the leaders of the Clan-na-Gael had taken and the reasons for it, for both said in Parliament, "there was nothing to fear from the Irish in America." Clansmen should look out, for there is something wrong about their leaders. Had the Irish destroyed that camp, it would have told England, in unmistakable terms, that so long as there are Irish in America, so long will it be impossible for her to recruit horses, mules and men on our soil. England would then learn that it would be for her best interests to allow the people of Ireland to govern themselves.

Irish enmity will live in all its bitterness till the people are free, and England will find this out when it is too late. She is now going to give them a land bill by which the tenants can, to a certain extent, buy the land of which they were forcibly robbed in years gone by; and I confess this will prove a great boon to them. I believe, however, that the concession is intended as a bribe, for England is frightened because the Irish have at last come to then: senses and cease to enlist in the army. Without the Irish, the British army would be helpless in a war with any country, for they are its very backbone and sinew of strength. The Scotch will think twice about enlisting, too, when they learn the Irish have cleared out, for they know that when it comes to a fight the Englishmen are not there, and if there are no Irish to call upon, why they, the Scotchmen, would have to stand the whole brunt. By the concession which England now makes, she hopes the Irish will feel grateful, to the extent of enlisting again in the army; but I hope they will have sense enough to do no such thing, as England grants nothing except when forced to it.

# Conclusion

Now my narrative is virtually at an end, but to be in fashion I must say another word to be called the "Conclusion."

Queen Victoria had a peaceful reign of some sixty-three years. Of this long period, only thirty-seven years were devoted to war against her own people in her own possessions. It was against the blacks, her own subjects, that her huge armies were principally employed. Her armies could easily account for 5,000 dead blacks annually, so that during the thirty-seven years of her long and peaceful reign of sixty-three years, there could be recorded in the annals of English History the names of some 185,000 of her black subjects who, innocent, helpless and unarmed, were deliberately shot down because they were native and rightful owners of lands that might be rich in gold and other precious minerals.

The venerable queen died in the year 1901 during her war in South Africa against an innocent, humane and Christian people who happened to have the richest gold-fields known. She was succeeded by her son who followed in her footsteps till the Boers finally consented to surrender in order to save all that remained of their women and children and therefore their race from extinction.

At last, England longs for peace. She has all the gold-fields with the exception of those in Alaska and she knows that by sending a titled person to the English Government in Washington, D. C., she can get all the gold she wishes in that land by the mere asking.

She is through with war and such is her condition financially that if any Power offers her an insult she must swallow it. The South African war absorbed all her money and today, (1903), she acknowledges the huge debt of £4,000,000,000. To pay the interest on that debt alone her population of 40,000,000 people must be taxed at the rate of three dollars per head annually for every man, woman and child.

Even bread, the sole food' of her thousands of starving poor, must be taxed in order that she may meet the interest of her heavy debt. She prays for peace not only because she is pressed to earth by the weight of her debt but also because the South African War demonstrated the extreme weakness of her army.

The Mad *Mullah* in line with the Boers, has also developed the fighting incapacity of her army, I wonder why they call him "Mad?" Is it because he has wiped out some English commands? It may be so, because General Cronje was called the "Butcher" when he wiped out some English commands.

The English Army having shown itself so pitifully weak in the presence of an armed though far inferior enemy, in numbers, the question arises, "Is her navy as weak as her army?" I don't know, but should her navy by accident run against either the; American or French navy, I have an idea that it would follow the same course and meet the same fate as the Spanish navy during the American-Spanish War.

That the English navy is huge in its number on paper I do not doubt, but that there is any effective; strength in its numbers, I seriously doubt, because so many of her principal ships are armed with old smooth-bone muzzle-loading guns, so many of the boilers; are burnt out and so many of the old hulks are rotten with age?

At any rate England is praying for continued peace and will not go to war unless actually driven to it. For 700 years she has tried to crush out the very life of the Irish people by thrusting them in prison, by starvation and by actually murdering them, yet, in the end she found them invincible and not to be destroyed. Now her king and queen go to Ireland and fairly kiss the Irish people's feet and tell them what a good, noble people they are and how dearly they love them. To be sincere, they should have added, "Now won't you enlist in our army, for we: can't possibly fight without your help?"

The English, of all people, are the least sincere officially and know best the value of flattery. It is for this reason, I think, that the British Empire has so long held together, but now the people of the Colonies are beginning to reflect, to think and reason, and the connecting links are growing weaker and weaker every day and some of them may, at any moment, snap.

As soon as peace was made in South Africa, the English with long faces and pleading tones, appealed to the Boers to forgive and forget, as there were no longer any reasons why they should live on unfriendly terms. Having robbed the Boers of their gold-fields, destroyed more than 22,000 of their women and children, all their homes and property, and then endeavoured to starve to death the whole population, she humbly begs them to forgive and forget. Yes, the Boers are sure to forgive and forget, but when?

The Eighty Years' War showed that the Dutch were the most determined fighters and the greatest lovers of liberty the world had ever known. Shortly after the conclusion of this war many of them went to South Africa and settled in Cape Colony. It was fight, fight and fight all the time for years, but, though they lost many of their women and children, yet they were determined and held their ground. Near the close of the 17th century many of the Huguenots driven from France also sought refuge in Cape Colony. The Boers of today are the descendants of those two races of people. This explains why they are such a determined race and such great lovers of liberty. The Dutch and French Huguenots, both being intensely religious, united, fought side by side during those fearful times and in the end became so intermixed that today there is not one individual Dutch or Huguenot family among the Boers.

After years of fighting the natives, wild beasts and starvation, they succeeded in establishing themselves in comfortable homes and converting a wilderness into a habitable, productive country.

Now the time was ripe for England to act and she fell upon them with her army and navy and deprived them of all their rights and liberties. They withstood English domineering for a few years, when many of them, driven to it, openly rebelled. The terrible murder scene at Slagter's Nek was the result. Here five men were hung in the presence of hundreds of men, women and children who had been driven to the scene at the point of English bayonets. When the five patriots were dropped, the scaffold broke and down all came, some half dead from choking, and all writhing in agony. The scaffold was partially repaired and all drawn up, so that they could die as horrible a death as possible. The Boers have never forgotten that awful day and that heartrending scene, and they never will.

During the recent war men, women and children were again forced to witness many such revolting scenes, and yet the English beg them to forgive and forget.

Back in the thirties, the English became so oppressive that life to the Boers was unendurable, so thousands of them banded together, left their dear old homes and all their property and started on the "Great Trek" to the unsettled country of Natal. Here again they had to contend with the savages, wild beasts and starvation. Hundreds of them were murdered, yet, in the end, they again established themselves in homes and made the wilderness bloom. No sooner were they comfortable, happy and in a flourishing condition than the English fell upon them again and drove them from the land. They now crossed the mountains and sought homes in the great deserts now known as the Transvaal and Free State. At last the English said they would no longer hound them and would allow them to live or die in the desert.

Again the Boers had to contend with the savages, wild beasts and starvation. Here they suffered terribly, hundreds of them died and hundreds of women and children were murdered by the savages. Yet they persevered and converted the desert into two of the richest and most flourishing little republics in the world. All this is as fresh as ever in the Boer memory, yet, after the late South African War, the English beg the Boers to forgive and forget.

Unfortunately for the Free State, as soon as she began to really flourish, the great diamond fields at Kimberly were discovered. Now England falls upon her, kills a lot of her people and, in the end, robs her of her diamond fields and establishes a little despotism in Kimberly. The diamond fields were alone cut off and annexed to Cape Colony, for there was nothing else in the Free State worth having as far as the English knew.

It is at Kimberly that the great "Compound System" was established and is still running in all its glory. Rhodes, Beit, Phillips and Bernato were the prime movers.

A large compound was built around the mines and all the employees locked within it. No employee can buy anything except from the Company and within that compound. On leaving the compound, the employees have to go through an ordeal that is simply beastly, because the Company fears that some of them may have swallowed a diamond. It requires a week to pass the last door and Everyone must swallow such purging drugs as the Company may command. The Compound is simply a little hell established by the civilized English.

They made a law in the Colony by which anyone caught with a rough diamond in his possession is sent to penal servitude for a term of years, the period raging from five to seven years. This law was especially enacted for the Diamond Company? now known as De Beers Company.

Anyone in Kimberly who might say anything about the Compound System would incur the displeasure of the Diamond Company.

That means that one of the Company's detectives would watch his chance and drop a rough diamond in the offender's pocket. In another five minutes the detective would arrest the offender and charge him with having a rough diamond in his possession. The offender would plead innocence, but the search brings out the diamond, the offender is hauled before the Company's judge and sentenced to five or seven years' penal servitude. I remember, in one instance, where the judge held a rough diamond in his hand and remarked to those in the court room that that one diamond had sent eleven men to penal servitude. Sure it is that under an English administration, there is no doubt that justice will be given.

This frightful state of affairs exists because Rhodes, Bernato, Beit, Philips, etc. must be pleased. Rhodes and Bernato are now dead, the one having been fatally shot by John Barleycorn, and the other having jumped overboard at sea that it might be recorded of him that he had at least done one good thing.

Having sliced off the diamond fields and annexed them to Cape Colony, the English now allowed the Free Staters to live in peace. The people of the Transvaal had long since established their government, but they were struggling hard to keep starvation from the door. There was no money in the treasury, the people had no money and every official gave his time and services free. There was no complaint, however, for all could be happy in their religion even if they had no money and starvation was staring them in the face.

While still struggling to live, a great misfortune fell upon them in the year 1887 by the discovery of the great Rand gold fields at Johannesburg. People from all parts of the world poured into the country and the Boers suddenly jumped from poverty into affluence. These fields became world known, all was flourishing in the Transvaal, and Boers and foreigners alike were all happy and prosperous. England, through the subsidized press soon manufactured an excuse to make war upon the Boers and rob them of their gold fields.

With the material assistance rendered by the English Government in Washington, D. C., she managed to succeed in her highway robbery and at the same time deprive two little republics of their independence.

Judging by what I read and hear, I am led to believe that President Roosevelt claims to be of Irish and Dutch extraction, but judging him by his conduct and the English proclivities of some of those who are his chief advisers, I should say that real English blood predominates over all others he may claim. Whatever the composition of his blood may be, certain it is that he helped England destroy two little republics in South Africa. The American people will wake up by and by and see to it that none but true Americans will hold office under the United States Government.

Having driven the Boers from pillar to post, hounded them, preyed upon them and robbed and murdered them for 250 years, and then deprived them of their liberty and independence, England now expects them to forgive and forget because there is no longer any reason for ill-feelings.

Will the Boers ever forget the sufferings and torture heaped upon their forefathers in Cape Colony? Will they ever forget what their fathers and mothers had to endure in Natal? Will they ever forget what they themselves have had to suffer in the Transvaal and Free State? Will they ever forget the 3,723 patriots who were killed or died of wounds during the late South African War? Will they ever forget the 22,000 women and children who were murdered in the English prison camps? Will they ever forget the many martyrs who were tied hand and foot, and deliberately shot in cold blood?

Go to the lone tent standing by the charred walls of the destroyed home and with the children listen to what is taught them by the mother, and you will hear the answer.

Such noble women as that grand matron, Mrs. Joubert, widow of the late Commandant-General Piet Joubert, would redeem any land or people. She is one of thousands of Africander mothers whose sons may forgive much, because they are Christians but will forget nothing because they are men. They will not have any of the amiable sentimentality of the Irish whose soft hearts and heads prompt them too often to let bygones be bygones. Nor will they have any of the vulgar admiration of success which makes the American parvenu cringe to the Englishman of rank or station, until the Yankee today, (1903), is more despised in Great Britain than his independent father was ever hated there which is saying a good deal.

The bible-loving Africanders may enjoy the following poem, with its Hebraic language of fierce denunciation. It is by an Irish-American without any Anglo "virus" in his system, James Jeffrey Roche, editor of the *Pilot*.

With it I conclude this story trusting and believing that it is anything but the concluding chapter to the Boer fight for freedom, the bravest and noblest ever fought since God taught men to love liberty.

*Her robes are of purple and scarlet,
And the kings have bent their knees
To the gemmed and jewelled harlot
Who sitteth on many seas.*

*They have drunk the abominations
Of her golden cup of shame;
She has drugged and debauched the nations
With the mystery of her name.*

*Her merchants have gathered riches
By the power of her wantonness,
And her usurers are as leeches
On the World's supreme distress.*

*She has scoured the seas as a spoiler;
Her mart is a robber's den,
With the wrested toll of the toiler,
And the mortgaged souls of men.*

*Her crimson flag is flying,
Where the East and the West are one;
Her drums while the day is dying
Salute the rising sun.*

*She has scourged the weak and the lowly
And the just with an iron rod;
She is drunk with the blood of the holy,
She shall drink of the wrath of God!*

# ALSO FROM LEONAUR
### AVAILABLE IN SOFTCOVER OR HARDCOVER WITH DUST JACKET

**AT THEM WITH THE BAYONET** by Donald F. Featherstone—The first Anglo-Sikh War 1845-1846.

**STEPHEN CRANE'S BATTLES** by Stephen Crane—Nine Decisive Battles Recounted by the Author of 'The Red Badge of Courage'.

**THE GURKHA WAR** by H. T. Prinsep—The Anglo-Nepalese Conflict in North East India 1814-1816.

**FIRE & BLOOD** by G. R. Gleig—The burning of Washington & the battle of New Orleans, 1814, through the eyes of a young British soldier.

**SOUND ADVANCE!** by Joseph Anderson—Experiences of an officer of HM 50th regiment in Australia, Burma & the Gwalior war.

**THE CAMPAIGN OF THE INDUS** by Thomas Holdsworth—Experiences of a British Officer of the 2nd (Queen's Royal) Regiment in the Campaign to Place Shah Shuja on the Throne of Afghanistan 1838 - 1840.

**WITH THE MADRAS EUROPEAN REGIMENT IN BURMA** by John Butler—The Experiences of an Officer of the Honourable East India Company's Army During the First Anglo-Burmese War 1824 - 1826.

**IN ZULULAND WITH THE BRITISH ARMY** by Charles L. Norris-Newman—The Anglo-Zulu war of 1879 through the first-hand experiences of a special correspondent.

**BESIEGED IN LUCKNOW** by Martin Richard Gubbins—The first Anglo-Sikh War 1845-1846.

**A TIGER ON HORSEBACK** by L. March Phillips—The Experiences of a Trooper & Officer of Rimington's Guides - The Tigers - during the Anglo-Boer war 1899 - 1902.

**SEPOYS, SIEGE & STORM** by Charles John Griffiths—The Experiences of a young officer of H.M.'s 61st Regiment at Ferozepore, Delhi ridge and at the fall of Delhi during the Indian mutiny 1857.

**CAMPAIGNING IN ZULULAND** by W. E. Montague—Experiences on campaign during the Zulu war of 1879 with the 94th Regiment.

**THE STORY OF THE GUIDES** by G.J. Younghusband—The Exploits of the Soldiers of the famous Indian Army Regiment from the northwest frontier 1847 - 1900.

### AVAILABLE ONLINE AT www.leonaur.com
### AND FROM ALL GOOD BOOK STORES

## ALSO FROM LEONAUR
### AVAILABLE IN SOFTCOVER OR HARDCOVER WITH DUST JACKET

**ZULU:1879** *by D.C.F. Moodie & the Leonaur Editors*—The Anglo-Zulu War of 1879 from contemporary sources: First Hand Accounts, Interviews, Dispatches, Official Documents & Newspaper Reports.

**THE RED DRAGOON** *by W.J. Adams*—With the 7th Dragoon Guards in the Cape of Good Hope against the Boers & the Kaffir tribes during the 'war of the axe' 1843-48'.

**THE RECOLLECTIONS OF SKINNER OF SKINNER'S HORSE** *by James Skinner*—James Skinner and his 'Yellow Boys' Irregular cavalry in the wars of India between the British, Mahratta, Rajput, Mogul, Sikh & Pindarree Forces.

**A CAVALRY OFFICER DURING THE SEPOY REVOLT** *by A. R. D. Mackenzie*—Experiences with the 3rd Bengal Light Cavalry, the Guides and Sikh Irregular Cavalry from the outbreak to Delhi and Lucknow.

**A NORFOLK SOLDIER IN THE FIRST SIKH WAR** *by J W Baldwin*—Experiences of a private of H.M. 9th Regiment of Foot in the battles for the Punjab, India 1845-6.

**TOMMY ATKINS' WAR STORIES: 14 FIRST HAND ACCOUNTS**—Fourteen first hand accounts from the ranks of the British Army during Queen Victoria's Empire.

**THE WATERLOO LETTERS** *by H. T. Siborne*—Accounts of the Battle by British Officers for its Foremost Historian.

**NEY: GENERAL OF CAVALRY VOLUME 1—1769-1799** *by Antoine Bulos*—The Early Career of a Marshal of the First Empire.

**NEY: MARSHAL OF FRANCE VOLUME 2—1799-1805** *by Antoine Bulos*—The Early Career of a Marshal of the First Empire.

**AIDE-DE-CAMP TO NAPOLEON** *by Philippe-Paul de Ségur*—For anyone interested in the Napoleonic Wars this book, written by one who was intimate with the strategies and machinations of the Emperor, will be essential reading.

**TWILIGHT OF EMPIRE** *by Sir Thomas Ussher & Sir George Cockburn*—Two accounts of Napoleon's Journeys in Exile to Elba and St. Helena: Narrative of Events by Sir Thomas Ussher & Napoleon's Last Voyage: Extract of a diary by Sir George Cockburn.

**PRIVATE WHEELER** *by William Wheeler*—The letters of a soldier of the 51st Light Infantry during the Peninsular War & at Waterloo.

AVAILABLE ONLINE AT **www.leonaur.com**
AND FROM ALL GOOD BOOK STORES

www.ingramcontent.com/pod-product-compliance
Lightning Source LLC
Chambersburg PA
CBHW021957160426
43197CB00007B/157